# Ships, Seas, and Scientists

# Ships, Seas, and Scientists

## U. S. Naval Exploration and Discovery in the Nineteenth Century

**VINCENT PONKO, JR.**

**Naval Institute Press**
**Annapolis, Maryland**

Scarce a sail . . .
But bears on board some authors, shipt
For foreign shores, all well equipt
With proper book-making machinery,
To sketch the morals, manners, scenery,
Of all such lands as they shall see,
Or not, as the case may be.

*Thoughts on Patrons*
Thomas Moore

# Preface

The writing of a book on the United States Navy and exploration in the mid-nineteenth century was first suggested by the late Mr. Frederick Hall of the Newberry Library, Chicago, Illinois. Mr. Hall was not responsible for the finished product, but he was certainly in the best sense of the term, the instigator of its inception. For the encouragement rendered the author in the beginning phase of this work, the author extends thanks to Dr. John Parker, James Ford Bell Library, University of Minnesota and to Rear Admiral E. M. Eller, USN (Ret.), the Director of Naval History, who made available basic source material from the library of the Navy Department. Mr. Walter Greenwood, Librarian, of the Navy Department's library and members of his staff were very cooperative in implementing this arrangement. To Mr. Benton Scheide, Director of Libraries of California State College, Bakersfield, and his staff the author is grateful for receiving sections of this material on an inter-library loan basis, seeing that it reached the author, and then handling the arrangements to send it back to Mr. Greenwood and the Navy Department's library at the appropriate times. Mr. Scheide and his staff were also very cooperative in obtaining books and other materials on an inter-library loan basis from other depositories. Without the help of those noted above, writing this book would have been much more difficult indeed.

For their help in obtaining other source material, their aiding the author in interpreting it, and their permission to use material written by them, special acknowledgement must be given among others to Mr. David H. Johnson, formerly Curator of the Division of Mammals, United States National Museum, Smithsonian Institution, and now a resident of Weed, California; Mr. Richard von Doenhoff, Division of Naval History, Department of the Navy, and Dr. Edward Caswell of Stanislaus State College, Turlock, California.

It must also be stated that the Smithsonian Institution gave financial help in the form of a small grant to enable the author to consult the Smithsonian's archives. The staff of the Smithsonian aided the author greatly in this endeavor and contributed through their kindness, cooperation and advice in no small way to the completion of this book. The author would also like to thank Ms. Helen J. Hutchinson, Secretary, Division of Mammals, United States National Museum, for her entirely voluntary and otherwise unrewarded work in compiling and sending to the author information about the holdings of the Division of Mammals pertinent to this study.

Special acknowledgment must be given to the National Archives and the Library of Congress, and to the many staff members of both, whose interest and cooperation greatly simplified research efforts.

With regard to the typing of the preliminary drafts as well as the copy of the manuscript, the author is very appreciative of the outstanding work done by Miss Janet Banion and Miss Claudia Lindley. He also extends his thanks to Miss Banion and Miss Lindley for their willingness on some occasions to act as research assistants and all-around general helpers. In these areas of endeavor, Miss Francie Yaksitch also merits a grateful thanks for her important assistance. A special debt is owed to Arnold S. Lott, Lieutenant Commander, U.S. Navy (Ret.) of the Naval Institute Press, for his editorial handling of the manuscript resulting in its improved factual presentation and clarity of style.

To everyone who in any way made this work possible the author expresses his gratitude. Of course, whatever shortcomings pertain to the book are the sole responsibility of the author.

# Contents

# Prologue

Until little more than six hundred years ago, the Mediterranean could be called the center of the European world. Viking ships crossed the Atlantic during the Middle Ages to the mainland of North America, and there is evidence that vessels from other Old World areas performed the same feat, perhaps in earlier times. It was the venturesome voyages of Prince Henry of Portugal's navigators, however, following upon the trips of fishermen in the late Middle Ages to the fishing banks off the new world, that opened the way into the Atlantic for European travellers less than a century before Columbus sailed to the new world. In the next century the Pacific was discovered and the world was rounded. By the time the American colonies were established, Cabot, Balboa, Magellan, Drake, and Cook had drawn new latitudes and longitudes across the charts until it appeared the world had indeed spread beyond the end of reckoning.

As colonization and the resulting commerce opened up new lands, exploration continued, with many nations participating in purposeful geographical discovery, scientific investigation, and charting; by the last decade of the nineteenth century there were few blanks left on the globe where details could be filled in by those lesser known men who followed the great explorers of the past. By that time, for instance, the United States had almost completed the westward movement across the continent whose vast interior was already fairly well known.

In this accomplishment of filling in the last unknowns, wherever they might be, the United States Navy was an active participant, especially in the twenty-five year period preceding the Civil War. From 1838 to 1861, for example, officers and men of the United States Navy conducted major exploring expeditions in at least eleven, sometimes overlapping but yet distinct, areas of the world purposely planned and aimed not only at discovery, surveying, and charting, but also the advancement of scientific inquiry.*

Some of these expeditions have received extensive treatment by historians in the past; others have been studied and publicized only in part, the

---

*This number does not include voyages performed exclusively or mainly for oceanographic and hydrographic purposes such as those of the USS *Dolphin* in 1849 and USS *Taney* between 1851 and 1854.

complete stories being known only to those familiar with the pertinent records and manuscripts in public documents and archives. In short, the published record of the U.S. Navy's part in exploration from 1838 to 1861 contains factual gaps and is deficient in synthesis. The Navy's part in the activity of exploration before the Civil War, for instance, has not received adequate treatment in monograph form. Few of these expeditions considered singly or as groups have received adequate recognition in general histories of either the Navy or of the United States.

Because of this situation, the Navy's role in exploration and discovery before the Civil War has not been appreciated adequately. In an attempt to improve this situation, the histories of the major exploring expeditions from 1838 to 1861 associated with the Navy have been examined individually (or re-examined where appropriate), condensed and brought together in this volume in distinct chapters, separated generally according to geographical area, preceded by two chapters of background material. Each chapter owes a debt to previously published or unpublished studies, as noted in the footnotes, but each one had to be based, at least in part, on independent research, including appropriate attention to what happened to the scientific data collected by each expedition, in order to tell as complete a story as possible about the expedition or expeditions discussed in it. In investigating these expeditions, it was concluded that no one man, agency, or cause was responsible for their origin considered collectively except insofar as the Navy was available as an instrument and the climate of the period induced men with curiosity, vision, and ambition to attract national and naval support for their formulation and implementation. Each of the expeditions had a life story of its own, and all of them make stimulating reading for their own sake. Thus, this book is not organized around a central theme of an ultimate cause or causes, and it does not pretend to be a synthetic history of U.S. naval exploration before the Civil War. For those specific expeditions that have received extensive coverage elsewhere, it is hoped that this format will provide a worthwhile condensation, advantageously arranged for reading, as well as a take-off point for additional inquiry. Corrections where relevant are also noted. Those expeditions not previously presented adequately will undoubtedly be the subject of longer and more detailed monograph accounts in the future, but until these are produced, the appropriate chapters in this book are offered as readable, balanced, and authoritative narratives of the essential elements in the origins, operations, and accomplishments of the expeditions in question.

Considered together, all the accounts in this book provide a new and hopefully better opportunity to reflect upon the more important phases of Naval exploration for the period 1838–61, particularly in relation to a proper appreciation of the importance of this work for the protection of commerce, the advancement of science, the history of the Navy, and the general welfare of the United States.

# Ships, Seas, and Scientists

# Chapter 1

# Early Naval Exploration
# and Scientific Discovery

The history of the United States is closely tied to the sea. The early explorers, discoverers, and adventurers all reached the North American continent by sea, and so came those who established the colonies in New England, along the Delaware, and on the Chesapeake. The early colonies, primitive coastal settlements facing the sea and surrounded by an unknown land which reached westward across a continent, were no more than small islands of civilization at the edge of a vast wilderness. The colonists came by sea, their only communication with Europe was by sea, and for nearly two centuries their main communication with one another was by sea.

Since most of the trade possible in early colonial times was moved more readily by sea, the colonists became shipbuilders, fishermen, and merchants; thus American interest in shipping and foreign trade stemmed from colonial times. British attempts to regulate and tax such trade and New England's profitable commerce in molasses and rum were strong factors in the Revolutionary War. After the colonies achieved independence, U.S. merchant ships took to the trade routes of the world—in the Atlantic, in the Mediterranean, and in the far reaches of the Pacific. During the late eighteenth century there was a steady increase in American foreign trade with the Mediterranean region; some eighty United States ships were reported as passing eastward through the Straits of Gibraltar in 1799 alone.[1]

During the War of 1812 and the period just preceding it, such commerce declined. Nevertheless, the trend for the period 1790–1861 was toward greater foreign trade, rather than in any reduction. In 1800, the value of exports in the United States was $70,972,000; the value of imports was $91,253,000. During the period 1830–1860 American registered gross tonnage increased from 1,191,776 gross tons to 5,539,813 gross tons.

Moreover, American ships traveled all over the globe. In this activity, the American merchant marine became dominant in certain trading regions. The development of the clipper ship allowed the United States to dominate the China trade. In 1855, of 58,000 tons of foreign shipping in Chinese water, 24,000 were under American registry while only 18,000 were British. Profits arising out of the situation were correspondingly large. During 1850, a cargo of tea brought to London by the American clipper ship, *Oriental,*

*1*

after a passage of 104 days, made a profit of $48,000 or a little more than two thirds of the vessel's entire cost. In this development, the mariners and merchants of New England and Middle Atlantic states led the way in terms of size, volume and variety of their interests, but by the 1850s Mobile and New Orleans had a flourishing export trade. The South was concerned about developing direct trading connections through Southern ports. The only problem with this overall expansion was that in 1850 British development of steam power allowed that country to capture a progressively greater share of ocean-going trade and thus began to weaken the mercantile marine of the United States.[2]

It was in response to the need to protect this merchant shipping and the demand for government protection, that the United States Navy had its origin. Moreover, after its inception the United States Navy was associated not only with the defense but also the furthering of American foreign commerce, as it expanded in volume and value. In its early days, the Navy gave convoy protection to American merchant shipping and put down pirates. Later this role was expanded to include expeditions aimed at charting the seas, making speedier trading voyages possible, and opening up new areas to American commercial activity. These expeditions also collected data and specimens for the advancement of science, although the importance and attention given to this objective varied in the organization and operations of each expedition.

This development began early in the last decade of the eighteenth century, when the depredations of Mediterranean pirates began to take a heavy toll of American shipping, since the United States neither made a treaty of mutual defense with the European powers nor purchased "protection" from the Bey of Algiers. After much debate in which some members of the House of Representatives from inland districts seemed to favor the loss of our commerce in the Mediterranean rather than the establishment of a Navy, Congress responded by ordering the construction of six frigates to protect American merchant shipping, an action that became law March 27, 1794. Although a law which went into effect on April 20, 1796, reduced the number of six to three, and although opponents of the Navy, mainly from states outside New England, came close to doing away with even this number, the Act of March 27, 1794, may be accepted as the legislative foundation of the United States Navy.[3]

For about six years after it was founded, the new naval force did not participate in combat against the pirates of the Barbary Coast. Instead, the United States entered into treaty relations with the Barbary states of Algiers, Tunis, Tripoli and Morocco, for the payment of tribute in return for their refraining from attacks on American merchant shipping. For many people in the United States, especially those members of the new

Navy who were involved in delivering the tribute, this was not a comfortable nor an honorable relationship, but treaty obligations were carried out.

In 1800, the Pasha of Tripoli demanded a new treaty calling for increased tribute. The United States refused his demand and in 1801 sent Commodore Richard Dale to the Mediterranean with three frigates and a schooner. Dale's instructions were to act against Tripoli and protect American shipping in the event that Tripoli declared war against the United States. When the squadron reached Gibraltar on July 1, 1801, Dale learned that Tripoli had declared war. All Dale could accomplish was to blockade two Tripolitan ships he found at Gibraltar, convoy American merchant shipping, and maintain a limited blockade of Tripoli itself.

In May 1802, a new force of five frigates and a schooner under the command of Commodore Richard Morris reached the Mediterranean to replace Dale and his ships. Morris did nothing to subdue Tripoli, except capture one Tripolitan ship which had been blockaded in Gibraltar, and convoy American merchant shipping. For this lack of definitive results, Morris' commissions were revoked and he returned home in 1803 after being relieved by Commodore Edward Preble.

Preble's force was inferior in size to Morris', but Preble did not let that deter him from taking forceful action against Tripoli and asking for reinforcements. By the summer of 1804, Tripoli was under blockade and being bombarded by Preble's ships. As part of this operation, the frigate *Philadelphia* ran aground in the harbor and was captured with all hands. This capture provided the opportunity for a daring exploit on the part of some of Preble's men. Under the command of Stephen Decatur, a party boarded the *Philadelphia* and completely destroyed the ship so that the enemy could not make use of her. The officers and crew of the *Philadelphia,* however, remained prisoners.

Before Preble could bring about the submission of Tripoli, it was decided in Washington to send a larger force to the Mediterranean and he was recalled to make way for a commander senior on the Navy register. A new force under Commodore Samuel Barron consisting of five frigates, three brigs, three schooners, ten new gunboats, and two bomb vessels took its place before Tripoli. At this time, moreover, naval action was co-ordinated with a land operation conducted under the supervision of William Eaton, a former American consul at Tunis.

This show of force led to the signing of a new treaty providing for the payment of ransom for the officers and crew of the *Philadelphia* and the promise by the ruler of Tripoli to refrain from attacking American shipping in the future. New demands by Tunis were settled by a cash payment of $10,000.

After the Tripolitan War ended no United States warships were sent to the Mediterranean until 1815. In their absence, Algiers, Tripoli and Tunis all preyed upon American merchant shipping or engaged in unfriendly acts against American privateers operating against Great Britain. In May 1815, a force under Stephen Decatur was dispatched to deal with the situation. Two months later in July 1815, reinforcements under William Bainbridge were sent. Such forceful action was taken against Algiers by Decatur and Bainbridge that by the end of June 1815, Algiers agreed not to capture any more American merchant ships without provision for tribute. Tunis and Tripoli soon followed suit. In October 1815, Decatur and Bainbridge sailed for home leaving four frigates and brigs behind to become the Mediterranean Squadron. Except for the period of the Civil War, the United States has maintained some sort of naval force in the Mediterranean ever since.[4]

Solicitude for American commerce in the South Atlantic and Pacific also contributed to the development of the United States Navy. As early as 1800, the USS *Essex*, a 32-gun frigate, convoyed 14 merchant ships, chiefly loaded with coffee, sugar, and pepper, from the East Indies to the United States. The termination of the War of 1812 brought a rejuvenation of trade with the Far East. In 1819 the 36-gun *Congress* sailed a two year cruise in East Indian waters for the protection of American commerce. In 1829, the *Vincennes* was ordered to visit various Pacific islands and Far East ports before returning home by way of the Cape of Good Hope. The ship arrived in New York on June 8, 1830, the first ship of the United States Navy to circumnavigate the globe.

As expanding trade with the Far East engendered the protection of the United States Navy, it also raised the idea of discovery, particularly of a new continent suspected to lie below the Antarctic Circle.

Some of the products exported to China were ginseng, opium, quicksilver, lead, iron, copper, steel, cotton, camlets, sandalwood, mother-of-pearl, edible birds nests, large worms called bêche-de-mer, and furs, as well as seal, sea elephant, and sea otter skins. Sandalwood, mother-of pearl, edible birds' nests, and bêche-de-mer were obtained from the Hawaiian and other island groups further south, such as the Society Islands and the Fijis. Furs and skins were secured from various source areas in the South Atlantic and the Pacific area, including the Northwest Coast of North America.

As the trade in furs and skins increased, it resulted in the need to find new supply sources of such mammals as the seal and sea otter almost every year. By 1805, the seal population had been so depleted by the slaughter of previous seasons, particularly in the much worked over area of the Falklands and Juan Fernandez group of islands, that American sailors began to search for new areas of supply further south. After this search was halted temporarily by the War of 1812, new seal beaches were found in 1819–1820 on a group of ten islands lying south and east of Cape Horn stretching in a northeast-southwesterly direction for some 250 miles. These islands were first called New South Britain, but their name was later changed to the New South Shetland group since they were on the same longitude as the original Shetland Islands. During the sealing season of 1820–1821, approximately forty American, English, Scotch and Australian ships were in competition for seal pelts in this area.

During this period, at least one American sealer, Nat Palmer, coasted along the shore of the Antarctic Peninsula in November, 1820. It is uncertain whether he fully appreciated the discovery and it appears that his feat did not receive adequate publicity until a few years later. Two other sailors visited the Antarctic early in 1821. Most probably a boat from the *Huron* of New Haven, commanded by Captain John Davis, landed in the region of Hughes Bay on the Antarctic Peninsula in February 1821; the *Jane Maria* under Captain Robert Johnson was at approximately latitude 66° south and longitude 70° west during the same period when land was sighted covered with ice and snow. The importance of these Antarctic landfalls also seems not to have been given significant publicity at the time.

Other sailors reached the shores of the Antarctic after 1821, but by this time they were beginning to better understand the importance of their accomplishments and to appreciate the value of keeping proper records for publication and as an aid to further and more comprehensive exploration. One such man was Benjamin Morrell who explored the area of the New South Shetlands in the 1820s and published a work in 1832 called *A Narrative of Four Voyages* containing descriptions of an ice-free South Polar Sea, and an Antarctic land mass which he called New South Greenland. Since accounts of Palmer's sighting of the Antarctic continent had been published a few years earlier, particularly in *Washington Intelligencer* for December 13, 1828, the public was not entirely surprised that sailors like Benjamin Morrell had explored the area close to the Antarctic land mass. Unfortunately, Morrell's book was written in a somewhat ornate way and his claims of having seen an ice-free Polar Sea as well as an Antarctic land mass were received by some people with skepticism.

Any public uncertainty as to whether to accept Morrell as a bonafide and accurate explorer did not seem to dampen a rising enthusiasm over the future of the United States and the Antarctic. By the 1830s, sealers, merchants, and financiers who supported sealing were not the only ones interested in what lay further south of the South Shetland Islands. While individual sealers were looking for new and hitherto untapped rookeries, John Cleves Symmes, a former United States Army captain, was advocating a theory that the earth was hollow and habitable within; it contained a number of concentric spheres one within the other, and that it was open at the pole twelve or sixteen degrees.

In 1825, Symmes was joined in this work by Jeremiah N. Reynolds, a former Ohio schoolteacher and newspaper editor, who a few years later disagreed with Symmes over which pole should be investigated. Reynolds believed that an expedition to the Antarctic offered the best hope of proving the hollow earth theory and then began to agitate for governmental support. By 1828 he seemed to have abandoned his concentric sphere and hollow earth theory in favor of discovery for the sake of what it might contribute to the national interest of the United States and the benefit of mankind. Reynolds urged Congress to sanction an expedition to the Antarctic to further science and to add something to the common stock of general information by investigating the interesting, extensive field of enterprise, in the Southern hemisphere. He was seconded by many citizens, particularly along the Atlantic seaboard, who especially hoped for the discovery of new sources of fish, whale oil and seal skins as well as the development of new markets.

Such individuals and groups maintained that it was for the best interest of the country to discover what resources could be drawn from the ocean. Legislative bodies, such as the Pennsylvania legislature, had earlier stated that while Reynolds' proposed expedition might not do spectacular deeds, it would provide much useful information on the hydrography and geography of the Antarctic regions, as well as important observations on atmospherical, magnetical, and electrical phenomena. By 1828, Reynolds had achieved such strong support that the House of Representatives passed a resolution on May 21, 1828, calling upon the Secretary of the Navy to send a small vessel for a surveying and exploration voyage to the Pacific Ocean and the South Atlantic. The expense of such a voyage was to be defrayed from funds already allocated to the Navy.

Secretary of the Navy Samuel Southard, with the approval of President John Adams, started very quickly to organize such an expedition. Unfortunately, Southard could not cover the cost of this expedition and the matter came to the attention of Robert Y. Hayne, senator from South Carolina, and Chairman of the Senate's Committee on Naval Affairs. That committee asked Southard why he had started to prepare for such an expedition without the approval of the Senate, demanded precise explanation of the purposes and objectives of the projected voyage, inquired about expenditures to date and the inability of the Navy to meet expected costs out of money already allotted. In his response, Southard noted that in relation to the hopes of the advocates of exploration, the addition of a scientific aspect necessitated additional personnel, equipment, plus another ship, the expenses for which could not be met out of regular funds. Southard's overall reply was not accepted and, with some general statements against overseas exploration in general, the committee scuttled the project.

As Reynolds worked to convince the public and Congress of the need for an Antarctic expedition, the government had already recognized the importance of American commercial activity in the South Atlantic and in the

Pacific by the establishment of the Pacific Squadron in 1822 and the Brazil or South Atlantic Squadron in 1826.

In the early 1820s, the New England merchant fleet in the Pacific numbered some 232 vessels employing 2,352 seamen. Later, the New England whaling industry assumed greater importance in the Pacific. Probably the first whaler in the Pacific was the English *Amelia,* owned by the London firm of Enderby and Sons, which reached the Pacific in 1789. Her success induced three whalers from Nantucket and one from New Bedford to go to the Pacific in 1791. Their voyages were also successful, and by 1843, out of 140 whalers arriving at the Hawaiian Islands, 132 were from the United States. Around this time, the whaling fleet of the United States numbered 675 vessels grossing over 200,000 tons, most of which cruised the Pacific; their combined crews numbered 15,000 to 16,000 men and the fleet had a value of about $225,000,000 with an annual return of around $5,000,000.

By the middle of the 1830s the whaling industry re-emphasized the economic importance of the South Atlantic and Pacific regions to the United States. This added new force to the demands for a governmentally financed voyage for surveying and exploration.

The refusal of the Senate's Committee on Naval Affairs to endorse exploration in the South Atlantic and Pacific in 1828 induced Reynolds, with the support of Edmund Fanning, a prominent New York merchant long active in the sealing industry, to organize a private voyage with two 100-ton brigs, the *Seraph* and the *Annawan,* commanded by former sealers, Nat Palmer and Benjamin Pendleton. They sailed in October 1829, for the South Shetland area with a party of scientists made up of Dr. James Eights, a naturalist of Philadelphia, John F. Watson, and Reynolds.[5]

This expedition was unsuccessful for the most part.[6] It encountered two problems which Reynolds and the captain could not handle: bad weather and discipline of the crew. Reynolds himself preferred not to return home with the *Seraph* and *Annawan* and obtained employment as private secretary to the commanding officer of the USS *Potomac,* then on its way to the East Indies under the command of Commodore John Downes.

Edmund Fanning, who did not sail with the expedition, renewed the agitation for an expedition conducted by the Navy. In the fall of 1832, he presented a memorial to the House of Representatives and at the same time sought the approval of the Secretary of the Navy, Levi Woodbury. When the Congress convened he presented an additional memorial to the Senate that estimated the cost of an expedition at $10,000, with a complement of about 90 or 100 people. In the meantime he published in 1833 an account of his maritime career called *Voyages Round the World* which gained considerable publicity for him and the question of discovery in the Antarctic.

When Reynolds returned to the United States in 1834, he published an account of his journey under the title *Voyage of the United States Frigate Potomac, Under the command of Commodore John Downes, During the circumnavigation of the globe in the years 1831, 1832, 1833 and 1834.* One of the features of the work was its presentation of the Navy's world-wide range of interests and capabilities. Reynolds had, in a sense, conducted his own exploring expedition, thus preparing the public for more such expeditions to follow.[7]

In response to agitation by Fanning and renewed activity by Reynolds, various groups with maritime interests, particularly in New England, began to petition Congress to appropriate money for an expedition to the South Atlantic and the Pacific. The East India Marine Society of Salem, composed of influential mariners, called for a survey to be made to correct the charting of islands, reefs, and shoals in both the South Atlantic and the Pacific.

In 1835, these petitions led to a movement in Congress to include money for an expedition to the South Atlantic and Pacific in the Navy Appropriation Bill of 1836, and Reynolds was invited to speak before it. The staunch advocacy of the merits of surveying and exploration for the country, by Representative John Reed of Massachussetts and Representative Thomas Hamer of Ohio, lent strength to his views against the attacks of many congressmen from inland states who opposed the use of government funds for maritime exploration, and convinced the House to vote $300,000 for such an expedition; the Senate also agreed. In this debate, Reed and Hamer urged congressmen to forget sectional interests and to look upon maritime surveying and naval exploration as in the national interest and national good. This was the inception of the United States Exploring Expedition, or Wilkes Expedition of 1838–1842.[8]

Thus began naval exploration in the United States. A century later the benefits of such work were still being realized. Land surveys had commenced very early in the history of the United States, and the Coast Survey, established in 1807, had been charting the U.S. coastline since 1816. But it is generally agreed that the "Wilkes Expedition" was a beginning point in U.S. naval exploration. The reasons given for its formulation, the way in which it obtained congressional approval, the manner of its organization and operation, all serve as a guide on which to base studies of subsequent explorations conducted by the U.S. Navy.[9]

# Chapter 2

# The Navy's Role in Economic and Scientific Development

The Constitution of the United States, in Article I, Section 8, gives Congress the power to "provide and maintain a navy." The same article and section gives Congress the authority and responsibility to "make rules for the government and regulation of the land and naval forces." From the early days of the government, as established under the Constitution, Congress has accepted this latter responsibility, and by 1830, naval regulations, uniform code, structure of rank, and pay and allowance scales within a matrix of tradition had been established.[1]

On the other hand, the history of the United States until the Civil War shows many occasions on which Congress seemed reluctant not only to provide but also to "maintain a navy." One element behind this was a continuous condition of uncertainty as to the value and purposes of a Navy.

By 1815, Congress had seemingly accepted the argument that one of the reasons for having a Navy was to protect United States shipping in all parts of the globe. It failed, however, to provide an acceptable definition as to how it was to be accomplished beyond the establishment of patrolling and escort service for needed occasions on the part of individual or small groups of the Navy's vessels, with punitive action when feasible and necessary.

In this situation the Congress was not helped by the executive branch of the government. Most of the Secretaries of the Navy during this period failed to advance what appeared to be the lesson of the War of 1812; that the United States should build enough ships capable of operating as a fleet, to break a blockade of the United States by defeating the enemy blockading force; or enforce a blockade against an enemy; or even by their mere being to dissuade an enemy from attempting a blockade. The principle of "command of the sea" was not used as a focal point of naval policy.

Some of the factors combining to make comprehensive, strategically purposeful decisions and determinations of this kind impossible were: (1) the continuous development of a far-flung seagoing commerce centered in the New England States, which seemed to indicate that naval ships should be stationed singly or in small groups on distant stations in order to protect and advance U.S. trade throughout the world; (2) a belief within the inland regions of the United States that a Navy was of no advantage—either in terms of economic activity or defense; (3) the geographical isolation of the various states which seemed to make it difficult for any foreign power to bring a large invasion fleet near the coast except at places which the U.S. could easily fortify; (4) the idea that the Royal Navy was the enemy to fear and so superior that any naval development by the United States would just contribute to an increase in the Royal Navy through its capture of U.S. ships; (5) a tradition of naval warfare in which battle involved ship-to-ship action and fleet actions were only dimly envisaged; and (6) demands by special interest groups that ships of the U.S. Navy be used for special purposes such as charting and exploring little-known regions of the globe.

All of these elements influenced the formulation of United States naval policy and development of naval strength, particularly after the War of 1812, in which the Navy fought so gallantly and so well that it convinced the new nation of its value and importance. In the period just after the war, for example, an atmosphere of good will toward the Navy existed and the executive branch of the government attempted to capitalize on this spirit. In his annual report for 1815, Secretary of the Navy Benjamin W. Crowninshield recommended that Congress appropriate funds for five warships annually. President Madison, in general accord with Crowninshield, passed this recommendation on to Congress. As a result of this recommendation, and the favorable atmosphere into which it was received, Congress passed an act on April 29, 1816, for the gradual increase of the navy of the United States, with one million dollars appropriated annually for eight years, to be used to build nine 74-gun line-of-battle ships and twelve 44-gun frigates. There is little evidence that this legislation was passed with the idea of promoting any strategic principles. Moreover, the act empowered the President to keep the new warships on the building ways and in a state of preservation until a public exigency might deem otherwise. Construction of the first of the line-of-battle ships, the *Columbus,* was started at the Washington Navy Yard in May 1816; she was launched in March 1819. Others were started about the same time or in subsequent years but never launched. The first frigate, the *Potomac,* was launched in 1821; the second, the *Brandywine,* in 1825; and the third, the *Columbia,* not until 1836.

In February 1816, Congress established the Board of Naval Commissioners consisting of three senior naval officers to handle the procurement of naval stores and materials; the construction, armament, equipment, and employment of vessels of war; and other matters connected with the naval establishment of the United States. On June 14, President Madison clarified some of the uncertainty in this language by saying that the Board was an instrument of the executive branch and therefore responsible to the President. In this relationship, the Board reported to the President through the Secretary of the Navy, who could determine its actual powers. Benjamin Crowninshield decided that the Board would be responsible for the building, repairing, and equipping of ships as well as the overseeing of dry docks, naval stations, and navy yards. As far as appointments, the ordering of officers to duty, disciplinary matters, and the movement of ships were concerned, the Board was to act merely in an advisory capacity to the Secretary of the Navy. For business, the commissioners first obtained the consent of the Secretary before handling it.

It was well that the Navy Department had settled down into the new and stronger organizational position in terms of meeting its workload and that the *Columbus* was launched in 1819, for in 1820 a movement in behalf of what may be called naval retrenchment developed in the House, and after that time a comprehensive and well-planned naval strengthening program proved almost impossible to carry out until the Civil War. In 1821, an act was passed, over the protest of the Department of the Navy, reducing from $1,000,000 to $500,000 the sum to be spent each year for new naval construction and authorizing this expenditure for only six more years. Annual appropriations fell from a yearly average of nearly $3,700,000 for the period 1817–21 to $2,900,000 for the period 1821–25.

During 1827 Congress debated another bill calling for the gradual improvement rather than the increase of the Navy. It provided for building two dry docks, the improvement of existing navy yards, and the establishing of an academy for officers, but no new ships. The provision for a naval academy was attacked as being an opening wedge toward the fostering of a naval class whose members would form a dangerous lobby working persistently for the construction and use of more and more warships. The bill finally passed, but without the provision for a naval academy. The strongest opposition came from the representatives of inland states and from the followers of General Andrew Jackson's new agrarian party.

Jackson became President in March 1829, and a policy embodying the principle that the United States needed no more ships of war in commission than were requisite to the protection of commerce as required by the distant-station system governed his eight years in office. Even the professional opinion of the leading naval officers of the period essentially supported this view. In March 1836 the Board of Naval Commissioners, over the signature of Commodore John Rodgers, submitted a report in which it was argued that in time of war the size of the Navy should be determined simply by the number of seamen that could be found to man the ships. Commerce, they thought, would inevitably be interrupted in a future war, allowing the Navy to enlist unemployed merchant marine seamen.

For peacetime, the Board endorsed the distant-station policy for the protection of national commercial interests and ignored the difficulties so presented in the development of a sea-going fleet powerful enough to send against any enemy. They further suggested that only five capital ships be kept in commission and that only two of these be on active duty at any one time. Training for officers or men would not extend very much beyond simple ship-handling.

This policy of "drift" controlled naval policy until about 1853, except for the period 1841–43 when Abel Upshur was Secretary of the Navy and for times of international crisis when naval affairs received greater attention.

In December 1841, Upshur submitted a report advocating the expansion of the Navy to at least half the naval power of the strongest maritime power in the world. He also recommended building more steam warships and establishing a naval training school for officers. To replace the Board of Naval Commissioners, Upshur supported a Bureau system without collective responsibility. He fought vigorously for his program but was only partially successful; he did not get enough money to expand the Navy as he desired, nor was a naval training school established, but in August 1842, the system of Bureaus was set up.

As on previous occasions, the debate and vote on Upshur's program revealed sectional cleavage based on the geographical and economic relationship of an area adjacent to the seaboard, limited and uncertain ideas about the value of the Navy to the United States, and desire for spoils. This approach to naval problems continued in subsequent years. Even the success of the Navy in maintaining command of the sea during the Mexican War failed to bring about a change. In 1848, Secretary of the Navy John Y. Mason declared that the only naval force needed in peacetime was a few ships of war to protect American interest abroad and to serve as a nucleus, capable of any degree of expansion, to meet wartime conditions.

With this type of executive leadership, the members of Congress conspicuously began to view the welfare of the Navy from the point of view of what advantage their votes and interests in naval affairs might bring to their constituencies; selfish and local interests took precedence over national interests. Ships were added to the Navy as the need arose, and as Congress could be persuaded to appropriate or not to prohibit the necessary expenditure. They were dispersed to the various stations either singly or in small groups to protect commerce and carry out other specially assigned duties such as transporting diplomatic missions or exploring and charting. By 1843, seven such stations had been established: the Mediterranean (1815), the West Indian (1822), the Pacific (1822), the Brazilian (1826), the East Indian (1835), the African (1843), and the Home (1841), each having its own squadron. Even when there were two or more ships on a station, they seldom trained or operated as a unit.[2]

Despite this diverse, and what proved to be very costly effort with respect to the naval strength achieved, the Navy in the period from 1816 until 1861 did have responsibilities for the national welfare, and all in all seems to have carried off these responsibilities reasonably well.

In that period, when the Navy still consisted largely of sailing ships, most of which were on distant stations for long periods of time, skill in ship-handling and the ability to maintain discipline were no small achievements. The maintenance of discipline was particularly valuable, especially after 1850, when flogging, long considered an adjunct of discipline, was abolished. Yet, between 1816 and 1861, the Navy produced officers who were skilled shiphandlers and strict disciplinarians.

In support of the distant-station policy, the Navy developed a widespread system of supply depots and naval agents. An adequate supply system was one of the most essential attributes of a strong naval force. Between 1815 and 1861, depots were established at Key West and San Francisco, and overseas at Rio de Janeiro, Manila, Singapore, Shanghai, Hong Kong, Macao, Monterey and Mazatlan in Mexico, Panama, Lima, Valparaiso, and in the Hawaiian and Cape Verde Islands, among others. Funds for local expenses were provided through drafts drawn on Baring Brothers, London, where the Navy kept an account, or by means of sight drafts drawn on the Department of the Navy. Supplies were shipped to the various stations periodically. The principal navy yards in the United States were at Boston, New York, Norfolk, Pensacola, and Mare Island, California; secondary yards were at Portsmouth, Philadelphia, and Washington. By the middle of the 1830s, dry docks were in operation at the Boston Navy Yard and at Norfolk.[3]

What the civilian and professional leadership of the Navy seemed to lack, in addition to failing to advance the idea of fleet operations as a means of best defending the interests of the United States, was an adequate grasp of the naval revolution about to take place with the use of steam power. Most senior naval officers and some Secretaries of the Navy considered the sailing ship to have reached a state of near perfection. Secretary of the Navy James K. Paulding declared in a report to the Senate, dated January 6, 1839, that he would never consent to let the old ships perish, and transform the Navy into a fleet of steam sea monsters. Nevertheless, officers such as Captain Matthew C. Perry, Captain Robert F. Stockton, Lieutenant William Hunter, and Secretary of the Navy Abel P. Upshur appreciated the advantage of steam power, and between 1820 and 1861 tried to induce the Navy to build steamships and train officers to operate them. It was mainly due to the support and effort of Perry and Upshur that the paddle-wheel steamships *Mississippi* and *Missouri* were completed in 1842. Small engines gave them a maximum speed of 9½ knots. The *Mississippi* was flagship of Perry's expedition to Japan in 1852–1854. Stockton was largely responsible for the building, in 1841, of the USS *Princeton,* the first screwdriven warship in any navy. In 1846, the United States Navy had only seven steam warships; by 1854, 18 steam vessels had been acquired. Great Britain then had 141 steamers of war, while France had 68.

In 1854, Congress, at the urging of Secretary of the Navy James C. Dobbin, appropriated $3,000,000 for the construction of six first-class steam frigates, *Merrimac, Wabash, Minnesota, Roanoke, Colorado,* and *Niagara,* with screw propellers as part of a comprehensive naval expansion program. With this appropriation, the period of "drift" in naval affairs turned to what might be called a policy of naval "rejuvenation" supported by the industrial northern states and the slave-owning southern states. The frigates, launched in 1855–56, were essentially sailing ships with auxiliary steam power. Later, a number of other steam frigates and shallow-draft sloops were authorized by Congress, but these were also wooden-walled and represented only a small proportion of our naval capability. On the eve of the Civil War the Navy had not one steam-propelled ironclad warship of the type being developed in European navies. The steam warships the Navy did have were dispersed like sailing ships according to the distant-station policy.

The lack of ironclads was not considered alarming by most statesmen and naval leaders. United States interests seemed to be best served by swift frigates and sloops, armed with the most powerful guns, and manned by crews willing to do ship-to-ship battle. Even the construction of more steam-propelled warships did not change ideas prevailing before the Civil War as to how best the ships of the Navy could be used both in peace and war.[4]

But seamanship, discipline, and fighting spirit were not enough to keep the Navy afloat and meet all of the demands upon its services. With the increasing use of steam power, the Navy was forced in 1842 to form a new corps of engineers as well as to develop other technical and support services.

Increasing operations in distant areas required accurate charts and navigation instruments, as well as the ability to use them. For this purpose, in 1830 the Navy organized a Depot of Charts and Instruments and in 1842 a Naval Observatory to provide astronomical data as an aid to navigation. Under the supervision of Lieutenant Matthew Fontaine Maury from 1844 to 1861, these offices helped the Navy in its basic mission. They also provided services oriented toward aiding commerce and science and for the advanced professional education of young officers. Merchants wanting more accurate charts, scientists wishing to know more about the secrets of the earth, and naval officers hoping to lead expeditions for this purpose found a friend in Maury. For his valuable work in marine meteorology and oceanography from data supplied to him by ship captains, explorers, and others, Maury received acclaim from European scholars and was awarded many foreign decorations.

As important as the Naval Observatory and the Depot of Charts and Instruments was the Nautical Almanac Office, established in 1849, at Cambridge, Massachusetts, to compile an American ephemeris. Its first officer in charge, Lieutenant Charles H. Davis, used some of the best scientists of the time, including Professor Benjamin F. Pierce, Professor

John D. Runkle, and Professors William Ferrel, Joseph Winlock and Simon Newcomb, all famous as mathematicians or astronomers.[5]

The Department of the Navy was headed by the Secretary of the Navy, a civilian, appointed by the President. From 1841 to 1861, Secretaries were usually southerners. Only Abel P. Upshur of Virginia, who served from 1841 to 1843, presented Congress with an overall naval legislation program that may be called comprehensive, and he of all the Secretaries of the Navy showed the most comprehension of the effect of steam power on the navy. It was Upshur who obtained the establishment of the Bureau system, and he was in office when the *Princeton, Mississippi,* and *Missouri* were completed. Other secretaries gained distinction by their attention to developing particular aspects of the Navy's role in furthering the national interests of the United States. John P. Kennedy, Secretary of the Navy from July 1852 to March 1853, was responsible for the dispatch of at least three exploring expeditions, and received much recognition from scientific societies and scientists in the United States for his strong advocacy of using the Navy for exploration and the advancement of science.

As long as the distant-station policy was not violated, the Secretary of the Navy exercised great influence as to the use of the ships, officers, and men of the Navy. His main limitations were money and whether he was sometimes willing to interpret broadly how Congress intended he should use the funds appropriated to the Navy when the wording of the legislation seemed to preclude a desired course of action. But even if he was willing to be bound by a strict reading of an appropriation bill, he could always ask Congress, with the approval of the President, for additional funds; whether he could get them depended to a great extent on how Congress viewed his "political" influence. In this regard, the secretaries used the pressure of expert testimony, individual and group memorials, as well as crisis situations to gain their objectives.[6]

In the middle of the 1840s, the 20-year old agitation for the establishment of a naval academy at last brought action. Until 1845 young officers were trained at sea, following preliminary education for midshipmen in schools established at various navy yards. Most midshipmen entered the Navy at the age of fifteen or sixteen and began training as a member of a ship's crew. Their education, for the rest of their careers, was primarily aboard ship, with promotion by seniority. Officers could request leave of absence to attend an institution of higher learning to enhance their professional qualifications.

The system of shipboard training supplemented by individual study with promotion by seniority had great disadvantages, although it functioned adequately between the War of 1812 and the Civil War. Some of the disadvantages were an excess of older officers in the senior ranks, the development of cliques, long demoralizing periods between promotions, and the automatic promotion of unqualified men. George Bancroft, Secretary of the Navy from 1845 to 1846, felt strongly about this situation, particularly with regard to the qualifications of officers, and in an attempt to help rectify it, in 1845 he moved the Philadelphia Naval School to Annapolis, supervised its reorganization, and enlarged it. During 1850–51, with Congressional approval, the school was renamed the Naval Academy; it was again reorganized, and a four-year course of study was adopted. The first Naval Academy class graduated in July 1846.

The establishment of the Naval Bureaus in 1842 also placed new emphasis on the principle of determining the qualifications of officers for appointment and promotion by means of examinations. Admission to the engineering corps, for example, required an applicant to pass a technical examination. In August 1846, Secretary Bancroft issued a general order for the establishment of an entrance examination for naval constructors, boatswains, carpenters, and sail-makers. As far as line officers were concerned, he recommended that promotion should be judged by examining boards or by efficiency reports. The examinations of candidates for assistant surgeons who were eligible for promotion, were prescribed by law in 1828, and in 1835, the first examinations were held for prospective professors of mathematics.

Through the activities of the Naval Retiring Board, brought into being by Congressional action in 1855, retired and reserved lists for officers came into existence. Certain officers placed on these lists who were too old or incapacitated for active duty but whose records indicated they should be retained on some naval list accepted the decision, understandably, with some bitterness.

During the period 1816–1861, enlisted men were usually "shipped" for three years and then discharged. There was no "career plan." Between enlistments, men were not considered subject to Navy regulations or discipline. Long-term training was unknown and it was difficult to meet manpower needs; ships sometimes sailed without a full crew. An apprentice system under which boys between fourteen and eighteen were enlisted, was tried but did not prove successful; it was abandoned by the beginning of the Civil War.

In 1852, Secretary of the Navy John P. Kennedy recommended the establishment of a permanent corps of seamen. In 1857, the ordnance ship *Plymouth*, commanded by Commander John A. Dahlgren, took seamen for a six-month cruise to learn the management of heavy ordnance in storm and calm. Essentially, however, the enlistment situation for seamen did not change between 1815 and 1861, and like officers, new recruits were expected to learn their trade through service aboard ships.[7] What did change for the better, however, were the living conditions within which this trade was acquired.[8]

In spite of the absence of fleet operations and deficiencies in ships and men, the Navy from 1815 to 1861 played a vital role in the furthering of United States foreign policy, commercial activity overseas, and the advancement of science. One of the cardinal points in American foreign policy before the Civil War was to promote and protect overseas commerce. By 1815, the Navy had contributed to the success of this effort in the Mediterranean region by convoy protection and by defeat of the Barbary pirates. It continued to aid American interests there by keeping the Mediterranean open to American shipping and by helping to negotiate treaties of benefit to American commerce. Commanders of the Mediterranean Squadron, such as Commodore William M. Crane and Commodore James Biddle, helped to bring about a treaty in 1830 with the Ottoman Empire that, among other results, opened the Black Sea to American ships. The first chargé d'affaires at Constantinople appointed under the terms of this treaty was a naval officer, Commodore David Porter.[9]

A similar sequence of events took place in the Pacific, except that the pursuit of science was a distinct but related element within the purpose of protecting and advancing American foreign commerce. The USS *Potomac,* during its cruise around the world between 1831 and 1834, had carried out orders to destroy the stronghold of pirates at Quallah Battoo in Sumatra who had captured the merchant ship *Friendship* of Salem, killing and wounding a number of officers and men. In 1844 the *Columbia* and *John Adams* performed a similar act of retaliation against various other pirate strongholds in Sumatra.[10]

Following efforts to subdue piracy, the Navy frequently assisted in negotiations aimed at opening new markets to American commerce. Naval officers negotiated commercial treaties with various native rulers in the Pacific and Indian Ocean areas. In 1846, Commodore James Biddle exchanged, with the Chinese, ratifications of the treaty of Wanghea that had been negotiated by Caleb Cushing and that opened certain Chinese ports to United States commercial activity. Later, Commodore Matthew C. Perry commanded an expedition to Japan and performed the diplomatic duty of negotiating a treaty which opened Japan to foreign trade (see Chapter 8).[11]

The use of ships, officers, and men to further the interests of the nation's commerce was very evident in the activity of the U.S. Navy in South America. There, as in the Pacific, the advancement of scientific knowledge was also a factor in the many expeditions the Navy conducted.

All such activity involved expenditures of government funds. Additional expense was incurred in the publication of charts, classification and description of specimen collections, and the printing of other data resulting from expeditions. Because the ships and men would have had to be paid for even if there were no expeditions and because complete financial records for each expedition have not been located, the total cost of the expeditions and their publications cannot be determined with accuracy. The exploration of the valley of the Amazon cost less than $5,000 (estimated), while the North Pacific-Bering Straits-China Seas voyage cost over $150,000. Publication of the results of the Perry expedition to Japan cost over $360,000. As contrasted with the ultimate economic and scientific benefit to the nation, however, the government probably never spent the taxpayers' money to better advantage.

# Chapter 3

# Wilkes' United States Exploring Expedition of 1838-1842

On August 19, 1838, a squadron of naval vessels, the *Vincennes, Peacock, Porpoise, Sea Gull, Flying Fish,* and *Relief* departed from Norfolk, Virginia. They were under the command of Lieutenant Charles Wilkes, who had orders to sail to Rio de Janeiro and then to Tierra del Fuego. From Tierra del Fuego, the ships were to attempt to penetrate the Antarctic ice in order to investigate whether a continent or a polar sea existed in the south polar region. Wilkes's orders further stated that when this had been accomplished, he was to make surveys of various Pacific Islands before going to Sydney, Australia, to refit and take on provisions for a second voyage of Antarctic discovery.*

In 1840, Wilkes was to take his ships from Sydney, during the southern hemisphere summer, on a voyage of exploration south of Van Diemen's Land, and as far westward as Enderby's Land. He would then sail north, surveying various island groups on the way to the Hawaiian Islands, after which he was to survey the northwest coast of North America and the seas off Japan. The orders stipulated that under no circumstances should Wilkes or any member of his command furnish anybody not belonging to the expedition with "copies of any journal, charts, plan, memorandum, specimen, drawing, painting, or information of any kind, which has reference to the objects or proceedings of the Expedition." It should be noted, however, that Wilkes did admonish his officers to keep a diary "in which will be housed all that related to public information, being a record of all objects of interest, however small, which may take place during the cruise, in the scientific or

---

*The following account of the United States Exploring Expedition draws heavily from two publications: Philip I. Mitterling, *America in the Antarctic to 1840* (1959) and David B. Tyler, *The Wilkes Expedition: The First United States Exploring Expedition,* (1838–1842), published in 1968. Many of the quotations used in this chapter can be found in Mitterling, but, except where otherwise noted, they have been taken directly from Wilkes' *Narrative of the United States Exploring Expedition, During the Years 1838, 1839, 1840,* 5 vols. The accounts of Mitterling and Tyler have been checked against this source as well as others listed in the footnotes.

any other department." He also stated that they could express opinions should they so wish.

The departure of these ships from Norfolk was the culmination of at least two years of preparation during which many false steps and unproductive procedures had been taken. In 1836, Congress had appropriated $300,000 for an exploration of the Antarctic region and the area of the Pacific ocean in which the United States had exhibited a commercial interest. The purpose of such an exploration was to make hydrographic surveys, chart unknown navigational dangers, and add to scientific knowledge through astronomical observations and the collection of specimens. Captain Thomas ap Catesby Jones was named to command the expedition, which was to include the frigate USS *Macedonian,* the brigs *Pioneer* and *Consort,* the schooner *Pilot,* and the provision ship *Relief.*

Subsequently, Jones became dissatisfied with the way the expedition was being organized and asked to be relieved of its command. There was some difficulty in naming an officer who would accept the assignment, and finally it was given to Lieutenant Charles Wilkes, who had already journeyed to England to buy instruments for the expedition. Wilkes was in command of the *Porpoise* searching for pirates off the southeast coast of the United States when he was selected to lead the expedition. He had entered the Navy as a midshipman on January 1, 1818. His previous experience in surveying Georges Shoal and Bank off the New England coast made him especially qualified for such duty. Second in command was Lieutenant William Hudson, who was two years senior to Wilkes but who accepted the position with the understanding that the voyage was to be purely civil and not military. To legitimatize and clarify this position, Secretary of the Navy Mahlon Dickerson issued an order stating that the expedition was to be purely scientific, entirely divested of all military character, and would return to the United States even if the nation became involved in war. Wilkes did not approve of this situation, but he accepted Hudson's appointment.

James Kirke Paulding, who succeeded Dickerson as Secretary of the Navy, gave Wilkes orders which read: "Cabals of discontented officers must be properly arrested and their leaders either kept in subjection or detached from the squadron as it is not to be endured that the purposes you are sent to attain are to be defeated by the fantastic claims of rank."[1] These orders were not made public nor given to any other officer.

Again conditions seemed propitious for the departure of the expedition, until reaction in the House of Representatives against expenditure of funds almost killed it. After a lengthy and bitter debate the necessary appropriation was passed by two votes. Debate in the Senate paralleled, but was much less extensive than that in the House, and the appropriation passed.

After the appointment of Wilkes, and during the debates in the House and Senate, Wilkes and the Secretary of the Navy agreed to replace the ships originally assigned to the expedition with the *Vincennes, Peacock, Porpoise, Flying Fish, Sea Gull,* and *Relief.*

More than five months after they left Norfolk, most of the squadron reached Orange Harbor, New Island, Tierra del Fuego, on January 26, 1839. The *Relief,* a more sluggish sailer, arrived a few days later. Almost immediately preparations were made for the cruise into the Antarctic. Time was limited because of the lateness of the season, but they could get some experience sailing in the Antarctic and possibly make a landing.

Here Wilkes split up his squadron. The *Vincennes* would survey in the vicinity of Orange Harbor; the *Relief* would examine the Strait of Magellan. The *Porpoise* (with Wilkes on board) and *Sea Gull* were to investigate the eastern shore of Palmer Land as far south as possible. The *Peacock* and *Flying Fish* were to sail at least as far as 105° west before turning toward what is now called the Palmer Peninsula. In their orders, Wilkes mentioned the possibility of Palmer Land being an island that could be circumnavigated.

On the morning of February 25, 1839, the ships got underway. The *Porpoise* and *Sea Gull,* on March 3, sighted land that was thought to be Mt. Hope or Hope Island, on the eastern end of Palmer Land. A landing was made impossible by drift ice and icebergs of which Wilkes later wrote: "I have rarely seen a finer sight. The sea was literally studded with these beautiful masses, some of them pure white, and others showing shades of opal, others emerald green, and occasionally here and there some would be black, a strong contrast to the pure white." Three large rocks that were discovered in the area were named the Adventure Islets.

By March 5, 1839, the decks of the ships were covered with ice, and the men were suffering, according to Wilkes, "not only for want of sufficient room to accommodate the numbers in the vessels, but from the inadequacy with which they had been supplied." There was constant danger in fog and mist, due to huge ice islands, and deceptive masses of submerged floe ice. A fierce gale beset the ice-encased vessels. Faced with this situation, Wilkes ordered the *Sea Gull* to sail to Deception Island and thence to Orange Harbor. He took the *Porpoise* toward the South Shetlands, but on arrival, the condition of the crew permitted only a hurried investigation of Elephant and Cornwallis Islands, after which the ship returned to Orange Harbor.

The *Peacock* and the *Flying Fish* also encountered such extreme weather conditions that they were unable to carry out their objectives. The day after they left Orange Harbor a fierce gale separated them and all efforts to join up again were futile. The *Peacock* under Lieutenant Hudson sailed southward in an effort to carry out orders, but misfortune followed her. Seaman William Stewart, captain of the main top, fell overboard, was rescued, but died of his injuries and was buried at sea. This saddened the crew, and their depression was increased by continuing strong gales, heavy seas, and thick fogs that destroyed visibility almost completely. Despite the terrible weather, the *Peacock* reached 68°8′S latitude, 95°44′W longitude on March 25, 1839, and sighted the *Flying Fish,* under Lieutenant Walker, who reported that his ship had reached 70° south on March 22, but could go no further because of ice. According to Walker's written account (narrated by Wilkes), "I did not know at first how I should proceed; but after a careful look around I ran over to the weather shore of the pond, stood along it in search of a passage that I could not find; but observing at intervals sutures in the ice, where it did not appear firmly formed, I resolved to take advantage of this, and, if possible, force passage, feeling it necessary at all hazards to extricate ourselves as soon as possible." For once the wind favored Walker's plan and the *Flying Fish* broke out of the ice.

Walker's report made Lieutenant Hudson decide to turn back toward Tierra del Fuego. The ships had little to show for their efforts except observations on the climate, currents, and the aurora australis, and some birds collected by Titian Ramsey Peale, the only scientist accompanying them.

By the middle of April, the *Porpoise, Flying Fish,* and *Sea Gull* were at Orange Harbor; the *Peacock* was at Valparaiso, Chile; and the *Relief* was off Cape Horn. The *Relief,* carrying most of the scientists, had not been able to enter the Strait of Magellan from the western side, and could not return to Orange Harbor against strong southwest winds. Finally, she found refuge in the unprotected harbor of a small island called Noir Island. After losing both anchors there, it was decided to go on to Valparaiso instead of trying again for Orange Harbor.

Wilkes, certain that the *Relief* would return to Tierra del Fuego, had ordered the faster-sailing *Sea Gull* and *Flying Fish* to wait there and carry the scientists to Valparaiso. They waited for 10 days and then set out around Cape Horn for Valparaiso. The *Sea Gull* became separated from the *Flying Fish* at midnight on April 26 and was never seen again, evidently a victim of the perilous waters off Cape Horn.

From Valparaiso, the *Vincennes,* the *Peacock,* the *Porpoise,* and the *Flying Fish* headed northward to Callao, Peru. There they took different routes into the Pacific to explore and survey the Tuamotus, the Society Islands, Samoa, the Fijis, New Hebrides, and New Caledonia. The *Relief* was ordered to go to Hawaii and Sydney, Australia, for provisions and then to return home. It took her 50 days to reach Honolulu, and after a two-week stay there, 41 days to Sydney. On March 28, 1840, the *Relief* arrived in New York, carrying many specimens of natural history taken aboard in her 19-month voyage.

After the surveys had been completed by the other ships, they were to rendezvous at Sydney, Australia, before again venturing into the Antarctic. By the first week of December 1839, all the ships had reached Sydney, and

Wilkes and his officers made the usual official and social calls. The crews were allowed ashore for recreation. Wilkes busied himself with his astronomical studies, the scientists made journeys inland for specimens, and the ships were repaired. By December 18, the astronomical studies were completed and work was begun in earnest to prepare the ships for the Antarctic.

The people of Sydney considered the expedition to be unprepared for its mission. Wilkes later wrote, ". . . they inquired whether we had compartments in our ships to prevent them from sinking? How we intended to keep ourselves warm? What kind of antiscorbutic [preventative for scurvy] we were to use? And where were our great ice-saws?" Wilkes had no positive answer. Once more, he decided he could do nothing constructive to improve the condition of his ships. The *Peacock* was in a deplorable condition; it would be impossible to repair her without giving up the Antarctic cruise. According to Wilkes, "We made up our minds that it was absolutely necessary for the credit of the Expedition and the country for her to perform it; for we were well satisfied that improper imputations and motives would be ascribed to us if she did not, and was detained undergoing repairs, in the state of inactivity, during the seasons for operations in the high southern latitudes. The necessity I felt of subjecting so many lives in so unworthy a ship, caused me great anxiety during the whole cruise."[2] It was no wonder that the Australians were certain that the Americans, although seemingly without worry, were probably going to freeze to death.[3]

On December 25, 1839, the ships left Sydney; despite strenuous efforts to stay together, they were soon scattered. The *Flying Fish* was out of sight of the others on January 1, 1840. The *Peacock* lost the *Vincennes* and *Porpoise* on January 3, and set out for Macquarie Island, the designated rendezvous if ships became separated.

Icebergs and icefields were met as they reached 61°8'S latitude, 160°32'E longitude on January 10. The icebergs were so numerous that by the time the ship reached the 65th parallel they blocked further progress directly south, and on January 15 the *Vincennes* turned westward to sail along the ice barrier.

On January 19, ice-covered elevations were seen, which Wilkes decided must be hills, but the *Vincennes* ran into fog and Wilkes was unable to see them distinctly. The only confirmation he had was a sighting made by a seaman Wilkes considered to be very experienced.

Still pushing southwestward, the *Vincennes* reached what seemed to be an open lead to the southward, and was blocked again at 67°5'S latitude, 137°30'E longitude. Wilkes named the place Disappointment Bay. Again the *Vincennes* went on southwestward, but on January 28 she met fog and seemed about to be trapped by heavy ice. She could not keep on her course and was in danger of sinking. In a violent snow storm, Wilkes maneuvered carefully through icebergs to open water.

On January 30, a small indentation was entered and black rocks were observed on an elevated snow-covered area about a mile and a half from the ship. Wilkes recorded this discovery and labeled his journal entry "Antarctic Land discovered beyond cavil."[4] Later, he wrote that he "gave the land the name of the Antarctic Continent." These highlands, about 3,000 feet high, stretched approximately 60 miles east and west at 66° 45'S latitude, 140° 2'E longitude.

The next day the assistant surgeon reported that 15 seamen were on the sick list and recommended that the ship turn northward. Wilkes did not change her course. He later explained that "in bringing myself to this decision, I viewed the case on all sides with fairness, and allowed my duty to my country, my care for those whom it had committed to my charge, and my responsibility to the world, each to have its due weight."

The *Vincennes* continued to push westward along the ice barrier, and indications of what seemed to be land were seen every day. On February 12, Wilkes climbed the mainmast to observe what appeared to be a snow-covered mountain range at 65° 20'S latitude, 112° E longitude. He wrote in his journal: "The . . . land clearly determines or settles the question of our having discovered the Antarctic Continent."[5] A boat was lowered, and men from the *Vincennes* landed on some ice islands containing embedded boulders and large pieces of rock. On February 21, after a month and eight hundred miles of sailing along the coast, the *Vincennes* headed back to Sydney.

When the *Peacock* reached Macquarie Island, no other ships were present. A landing party went ashore to investigate the rookeries of penguins and other water fowl. On January 12, 1840, the *Peacock* passed within a degree of the supposed position of Emerald Island, but no land was seen.

On January 15, the *Peacock* sighted the *Porpoise* and *Vincennes* at 66° 01'S latitude, 165° E longitude. The ships did not remain together; they took different tracks along the ice barrier. On January 19 and January 23, the *Peacock* sighted what seemed to be land to the south. They captured a large king penguin carrying 32 pebbles of various sizes in its craw. In addition to the sightings, soundings showed "slate colored mud" at 320 fathoms, evidence that seemed to indicate they were near land.

Soon after these observations, the *Peacock* hit an ice floe that carried away one of the wheel ropes, disjointed the neck of the rudder, and made the rudder useless. The carpenter tried to repair the damage while the crew tried sails and ice anchors to work the ship toward a more open sea. The *Peacock* began to drift, hit more ice, and smashed her stern davits, stern boat, and spanker boom. She finally reached open sea on the morning of January 25. There the crew repaired the rudder and then sailed for Sydney to complete repairs and to be ready to join the squadron again as soon as possible.

The *Porpoise,* under the command of Lieutenant Cadwallader Ringgold, had a similar experience. Ringgold thought he saw land beyond the ice shelf, and reached 66°49′S latitude, 151°24′E longitude, without making any definite contact. On January 27, the *Vincennes* was within hailing distance, and both ships compared chronometers before separating once again. On January 30, 1840, the *Porpoise* met a French expedition and tried to pass within hailing distance of them. To Ringgold's surprise, however, the French ships sailed away without making any attempts to contact the Americans. Later, the commander of the French expedition, Captain Jules Sebastian Cesar Dumont d'Urville, who had the ships *Astrolabe* and *Zelee,* explained that he had estimated the *Porpoise* was sailing at a relatively faster pace and would pass the *Astrolabe* and *Zelee* unless the *Astrolabe* could accelerate by opening its sails to the wind. This maneuver, however, resulted in his ships' pulling away from the *Porpoise.* Later d'Urville shortened sail, proceeding slowly on his course to speak to the Americans if they returned.

After their disappointing failure to contact the French expedition, the crew of the *Porpoise* was fully occupied with the task of survival. The weather was terrible, and nothing of interest occurred until February 12 when "many strong indications of land presented themselves." At 64°54′S latitude, 105° E longitude, the ice shelf seemed to show "numerous stratified veins of earth and rock, with lofty and conical peaks." That day Ringgold secured some specimens of rocks from the iceberg area, and then ordered the *Porpoise* to stand to the northeast for Auckland Island, where she anchored in a harbor called Sarah's Bosom on March 17. After taking on wood and water, the *Porpoise* sailed to the Bay of Islands, North Island, New Zealand.

When the *Flying Fish* left Sydney, her acting master, George T. Sinclair, was of the opinion that no vessel had ever sailed with such a miserable crew. She had no cook and only seven seamen. Sinclair was in command because Lieutenant R. F. Pinkney, the actual commanding officer, was ill with little prospect of regaining his health. The only bright spot was that on December 28, the *Flying Fish* got a cook from the *Vincennes.*

Under such conditions, exploring prospects were not bright, and they grew dimmer. On January 1, 1840, strong winds carried away some of the sails. This prevented the *Flying Fish* from keeping up with the other ships, and the crew, somewhat amazed, watched the *Vincennes, Peacock,* and *Porpoise* continue on their way without giving any assistance.

On January 9, the *Flying Fish* sighted Macquarie Island. The *Peacock* was anchored there, but left in a heavy fog before the two ships could make contact.

The *Flying Fish* passed the supposed location of Emerald Island, but like the other ships, did not find it. She also reached the ice barrier, which Sinclair described as "masses of ice of different sizes, so closely packed and wedged together that it would be utterly impossible to penetrate it."[6] Like the other ships, the *Flying Fish* sailed westward along the ice barrier, and

*25*

her crew noticed the usual evidence of land, but were too busy keeping their ship afloat to give serious consideration to what appeared to be ice-covered highlands beyond the barrier.

On February 5, Sinclair decided that the *Flying Fish* would founder if the wind did not abate in the next 24 hours. If the ship stayed afloat that long, Sinclair would turn northward toward New Zealand. To this decision Pinkney gave no objection. On March 9, the *Flying Fish* entered the Bay of Islands; her crew felt that prayer and only the will of God had prevented them from spending their days in a watery grave. The *Porpoise* came in 17 days later.

From Sydney, the *Vincennes* joined the *Flying Fish* and *Porpoise* in the Bay of Islands. The *Peacock* remained in Australia for repairs, and was ordered to join the squadron at the Tonga or Friendly Islands.

After remaining at the Bay of Islands for only a short time, the *Vincennes, Porpoise,* and *Flying Fish* made an 18-day passage to Tonga. The *Peacock* arrived on May 1, and that same day all the ships sailed for the Fiji Islands, where Wilkes wanted to survey as many of the 150 islands in the group as possible. He also wanted to locate a port that could be used by whalers. In Fiji, Wilkes used the procedure of having ships and boats work in pairs as survey parties with assigned responsibility for specified areas. Each boat carried sails, tents, arms, and provisions for the number of days she would be away from headquarters located on the Island of Ovalou. An observatory was set up at Levuka on a high point of land.

The survey continued from early May to the last part of August. Except for minor accidents that incapacitated some men, everything went well until one day when Lieutenant Joseph A. Underwood and Midshipman Wilkes Henry were killed by natives as they tried to bargain for food and a seaman with them was seriously injured. After burying Underwood and Henry, Wilkes led a force of about sixty men in an attack on two villages from which the murderers were supposed to have come. The villages were destroyed and many natives killed. Wilkes forced the survivors to make their submission by crawling on their hands and knees before him. Peace was then proclaimed on the condition that the natives bring provisions for the ships on the following day, which they did.

On August 11, the squadron started for the Hawaiian Islands. En route, various islands along the way were investigated and surveyed. By October 7, all the ships were together again at Honolulu, where they began a general overhaul. The crews were given time for rest and recreation, and charts were prepared. Since most of the men had enlisted for a 3-year cruise which ended on October 31, 1840, new shipping articles extending their time to May 31, 1842, were drawn up. After some persuasion, all but 23 men signed the new articles; those who refused were left in Hawaii and replaced by Hawaiians.

By the middle of November, repairs and chart-making were completed, and the squadron resumed surveying and exploration. On November 16, the *Porpoise* was sent to survey the southern shore of the island of Ovalou, Samoa, and certain of the Society Islands. The *Peacock* and *Flying Fish* departed on December 2 to survey islands in the central Pacific. Wilkes led a party to the top of Mauna Loa on the island of Hawaii to make scientific observations to be compared with those performed at sea level.

By March 24, 1841, the *Porpoise* had returned to Honolulu. On April 5, the *Vincennes* and *Porpoise* sailed to the Pacific Coast of North America to map the Columbia River region in the Oregon Territory. They arrived off the Columbia River on April 28. On May 1, they entered the straits of Juan de Fuca and the next day anchored near the eastern end. At Fort Nisqually, the nearest outpost of the Hudson's Bay Company, a pilot was obtained who took the *Vincennes* through the narrows dividing Admiralty Inlet from Puget Sound. She then anchored opposite the fort.

Again the work of mapping and charting was resumed. The *Porpoise* was detailed to survey Puget Sound and the coast as far as Fraser's River, and a boat party was detailed to survey Hood's Canal. Land parties, accompanied by Hudson's Bay Company men and Indians, were dispatched to map the area east of the Cascades and to visit Astoria, Vancouver, the Willamette Valley, and the Columbia River as far up as Walla Walla. An observatory was set up to make necessary observations.

On July 17, the *Vincennes* left Fort Nisqually and met the *Porpoise* on July 20 at New Dungeness Roads for more mapping and surveying. One group surveyed New Dungeness Bay and Protection Island; another, a stretch from Hood's Canal to Whidby's Island that had not been surveyed previously. The *Porpoise* was sent through Johnson's Straits and around the north end of Vancouver Island to Nootka Sound.

In the midst of this work news arrived that the *Peacock* had been wrecked on the bar at the entrance to the Columbia River. On July 31, the *Vincennes* and *Porpoise* sailed to her rescue. As they approached Cape Disappointment on August 6, the *Flying Fish* arrived. Lieutenant William Hudson of the *Peacock* came on board the *Vincennes* from the camp, called Peacockville, which his officers and men had erected near Astoria. Fortunately, no lives were lost. The place where the ship was wrecked was (and still is) called Peacock Spit.

The loss of the *Peacock* was compensated for to some extent by the purchase of a brig which happened to be at Fort George under charter to the Hudson's Bay Company. Wilkes paid $9,000 for her and named her *Oregon*. With this ship, in addition to the *Porpoise* and *Flying Fish*, charting and surveying were continued from the mouth of the Columbia River and up stream to the head of navigation in the Cascades. The Willamette River was also surveyed as far as its falls. While this work was underway, a party under Lieutenant George F. Emmons, consisting of 39 men and 76 horses and mules, started off from a camp near Astoria on the Willamette River. The party was to map a route to San Francisco and meet the squadron there. Meanwhile, the *Vincennes* sailed to San Francisco, arriving there on August 14.

By the second week of October, the *Porpoise* and *Oregon* were en route to San Francisco to join the *Vincennes*. The *Porpoise* arrived on October 19, and the *Oregon* a day later. The party under Emmons reached San Francisco the last week of October. On October 31, with all the members of the expedition on board again, the squadron sailed for Hawaii, where all ships arrived on November 17 within a few hours of each other.

After making repairs and taking on provisions, the ships sailed on November 28, en route for the United States by way of the Cape of Good Hope with a rendezvous at Singapore, hopefully during the first week of February. On the way, the *Porpoise* and *Oregon* investigated islands and reefs to the northwest of the Hawaiian Islands and then sailed straight to Singapore.

The *Vincennes* and *Flying Fish* sailed in company from Honolulu, but soon separated because the *Flying Fish* could not keep up. Both ships reached Manila Bay on January 12, 1842. The *Flying Fish* had narrowly escaped being wrecked off Cape Espiritu Santo on the northeast point of Samar Island.

After eight days of rest and relaxation, both ships sailed on January 21, 1842. The *Flying Fish* surveyed the strait between the islands of Mindoro and Palawan, and arrived at Singapore on February 15, 1842. The *Vincennes* made a quick survey of the harbor of San Jose, part of the Island of Panay, and the harbor at Caldera before proceeding to the Island of Sulu, a rendezvous for pirates, where Wilkes negotiated a treaty of commerce with Sultan Mohammed Damaleil Kisand. This treaty stipulated that United States citizens could carry on trade and contained the promise that the natives would protect the property and persons of Americans in case of shipwreck or injury of any kind.

After surveying the harbor and making astronomical and magnetical observations, the *Vincennes* sailed on February 6, 1842. She investigated the Mansee Islands at the entrance to the Straits of Balabac, and anchored at Singapore on February 18, 1842.

At Singapore the *Flying Fish* was sold for $3,700 and her officers and crew assigned to other ships of the expedition, which sailed on February 26, 1842, for Cape Town, where they arrived on April 14.

Three days later, the *Vincennes* left for St. Helena, arriving there on April 25. On May 1, the ship departed for New York, where she arrived on June 10, 1842. The *Oregon* and *Porpoise* stopped at Rio de Janeiro en route and reached New York on June 29 and July 2, respectively.

The officers and men of the United States Exploring Expedition came home wearied of seeing or talking to each other, to a government and public that seemed more interested in criticizing that in honoring their achievements. Wilkes stated that ". . .all of the officers and men . . . had naturally expected to be welcomed home with some cordial and commendatory words from the government of their country. He had found, instead of this, a cold insulting silence. His reception by President John Tyler was cool and indifferent, as was his meeting with Secretary of the Navy Abel P. Upshur.

The claim made by Wilkes that the expedition had discovered the Antarctic Continent was challenged on the basis of statements from Captain Sir James Clark Ross, the British explorer who had taken an expedition to the Antarctic just after Wilkes and who stated that he had sailed over areas laid down as land by Wilkes, intimating that Wilkes was guilty either of incompetence or lying. Two disgruntled officers of the expedition used this situation to bring charges which led to court-martial proceedings against Wilkes for scandalous conduct tending to the destruction of morals because he had deliberately and willfully lied when he stated he had discovered land on January 19, 1840. Other officers preferred additional charges.

The court martial lasted from August 17 to September 7, and Wilkes was tried on 26 specifications including one based on the charge noted above. Wilkes was found not guilty and the specifications were not proven in every case except one charging illegal punishment for seamen. For this, he received a letter of reprimand from the Secretary of the Navy.

The overall atmosphere surrounding the return of the expedition was not improved when Wilkes, in turn, preferred charges against some of his officers that resulted in court-martial proceedings against them. As a result, one officer was reprimanded by the Secretary of the Navy, one was suspended without pay or emoluments for twelve months, and a third was reprimanded and suspended from duty for six months.

While these trials were in progress, Congress on August 26, 1842, passed a bill calling for all the written material of the expedition and its collection of natural history specimens to be deposited with the Library Committee of the Senate. The Library Committee then persuaded the Secretary of the Navy to issue orders to Wilkes to write the history of the expedition and to do reports on hydrography, magnetism, and meteorology.

By January 1844, Wilkes had completed work on a five-volume *Narrative* totaling some 2,500 printed pages. There were 250 copies of this work printed, 100 copies at government expense and the rest at the expense of Wilkes, who obtained the copyright to this edition and obtained permission to publish an additional 1,000 copies of a slightly different-size version to sell for his private benefit. The demand for the *Narrative* proved good, and additional printings and editions were issued in subsequent years. Of these, one appeared in London, and another, a German language edition, in Stuttgart.

While writing the *Narrative,* Wilkes also, with the assistance of a number of junior officers who had been with the expedition, prepared the expedition charts for publication.

The scientists and scientific collections associated with the expedition did not fare so well. The scientists were dismissed by the Secretary of the Navy, and the collections were deposited with the National Institute in the Great Hall, or National Gallery as it came to be called, of the Patent Office. Mismanagement in the unpacking and labeling of the specimens destroyed the scientific value of many of them. Charles Pickering, the biologist of the expedition, was eventually placed in charge of the collections and some of the expedition scientists were employed to prepare them for exhibition. The botanical specimens eventually were moved to the Botanical Garden in Washington, D.C. In June 1843, Pickering resigned his position and Wilkes took over his duties.

Wilkes remained in charge of the specimen collection until the outbreak of the Civil War. Under his supervision 19 scientific reports, some of which were never published, were written at a cost to the government of nearly $300,000.

Wilkes published his narrative in 1844 as the first five volumes in this series. In 1846, Volume 6, *Ethnography and Philology,* by Horatio Hale, was published. The same year, *Zoophytes,* by James D. Dana, appeared as Volume 7, with an atlas printed in 1849. Titian Peale produced *Mammalogy and Ornithology,* which was published in 1848 as volume 8 and revised in 1858 by John Cassin.

Also, in 1858, Cassin's revised version of Charles Pickering's *Races of Man* was printed as Volume 9. Volume 10, *Geology,* by James D. Dana, was published in 1849. In 1851 Charles Wilkes' work, *Meteorology,* appeared as Volume 11. A. A. Gould's *Mollusca & Shells* was added to the list in 1852 as Volume 12, with an atlas dated 1856.

*Crustacea,* Volume 13–14, by James D. Dana, appeared in 1852–53 and an atlas was published in 1855. Volumes 15 and 16 on botany by Asa Gray and William D. Brackenridge appeared in 1854 with atlases dated 1855 and 1856. Another work on botany, Volume 17, was finished in 1874 but never officially distributed. Volume 23, *Hydrography,* by Wilkes appeared in 1861, preceded in 1850 and 1858 by two volumes of charts.

Completed but never printed were Volume 18 on botany by Asa Gray, Volume 19 on the geographical distribution of animals and plants by Charles Pickering, Volumes 21–22 on ichthyology by Louis Agassiz, and Volume 24 on physics by Charles Wilkes. Parts 1 and 2 of Volume 19 were issued privately by Pickering in 1854 and 1876 respectively.[8]

World-wide, although limited, distribution of the reports prepared by the expedition was arranged for by the Congress which on February 20, 1845, ordered that 58 copies of each report

. . .shall be delivered to the Secretary of State, to be distributed as follows, that is to say: To each of these United States, one copy; to the Government of France, two copies; Great Britain, two copies; Russia, two copies; and one copy each to Sweden, Denmark, Prussia, Austria, Bavaria, the Netherlands, Belgium, Portugal, Spain, Sardinia, Greece, Tuscany, the Ecclesiastical States, the Two Sicilies, Turkey, China, Mexico, New Granada, Venezuela, Chili, Peru, the Argentine Republic, Brazil, Texas, and the Sandwich Islands; and one copy to the Naval Lyceum in Brooklyn, New York.

Wilkes was promoted to the rank of Commander in 1843 and to Captain in 1855. When the Civil War erupted in 1861, Wilkes was given command of a steamer, *San Jacinto,* and ordered to capture Southern blockade runners. On November 8, 1861, he sent a party aboard the British mail steamer *Trent* to remove two Confederate commissioners, John Slidell and James Mason, and their secretaries. For this action he was applauded by the public and congratulated by Congress. In the end the United States government decided that by taking it upon himself to remove and imprison the Confederate commissioners without bringing the *Trent* into port for the case to be adjudicated by a proper court, Wilkes was exercising a right of search which the United States held to be illegal. The commissioners and their secretaries were released from custody.

On July 16, 1862, Wilkes was promoted to the rank of Commodore and given command of a special squadron in the West Indies. A disregard for the rights and feelings of neutral powers in the area brought about his recall in June 1863. It was then discovered that he was three years older than indicated in his records. This situation was used as a pretext to demote him and place him on the retired list because of age.

As a retired officer, Wilkes continued to exhibit the energy and independence of mind he had when in service. He was promoted to Commodore on the retired list, but during March and April of 1864 he was court-martialed and found guilty of disobedience, disrespect, insubordination, and conduct unbecoming an officer. He was sentenced to be reprimanded and suspended from duty for 3 years, a space of time which was eventually reduced to one year. He died on February 8, 1877, in Washington, D.C.

When the United States Exploring Expedition returned to the United States in 1842, after an absence of nearly four years, it had sailed about 85,-000 miles, surveyed about 280 islands, 800 miles of streams and coastline in the Oregon Territory, and 1500 miles of the Antarctic coastal region. Hundreds of new species of fish, reptiles, and insects were brought back for classification and study. Published accounts of the expedition, prepared over the next 30 years covered hydrography, geology, ethnography, meteorology, botany, zoophytes, and crustacea. Relatively unknown, these volumes contain a wealth of information on the Pacific Ocean areas. The value of the expedition, to U.S. commerce and the world at large, has probably never been fully appreciated, except by scientists.[7]

The United States Exploring Expedition was the first large-scale exploring expedition sent out by the United States Navy. More expeditions were to follow, but all subsequent expeditions took their tone from this one. Moreover, its success stemmed to a great extent from the fact that Wilkes had strong convictions and stood up for them. This conviction brought him into conflict with both junior and superior officers and contributed to his being involved in controversy, such as that with Sir James Ross, but it was invaluable to his successful completion of his tasks. It is appropriate that the best monument to Wilkes' determination and ability is the hundreds-of-miles-long sector of the Antarctic continent, south from Australia, which is now named Wilkes Land.

# Lynch Expedition to the Dead Sea and the River Jordan, 1847-1849

On November 20, 1847, the USS *Supply,* a storeship under the command of Lieutenant William F. Lynch, got underway from the Brooklyn Navy Yard and anchored off the Battery to await weather suitable for passage through the Brooklyn Narrows and into the Atlantic Ocean. Six days later, on November 26, when the weather turned favorable, the USS *Supply* sailed into Raritan Bay, discharged the pilot off Sandy Hook, and headed for the Mediterranean Sea and the Levant.

Lieutenant Lynch's orders were, upon reaching the Mediterranean, to deliver needed provisions to the United States Mediterranean Squadron and then sail the *Supply* to Smyrna. While the *Supply* remained at Smyrna, Lynch was directed to go to Constantinople and, through Dabney Carr, United States Minister, apply to the Ottoman government for permission to pass through its territory for the purpose of exploring the River Jordan and the Dead Sea.

If the prerequisite permission was obtained, Lynch was to return to Smyrna, take the *Supply* to "such point on the coast of Syria as shall be deemed most advantageous for the purpose,"[1] turn her over to the first lieutenant, and then land his party to begin exploration. The ship then was to deliver more stores to ships in the Mediterranean Squadron and return to Beirut in time to pick up the Lynch party at the end of their labors. In the event that approval to pass through Ottoman territory was refused, Lynch had permission to turn the *Supply* over to the first lieutenant, consider himself on leave, proceed on his own to carry out whatever exploring plans he had in mind, and return to the United States within a year.

With these orders, Lieutenant Lynch hoped to fulfill the yearnings of some twenty years. Twice before he had contemplated visiting the region of the Jordan and the Dead Sea, but had been prevented from doing so first by duty and then by ". . . a domestic calamity."[2] In the early months of 1847, however, Lieutenant Lynch found himself without a command. He had

---

*Most of the quotations in this chapter can be found in Lieut. W. F. Lynch, *Narrative of the United States Expedition to the River Jordan and the Dead Sea* or in his *Letters written to the Secretary of the Navy during the Expedition;* see f.n. 15, p. 236.

made repeated but unsuccessful requests to the Secretary of the Navy for the command of various vessels. This inability to secure a command of his own was not due to his record. Born in Norfolk, Virginia, on April 1, 1801, Lynch was appointed a midshipman in 1819 and commissioned a lieutenant on May 17, 1828. As a midshipman he served in the USS *Shark* off the coast of Africa and on vessels of Commodore David Porter's "Mosquito Fleet" for the suppression of piracy in the West Indies. After being commissioned, Lynch saw service in the Mediterranean, the Gulf of Mexico, and on board the side-wheel steamer *Fulton*. He later commanded the USS *Poinsett* and USS *Colonel Marney,* War Department steamers taken over by the Navy after the Seminole War. While in command of the *Colonel Marney,* Lynch was commended by the Secretary of the Navy for his zeal in executing the orders of the Navy Department to report about depredations on public timber lands during a cruise around Florida and along the Gulf Coast to New Orleans made in the winter of 1844.

In September 1846, Lynch's only daughter died, and he took three months leave, following which he requested a new command. The Secretary of the Navy replied that although his record indicated he should be given a command, there were no suitable ships available.[3] The problem was that even though the Navy was involved in the war with Mexico and exerting all its efforts to reduce Vera Cruz, there were not enough ships to meet the command aspirations of all officers. With the fall of Vera Cruz the lack of ships became more acute. At that time Lynch put in writing a scheme that had long been germinating in his mind. On May 18, 1847, he proposed to the Secretary of the Navy that he be ordered to "circumnavigate and explore the Lake Asphaltites or Dead Sea and its entire coast."[4] The expense involved in such a project would be trifling, he asserted, and he was confident that the proposal could easily be achieved. The Navy's ships touched at Acre in Syria, only 40 miles from the foot of Lake Tiberias or Sea of Galilee. It was only 60 miles from the Sea of Galilee down the Jordan to the Dead Sea. The expedition could sail to Acre, land boats, and haul them overland to Lake Tiberias. Once at Lake Tiberias they could descend the Jordan to the Dead Sea and be back at the coast in 15 days.

As justification for the expenditure of the Navy's time and money, Lieutenant Lynch stated that the expedition would advance the cause of science by obtaining information that would provide answers to questions about the Jordan and the Dead Sea—questions that were burning issues among scientists in the second quarter of the nineteenth century. In 1837, the scientific world for the first time became aware that the surface of the Dead Sea was below that of the Mediterranean, and with this awareness came a strong desire to know exactly what the difference was. Moreover, desire was voiced for geological data and specimens that would permit a thorough scientific appraisal of the cause of this phenomenon and its relationship to conflicting reports on the existent or non-existent animal and plant life in the region. Other questions such as whether the Jordan did indeed meander, what the river's velocity and elevation were at selected points, and the exact size, depth, and temperature of the Dead Sea also agitated scientists at this time.

During the first half of the nineteenth century, a number of people visited the Jordan and Dead Sea in an attempt to answer some of these questions. As early as 1835, an Irishman named Christopher Costigan circumnavigated the Dead Sea in eight days, but he died at the end of his trip without leaving a journal. In 1837, W. G. Beke and two other Englishmen estimated that the Dead Sea was 500 feet below the Mediterranean by timing the boiling point of water at various locations. They also transported a boat from Jerusalem to the Jordan at Jericho, sailed into the Dead Sea, took some soundings, and examined part of its shores. Later Lieutenant Symonds, RN, computed by triangulation that the Dead Sea was 1,312 feet below the level of the Mediterranean. Other visitors gave various and often conflicting estimates of its size and shape.

In 1847 this activity and the often contradictory statistics that it engendered induced Dr. Edward Robinson of the Union Theological Seminary in New York to read a paper before the Royal Geographical Society in which he called on "all European governments to combine their resources to solve this burning problem" and "speedily cause the questions raised to be put to rest forever" within the year.[5]

In addition, the expedition proposed by Lynch would gratify the Christian world because the observations made and the data brought back would contribute to a better appreciation and understanding of the Old and New Testaments. Voltaire, in his *Philosophical Dictionary,* for example, had questioned the biblical account of the destruction of Sodom and Gomorrah, particularly the belief of his contemporaries that this destruction had resulted in the formation of the Dead Sea.[6] This question was still being debated in the first part of the nineteenth century, and Lynch hoped to settle it by finding physical evidence of the fate of Sodom and Gomorrah.

Thus, the Dead Sea was still a mysterious entity to scientists and "of thrilling interest to the Christian."[7] Lynch hoped that the U.S. Navy would gain prestige and glory by finding answers to the still unanswered questions about this region. Since books dealing with the Holy Land were popular (witness the record of J. S. Stephens' *Incidents of Travel in Egypt, Arabia, Petraea, and the Holy Land*);[8] such an expedition would also arouse the interest of many ordinary citizens.

The Secretary of the Navy's initial reply to Lynch's proposal was that he was favorably disposed and would consider implementing Lynch's project at the opportune moment. On July 31, the Secretary authorized Lynch to start preparations for the exploring trip and said that additional orders involving transportation and other matters would be given him at the first opportunity.[9] In the fall of 1847, this opportunity arrived when the storeship

USS *Supply* was chosen to transport provisions to the Mediterranean Squadron.

On October 2, 1847, Lynch received orders to take command of the USS *Supply,* and he was soon busily engaged in organizing and fitting out his expedition.

Lynch had read widely in the literature pertaining to the Jordan and the Dead Sea region in planning the expedition, and he used imagination in carrying it out. An example was the first use of "prefabricated" boats. Two such boats were purchased from the patent owner, Joseph Frances of New York City. One boat was copper and the other was galvanized iron, both constructed in 12 sections so they could be knocked down for shipping and re-assembled when they were to be used. However, they were loaded aboard the *Supply* in a completed condition. In addition, Lynch had two four-wheel carriages or trucks, for hauling the boats, also constructed so that they could be knocked down for shipping and stowed in sections. It was Lynch's hope to transport the boats in a completed form on these carriages from Acre to Lake Tiberias. No horses were loaded. In his letter to the Secretary of State, Lynch had mentioned that camels could be used to draw the carriages and boats, but he only took harness for horses.

In addition to the boats, Lynch secured instruments necessary to complete his mission. Among them were self-registering thermometers, barometers, boiling water apparatus, surveying equipment including a Troughton spirit level and theodolite, and a Stell-wagen cup lead and line; two pocket chronometers from London were to be delivered in Gibraltar. Airtight gum-elastic bread-and-water bags were also procured, which, when empty, could be inflated for use as life preservers. The expedition was also equipped with a veritable armory of arms and ammunition, consisting of "a blunderbuss, fourteen carbines with long bayonets, and fourteen pistols, four revolving and ten with bowie-knife blades attached." Each "officer carried his sword, and all officers and men were provided with ammunition belts." Lynch was not going on a pilgrimage but on an official expedition under orders, and he was not going to be deterred by violence if he could help it; the Christian world would be gratified by the information he brought back even if conflict with the people living in the region could not be avoided and the expedition's days were not all peaceful. The party was also equipped with tents, sails, oars, salted pork, coffee, tobacco, and cooking utensils.

Equal attention was given to the party's physical and psychological characteristics. Lynch had permission to select 10 seamen for his expedition and went to great lengths to secure "young, muscular, native born Americans, of sober habits, from each of whom I exacted to abstain from all intoxicating drinks." Lynch felt that adherence to this provision was principally responsible for his party's being able to endure the extreme prostration caused by the severe privations and great exposures to which they were unavoidably subjected. One of his first moves was to recruit a good metalsmith with the rank of Master's Mate, Joseph C. Thomas. The other seamen selected were George Overstock, Francis Williams, Charles Homer, Hugh Read, John Robinson, Gilbert Lee, George Lockwood, Charles Albertson, and Henry Loveland. At least one of them had lived and worked on a farm and was used to handling horses. Another was trained to blast rocks in case it was necessary to make a passageway through the mountains to the Jordan valley. Two young officers, Lieutenant J. B. Dale and Passed Midshipman A. Aulick, both excellent draughtsmen, were detailed to help Lynch in the projected enterprise. Lynch's son, Francis, joined the expedition as the person responsible for the collection of plant specimens. No other civilian scientists were in the expedition when it left New York, nor did Lynch try to add any to his group. He did, however, correspond with Professor Samuel S. Haldeman of Philadelphia, Pennsylvania, a trained and competent scientist, who made suggestions about the kinds of specimens Lynch should gather. Lynch also received advice from Dr. Edward Robinson[10] who had visited Palestine in 1838, and from the traveler and author J. S. Stephens.

At the time he authorized the expedition, Secretary of the Navy John Mason had also written to Secretary of State James Buchanan, requesting that Dabney Carr secure permission from the Ottoman government for Lynch's journey into the Jordan and Dead Sea region. The Department of State was willing to help obtain such permission, but expressed doubts as to the expedition's value to United States relations with the peoples and countries of that area. The State Department felt that it was very risky to land a party of sailors on an official U.S. mission when the United States would inevitably become involved in the political problems of the region should the party run into trouble. Despite this doubt, Secretary Mason did not withdraw his approval, but in final orders issued to Lynch, stipulated that if for any reason the Ottoman Empire refused to grant permission for the expedition, Lynch was not to undertake it as an officer of the United States Navy, and he was not to use the crew or facilities of the Navy. If the Sultan refused to grant a firman, or document of authorization for the trip, however, Lynch was granted permission to take leave from the Navy for a year to conduct the expedition at his own expense. The problems of international relations must have been very carefully explained, for Lynch was called to Washington for a personal consultation with the Secretary of the Navy before he received his final orders.[11]

In its final form, the expedition's objective was somewhat enlarged; besides descending the Jordan from Lake Tiberias to the Dead Sea and circumnavigating and exploring the Dead Sea, it also was to determine how far the surface of the Dead Sea was below that of the Mediterranean and how high the intervening mountains were; investigate the source of the Jordan; and gather pertinent information about the commercial situation and potential of the area. In a confidential letter dated November 11, 1847, the objective of the expedition was described by the Secretary of State as being to "promote the cause of science, and advance the character of the naval service."[12] Lynch was not given any instructions relative to the scientific procedures he should follow, but he was urged to be "circumspect, conciliatory and forbearing," and to refrain "from committing the slightest act of aggression." At the same time, he was warned "to practice the strictest economy . . ." and to keep an account of each item for which money was expended.

The general public and Congress knew very little about the expedition or its purpose until shortly before it sailed. The *New York Herald* on Saturday, November 13, 1847, printed a short article about the expedition that cast doubt on the value of the venture with statements such as, ". . . but what object is intended other than scientific research, we cannot at present say." This attitude of blasé skepticism was taken up by the *National Intelligencer* in Washington, D.C., which on Wednesday, November 24, 1847, pointed out that the *New York Herald,* as well as other newspapers, had expressed some reservations about the expedition. Such lack of enthusiasm on the part of the press prompted Lynch to write a letter to the *Herald* to explain the purposes of the expedition and to try to allay the doubts expressed by the *New York Herald* and other newspapers. The *Herald* printed this letter on Saturday, November 20, 1847.

Since the *Herald* had given the first public intimation of the trip, Lynch felt it was only proper that the *Herald* print his letter as a defense of the enlightened statesman who had authorized the expedition. After some comments on what the world did not know about the Jordan and the Dead Sea, Lynch added that the object of the expedition was to ascertain with certainty if the Dead Sea and its shores had been caused by volcanic or non-volcanic action as well as "to refute the position of infidel philosophers with regard to its formation. The elucidation of this subject is a desideratum to science and would be most gratifying to the whole Christian world." The waters of the Dead Sea "will reveal those ruins upon the non-existence of which the unbeliever stakes his incredulity." Expected hardships and " small pecuniary considerations" should not stand in the way of such an undertaking, for the United States owed "something to the scientific and the Christian world, and while extending the blessings of civil liberty in the south and west, may well afford to help science and strengthen the bulwarks of Christianity in the east." Lynch ended his letter with the query, "Are the questions answered?"[13]

Lynch's letter, however, did not end questions about the value of the expedition. In December, in a preface to a short article entitled "Notes on the Dead Sea," *Littell's Living Age* printed the following:

> The following notes have been drawn up with much seeming care, and possess at present a more than usual interest, since, within the last month,

one of our public vessels has gone to the Mediterranean with a party of officers of the Navy to survey this region.

We do not perceive what practical benefit can arise therefrom, but as a matter of curiosity it is certainly as worthy the attention of our people as it has been that of the inhabitants of other countries.[14]

The lack of enthusiasm on the home front was the harbinger of other difficulties in getting the expedition started. The passage across the Atlantic, a particularly stormy one, took 23 days.[15] When the *Supply* arrived at Gibraltar, Lynch found that the Mediterranean Squadron had sailed for Port Mahon two days before, and that the pocket chronometers from London had not arrived. Lynch's enthusiasm, however, had not abated. In his letter to the Secretary of the Navy dated December 19, 1847, Lynch expressed the desire he had communicated to the Secretary of the Navy before he left New York: that the Secretary authorize the expedition to proceed beyond the southern borders of the Dead Sea to the mouth of the Euphrates River. In Lynch's mind, the expedition had grown into a general reconnaissance of the area to the north of Arabia. Lynch was so engrossed in his expedition that he was prepared to proceed immediately to Smyrna after the arrival of the chronometers, disregarding an order from the Mediterranean Squadron commander, Commodore George C. Read, USN, that the *Supply* proceed immediately to Port Mahon to supply the squadron. At Gibraltar, Lynch purchased an herbarium and some chemical tests for use by the expedition.

While awaiting the arrival of the pocket chronometers, Lynch and a seaman contracted smallpox. As soon as he became aware of his condition, Lynch sailed immediately for Port Mahon. Luckily the authorities there allowed the *Supply* to offload cargo while Lynch recuperated from sickness; the seaman, although he eventually recovered, was still ill when the ship sailed and had to be left in Malta. During this time, Lynch learned that an English naval officer, Lieutenant Thomas Howard Molyneaux, had traveled to and circumnavigated the Dead Sea, only to die when he arrived back on board his ship. The notes he left read like an adventure story and were of little immediate value in solving the questions about the region.

The tragedy did nothing to lessen Lynch's ardor; rather, it spurred him on to reach Smyrna. Before he left Port Mahon, Lynch held conversations and exchanged correspondence with Commodore Read that seemed to indicate Read's willingness to cooperate and to send the *Supply* to meet Lynch's expedition at Beirut by July 1, 1848.

On February 17, 1848, Lynch wrote the Secretary of the Navy from Smyrna, again asking permission to extend his expedition to the Euphrates River and reporting that he was on his way to Constantinople to secure the necessary firman, or document of permission. With the help of the United States Minister in Constantinople, Dabney Carr, and after almost two weeks of waiting, Lynch received authority to travel anywhere within the

Ottoman Empire. In reporting this fact to the Secretary of the Navy, Lynch wrote: "You may be pleased to direct my footsteps. The objections of the Secretary of the State are consequently removed and I trust that the expedition will be permitted to carry out the plan which you with such judgement and sagacious liberality designed." Lynch noted that the Constantinople press had given him favorable notice. On the other hand, he stated that the captain pasha, or head of the naval forces of the Ottoman government, had asked his opinion about an English steamer of 1,400 tons and that Lynch had given an unfavorable one. Lynch feared that the English press might comment unfavorably on his interfering in a matter which did not concern him, and that this in turn would raise trouble for him in Washington. While in Constantinople, Lynch added Henry Bedlow, who happened to be traveling in Asia Minor, to the exploring group. It appears that an adventurous spirit and Dabney Carr's recommendation constituted Mr. Bedlow's qualifications for his new position.

With the permission to travel through the Jordan and Dead Sea region in hand, Lynch returned to Smyrna and with his party proceeded in the *Supply,* first to Beirut and then to the Bay of Acre. At Beirut, Henry J. Anderson, M.D., of New York, a former Columbia College professor of mathematics and astronomy whose recent conversion to Catholicism had led to his extended visit to the Holy Land, was added to the group as medical officer and geological reporter. Since the health of the party remained strong until the last days of their stay in the Levant, Dr. Anderson was occupied mainly in studying the geological features of the region. Lynch was fortunate also in hiring at Beirut a dragoman, or interpreter, and a cook for the officers, both of whom served the expedition in excellent fashion.

On Wednesday, March 29, 1848, the *Supply* anchored "under Mount Carmel, before the walled village of Haifa" across from Acre. High and rough surf prevented landing the metal boats, the parts for the carriages, and the effects of the party until Friday. The people of the area crowded around to watch the activity, and the seamen had great fun putting the carriages together while trying to prevent the theft of copper thole-pins by natives who thought they were gold. The seamen also erected their tents, which were circular and constructed so that the masts of the boats could be used as tent-poles. Each officer and seaman had a two-yard piece of India-rubber cloth to sleep on and a blanket or comforter to cover them. The seamen "were full of jokes and merriment, at the beginning of camp life," and that night the members of the expedition slept in tents for the first time upon the beach outside of Haifa with the American flag flying above them.

Saturday morning Lynch was shocked by the condition of the horses he had requested and received from the Governor of Acre, Sa'id Bey.

With the first ray of light, we saw that our Arab steeds were the most miserable galled jades, and upon trial entirely unused to draught. It was ludicrous to see how loosely the harness we had brought hung about their meager frames. On trial as an exhibition of discontent, there was first a general plunge, and then a very intelligible equine protest of rearing and kicking. After infinite trouble, and shifting the harness to more than a dozen horses, we found four that would draw, when once started. But the load was evidently too much for them . . . so that we were compelled to relaunch the boats and send them to the ship, which had sailed over, and was then blazing away, returning a salute of the town. With a sailor mounted on each of the trucks, the horses were at length made to draw them, by dint of severe beating.

By afternoon the caravan of carriages reached the beach outside of Acre's walls, and the *Supply* landed the boats and materials sent back that morning. The governor of Acre, with his staff, came down to view the scene, followed by "nearly the whole population of the town." Lynch requested the governor to have his police clear the area, but the governor declared he did not have the power to prevent the people from congregating in the area.

Since the authorities could not or would not protect us, we determined to take the law into our own hands and protect ourselves, and accordingly posted sentinels with fixed bayonets to keep off the crowd. Jack did it effectually, and the flanks of two or three bore witness to the "capable impressure" of pointed steel; after which we were no more molested.

Late Saturday afternoon, Lynch received an invitation from Sa'id Bey, to come to his palace, where the governor told Lynch that he had just received word from a Bedouin chief, Akil Aga el Hassée, that the spirit of the Arab tribes bordering the Jordan was very hostile at that particular time, that they were up in arms, "at war among themselves, and pillaging and maltreating all who fell into their hands." The governor voiced the opinion that Lynch's group could not proceed in safety without a guard of at least 100 soldiers, adding that if Lynch would agree to pay 20,000 piastres (about 800 dollars), he would procure better means for the transportation of the carriages and boats and guarantee the safety of Lynch and his men. Lynch replied that he was willing to pay fairly for transportation animals and a few soldiers to act as scouts, but that his group did not need further protection since they were well armed and able to protect themselves. On this note of defiance, Lynch ended his conversation with the governor and left the room.

Outside, Lynch met the Bedouin chief who supposedly had brought news of the hostile spirit of the Arab tribes along the Jordan to the governor. Lynch showed him his sword and revolver, and described the amount of arms and ammunition that the exploring party carried with it. The chief was very impressed and remarked that if any group could explore the Jordan and Dead Sea region, the Lynch party could. Later Lynch met another Arab leader, called Sherif Hazza of Mecca, who claimed to be the 33rd lineal descendant of the Prophet, and who agreed to accompany the group on its journey. The Bedouin chief, Akil Aga el Hassée, again met Lynch's group on their way to Lake Tiberias, and Lynch was able to persuade him to accompany them as guide and advisor. These men were known and respected figures among the Arabs of the Jordan region, and their presence helped to facilitate the passage of the expedition through this territory. Lynch was a courageous and forthright person, albeit stubborn and ill-equipped to understand Islam, and he got along well with the Arabs he met. This ability to secure the compliance, if not the cooperation, of the local people contributed a great deal to the success of the expedition. Both Costigan and Molyneaux had been hindered greatly in their work by the opposition of Arabs; Lynch, on the other hand, was helped by the local population who furnished guides, guards, and in some instances, camels and food.

In scorning the governor's offer, however, Lynch had not solved the problem of transporting the boats from Acre to Lake Tiberias. There seemed to be no alternative but to take the boats apart and carry them in sections to Lake Tiberias unless camels could be made to pull in harness, and Lynch decided to try this method, which was successful; the "huge animals, three to each, marched off with the trucks, the boats upon them, with perfect ease." Elated, Lynch felt free of the governor because camels could be hired in abundance. With animals found to pull the carriages, the group left Acre for Lake Tiberias on April 4, 1848. The party was large: Lynch, his officers, the seamen, the dragomen, Bedlow and Sherif Hazza, each rode a saddle horse, for a total of 16 horses. Twenty-nine camels were with the party: to pull the carriages, three to a carriage; six in reserve; and seventeen pack animals. One mule, led by the cook, carried supplies, and about 15 mounted Bedouin and an unspecified number of camel drivers accompanied the party. Dr. Anderson met the group on the road to Lake Tiberias.

There were no roads, and the expedition encountered severe difficulties in hauling the boats across the mountainous terrain, such as narrow gorges, wet ground, broken and rocky country, and seemingly impassable ridges. By making detours, filling up hollows, and otherwise constructing a passable way, however, such obstacles were passed. Finally, after five days of arduous travel, the party brought the carriages and boats down the steep slope to the shores of the Sea of Galilee. At 2 p.m., on Saturday, April 8, 1848, the boats were launched. On this momentous occasion, Lynch opened a letter he had previously written to the Secretary of the Navy to add the following expression of delight: "I have opened this letter to communicate the intelligence that the 'Two *Fannies*' each with the Am: ensign flying are now afloat upon the Sea of Galilee."

At Tiberias, Lynch, his officers, the seamen, Bedlow, and Dr. Anderson secured quarters in the home of Heim Wiseman. After the boats were launched on the Sea of Galilee, the carriages, harness, and other unneeded effects were given to Wiseman for return to Acre. The horses, camels, and camel drivers were sent back to Acre. With the help of the Bedouin, Lynch secured the services of new horses and 11 new camels with their drivers, plus a donkey for carrying the cooking utensils.

Lynch was surprised and shocked to find only one boat on the Sea of Galilee. The owner was willing to sell it for 600 piastres (or about twenty-one dollars). Lynch added it to his flotilla, christened it *Uncle Sam,* and hired an Arab crew to man it. He noted that although fish were available, no native seemed interested in supplementing their meager food resources by fishing. He also compared the New Testament account of life there to what he considered its backward state two millenniums later. That was not the last comparison of the sort to be made by Lynch. Lynch was deeply religious, and his official reports and books indicate that he was familiar with the Scriptures as well as classical mythology, history, and literature.

On April 10, 1848, the exploring party, divided into two groups, began its journey to the Dead Sea. A land party under Lieutenant Dale consisting of Dr. Anderson, Bedlow, Francis Lynch, the cook with his donkey, the 11 camels with the heavier baggage and camel drivers, and the Akil Aga el Hassée and Sheríf Hazza with 10 of their men on horseback, set out to observe the country, collect specimens of plants, guard against attacks, and prepare nightly camps on the river bank. The boat party, under Lynch's command, started down the Jordan. To Passed Midshipman Aulick, Lynch assigned the task of making a topographical sketch of the river and its shores. Lynch observed and recorded "the course, rapidity, color, and depth of the river and its tributaries,—the nature of its bank, and of the country through which it flowed— the vegetable production, and the birds and animals we might see, with a journal of events." He also measured how far below the surface of the Mediterranean the Jordan was at selected points.

The land party started off through the streets of the town, toward the northern gate, at about the same time the boat party pushed off from the shelving beach with snow-white awnings spread and colors flying, steering directly for the outlet of the Jordan. "The *Fanny Mason* led the way, followed closely by the *Fanny Skinner;* and the Arab boatmen of the *Uncle Sam* worked vigorously at the oars to keep their place in the line." Along the shore, "eleven camels stalked solemnly ahead, followed by the wild Bedawin on their blooded animals, with their abas flying in the wind, and their long gun-barrels glittering in the sun; and Lieutenant Dale and his officers in the Frank costume brought up the rear."

Lynch was determined to adhere to his plan to travel from the Sea of Galilee to the Dead Sea by water, as his letters, notes, and book later showed. Only an hour after departing, the boat party encountered the first of many rapids that Lynch would not allow to be bypassed by portage. This meant that the boat crews had to go overboard to guide the boat through dangerous places. Sometimes, as Lynch melodramatically put it, ". . .

placing our sole trust in Providence we had to plunge with headlong velocity down appalling descents." The course of the river was so tortuous that the boat made only 12 miles in a direct line from Tiberias in the first two days. Moreover, the *Uncle Sam* was damaged so badly during the first two days that it had to be abandoned on the morning of the third, and the Arab boatmen sent back to their homes.

During the trip, the condition of banks of the river, and the flora and fauna along its course, varied but little. Although observations were taken and sketches made from which a chart was constructed, the manner of travel prevented the accurate charting Lynch himself had hoped to do. Perhaps the expedition's main contribution to the geographic knowledge of the region was the discovery that there were at least "twenty-seven threatening rapids, besides a great many of lesser magnitude," in the river, plus the observation that "in the depression between Lake Tiberias and the Dead Sea, the Jordan River wandered at least 200 miles in a straight line distance of sixty miles."

Each night, the land party selected a camp site. The busy scene, putting up the tents, driving in tent-pins, observing the wearied camels standing by waiting to be unloaded—all these things reminded Lynch of "the graphic descriptions of the Bible." Moreover, everything bore the aspect of a military expedition through hostile territory. In most instances, the boats were securely moored and guarded by a man with a blunderbuss, while the baggage was piled between the tents. At all times U.S. sentries were placed along the perimeter of the camp, and Bedouin were posted as lookouts on the highest ground available. When possible, the horses and mule were allowed to graze; where there was nothing growing, they could eat forage that the expedition brought with it. As darkness fell, they were tethered. The camels were usually hobbled and left to find food for themselves.

For dinner, the exploring party brought along salted pork, rice, bread, and coffee. Lynch, his officers, and the volunteers were served by the Arab cook; the seamen took turns cooking for the others. Since Lynch limited expedition members to two meals a day, one in the morning and one in the evening, the group usually ate with vigor. In many instances, the Bedouin brought them a sheep or a lamb as a gift for which Lynch paid them appropriately. For some dinners, the Bedouin cooked a whole sheep with rice, and everyone feasted. The nights along the Jordan for the exploring party were often memorable: "Around the blazing fires, which shot long, flickering tongues of flame into the night, and seemed to devour darkness, were gathered in circles, groups of Franks and wild Bedawin, solemnly smoking the chibouque, drinking coffee, or listening eagerly, as, with wild gesticulations, one related an adventure of the day or personal incident of times gone by," or listening to an Arab bard "who sang Arabic love-songs to the accompaniment of his rebabeh, or viol of one string."

In mid-afternoon on April 18, 1848, the boat party entered the Dead Sea.

As they did so, a gale force wind began to blow from the northwest, so agitating the sea that for the next two and one-half hours, the crews had to fight to keep the boats from foundering. Lynch later wrote:

> Our arms, our clothes and skins were coated with a greasy salt; and our eyes, lips, and nostrils, smarting excessively. How different was the scene before the submerging of the plain, which was even as the garden of the Lord. At times it seemed as if the Dread Almighty frowned upon our efforts to navigate a sea, the creation of his wrath.

At 5:58 p.m., the wind began to subside, and twenty minutes later the sea became placid. By 8:00 p.m. the boat party found the camp which the land party had established in a cane brake, beside a brackish spring on the shore. The shipboard experience and the undesirable camp site foreshadowed events in the days ahead. The greatest problems faced by the exploring party on the Dead Sea were brief but violent gales, the irritation of salt in the spray and air, heat, unpleasant odors, especially that of sulphur, and a scarcity of fresh water. For a few days, food and forage were scarce. Lynch, however, discharged the Bedouins with their horses, except for Sheríf Hazza; released his camel drivers and all the camels except one; sent an unspecified number of saddles, bridles, holsters, and all but a few articles of clothing to Jerusalem; and obtained from Jerusalem a fresh stock of bread along with some salted pork he had sent there from Beirut. The party also obtained the services of four Turkish soldiers from Jerusalem to guard the camp while the boats were on the sea. From Lynch's reports it is evident that the group also had an unspecified number of horses, but whether they were brought from Tiberias or obtained from the Arab tribes of the district is not clear.

On Friday, the expedition moved to a camp near the oasis called Ein Gedi, which Lynch christened "Camp Washington." On Saturday they were established in this camp around which the "whole aspect of the country . . . was one incinerated brown." That afternoon they began a series of barometrical and thermometrical observations and surveyed the ground for a base line. For the next 21 days, they "carefully sounded the sea, determined its geographical position, [took] the exact topography of its shores, ascertained the temperature, width, depth, and velocity of its tributaries, collected specimens of every kind, and noted the winds, currents, changes of weather, and all atmospheric phenomena." Lynch's boats were the first modern boats to enter the southern section of the Dead Sea. The water was only six inches deep half a mile off the shore, where "many fathoms deep in the slimy mud beneath it lay embedded the ruins of the ill-fated cities of Sodom and Gomorrah." Lynch's expedition was also the first in modern times to explore the ruins of Masada. On April 29, 1848, a party under Lieutenant Dale climbed the 1,200 to 1,500-foot cliffs rising almost perpendicularly from the seashore to examine the fortalice, the caves, and other constructions of Herod and his besieged people.[16]

Except for one seaman who was slightly ill, the group rode into the mountains for a two-day visit to the fortress town of Kerak. Horses and mules for this trip were furnished by the Arab and Christian leaders of the city. Lynch found the Muslim-dominated Christian community very considerate and accepted a letter from them addressed to the Christians of the United States in which they asked for money to build a new church. Lynch considered the Muslims very insolent. The son of their leader demanded a gift of guns and ammunition, and when Lynch refused, a quarrel almost ensued. To avoid such an eventuality, Lynch took the Muslim leader's son into custody on the way back to the Dead Sea and kept him captive until the party reached the boats.

The letters Lynch wrote from the scene, as well as his later official report and his books, showed that he had feelings of both awe and gladness to be exploring a region so important in the history and religion of the ancient world. "So sudden are the changes of the weather, and so different the aspects it presents as at times it seems as if we were in a world of enchantment." Of his exploration in the southern part of the Dead Sea he wrote:

> It was indeed a scene of unmitigated desolation. On one side, rugged and worn, was the salt mountain of Usdum, with its conspicuous pillar, which reminded us at least of the catastrophe of the plain; on the other were the lofty and barren cliffs to Moab, in one of the caves of which the fugitive Lot found shelter. To the south was an extensive flat intersected by sluggish drains, with the high hills of Edom semi-girdling the salt plain where the Israelites repeatedly overthrew their enemies; and to the north was the calm and motionless sea, curtained with a purple mist. . . . The glare of light was blinding to the eye, and the atmosphere difficult of respiration. No bird fanned with its wing the attentuated air through which the sun poured his scorching rays upon the mysterious element on which we floated, and which, alone, of all the works of its Maker, contains no living thing within it.

Before leaving the Dead Sea, Lynch moored a specially constructed float flying the flag of the United States in 80 fathoms of water beyond the reach of anyone not having a boat. On May 10, 1848, the group left the shores of the Dead Sea, one of their prime objectives accomplished. En route to Jerusalem, Lynch wrote "I scarce realized my position. Could it be, that with my companions I had been permitted to explore that wondrous sea, which an angry God threw as a mantle over the cities he had condemned, and of which it had been heretofore predicted that no one could traverse it and live. It was so, for there, far below, through the descending vista, lay the sombre sea."

In gathering data about the Dead Sea, Lynch had not completely carried out his orders. He still had to measure the relative levels of the Dead Sea, and the mountains between the Dead Sea and the Mediterranean with respect to the surface of the Mediterranean, and locate the source of the Jordan River. In order to accomplish this as precisely as possible, Lynch's party used the theodolite and spirit level brought from New York. The party ran a "line of levels," or obtained a series of relative measurements at selected points which established the Dead Sea's distance below sea level and the relative height of the mountains. This process, while fairly accurate, was slow and required much walking over rough country. Because of these and other difficulties, it took seven days to run the level to the highest peak northwest of Jerusalem. Observations showed the surface of the Dead Sea to be 1,316.7 feet below the surface of the Mediterranean.

In approaching Jerusalem, Lynch could hardly contain his excitement.

> Before me, on its lofty hill, four thousand feet above that sea, was the queenly city. I cannot coincide with most travellers in decrying its position. To my unlettered mind, its site, from that view, seemed, in isolated grandeur, to be in admirable keeping with the sublimity of its associations. A lofty mountain, sloping to the south, and precipitous on the east and west, has a yawning natural fosse on those three sides, worn by the torrents of ages. The deep vale of the son of Hinnom; the profound chasm of the valley of Jehoshaphat, unite at the south-east angle of the base to form the Wady en Nar, the ravine of fire, down which, in the rainy season, the Kidron precipitates its swollen flood into the sea below.
>
> Mellowed by time, and yet further softened by the intervening distance, the massive walls, with their towers and bastions, looked beautiful yet imposing in the golden sunlight; and above them, the only thing within their compass visible from that point, rose the glittering dome of the mosque of Omar, crowning Mount Moriah, on the site of the Holy Temple. On the other side of the chasm, commanding the city and the surrounding hills, is the Mount of Olives, its slopes darkened with the foliage of olive-trees, and on its very summit the former Church of the Ascension, now converted into a mosque.
>
> Many writers have undertaken to describe the first sight of Jerusalem; but all that I have read convey but a faint idea of the reality. There is a gloomy grandeur in the scene which language cannot paint. My feeble pen is wholly unworthy of the effort. With fervent emotions I have made the attempt, but congealed in the process of transmission, the most glowing thoughts are turned to icicles.

The expedition camped outside of Jerusalem until May 22, making astronomical observations and reconnoitering the best route to the Mediterranean, and everyone visited the Holy City and the garden of Gethsemane.

> It is enclosed by a high stone wall, and when we saw it, the trees were in blossom; the clover upon the ground in bloom, and altogether, in its aspect and its associations, was better calculated than any place I know to soothe a troubled spirit.
>
> Eight venerable trees, isolated from the smaller and less imposing ones

which skirt the base of the Mount of Olives, form a consecrated grove. High above, on either hand, towers a lofty mountain, with the deep, yawning chasm of Jehoshaphat between them. Crowning one of them is Jerusalem, a living city; on the slope of the other is the great Jewish cemetery, a city of the dead. Each tree in this grove, cankered, and gnarled, and furrowed by age, yet beautiful and impressive in its decay, is a living monument of the affecting scenes that have taken place beneath and around it. The olive perpetuates itself, and from the root of the dying parent stem, the young tree springs into existence. These trees are accounted 1000 years old. Under those of the preceding growth, therefore, the Saviour was wont to rest; and one of the present may mark the very spot where he knelt, and prayed, and wept. No cavilling doubts can find entrance here. The geographical boundaries are too distinct and clear for an instant's hesitation. Here the Christian, forgetful of the present, and absorbed in the past, can resign himself to sad, yet, soothing meditation. The few purple and crimson flowers, growing about the roots of the trees, will give him ample food for contemplation, for they tell of the suffering life and ensanguined death of the Redeemer.

On the same slope and a little below Gethsemane, facing the city, are the reputed tombs of Absalom, Zachariah, St. James, and Jehoshaphat, the last giving its name to the valley. Some of them are hewn bodily from the rock, and the whole form a remarkable group. That of Absalom in particular, from its peculiar tint, as well as from its style of architecture, reminded us of the descriptions of the sepulchral monuments of Petra. It is eight feet square, surmounted by a rounded pyramid, and there are six semi-columns to each face, which are of the same mass with the body of the sepulchre.

The tomb of Zachariah is also hewn square from the rock, and its four sides form a pyramid. The tomb of Jehoshaphat has a handsomely carved door; and a portico with four columns indicates the sepulchre where St. James, the apostle, concealed himself.

It was in the valley of Jehoshaphat that Melchisedec, king of Salem, met Abraham on his return from defeating the five kings in the vale of Siddim. In the depths of this ravine Moloch was worshipped, beneath the temple of the Most High, which crowned the summit of Mount Moriah.

In the village of Siloam, the scene of Solomon's apostasy, the living have ejected the dead, and there are as many dwelling in tombs as in houses. Beneath it, at the base of the Mount of Offence, is the great burial-ground, the desired final resting-place of Jews all over the world. The flat stones, rudely sculptured with Hebrew characters, lie, as the tenants beneath were laid, with their faces towards heaven. In the village above it and in the city over against it, the silence is almost as death-like as in the grave-yard itself. Here the voice of hilarity or the hum of social intercourse is never heard, and when man meets his fellow there is no social greeting. The air here never vibrates with the melodious voice of woman, the nearest approach to a celestial sound; but, shrouded from head to foot, she flits about, abashed and shrinking like some guilty thing. This profound silence is in keeping with the scene. Along the slope of the hill, above the village, the Master, on his way to Bethany, was wont to teach his followers the sublime truths of the gospel. On its acclivity, a little more to the north, he wept for the fate of Jerusalem. In the garden below, he was betrayed, and within those city walls he was crucified. Everything is calculated to inspire with awe, and it is fitting that, except in prayer, the human voice should not disturb these sepulchral solitudes.

From the slope of the Mount of Olives projects a rock, pointed out by tradition as the one whereon the Saviour sat when he predicted and wept over the fate of Jerusalem. It is further alleged that upon this spot Titus pitched his camp when besieging the city. Neither the prediction nor its accomplishment required such a coincidence to make it impressive. The main camp of the besiegers was north of the city, but as the sixth legion was posted on the Mount of Olives, the tradition may not be wholly erroneous.

A little higher, were some grotto-like excavations, hypothetically called the Tombs of the Prophets; and above them, were some arches, under which, it is said, the Apostles composed the creed. Yet above, the spot is pointed out where the Messiah taught his disciples the Lord's Prayer,— that beautiful compend of all that is necessary for man to ask, whether for time or eternity.

On the summit of the mount are many wheat-fields, and it is crowned with a paltry village, a small mosque, and the ruined church of the Ascension. In the naked rock, which is the floor of the mosque, an indentation is shown as the foot-print of the Messiah, when he ascended to heaven. Apart from the sites of the Temple, of Calvary, and of the Holy Sepulchre, the assigned localities within the city walls, such as the Arch of the Ecce Homo, and the house of the rich man before whose gate Lazarus laid, are unworthy of credit. But those without the walls, like the three first-named within them, are geographically defined, and of imperishable materials. While one, therefore, may not be convinced with regard to all, he feels that the traditions respecting them are not wholly improbable.

From the summit, the view was magnificent. On the one hand lay Jerusalem, with its yellow walls, its towers, its churches, its cone-roof houses, and its hills and valleys, covered with orchards and fields of green and golden grain, while beneath, distinct and near, the mosque of Omar, the Harem (the Sacred), lay exposed to our infidel gaze, with its verdant carpet and groves of cypress, beneath whose holy shade none but the faithful can seek repose. On the other hand was the valley of Jordan, a barren plain, with a line of verdure marking the course of the sacred river, until it was lost in an expanse of sluggish water, which we recognised as the familiar scene of our recent labours. The rays of the descending sun shone full upon the Arabian shore, and we could see the castle of Kerak, perched high up in the country of Moab, and the black chasm of Zerka, through which flows the hot and sulphureous stream of Callirohoe.

No other spot in the world commands a view so desolate, and, at the same time, so interesting and impressive. The yawning ravine of Jehoshaphat, immediately beneath, was verdant with vegetation, which became less and less luxuriant, until, a few miles below, it was lost in a huge torrent bed, its sides bare precipitous rock, and its bed covered with boulders, whitened with saline deposit, and calcined by the heat of a Syrian sun. Beyond it, south, stretched the desert of Judea; and to the north, was the continuous chain of this almost barren mountain. These mountains were not always thus barren and unproductive. The remains of terraces yet upon their slopes, prove that this country, now almost depopulated, once maintained a numerous and industrious people.

North of Gethsemane, nearer the bed of the ravine and the one-arched bridge which spans it, is a subterranean church, in a grotto reputed to contain the tomb of the Virgin Mary. Having no faith in the tradition, which is based on an improbable legend, I did not visit it; but in passing by, just from the garden, and accoutred in a soiled and salt-encrusted dress, the only one I had, I saw a European fop ascending the flight of steps, attired in a short frock, tightly-fitting pants, a jockey-cap upon his head, a riding-whip in his hand, and the lines of his face wreathed in a smile of smirking self-conceit,—not one feature of the man or his dress in keeping with the scenes around him.

On the way to Jerusalem, Sheríf Hazza of Mecca left the group, and when the party had established itself in camp outside of Jerusalem, Dr. Anderson took his departure. The camels that had carried the boat sections, specimens, and other baggage were replaced by mules. It is uncertain whether the Americans walked or rode from the Dead Sea to Jerusalem, but if they walked they secured horses in Jerusalem, for it seems clear that they rode from this point on.

There was a road the party could use "which was frightful," and even without having to pull the carriages, it took eight days, from May 22 to May 29, to travel about 100 miles and plant the "level on the margin of the Mediterranean, about one and a half miles south of Jaffa." Once a local sheikh tried to prevent them from passing through his territory, but backed down when Lynch stated that they were determined to pass, come what may. For the most part, the people were curious about the operations of the Americans, and "all desired to look through the telescope, and even little children were held up for a peep."

At Jaffa, Lynch, his officers, and the seamen were allowed to use the house belonging to the United States consular representative, Mr. Murad Serapion. They remained in Jaffa until June 6. The mules were sent back to Jerusalem, an Arab brig was chartered to transport the party to Acre, and the members of the expedition "found full occupation in bringing up our work, particularly the astronomical and barometrical observations, and the measurements of the level and rebuilding our boats by putting their sections together. The physical repose was truly grateful."

The Arab brig, however, would not take all of them as well as the boats and baggage. Thus, a group under Lieutenant Dale started on horseback for Acre while Lynch and the rest embarked on the brig, hoisted the United States flag, and sailed with their supplies and boats to Acre where they arrived the next day. The land party arrived June 9. On the way, seaman

Charles Homer was wounded in the arm by the accidental discharge of a gun. He was taken aboard the brig, along with the dismantled carriage trucks, boats, specimens, and some miscellaneous baggage, and the craft sailed to Beirut under the care of Passed Midshipman Aulick, Mr. Bedlow, and three seamen. On arrival, Homer was placed under the care of the Sisters of Charity and "a French surgeon of eminence."

On Saturday, June 10, the rest of the group left for Mount Hermon by horseback, to view the source of the Jordan. It is surmised that mules transported their baggage. From Acre the party took a different route to Tiberias and made a detour to Nazareth, where Lynch wrote:

> Feelings are inexpressible which overpower one in passing to and fro amid scenes which, for the greater portion of his mortal existence, were frequented by our Saviour. In Jerusalem, the theatre of his humiliations, his sufferings, and his death, the heart is oppressed with awe and anguish; but in Nazareth, where he spent his infancy, his youth, and his early manhood, we yearn towards him unchilled by awe, and unstricken by horror.
>
> In its secluded position, with a narrow valley before it, and mountains in every other direction, we liked Nazareth better even than Bethlehem, and thought it the prettiest place we had seen in Palestine. The streets were perfectly quiet; there was an air of comfort about the houses, and the people were better dressed, and far more civil, than any we had encountered.
>
> Nazareth contains about 5000 inhabitants, four-fifths Christians, the remainder Muslims. It has twenty-two villages in its district, which is subordinate to the Pashalic of Acre. While here, we paid a visit to a Turkish tax-gatherer, who, from his books, furnished us with much statistical information with regard to the tenure and the cultivation of land, and the land-tax, the poll-tax, and the "kharaje," or blood-tax, paid by the Christians. This tax-gatherer was an Egyptian, with a dark complexion, and short, crisp, black hair; his wife, a native of Aleppo, in the north of Syria, had a white skin, and chestnut ringlets; and their servant woman was a Maronite of Mount Lebanon, with high cheek-bones, a freckled face, and reddish-brown hair.
>
> Napoleon stopped at Nazareth after having rescued General Kleber in his desperate engagement with the Syrian army, in the plain of Esdraelon, about two hours distant.
>
> We found here the heliotrope, the pink, the pheasant's eye, and the knotty hartswort. The roots and seeds of the latter are medicinal, having similar properties to those of the carrot. The Turks are said to eat the young shoots as a salad.

Early on June 14, they began to ascend the hills before Mount Hermon. After "a toilsome ascent of an hour," they reached the summit of the first hill overlooking the plain and from it had a fine view of the Sea of Galilee and the Jordan. From this point they had to alternately descend and ascend until they reached the plateau which "breaks down towards lake Huleh," and soon they could see Mount Hermon.

On June 16, after 200 miles of travel, much of it over uneven ground and at altitudes which tired them quickly, Lynch, Lieutenant Dale, and the seamen viewed one of the places where the Jordan bursts through the surface in the southernmost section of Lebanon near a village called Hasbaya. Lynch declared the place was a "fitting fountain-head of a stream which was destined to lave the immaculate body of the Redeemer of the world." There are six such springs in this region, and the Lynch party seems to have seen the principal one. In his letters, his report, and his later book, Lynch, however, mentions only the spring he saw as the source of the Jordan. Moreover, he also does not recognize the River Banias or the spring near Dan, as two other principal sources of the Jordan.

While climbing Mount Hermon, Lynch observed the jealousies of the Christian population with sadness and remarked upon the strength of the Druse element in the area. He also commented favorably upon the terraced agriculture of the region.

Lynch decided by Sunday, June 18, that the party was too inactive for "an elevated region," and on Monday, June 19, the group left for Damascus. To get there, they crossed the mountains known as the Anti-Lebanon through a gorge (the Wistanee) that lay

between Mount Hermon and the next peak to the southward. The two crests were covered and many clefts on both sides filled with snow. From the summit, the country below, which had seemed so mountainous to the upward view, appeared an immense rolling plain. Far to the north-west, at the verge of the seeming plain, were the red sands, a dazzling line of gold separating the luxuriant green of the plain from the light azure of the far-stretching sea. Upon the line of sand, like clustering dots upon a chart, were the cities of Tyre, Sidon, and Beirut. Another plain stretched, from the opposite side, south to the Hauran, and to the east until it was lost in the great desert. On the northern margin of that plain, but yet in the far distance, lay the city of Damascus, Es Sham (the Holy), embosomed in groves and meadows. We made an attempt to ascertain the height of Mount Hermon with our boiling-water apparatus, but the thermometer attached to it was not graduated sufficiently low. The summit is estimated to be about 9000 feet above the level of the sea, which is, perhaps, but little more than the actual height. As we ascended, we suffered from a stricture about the temples, but nearer the summit, the feeling passed away, and was succeeded by great nervous exhilaration.

We found snow some distance down the eastern slope; and the descent was gradual; but, from the nature of the road, very slow and excessively fatiguing. As we descended, the limestone rock disappeared, giving place to sand-stone and trap; and, lower down, serpentine occasionally cropped out. At "Ain Ennahad" (Copper Fountain), the water was deeply impregnated with iron; the dry bed of one of its branches was coated with the yellow oxide of the same metal, and the rocks around bore marks of metallic corrosion. Near the base of the mountain, there was a profusion of wild roses.

The next day their route lay over a high, rolling plain, their travel became easier, and by late afternoon they were within the walls of the city. When entering the city they were advised to furl the flag of the United States, but Lynch refused because they "had carried it to every place we had visited, and, determining to take our chances with it, we kept it flying." Despite angry comments by the populace at the spectacle of a foreign flag entering the city, there were no violent incidents. Lynch was very impressed with Damascus and visited as much of it as he could; in turn, he was visited by the important people of the area, including the Great Sheikh of the Anazeh tribe who exercised paramount power in the desert region from Damascus southward to Basra.

On June 25, because of oppressively hot weather and complaints by the seamen, Lynch decided to leave Damascus by horseback and head for Beirut. Early in the afternoon of June 27, they sighted the ruins of Heliopolis, at Ba'albek, and camped just outside the village. On Wednesday, June 28, the group started to explore the ruins, but by mid-day the heat became oppressive and Lynch decided to start again for Beirut. Their march on this day was long, and they did not make camp until 9:45 p.m.

That night two seamen became sick and Lynch thought that they had "imbibed the disease which has heretofore prostrated all who have ventured upon the Dead Sea." It could have been cholera. "As I looked upon my companions dropping around me, many and bitter were my self-reproaches for having ever proposed the undertaking." The area was unsuitable for nursing sick men, so they pushed on slowly, with additional men falling ill, until they reached Beirut the last day of June.

The expedition was to rendezvous with the *Supply* on July 1, but the ship was not at Beirut. The entire month of July passed without word of it. The United States Consul at Beirut found quarters for the officers and seamen, but Lynch had to pay rent and buy food. By July 14, even though their horses and baggage animals had been sent back to Acre, Lynch was complaining of the expense involved. Even then, Lynch still hoped to receive authorization to explore the course of the Euphrates to its mouth on the Persian Gulf. Secretary Mason had written to him months before that he could not do this, but it seems that Lynch never received the Secretary's letters.

In the meantime, all of the sick men, except Lieutenant Dale, recovered from what was described as "attacks of high febrile character." As the men recovered from their sickness, they began getting the boats and other equipment ready for loading on the *Supply,* while Dale went up into the mountains to the village of Bhamdun in hopes of recovering more quickly. On July 17, Lynch received word that Dale, in the house of the Rev. Mr. Eli Smith of the American Presbyterian Mission, was very ill. Dale died on July

24, despite the attentions of Dr. De Forest of the American Evangelical Mission, his wife, and a Dr. Vandyke. This unfortunate event hit Lynch hard, and he determined to take Dale's remains home. Dale's body was brought back to Beirut, placed in "three coffins, (one metallic, and two wooden ones) and laid in a vacant building."

By July 30, Lynch decided not to wait any longer for the *Supply*. On May 25, he had sent a letter to Lieutenant Pennock, the acting captain of the *Supply,* via the United States Consul at Malta, enjoining Pennock to be at Beirut on or before July 1, 1848. The consul sent a copy of this to Commodore Read in Sicily, but it does not appear that Pennock received a copy. Subsequently, while in Beirut, Lynch sent additional letters for Pennock via the Consul at Malta and the Consul in Marseilles. These men forwarded copies of the letter to various ports at which the *Supply* could be expected to visit.

Late in July, Lynch received notification from the United States Consul at Malta that as far as he knew, the *Supply* was at Spezia in the first week of July and could not get to Beirut that month. It appears that after the Lynch party left the ship, the *Supply* returned to the western part of the Mediterranean to provision the U.S. ships scheduled to call at various ports in the area during April. Late arrivals and quarantine restrictions, as well as Read's decision to use the *Supply* as a warship for the protection of American interests during the 1848 European revolutions in places which could not be visited by the small number of regular United States ships of war, found the *Supply* still in the western Mediterranean in July.

This failure to make the rendezvous, coupled with Dale's death, induced Lynch to ask the Secretary of the Navy for an investigation into Read's conduct, whom he blamed for not seeing that the *Supply* met its schedule. In Lynch's view, if the *Supply* had been at Beirut when it should have and had the expedition left the area quickly aboard it, the resulting sea voyage would have cured Dale. It was with some anger, therefore, that Lynch chartered a small French brig to convey the exploring party to Malta. In loading the brig, however, some unspecified trouble with the coffins, as well as the reluctance of the French captain and crew to have the body on board, induced Lynch to agree to bury Dale outside of Beirut. "About sunset, as the Turkish batteries were saluting the first night of Ramadan, we escorted the body to the Frank cemetery, and laid it beneath a Pride of India tree. A few most appropriate chapters in the Bible were read, and some affecting remarks made by the Rev. Mr. Thompson; after which, the sailors advanced, and fired three volleys over the grave; and thus, amid unbidden tears and stifled sobs, closed the obsequies of our lamented companion and friend."

The United States exploring expedition left Beirut on July 30, 1848, and reached Valetta on Malta, after a tiresome, 1,050-mile voyage of 38 days. When the *Supply* finally arrived at Beirut on August 22, the Lynch party was gone and cholera was rampant in the city. Consequently, the *Supply* quickly sailed away for Valetta, where she arrived on September 12. Lynch reassumed command of the vessel when it arrived and departed almost immediately for the United States.

While waiting for the *Supply* to arrive at Malta, Lynch had received a letter from Commodore Read declaring that Lynch was at fault for the *Supply's* not being at Beirut on July 1, since Lynch had been authorized orally by Read to retain the ship off the coast of Lebanon until the expedition had finished its work. To this charge, Lynch referred to a letter he had written to Read in February while they were at Port Mahon in which Lynch declared that in responses to Read's wishes made to him orally, Lynch would see that the *Supply* left the coast of Palestine in time to be back at Malta early in April. Lynch also stated that it was his understanding that the *Supply* would return to Beirut on or before July 1, 1848.

On Thursday, December 7, 1848, the *Supply* picked up a pilot off Norfolk, Virginia, and sailed up Hampton Roads to an anchorage off the Gosport Navy Yard. By Monday, December 11, 1848, all hands were paid off, and the *Supply* with its cargo of specimens was put under control of the Navy Yard's commander. While the seamen scattered to various destinations, Lynch and Passed Midshipman Aulick were detailed by the Secretary of the Navy to finish the official report which Lynch had started while at sea. The collection of specimens from the *Supply* was turned over to Lynch. At the same time, Lynch received permission to write an account of the expedition that could be published and sold to the public. The proceeds of this work, the Secretary expected, would be used to help the widow and children of Lieutenant Dale. Dr. Anderson returned to the United States on his own, and in January 1849, he traveled with Lynch to the Gosport Navy Yard to collect the geological specimens from the *Supply*. [17]

Lynch was somewhat disappointed in the reception given the return of his group. There were no dignitaries waiting to greet him and his crew as the ship was anchored, and the newspaper accounts were not as enthusiastic as they could have been. The *Norfolk Beacon* printed an account of some of the more noteworthy of the specimens brought back by Lynch; the *New York Herald* published a small article refuting a statement in the *Norfolk Beacon* that Lynch believed the specimen of salt from the salt pillar at Usdum was actually part of Lot's wife by saying that Lynch had no opinion on the matter one way or another;[18] and other newspapers noted the return of the expedition to the United States. Generally, however, the notice given to the return of Lynch, his officers, and his men by the government and the general public could only be called commonplace.[19] On the other hand, Lynch was pleased with the reception given his ideas and work by scientists both within and without the Navy. Matthew Fontaine Maury, for example, had published an article in the *Southern Literary Messenger* dated September 1848, that defended the expedition from the standpoint of the advancement of science and the contribution it was making "to the glory of the Navy and the honor of the nation." Dr. Edward Robinson wrote to the Secretary of the Navy and to Lynch even before the expedition returned to the United States asking for the data the group had collected for incorporation into a new account of the region that he hoped would be definitive. In a letter to the Secretary of the Navy dated June 9, 1848, Lynch wrote: "The expedition may encounter ridicule at home, but from all quarters I have received assurances that the literary circles of Europe are much interested in the results." The work of the Dead Sea expedition was also reviewed favorably, from the scientific viewpoint, by Benjamin Silliman in the *American Journal of Science and Arts* for November 1849. Favorable comments also appeared in newspapers and other similar journals.[20]

Lynch's spirits were further lifted when, in February, the Senate passed a resolution asking for the submission of his official report. With the help of Passed Midshipman Aulick, Lynch sent in his official report on February 3, 1849. In addition to a narrative of events, a traverse diagram of the country between the Dead Sea and Jaffa showing the actual difference of level, and hydrographic data, the report also included some commercial information from Beirut and Jaffa as well as sections dealing with the interpretation and classification of the ornithological, botanical, chronometrical, and meterological information the group had brought back; it did not, however, include a geological report.

The ornithological section was written by John Cassin, who had performed similar work for the Wilkes Expedition. For the botanical section, Lynch secured the services of Dr. R. E. Griffith, Vice President of the Philadelphia Academy of Natural Science. The report was submitted to the Senate on February 26, 1849, read on February 27, referred to the Committee on Commerce, and ordered to be printed. Lynch requested and received permission to supervise its printing, and despite his complaints that the workmanship and materials involved were of inferior quality, the report appeared as "Report of the Secretary of the Navy, with a Report Made by Lieutenant W. F. Lynch of an Examination of the Dead Sea."[21] Soon afterward, Lynch's *Narrative of the United States' Expedition to the River Jordan and the Dead Sea* appeared. In the same year an anonymous *Narrative of the Late Expedition to the Dead Sea From a Diary of One of the Party,* edited by Edward P. Montague, was also printed.

The printing and publication of these volumes heightened public interest in the expedition. The *Narrative* went through eight editions and was fairly well received by the press. The *New York Tribune* expressed its thanks to Lynch for the "gratification and instruction" it received from a very able volume. In the *New York Commercial Advertiser,* the reviewer ended his favorable evaluation with the statement that "the record he has given of the scenes through which they passed will be eagerly perused by his countrymen, and will be a lasting memorial of a great national enterprise skillfully consumated." Periodicals such as *Littell's Living Age* gave praise to the achievements of the Lynch expedition and to his book.[22]

However, there were some dissonant voices, mainly regarding the style of Lynch's narrative. The *Boston Post* called certain of Lynch's expressions well meant, but "fudge-like." Other descriptions and statements were called ". . . the clearest examples of bathos, commonplace and downright twattle extant." Then the reviewer relented somewhat, adding:

> . . . the book is really interesting and instructive, and is really and obviously the work of an able, well educated and enlightened man. How such silly defects of style should coexist with the more essential merits of the text is almost unintelligible; and, indeed, were we upon oath for our opinion at this moment, we should say that one man must have written the twattle, the triteness, the bad grammar and the bad taste, while another furnished the learning and narrated the facts.[23]

The *Southern Quarterly Review* criticized the expedition for its failure to provide more information of practical value to trade and commerce. The financial records of the expedition evidently have been lost, but from Lynch's letters it appears that when they reached the Dead Sea, Lynch had already spent $700 for the expenses of the trip from Acre. Since Lynch negotiated a draft for £1500 at Smyrna in March 1848, and one for £250 at Malta in September 1848, the total cost of the expedition must have been much higher than $700, and some members of the press felt the public had not received its money's worth in practical advantages.[24] In spite of such criticism, Lynch was promoted to the rank of Commander late in 1849.

In 1850, Lynch brought out his *U.S. Expedition to the River Jordan and the Dead Sea, a New and Condensed Edition,* which went through 10 editions. It was not until 1852 that the work of writing the report about the geology of the region based on the observations of Dr. Anderson and the specimens brought back was finished. This report was incorporated in *Official Report of the United States' Expedition to Explore the Dead Sea and the River Jordan by Lieutenant W. F. Lynch, USN.*[25] The first part of this volume contains Lynch's report with its scientific sections as printed in 1849; the second contains the geological report written by Dr. Anderson.

In 1852 *Harper's New Monthly Magazine* also printed a series by Jacob Abbott about the River Jordan, the Dead Sea, and the sources of the Jordan, based to a great extent on Lynch's official reports and his published work, in which Lynch and his crew were given high praise. The expedition's work was also noted in an article on the work of the French explorer, de Saulcy, which appeared in the December 1854–May 1855 issue of *Harper's New Monthly Magazine.*[26]

Because of the heat and problems of transportation, most of the specimens of fauna collected by the expedition perished on the way to the United

States. A relatively small number of the flora were also mutilated to the point where retention seemed inadvisable, but it appears that what was left after classification was deposited either with the museum supervised by the Patent Office or with the Smithsonian Institution. At one time the Secretary of the Navy ordered Lynch to deposit the seeds he brought back with the Patent Office, and it is possible that other specimens were sent there as well. In the *Annual Reports* of the Smithsonian Institution for 1849, 1850 and 1851, there is no mention of the Dead Sea Expedition. In the *Seventh Annual Report* for 1852 of the Smithsonian Institution, Lynch is mentioned in connection with a reconnaissance of the West African Coast he was making that year, and his work on the Jordan and Dead Sea is praised, but there is no mention of the receipt of any specimens. In 1867, the Smithsonian listed the expedition as a specimen source without any explanation.[27]

Despite confusion over the exact placement of the specimens, the Dead Sea Expedition's astronomical, meterological, hydrographical, and other observations "became the foundation on which all subsequent knowledge of the river and its valley was built and until the 1930's remained the main source of technical information on both the Jordan and the Dead Sea."[28]

Especially interesting to Lynch himself was what he considered to be the discovery that ". . . our soundings ascertained the bottom of the Dead Sea to consist of two plains, an elevated and a depressed one averaging, the former 13, and the latter 1300 feet, below the surface. Through the northern, and largest and deepest one, is a ravine, which seems to correspond with the bed of the Jordan to the north, and the Wady el Jerb, or ravine within a ravine, at the south end of the Sea." Furthermore, geological evidence, according to Lynch, indicated that this depression was caused by "a general convulsion" of volcanic activity, "preceded, most probably, by an eruption of fire, and a general conflagration of the bitumen which abounded in the plain. After twenty-two days' close investigation, if I am not mistaken, we are unanimous in the conviction of the truth of the Scriptural account of the destruction of the cities of the plain. I record with diffidence the conclusion we have reached, simply as a protest against the shallow deductions of would-be unbelievers."

If Dr. Anderson had voiced this conclusion in 1849, he changed his mind later, for his geological report stated the evidence collected indicated that the rearrangement of the earth which formed the depression of the Dead Sea either by fissure or volcanic action had occurred before the historic era. This new knowledge seemingly disproved the thesis that "the eruption by which the four cities [Sodom, Gomorrah, Admah, and Zeboiim] were destroyed had produced the chasm of the Dead Sea," and was given praise in such periodicals as the *Journal of Sacred Literature* as settling one facet of the long-standing argument about the origin of the Dead Sea. The question of whether these cities were located along the shores of the Dead Sea, however, and whether their remains were at its bottom still remained a subject for discussion.[29]

Between the time his *Condensed Version* of the expedition appeared and the publication of the 1852 *Official Report,* Lynch interested himself in the welfare of Dale's children who were orphaned by the death of their mother in February 1849, and in writing an account of naval life which in some respects is autobiographical in content. Through his initiative, the pension paid to Mrs. Dale was transferred to the children, and in 1851 Lynch published *Naval Life; or Observations Afloat and On Shore* (New York: C. Scribner's, 1851). During that period his controversy with Read was not made public and no investigation of Read seems to have been made.

Despite the fact that he was now 50 years of age and known for one successful exploring venture, Lynch's spirit of adventure remained high. He tried early in 1850 to interest Edward Fitzgerald Beale in joining him on an expedition in search of Sir John Franklin, and in 1852 he reconnoitered the coast of West Africa as a preparatory step for a fuller exploration which never materialized.[30]

It is noteworthy, moreover, that Lynch's interest in the Levant and in its exploration did not lessen. In 1860 he made a speech in New York in which he said the region of the Jordan is

> a land so remarkably situated that it forms a bridge between two continents, and a gateway to a third. Were the population and wealth of Europe, Asia and Africa condensed to a single point, Palestine would be the centre of their common gravity and with the amazing facilities of modern intercourse and the prodigious extent of modern commerce, who can estimate the commercial grandeur to which a country may attain, planted as it were, on the very apex of the old world, with its three continents spread out beneath it, having the Dead Sea and the Persian Gulf on one side, to bring it the golden treasures and the spicy harvests of the East, and the Mediterranean floating in on the other, the skill and knowledge and enterprise of the West?

The *sine qua non,* Lynch went on to say, for such a situation was the development of a new route to the East through the Holy Land:

> where the representatives of the West may harmoniously meet and remove the barrier to the regeneration of the East.
>
> Against that barrier the tide of commerce chafes—remove it and deep and full the stream will flow at once.
>
> And more than all—far beyond all—Civilization will be introduced, and Christianity, the hand-maid of Civilization, will dispense its blessings upon the benighted nations in its path.
>
> The first step in this great work is exploration, and they who by encouraging it, remove the obstruction to Commerce, Civilization and Christianity will become the benefactors of mankind—and the grateful pen of

history will record the names of those, who, each greater than a Hercules, assisted in opening the way. . . .[31]

Except for the substitution of commerce for science as a justifying factor, the last statements of this speech are similar to the expressions Lynch used in his letter of November 1847, defending the decision to dispatch a naval expedition to explore the River Jordan and the Dead Sea. It is suggestive in this regard, that in his letters and later in his books, Lynch not only revealed a strong desire to expand the scope of his expedition to include the survey of a path to the mouth of the Euphrates that could be developed into this bridge of commerce he mentioned in his 1860 talk, but also alluded more than once to the need and possibility of the Levant's regeneration with the help of Europe and the United States.

Thus, from this standpoint, despite its avowed limitation as primarily a scientific enterprise,[32] the exploring expedition to the River Jordan and the Dead Sea under the command of Lieutenant William F. Lynch, deserves to be included as a manifestation of expansionism and transcontinentalism that permeated the spirit of the United States in the 1840s and 1850s. The Dead Sea Expedition has a singular appeal for historical study; it has a place in the history of the Holy Land and of science; but it takes its larger meaning from the climate of the age and a comparison with subsequent naval exploring expeditions of the period.

# Chapter 5

# Herndon-Gibbon Expedition to the Region of the Amazon, 1851-1852

Until 1867, Brazil refused to allow free navigation of its rivers. One of the most forceful and vigorous opponents of the Brazilian policy of excluding foreign shipping from its inland districts was Lieutenant Matthew Fontaine Maury. During the late 1840s, Maury viewed the internal political problems of the United States as being motivated at least in part by the growing estrangement of the South and the North. As a Virginian, his sympathies were with the South, and he was involved with trying to develop the commercial and economic strengths of the South to a point where the southern part of the United States might rival the North in wealth and industry.

Maury, who served as Superintendent of the United States Naval Observatory from 1844 to 1861, believed that the winds and currents of the South Atlantic and the Gulf of Mexico dictated that the trade of the eastern ports of South America should flow to southern ports in the United States. Any improvement in the commercial relations between the interior of Brazil and its seacoast, which resulted in a greater volume of overseas trade, would particularly benefit the southern states. For the general welfare and especially to help the South, Maury favored the economic betterment of Brazil and the results it would have in the South.

For Brazil to achieve a more satisfactory rate of economic progress, its inland waterways, in Maury's view, had to be open to foreign commercial development. As a first step, it seemed necessary both to determine which waterways were navigable and which were not and to ascertain the conditions of life within Brazil's interior. This information would determine the courses United States citizens ought to pursue in relation to marketing goods in Brazil, buying Brazilian products, or trying to establish commercial and agricultural centers there. Moreover, there is evidence to suggest that Maury entertained the idea that the Valley of the Amazon might be colonized by southern slave holders as a counterweight to the power of the North or if slavery were discontinued in the United States.

As Superintendent of the Naval Observatory, Maury was engaged in charting the winds and ocean currents of the earth, in showing ship-masters how to use his charts in making faster and more economical voyages, and in theorizing about such physical phenomena as ice-free oceans at the poles.

To help with this work, Maury wanted to obtain scientific data on the meteorology and other natural phenomena in the upper reaches of the Amazon River.

To obtain such data, a scientific mission was required. Maury, sometime in the late 1840s, conceived the idea of a naval expedition to the valley of the Amazon. Finally, on March 29, 1850, Maury outlined his scheme for such an expedition in a letter to the Secretary of the Navy, William B. Preston. The expedition, when eventually undertaken, was led by Maury's brother-in-law, Lieutenant William Lewis Herndon.

The Cabinet discussed the expedition for two weeks. By May 2, Maury was confident of the outcome and wrote that "I consider the matter now as settled." The next day Secretary Preston seemingly told Maury that the expedition had been authorized and that Herndon, then serving aboard the *Vandalia* in the Pacific Squadron, would be ordered to command it.[1] In the first week of August that year, the *Vandalia* was at Valparaiso, where a letter from Maury led Herndon to believe that he would soon receive orders to explore the Valley of the Amazon.[2] On August 6, the *Vandalia* sailed for the Hawaiian Islands. Herndon secured permission from his commanding officer, Captain William H. Gardner, to wait in Valparaiso for his orders.

As matters turned out he had to wait a long time. Despite persistent attention from Maury, procedural and political maneuverings in the government delayed the orders through May and June.

On July 9, 1850, President Zachary Taylor died and problems associated with the installation of his successor, Millard Fillmore, created further delays.

In November, Maury addressed the new Secretary of the Navy, William A. Graham, about the desirability of exploring the Amazon and repeated the arguments he had made to Preston. In this letter, as in his previous one, Maury took the position that the expedition be considered as the first step toward a more elaborate one using a steamship to ascend the Amazon from its mouth. He also wrote to Herndon chiding him for leaving his ship at Valparaiso and saying that he had no idea when the new Navy Secretary would see fit to implement the Amazon exploration scheme.[3] Finally, on January 20, 1851, Herndon received the following instructions from the Secretary of the Navy, William A. Graham:

October 30, 1850

Sir: Proceed to Lima for the Purpose of collecting from the monasteries, and other authentic sources that may be accessible to you, information concerning the head waters of the Amazon and the regions of country drained by its Peruvian tributaries. You will then visit the monasteries of Bolivia for a like purpose, touching the Bolivian tributaries of that river, should it in your judgment be desirable.

The object of the department in assigning you to this service is with the view of directing you to explore the Valley of the Amazon, should the consent of Brazil therefore be obtained; and the information you are directed to obtain is such as would tend to assist and guide you in such exploration, should you be directed to make it.

As this service to which you are now assigned may probably involve the necessity of the occasional expenditure of a small amount on government account, you are furnished with a bill of credit for one thousand dollars, for which you will account to the proper office.

Also, enclosed you will find a letter of introduction to Messrs. Clay and McClung, chargés d'affaires near the governments of Peru and Bolivia.

On January 25, Herndon left for Lima, Peru, where he arrived on February 6. Almost immediately he arranged with the superintendent of the public library to read all available information, which he found "small and unsatisfactory," about the problems of traveling from Peru to the Brazilian seacoast by way of the Amazon. With such limited help, and through conversations with men who had ventured over the mountains into Peru and Brazil, Herndon began planning his route.[4] Meanwhile he received, on April 4, 1851, his final orders dated 15 February which stated, in part:

> The government desires to be put in possession of certain information relating to the valley of the river Amazon, in which term is included the entire basin, or water-shed, drained by that river and its tributaries.
>
> This desire extends not only to the present condition of that valley, with regard to the navigability of its streams; to the number and condition, both industrial and social, of its inhabitants, their trade and products; its climate, soil, and productions; but also to its capacities for cultivation, and to the character and extent of its undeveloped commercial resources, whether of the field, the forest, the river, or the mine.
>
> You will, for the purpose of obtaining such information, proceed across the Cordillera, and explore the Amazon from its source to its mouth.

The orders stated that Passed Midshipman Lardner Gibbon had been selected to accompany Herndon, and would bring with him a few instruments; that the Navy agent at Lima had been instructed to furnish funds not to exceed five thousand dollars, which were to be used only for *necessary* expenses; and that on his arrival at Pará, he was to take the first available ship back to the United States to report on his activities. He was to investigate the silver mines of Peru and Bolivia; ascertain what inducements those nations offered to emigrants; determine the size and character of the population and their principal products; make geographical and scientific observations; and bring back specimens, samples, seeds and plants.

While these orders were comprehensive, they were but a restrained embodiment of Maury's ideas. In a long and detailed letter to Herndon written between April 20 and May 3, 1850, Maury had expressed stronger opinions about the work and results of Herndon's trip than those contained in Herndon's official orders, which Maury must have had a hand in writing.[5] Moreover, in a letter dated July 10, 1851, to Secretary of the Navy William

Graham, Herndon stated approval of the purpose and objectives of his expedition as set forth by both his brother-in-law and his orders from the Secretary of the Navy.[6] In other words, Herndon considered his orders and Maury's concerns compatible; he was prepared for the tasks asked of him; and, as the record will show, he tried wholeheartedly to carry out both the spirit and the letter of his orders, as well as adhering to Maury's strictures.

Since his orders left the selection of a route to his discretion, and keeping in mind the objectives of his mission, Herndon decided to journey from Lima through the cities of Tarma, the mining districts of Peru, to the Huallaga River. His party would travel by mule and on foot to the Huallaga, which emptied into the Amazon, and from there to the Atlantic Coast of Brazil by whatever water conveyance was most appropriate.

After the route was determined, Herndon and his companion, Passed Midshipman Lardner Gibbon, began the necessary preparations. Manuel Ijurra, a young Peruvian who had traveled the Amazon a few years before, was engaged as interpreter. From the frigate *Raritan,* then at Callao, the services of Master's Mate Henry J. Richards were obtained as well as some equipment—India-rubber bags, carbines, pistols, ammunition, and a tent—and from the *St. Mary's,* more arms and some 1,500 fathoms of fishing line for soundings.

Herndon also purchased four "young, sound, and well bitted: but unshod mules as well as about a thousand yards of coarse cotton cloth for trading purposes", plus "hatchets, knives, tinder-boxes, fish-hooks, beads, looking-glasses, cotton handkerchiefs, ribbons, and cheap trinkets," for possible barter for food and services where money was not needed or known. Everything was packed in bundles of "half a mule-load."

The scientific equipment included instruments for skinning birds and dissecting animals; a medicine chest containing arsenical soap for the preservation of skins; some reams of coarse paper for drying leaves and plants; chart paper, notebooks, pencils; plus instruments such as a sextant, artificial horizon, boiling point apparatus, camera lucida, spy-glass, chronometers, and barometer brought by Gibbon. Gibbon carried a chronometer in the saddle pocket of his mule, and a barometer, slung in a specially made leathern case, at the saddle-bow. Passports and other papers were carried in a tin case. The group's personal effects were far from elaborate.

> Our bedding consisted of the saddle-cloths, a stout blanket, and anything else that could be packed in the India-rubber bag. An Englishman from New Holland, whom I met in Lima, gave me a coverlet made of the skins of a kind of raccoon, which served me many a good turn; and often, when in cold of the Cordillera I wrapped myself in its warm folds, I felt a thrill of gratitude for the thoughtful kindness which had provided me with such a comfort. We purchased thick flannel shirts, ponchos of India-rubber, wool, and cotton, and had straw hats, covered with oilcloth, and fitted with green

veils, to protect our eyes from the painful affections which often occur by the sudden bursting out of the sunlight upon the masses of snow that lie forever upon the mountain tops.

We carried two small kegs—one containing brandy, for drinking, and the other, the common rum of the country, called Ron de Quemar, for burning; also, some coarse knives, forks, spoons, tin cups and plates. I did not carry, as I should have done, a few cases of preserved meat, sardines, cheese, etc., which would have given us a much more agreeable meal than we often got on the road; but I did carry, in the India-rubber bags, quite a large quantity of biscuit, which I had baked in Lima, which served a very good purpose, and lasted us to Tarma.

On May 15, Herndon hired an *arriero,* or muleteer, Pablo Luis Arredondo, with seven mules to carry the baggage from Lima to Tarma for 10 dollars the head, with the provision that they stop wherever they pleased, as long as they pleased. An Indian named Mauricio was also engaged. The party finally left Lima on Wednesday, May 21, 1851, on the road to Tarma with a passport from the Peruvian government.

On that first day of a long and arduous journey, the party traveled on a level but stony road at first bisecting green fields, but later traversing barren and rocky ground. They spent the night at a hacienda called Pacayar where they slept in the one-room adobe house of the estate. Supper was a thin soup and a broth of potatoes, cheese, lard and some meat called chupe, a concoction extensively used in the mountainous regions of Peru. The next morning they had a breakfast of eggs and chupe at a nearby roadside inn.

The expedition either purchased food or received it as gifts, and managed to sleep under shelter, however rudimentary, on the first part of their journey. Herndon observed and recorded everything he could about the country and its inhabitants. As the elevation increased, the road cut into the rock on the sides of the hills, became narrower, precipitous, and dangerous. There was little pasturage for the mules and other food was very difficult to find or buy.

On May 27, they camped at the village of San Mateo, located on both sides of the Rimac River at an elevation of 10,200 feet. The next day Herndon and Gibbon, guided by a native boy, visited the mines at the hacienda of San Jose de Parac, a three-hour ride "over the worst roads, bordered by the highest cliffs and deepest ravines we had yet seen." Herndon carried letters of introduction to the superintendent, Don Tarribio Malarin, who gave them a warm welcome to the hacienda, which was

situated near the head of a small valley, which debouches upon the road just below San Mateo; the stream which drains it emptying into the Rimac there. It is a square, enclosed with one-story buildings, consisting of the mill for grinding the ore, the ovens for toasting it when ground, the workshops, store-houses, and dwelling-houses. It is managed by a superintendent and three mayordomos, and employs about forty working hands.

These are Indians of the Sierra, strong, hardy-looking fellows, though generally low in stature, and stupid in expression. They are silent and patient, and, having coca enough to chew, will do an extraordinary quantity of work. They have their breakfast of caldo and cancha (toasted maize), and get to work by eight o'clock. At eleven they have a recess of half an hour, when they sit down near their place of work, chat lazily with each other, and chew coca, mixed with a little lime, which each one carries in a small gourd, putting it on the mass of coca leaves in his mouth with a wire pin attached to the stopper of the gourd that carries the lime. Some dexterity is necessary to do this properly without cauterizing the lips or tongue. They then go to work again until five, when they finish for the day, and dine off chupe. It has made me, with my tropical habit of life, shiver to see these fellows puddling with their naked legs a mass of mud and quick-silver in water at the temperature of thirty-eight Fahrenheit.

These Indians generally live in huts near the hacienda, and are supplied from its store-houses. They are kept in debt by the supplies; and by custom, though not by law, no one will employ an Indian who is in debt to his patron; so that he is compelled to work on with no hope of getting free of the debt, except by running away to a distant part of the country where he is not known, which some do.

The diseases incident to this occupation are indigestion, called empacho, pleurisy, and sometimes the lungs seem affected with the fumes and dust of the ore; but on the whole, it does not seem an unhealthy occupation.

The four mines belonging to the hacienda employed about 60 workmen, "though more could be employed to advantage." These men were divided into two gangs for each mine, each gang being headed by a corporal under a majordomo. Herndon noted that the laborers who went to the mines as eight-year-old boys, worked for 24 hours at a time, with a two-hour break, and carried out loads of ore weighing 150 pounds from a depth of over 500 feet. The ore was refined in ovens fired by dried cattle dung, of which Herndon noted that particular hacienda used 1,500,000 pounds annually.

For the next two days, Gibbon was sick with chills and fever. On June 1, they returned to camp to find Richards ill. Nevertheless, by 11:00 a.m. the party was on the road again.

At twelve the valley narrowed to a dell of about fifty feet in width; the stream occupying its whole breadth, with the exception of a narrow, but smooth and level mulepath on its right bank. This is a very remarkable place. On each side the rock of red porphyry rises perpendicularly for full five hundred feet. In places it overhangs the stream and road. The traveller feels as if he were passing through some tunnel of the Titans. The upper exit from the dell is so steep that steps have been cut in the rock for the mule's feet; and the stream rushes down the rock-obstructed declivity in foaming fury, flinging clouds of white spray over the traveller and rendering the path slippery and dangerous.

The next day, June 2, an extraordinary event occurred. Herndon met a traveller "who proved to be an old schoolmate of mine, whom I had not seen, or even heard of, since we were boys." This unnamed man was head machinist at the mines near Morococha, and he gave Herndon a note to the administrator of that place which helped the expedition, particularly in finding food for the mules.

At the highest point of the road, called the pass of Antarangra, or copper rock, the barometer indicated an altitude of 16,044 feet. Herndon was disappointed with the "quiet beauty" of the scene, so very distinct from the "savage and desolate grandeur" he had expected. "Gibbon, with the camera lucida, sketched the cordillera. I expended a box of matches in boiling the snow for the atmospheric pressure; and poor Richards lay shivering on the ground, enveloped in our pillows, a martyr to the *veta.*" The party was still within 60 miles of the Pacific, but it had reached the "divide" which separated the watershed of the Atlantic from that of the Pacific Ocean.

At 5:00 p.m. the party reached the copper mining hacienda of Morococha, "belonging to some German brothers named Pflucker, of Lima who own, also, several silver mines of the neighborhood." Herndon hoped to visit the mines and observe the process by which the ore was extracted and smelted, but was unsuccessful because no one seemed to be at work when he was there. He also failed to get statistics about their yield and costs and thought he "noticed some reserve upon this subject."

However, he did observe everything possible about the administration of the hacienda and mines, the number and types of workmen employed, and the standard and quality of life in the area. The silver ore was rich and yielded "one thousand, and even fifteen hundred, marks to the caxon." (A caxon was 6,250 pounds and a mark was worth $8.50.)

On June 4, 1851, the group left Morococha without Richards, who was too sick to travel. They rode through the "Valley of the Lakes" to the village of Pachachaca. The next day they continued down the valley from Pachachaca and passed a

> very curious-looking place, where a small stream came out of a valley to the northward and westward, and spread itself over a flat table-rock, soft and calcereous. It poured over this rock in a sort of horse-shoe cataract, and then spread over an apparently convex surface of this same soft rock, about two hundred and fifty yards wide, crossing the valley down which we were traveling. This rock sounded hollow under the feet of the mules, and I feared we should break through at every instant. I am confident it was but a thick crust; and, indeed, after crossing it, we observed a clear stream of water issuing from beneath it, and flowing into the road on the farther side.

About two miles from Pachachaca, the expedition turned "to the northward and eastward." At first the country offered some pasturage, but became more barren as the party advanced. Around 2:30 p.m. the chain suspension bridge of Oroya was reached. This bridge was about 50 yards long and 50 feet above the Jauxa River and swayed as they crossed. It was necessary to partially unload the mules and carry some of the cargo across on the shoulders of the bridgekeeper and his assistants. The toll was 12½ cents per mule and the same for his cargo.

They camped at Oroya, where barley straw was purchased for the mules and the men got "a beef chupe, with eggs and roasted potatoes." The next day they reached Tarma around 4:00 p.m. The ride was "a long and tiresome one, being mostly a bone-shaking descent. . . ."

In 10 days at Tarma Herndon observed everything he could about the people and resources of the region. On June 16, the party left Tarma for a visit to "the Chanchamayo." The mulekeeper from Lima had been paid off and helped to secure "two asses and a saddle mule" along with two peons (workers). As it turned out, however, the owners of these animals were forced to rent their beasts against their will, and the two workmen had no desire to leave Tarma. Herndon regretted applying to the authorities for help since his application had given rise to "injustice and oppression," but he took mules and workmen and "rode off, followed, I have no doubt, by the curses of the community."

The ride was the wildest they had had up to that time. "The ascents and descents were nearly precipitous," and at one point it appeared that Gibbon would be forced over the side of the road, possibly to his death.

The next day was "the longest and hardest day's ride." The road was rocky, rough, steep, and at one place blocked by a fallen rock. This meant that the party had to cross a steep hill called the "Cuesta de Tangachuca" or "Hill of take care of your hat" to descend to the montana of Chanchamayo. The crossing proved steep and "trying to man and beast," while the descent into the montana was so circuitous and precipitous that, except for Gibbon, everyone went by foot. That night the expedition stopped at the hacienda of Don Jose Manuel Gardenas.

The following day, June 19, the Peruvian military post of San Ramon was reached at an altitude of 2,610 feet. Here Herndon computed that they had traveled 193 miles since leaving Lima with an ascent of 232 feet to the mile on the western slope of the Andes and a descent of 152 feet to the mile on the eastern side. He also estimated that he was still about 4,000 winding river miles from the Atlantic Ocean.

The fort of San Ramon was situated at the junction of the Chanchamayo and Tulumayo rivers. On the side of the Chanchamayo on which it stood there were farming haciendas; on the other side was the territory of Chuncho Indians determined "to dispute the passage of the rivers and any attempt at further conquest." Herndon recorded the actions of the Indians, the response of the Peruvian authorities, the manner in which the farms were worked, the conditions of the laborers, the type of crops grown, and described the agricultural operations and opportunities in the montana for possible use by colonists from the United States.[7]

Herndon's description of the principal agricultural products of the district were precise. He elaborated on the multiple uses of sugar cane; the stimulating effects of the leaves of the coca bush; the excellence of the coffee and the manner in which it was cultivated; the quality of the cotton produced from the various cotton trees; the planting and consumption of yucca (cassava root); the care and preservation of Indian corn; the many ways in which *plantanos* (plantains, or bananas) were cooked and eaten; and the variety of fruits in the district, such as pineapple, *sour sop* (a kind of chirimoya), and papayas.

In addition, Herndon commented on the scarcity of farming tools in the district, and the absence of good grazing land. The difficulty in breeding cattle because of a species of worm present which destroyed the animals was also detailed.

Finally, before leaving the area, Herndon described the construction of the houses on the haciendas, and ended his account of the district on a promising note:

> Many acres of fine land are lying uncultivated in Chanchamayo; and several of our Tarma friends offered us title deeds to large tracts of land there, because a feeling of insecurity regarding the stability of the government prevented them from expending time and money in the cultivation of them. Another such administration as that just closed under President Castilla will dissipate this apprehension; and then, if the Peruvian government would invite settlers, giving them the means of reaching there, and appropriating a very small sum for their maintenance till they could clear the forest and gather their first fruits, I have no doubt that fifty years would see settlements pushed to the navigable head-waters of the Ucayali, and the colonists would find purchasers for the rich and varied products of their lands at their very doors.

On June 23, the party began its return to Tarma—a three-day trip—accompanied by the commandant of San Ramon and his servant. The Indian servant hired at Tarma was discharged because he could not be trusted. A few days later Herndon decided to split his party, sending Gibbon to explore the Bolivian tributaries of the Amazon while he worked his way through the valley of Acombamba, the plain of Junin, and the mining district of Cerro Pasco to the headwaters of the Huallaga River. He planned to travel the Huallaga to the upper reaches of the Amazon and follow that river to the Atlantic at Pará, Brazil.

Herndon left Gibbon approximately half of their trading equipment, arms and ammunition, and $1,500 as well as all the instruments, except some thermometers and the "boiling-point apparatus." Sextants and chronometers had already been carried over Herndon's proposed route; Gibbon "might go where these had never been." Gibbon was to hire a guide at Tarma and to take Richards with him as soon as he could travel.

On July 1, 1851, at the entrance to the Acombamba Valley, Herndon parted from Gibbon and Richards.

I had deliberated long and painfully on the propriety of this separation; I felt that I was exposing him to unknown perils; and I knew that I was depriving myself of a pleasant companion and a most efficient auxiliary. My manhood, under the depressing influence of these feelings, fairly gave way, and I felt again that "Hysterica passio," that swelling of the heart and filling of the eyes, that I have so often been called upon to endure in parting from my gallant comrades of the Navy.

That day, Herndon, Ijurra, and Mauricio reached Palcamayo, a village of about 1,000 people at an elevation of 10,539 feet. For reasons not clearly stated, all of the officials in the town were drunk, and Herndon had to give them some money before his men and animals could get anything to eat.

The next day the group traveled 18 miles to the plains and town of Junin, 12,947 feet above sea level; next day they went 21 miles over a broad and elevated road, "built of stones and earth," without which, Herndon noted, the plain of Junin would be impassable in the rainy season. The night of July 3–4 was spent at the tambo (roadhouse) of Ninacacca. Another 18 miles took them to Cerro Pasco on July 5th:

The view from this point is a most extraordinary one. I can compare it to nothing so fitly as the looking from the broken and rugged edges of a volcano into the crater beneath. The traveller sees small houses, built, without regard to regularity, on small hills, with mounds of earth and deep cavities in their midst; the mud chimneys of ancient furnaces, contrasting strikingly with the more graceful funnel of the modern steam engine; the huge cross erected on the hill of Sta. Catalina, near the middle of the city, which his fancy may suppose placed there to guard, with its holy presence, the untold treasures beneath; two beautiful little lakes, only divided by a wide causeway at the southern extremity of the crater, and another embedded among the hills to the westward; hills (on one of which he stands) of five hundred feet in height, with bold white heads of rock, surrounding these; and the magnificent Cordillera from the right and left overlooking the whole.

These are the objects that strike the eye of the traveller at his first view. As he rides down the hill, he sees the earth open everywhere with the mouths of mines now abandoned; he is astonished at their number, and feels a sense of insecurity as if the whole might cave in at once and bury him quick. He rides into the narrow, ill-paved streets of the city, and, if he can divert his attention for a moment from the watching of his horse's footsteps, he will observe the motliest population to be met with anywhere out of the dominions of the Sultan. I believe that he may see, in a single ride through the city, men of all nations, and of almost every condition; and if he don't see plenty of drunken people, it will be a marvel.

I was delighted when we turned into the patio of the house of the sub-prefect of the province, Don Jose Mier y Teran, and escaped the rude stare and drunken impertinence of the Indians, thronging the streets, and doors of the grog-shops. This gentleman, whose kindness we had experienced at Tarma, gave us quarters in his house, and pressed us to make ourselves at home, to which his blunt, abrupt, and evidently sincere manners particularly invited.

After a wash, to which the coldness of the weather and the water by no means invited, I put on my uniform in honor of the day, and went out to see Mr. Jump, director of the machinery, and Mr. Fletcher, an employe of the *Gremio* (Board of Miners) to whom I brought letters of introduction from Lima. These gentlemen received me with great cordiality. Mr. Jump offered me a room in his house, and Mr. Fletcher handed me a number of letters from friends at home, at Lima, and at Santiago. These letters were cordial medicines to me; I had arrived cold, sick, and dispirited, and but for them should have passed the first night of mental and physical suffering that I had been called upon to endure since leaving Lima.

Herndon recorded everything he could about the mines around Cerro Pasco, despite the weather being so cold and rainy that on at least two days he was almost too sick to walk. For example, he discovered that:

... The most common and easily obtained ores here are called "casajos." They do not require roasting, as do the ores at Parac; but otherwise the silver is got out in the same manner as I have described it to be at that place. Instead, however, of the ground ore being placed in small piles, and, after being mixed with salt and mercury, trodden with the feet, and worked with hoes as it is at Parac, a large quantity is placed in a circular enclosure, with a stone floor and mud wall, and it is trodden with horses (as we used in old times to "tread wheat" in Virginia) until the amalgamation is completed. The general yield of the casajos is six marks to the caxon. Their cost, according to the hardness of the rock in which they are enclosed, or their distance from the surface, is from six to sixteen dollars. Here is a calculation to show that, even at their highest price, of sixteen dollars, (being assured by the guia that the caxon will yield six marks,) their working, or benificiation, as it is called here, will pay. The complete amalgamation in the "circo," or circle, requires from forty to fifty days.

| | |
|---|---:|
| Dr. Circo of six caxones, @ $16 caxon | $96 00 |
| 150 mule loads, (transportation to the hacienda,) @ 25 cents | 37 50 |
| Grinding, @ $10 | 60 00 |
| Magistral, (calcined iron pyrites,) 1 arroba | 1 00 |
| 40 arrobas of salt, @ 50 cents | 20 00 |
| 5 tramplings by horses, @ $5 | 25 00 |
| Working and washing the amalgam | 11 50 |
| Loss of 35 lbs. quicksilver, @ $1 | 35 00 |
| | $286 00 |

| | |
|---|---:|
| Cr. 6 caxones, @ 6 marks caxon, 36 marks. (Mark is worth in Cerro Pasco $8 50) | $306 00 |

I had this statement from Mr. Jump. I did not examine it at the time, but I observed afterwards that there is no charge for driving off the mercury of the amalgam, and leaving the pure silver, which is worth eight dollars and fifty cents the mark. This would amount to six dollars more, leaving the profit to the purchaser, for the two months that he has been engaged in getting his silver, but fourteen dollars. This, of course, is but a poor business; for, though any quantity of the ore may be purchased, there are not haciendas enough to grind, or circos to amalgamate, a sufficient quantity to make the speculation good; and thus many millions of this ore are left unworked. The ore, however, rarely costs sixteen dollars, and will frequently give seven or eight marks to the caxon.

Statement showing the cost of a mark of silver placed on board ship for export:

| | |
|---|---:|
| Cost of a mark of pina in the Cerro | $8 50 |
| Impost for steam machines for pumping water from the mines. (This has been 12½ cents, and soon will be 50 cents) | 25 |
| Socabon (or great dran) duty | 12½ |
| Public works | 6¼ |
| Government or export duty | 50 |
| Mineral tribunal duty | 12½ |
| Loss in running the pina into bars | 12½ |
| Carriage to Lima, and other petty expenses | 6¼ |
| Profit of the purchaser in the Cerro | 37½ |
| | $10.12½ |

Twelve dwts. is the standard of pure silver in the mint at Lima. All the bars that go from this place are marked 11.22. They are assayed in Lima. If they come up to that standard they are worth $8.6746 the mark. For every grain under this 11.22 there is a deduction in the price of .0303 of a dollar.

Herndon, Ijurra, and Mauricio left Cerro Pasco on July 13, but not without much trouble. Herndon had unknowingly elected to depart on the occasion of the first regular bull fight ever seen in Cerro Pasco. Because of this, his muleteers got drunk, and it was only after cajolery and threats to ask the military for assistance that they finally loaded the mules.

Seven miles in a N.N.E. direction, and passing many haciendas for the grinding of ore, brought us to the village of Quinua, where a mint was established several years ago, but is now abandoned. The machinery for coining is much better than any I have seen in South America. It was made by a Boston man, named Hacket, who also made nearly all the machinery for the sugar-mills near Huanco. There are goldmines in this neighborhood, but I think they are not worked. This village is just at the point where leaving the sterility of the Cerro we fall in with bushes and flowers.

Four miles further we stopped for the night at a hacienda called Chiquirn, (elevation 11,542) which appears once to have been flourishing, but which is now nearly abandoned, being only tenanted by an old man to take care of the house . . . we could get no supper at this place. I was tired enough to care little about it.

In two days they crossed the boundary between the provinces of Pasco and Huanuco and entered an agricultural area. This transition was very agreeable to the group, the only problem with Herndon being excessive fatigue: ". . . when I arrived (at five) at the hospitable gates of the hacienda of Quicacan, and with difficulty lifted myself out of the saddle, it was with the deep sigh which always accompanies relief from pain, and which was much more pleasurable than the sight of waving fields and babbling brooks."

The hacienda was owned by an Englishman named Dyer. Since his place was on the trail from the interior city of Huanuco to Lima, he usually had someone staying with him. Herndon's arrival occasioned no great surprise, and he was accepted as a member by a group on their way to Lima already at the hacienda. Thus, he was treated to good company, entertaining conversation, and a very satisfying dinner. Toward nightfall, the servants started "dragging out mattresses and bed-clothing from some obscure room, and going with them to different parts of the house to make pallets for the visitors who intended to spend the night," and Herndon was "carried back to my boyish days, and almost fancied that I was at a country wedding in Virginia." Dyer gave Herndon a wide "four-poster" with clean linen sheets and a "pillow with a frilled case to it."

After observing the operations of the sugar-mill at Quicacan, Herndon and his group went on to the hacienda of Colonel Lucar at Huanuco where they arrived at 4:30 p.m., July 17, 1851. Again they were very kindly received and given accommodations in the main house.

During the next five days, Herndon took time to observe life in Huanuco, and get information about the areas he intended to visit next. He arranged to sell his mules to Colonel Lucar for half the price he had paid for them on the condition that Herndon and his men could ride them out of Huanuco as far as possible and then send them back by the arriero.

On July 22, 1851, the group was ready to leave when it was discovered that Mauricio had deserted. This was a great annoyance, but it did not stop the departure at noon.

After four days of rough travel, alternating between ascending and descending hills, but generally always downward to a lower elevation, they reached the hacienda of Chihuangala. Beyond this point it was not practicable to go by mule, and Herndon and Ijurra settled down to wait for some porters requested by a letter to the governor from the village of Tingo Maria.

The wait was a trying one. There was rain part of the time, and they began to suffer from lack of food:

> No eggs; no potatoes; nothing in fact, but yuccas and bananas. There were turkeys, chickens, and a pig, running about the chacra; but no entreaty, nor any reasonable offer of money could induce the people to sell us one. I offered the patrona a dollar and a half for a half-grown turkey; but she said she must wait till her husband came in from his work, so that she might consult him. When he came, after long debate, it was decided that they would sell me a chicken for breakfast tomorrow. I tried hard to find out why they were so reluctant to sell, for they do not eat them themselves; but did not succeed. I believe it to be something like the miser-feeling of parting with property, the not being used to money, and also a dislike to kill what they have reared and seen grow up under their own eye.

On July 28, Herndon and Ijurra walked about three miles to visit another hacienda, that of Cucheros. There Herndon obtained information about the production of coca and met an English botanist by the name of Nation, the gardener for Souza Ferreyra, the Brazilian chargé d'affaires at Lima. Nation was collecting plants for his employer and had had a very rough time of it. Herndon and Ijurra took him with them to Tingo Maria.

On the return from Cucheros, Herndon and Ijurra stopped at the house of a man who had promised to sell them a turkey. He now refused, but Ijurra refused to take no for an answer and shot a turkey before Herndon was aware of what he intended to do. Fortunately, the resultant furious outcry was smoothed over by kind words and the payment of a dollar and a half. Herndon, however, admonished Ijurra not to be so precipitate again.

The Indian porters from Tingo Maria arrived on July 30, and at noon Herndon and Ijurra, with their baggage, started off toward Huallaga River. After two days of very tiring travel through thick bush and heavy rain showers, they reached the pueblo of San Antonio del Tingo Maria on the Huallaga. "The governor, an intelligent and modest young man, a former friend of Ijurra, welcomed us cordially, and gave us a capital breakfast of chicken broth."

While at Tingo Maria, Herndon estimated they had traveled 335 miles from Lima in 21 days, a little less than 16 miles per day, most of it on muleback. They walked the last 30 miles from Chihuangala to Tingo Maria.

From Tingo Maria, Ijurra and Herndon traveled by water down the Huallaga to the Maranon (as the upper portion of the Amazon was called), thence to the Amazon, and on the Amazon, except for an excursion up the Ucayali River, to the sea at Pará, Brazil. They left Tingo Maria on August 4, in two canoes, hollowed out from single logs, and manned by "a pintero, or bowman, who looks out for rocks or sunken trees ahead; a popero, or steersman, who stands on a little platform at the stern of the boat and guides her motions; and the bogas, or rowers, who stand up to paddle, having one foot in the bottom of the boat and the other on the gunwale."

When there were no obstructions in the river, they relaxed, and the canoe drifted with the current. As they approached an area of rapids, or mal-paso, however, the bowman indicated the channel to the steersman who directed the boat in the proper course, while the oarsmen went to their task with a will as every Indian emitted a "wild, triumphant, screaming laugh."

In this manner, Herndon estimated they traveled about 45 miles in a nine-hour day that included a mid-day break for lunch. The fare for all meals varied in relation to the animals and plants killed or discovered. Monkeys were roasted without skinning or cleaning. Herndon tried a piece and found it so tough that his teeth made no impression on it. As he put it later, "Jocko, however, had his revenge, for I nearly perished of nightmare. Some devil, with arms as nervous as the monkey's, had me by the throat, and staring on me with his cold, cruel eye, expressed his determination to hold on to the death. I thought it hard to die by the grasp of this fiend on the banks of the strange river, and so early in my course; and upon making a desperate effort, and shaking him off, I found that I had forgotten to take off my cravat, which was choking me within an inch of my life."

On August 7, 1851, the river town of Tocache was reached. Here the Indian boatmen from Tingo Maria left, and Herndon hired a new crew with the help of the governor of Tocache. He paid them in advance with a quantity of the cotton cloth brought from Lima. A hog was purchased, killed, and salted, and some chickens were obtained at a total cost of nine dollars. This purchase was of little benefit to the party, however, for half of the meat was stolen, and the rest spoiled before it could be eaten.

On August 12, Herndon and Ijurra left Tocache with two canoes and 12 boatmen. The river there was 50 yards wide, 18 feet deep, with a current of 3 miles per hour. Further down stream were rapids and other river towns. Herndon continued to record faithfully all he saw and heard. At time, food was a problem, but otherwise nothing delayed the journey except stops to change crews and visits to side areas.

On September 3, the travellers arrived at the junction of the Huallaga with the Amazon.

> The Huallaga, from Tingo Maria, the head of canoe navigation, to Chasuta, (from which point to its mouth it is navigable for a draught of five feet at the lowest stage of the river), is three hundred and twenty-five miles long; costing seventy-four working hours to descend it; and falling four feet and twenty-seven hundredths per mile. From Chasuta to its mouth it has two hundred and eighty-five miles of length, and takes sixty-eight hours of descent, falling one foot and twenty-five hundredths per mile. It will be seen that these distances are passed in nearly proportional times. This is to be attributed to the time occupied in descending the malos pasos, for the current is more rapid above than below. The difference between the times of ascent and descent is, on an average, about three for one. It is proper to state here that all my estimates of distance, after embarkation upon the rivers, being obtained from measurement by the logline, are in geographical miles of sixty to the degree.

Herndon was greatly impressed with his first vision of the Amazon.

> The march of the great river in its silent grandeur was sublime; but in the
> untamed might of its turbid waters as they cut away its banks, tore down
> the gigantic denizens of the forest, and built up islands, it was awful. It
> rolled through the wilderness with a stately and solemn air. Its waters
> looked angry, sullen and relentless; and the whole scene awoke emotions of
> awe and dread—such as are caused by the funeral solemnities, the minute
> gun, the howl of the wind, and the angry tossing of the waves, when all
> hands are called to bury the dead in a troubled sea.
>
> I was reminded of our Mississippi at its topmost flood; the waters are
> quite as muddy and quite as turbid; but this stream lacked the charm and
> the fascination which the plantation upon the bank, the city upon the bluff,
> and the steamboat upon its waters, lend to its fellow of the North;
> nevertheless, I felt pleased at its sight. I had already travelled seven
> hundred miles by water, and fancied that this powerful stream would soon
> carry me to the ocean; but the water-travel was comparatively just begun;
> many a weary month was to elapse ere I should again look upon the fa-
> miliar face of the sea; and many a time when worn and wearied with the
> canoe life, did I exclaim, "This river seems interminable."

The river indeed proved to be a highway, for by noon on September 9—
after six days of travel—Herndon and Ijurra reached the town of Nauta,
210 miles downstream. Nauta was essentially a fishing village of about 1,000
inhabitants, mostly Indians, but it was also the headquarters of the
governor-general of the "Missions of Marnas," consisting of 17 villages of
3,789 people. Herndon investigated the area's governmental, economic, and
social life, including the costs and probable profits of fishing, gathering sas-
parilla, and running a steamer line. In his report to the Secretary of the
Navy on the economic future of the Nauta region, Herndon estimated:

> . . . the annual cost of running a small steamer . . . between Loreto, the
> frontier port of Peru and Chasuta, a distance of eight hundred miles, en-
> tirely within the Peruvian territory, at twenty thousand dollars, including
> the establishment of blacksmiths' and carpenters' shops at Nauta for
> repairs. According to the estimate of Arebalo, (and I judge that he is very
> nearly correct,) the value of the imports and exports to and from Brazil is
> twenty thousand dollars annually. I have no doubt that the appearance of a
> steamer in these waters would at once double the value; for it would, in the
> first place, convert the thousand men who are now employed in the
> fetching and carrying of the articles of trade into producers, and would
> give a great impulse to trade by facilitating it. A loaded canoe takes eighty
> days to ascend these eight hundred miles. A steamer will do it in twelve,
> giving ample time to take in wood, to land and receive cargo at the various
> villages on the river, and to lay by at night. When the river becomes better
> known she can run for a large part of the night, and thus shorten her time
> nearly one-half. Men shrink at the eighty days in a canoe, when they will
> jump at twelve in a steamer.

The steamer will also increase commerce and trade by creating artificial wants; men will travel who did not travel before; articles of luxury—such as Yankee clocks, cheap musical instruments, &c.—will be introduced, and the Indians will work to obtain them; and, in short, when the wonders that the steamboat and railroad have accomplished are taken into consideration, I shall not be thought rash in predicting that in one year from the time of the appearance of the steamer Arebalo's twenty thousand dollars will be made forty thousand.

Thus we shall have twenty thousand dollars worth of goods going up from Loreto to Chasuta, paying at least one hundred per cent; and twenty thousand dollars going down, paying another hundred per cent; giving to the steamboat company (who would monopolize the trade) forty thousand dollars a year, against twenty thousand dollars of expenses.

At Nauta, Herndon purchased for 60 dollars a *garretea*—a boat 30 feet long, seven feet at its widest section, and three feet deep, partially decked and covered. He hired 12 rowers, a popero, and an Indian servant, and purchased some Portuguese axes, small fishhooks, and white beads for trading purposes. So equipped, he left Nauta on September 25, 1851, to explore the Ucayali River which emptied into the Amazon some 55 minutes of canoe travel from Nauta. Almost a month later, on October 18, they arrived at the principal Indian village of Sarayacu, which stood on a level plain with a "delightful" climate. With its environs, Sarayacu had a population of about 1,000 inhabitants under the direction of four Franciscan friars from "the College of Ocopa."

Between Sarayacu and the military post of San Ramon on the Chanchamayo, the land was inhabited for the most part by hostile Indians. When he left Nauta, Herndon had intended to ascend the Ucayali as far as Chanchamayo and also to explore the Pachitea River. At Sarayacu, however, he was unable to induce any more than eight Indians, at double pay, to accompany him. Since it was estimated that a force of at least 25 men was needed, Herndon was forced to abandon an enterprise on which he had set his heart,

... for I thought it possible that I might gather great reputation with my Chanchamayo friends by joining them again from below, and showing them that their darling wish (a communication with the Atlantic by the Perene and Ucayali) might be accomplished.

I felt, in turning my boat's head downstream, that the pleasure and excitement of the expedition were passed; that I was done and had done nothing. I became ill and dispirited, and never fairly recovered the gaiety of temper and elasticity of spirit which had animated me at the start until I received the congratulations of my friends at home.

From Sarayacu to the mouth of Ucayali, Herndon estimated the distance at 275 miles. On October 28, 1851, at 10 a.m., Herndon and Ijurra began the return trip down stream. With enough help they reached Nauta in eight days. They spent only two days in Nauta, then began the trip down the Amazon to Pará.

On December 4, 1851, the explorers arrived at the Brazilian frontier town of Tabatinga. The passage had gone smoothly except that it became almost impossible to keep the live animal specimens from fighting and killing each other.

> I had two little monkeys not so large as rats; the peccary ate one, and the other died of grief. My howling monkey refused food, and grunted himself to death. The friars ate their own tails off, and died of the rot; the mongoose, being tied up on account of eating the small birds, literally cut out his entrails with the string before it was noticed. The peccary jumped overboard and swam ashore; the tuyuyus grabbed and swallowed every paroquet that ventured within reach of their bills; and they themselves, being tied on the beach at Eyas, were devoured by the crocodiles. My last monkey died as I went up New York bay; and I only succeeded in getting home about a dozen mutuns, or curassows; a pair of Egyptian geese; a pair of birds, called pucacunga in Peru, and jacu in Brazil; a pair of macaws; a pair of parrots; and a pair of large white cranes, called jaburu, which are the same, I believe, as the birds called adjutants in India.

Ever since leaving Nauta, Herndon had flown the U.S. flag over his boat. When he reached Tabatinga, this flag was replaced by a Brazilian flag when Herndon, dressed in uniform, landed to present his Brazilian passport to the commandant. The fort was garrisoned by 20 soldiers, a corporal, a sergeant, and two officers, and Herndon was accorded a seven-gun salute from two long brass 12-pounder field guns. The commandant received him ceremoniously but with civility. The commandant's problem of how to get around the Brazilian law forbidding foreign vessels from navigating Brazil's inland waterways was finally solved by Herndon's agreement to use the commandant's boat in lieu of his own, "thus enabling him to say, in a frontier passport which he issued to me, that I was descending the river in Brazilian vessels."[8]

On December 6, 1851, Herndon and Ijurra left Tabatinga, accompanied for a short distance down river by the fort's officers and the commandant, who was received aboard with "a salute of, I should think, at least one hundred guns; for Ijurra did not leave off shooting for half an hour."

The group reached the village of San Paulo, 95 miles from Tabatinga, on December 8. Herndon continued to take soundings, ascertain the temperature of the water, and record everything about the life and environment of the region that seemed compatible with his instructions. On December 17, 1852, they arrived at a village of some 800 people, called Egas, still some 1,800 miles from the sea.

At Egas the party spent Christmas enjoying the hospitality of its military commandant, and left on December 28, 1852. All the boatmen from Sarayacu but one planned to return home; Indians from Tabatinga continued with them. The party took with them some bread—the first they had had in five months, a gift of the commandant.

During the first week of travel, the mouths of the Purus River were passed, and on January 6, 1853, they sailed into the Rio Negro and arrived at the town of Barra. Barra supported a colony of persons (including an Italian named Enrique Antonini) who had traveled from Europe to make Brazil their home, or who were visiting Brazil for adventure, for business, or for reasons connected with the advancement of science. There was one American, Marcus Williams, who did business as a general merchant. Thus, Barra had regular connections with the outside world, and Herndon particularly enjoyed the New York newspapers available there.

Herndon remained at Barra for the next six weeks, recuperating, looking for Gibbon, observing, recording, and planning the last stage of his passage to the sea. Ijurra and the Indians from Tabatinga left him there, and since he did not make contact with Gibbon, he had to go on alone. On February 18, 1852, he departed after securing the services of six Indians and asking his friend Antonini to look out for Gibbon, from whom he had been separated since July 1, 1851.

Two weeks later, on March 1, 1852, Herndon reached the town of Santarem, 650 miles from the sea. He changed boat crews again, restocked some supplies, and left on March 28. At 9:00 p.m. on April 11, 1852, he arrived at Pará, Brazil, the end of his river journey. He had left Lima nearly a year earlier, on May 21, 1851.

Herndon remained in Pará for a month while he investigated and recorded everything he could about the city and its environs. He was particularly attracted by the number of "curious and beautiful animals in Pará." One of these was the electric eel.

> Electric eels are found in great numbers in the creeks and ditches about Para. The largest I have seen was about four inches in diameter, and five feet in length. Their shock, to me, was unpleasant, but not painful. Some persons, however, are much more susceptible than others. Captain Lee, of the *Dolphin*, could not feel at all the shock of an eel, which affected a lady so strongly as to cause her to reel, and nearly fall. Animals seem more powerfully affected than men. Mr. Norris told me that he had seen a horse drinking out of a tub, in which was one of these eels, jerked entirely off his feet. It may be that the electric shock was communicated directly to the stomach by means of the water he was swallowing; . . . ."

On May 12, Herndon departed from Pará for the United States in the USS *Dolphin,* after having shipped his collections previously on the clipper barque *Peerless* belonging to Henry L. Norris, the U.S. Consul at Pará.

Before they separated at Tama, on July 1, 1851, Herndon gave Gibbon detailed instructions; to proceed to "Cuzco," to seek a river believed to empty into the Amazon, to round Lake Titicaca if necessary, to La Paz in Bolivia, to ascend the Amazon to "Barra do Rio Negro" and there to wait for Herndon. A copy of their basic instructions from the Navy Department was also given Gibbon.

On July 9, 1851, Gibbon, Richards, and a guide named Jose Casas, with an arriero and young son, set out for Cuzco, riding mules, on a 45-day trip.[9] They reached Cuzco on August 19, just in time for a good dinner: "soup, fish from the Apurimac, beef, poultry, potatoes, yucca, rice, and salad, with pine-apples, chirimoyas, plantains, oranges, and granadillas." They remained there for a month, and then left to search for the headwaters of the Madre de Dios or Purus River. The next evening Gibbon met a young Philadelphian, Charles Leechler, who "engaged in collecting Peruvian bark for a number of years. At first, he spoke with difficulty in his native language, but with a true American spirit assured me I might depend upon him as a companion. He knew parts of the country I was directed to explore; his services were the more acceptable. He joined me."

By Monday, September 22, the explorers arrived at the frontier farm of San Miguel, "where a number of houses are built in a hollow square, with a little wooden church, and fine orange trees in the centre, under the shade of which I was embraced by Padre Julian Bovo de Revello, a Franciscan missionary, honorary member of the Agricultural Society in Santiago de Chili."

San Miguel was the end of the road for mule transportation. The next day, leaving Jose Casas in charge of the animals, Gibbon took Leechler, Padre Julian, and four Indians in the direction of the supposed headwaters of the Madre de Dios. Twelve hours of difficult travel through thick undergrowth brought them to the bank of the "Cosnipata river, in the territory of the Chuncho savages," nine miles from San Miguel.

That night they ate wild turkey, fish, boiled rice, and parched corn; all were bitten by ants and bees, but were nonetheless able to sleep on the bare ground in a "bush house."

The next morning Gibbon, Leechler, and one old Indian tried to cross the river on a raft constructed of balsa logs. The swift current forced them to land on a rocky little island in the middle of the river, and in trying to swim back, Leechler lost their raft. More balsa logs were cut, but there was not enough daylight left to make another raft. Leechler swam to the island to spend the night with Gibbon and the Indian, but a heavy rain swelled the river and no one slept because they feared drowning. The next day the water subsided enough to allow them to reach shore, but another balsa raft was lost, and "another night was spent with the party divided."

By the evening of September 28, the group was back at San Miguel. On October 1, 1851, Gibbon, Leechler, and Jose Casas started for Portocambo and Cuzco. Leechler left them enroute. Six days later, Gibbon and Jose Casas reached Cuzco; they had been away 21 days.

In South Peru and Bolivia, about a day's journey apart, there were accommodations for travellers called post-houses. After deciding to stop each night at a post-house and to obtain new mules and a new arriero at each, Gibbon, with Jose Casas and Richards, left Cuzco on October 28, 1851, on the road to Lake Titicaca and La Paz, Bolivia. As he had done before, Gibbon made daily observations with the sextant and artificial horizon and took various meteorological measurements.

On November 18, 1851, the Gibbon party entered Bolivia across a bridge over the Desaguedero River, 50 yards wide. On the Bolivian side,

the military commandant was very civil, he requested the custom house officer to let us off easy, saying "they came to serve our country." The baggage was all taken off the backs of the mules; one or two trunks examined. The commander took great interest in our instruments; a woman in her riding dress begged permission to examine a needle and thread case which struck her fancy; she seemed to think it hard that a man had to do his own sewing.

Some three days later, the travellers first saw the city of La Paz, near the base of the great snow-capped mountain, Illimani. They soon entered the city and were received hospitably in the home of a man to whom they had been given a letter of introduction.

The most tiresome and troublesome part of the journey is the day of arrival in a large town, where we generally remain long enough to rest and pick up information. There are no hotels to which a traveller may go and make himself independently comfortable. Walking into a man's private house, bag and baggage, and handing him a letter of introduction, which plainly expresses that the bearer has come to make his house his home, is the custom of the country. We entered the most elegant house I saw in South America.

The gentleman of the house was not at home; he was engaged superintending the Indians at the gold mines and washings of Tipuani, situated north of La Paz, on a tributary of the river Beni, and to the east of the Sorata mountains. His daughter received the letter, smoking a large cigar, and invited us to join. Her husband was prefect of the province of Yungas, where is gathered the best cinchona bark. As it was Saturday, and 4 o'clock, the officers had left the custom-house, and the baggage could not be examined before Monday morning. Notwithstanding the lady of the house sent our letters to the prefect, and asked that we might have our clothing. We were in a house with four young ladies and no gentleman, so there was a poor chance of borrowing.

The party was a good deal sun-burnt, dusted, and harassed over the hot plains since leaving Cuzco, and all well tired out. Richards suffered, though he stood the travel better than was expected. Jose's beard had grown, and he had pulled an old white hat about so much to get it on the sunny side of his head, that he at once applied for part of his wages to purchase a new one. When we arrive, Jose always goes at once to pay his respects to the lady of the house, and through him a general sketch of our duties and characters are obtained. He is so polite, and of such an obliging disposition, that he seems to attract attention wherever he goes. He is fond of travelling, and, for so old a person, bears his part well, sleeps sound, and enjoys good health.

Helped by these accommodations, the group relaxed somewhat, and Gibbon began to investigate the manner of living in the La Paz region. Much time was spent in examining how much gold might be obtained from the streams and mountains a short distance from the city, and how cinchona bark was gathered to produce quinine. In all this, Gibbon was not seriously hampered by the people of La Paz, although some of them voiced mild but also amused apprehension about the ultimate purpose of the United States in sending him to Bolivia.

During a dinner party one evening, Gibbon's place

was next the lady of the house, who presided. She was very intelligent, and had greater advantages of education than most of her countrywomen. She seemed particularly fond of the United States—asking many questions— expressing her admiration of the people, but disapproving of some of their actions. She thought the country too warlike; and although we had conceived our answers satisfied her, with regard to Texas and California— of which she had very incorrect ideas—she asked me to explain to her the meaning of all the articles she saw published in the newspapers of La Paz, upon the subject of Cuba. Turning suddenly, she looked up and said: "What are you doing here, Senor Gibbon; do you want Bolivia, also?" After setting forth the advantages of trade through the rivers of Bolivia, and the difficulties the people of her country now labored under to avail themselves of foreign commerce, she approved of the enterprise, and expressed herself friendly to it; but concluded by saying—"I believe the North Americans will some day govern the whole of South America.'"

Our conversation was disturbed by the entrance of an Indian servant girl, with her mistress's youngest child, which was seated between us. The Indians teach the children their own language. The habit of using the most easily pronounced words in Aymara and Spanish had produced a very curious mixture. The Aymara for baby is "wawa." A gentleman seated opposite inquired if I was fond of them. Never having heard the word "wawa" before, and believing he said "guavas"—a fruit upon the table—I answered in the affirmative, with the addition that they "were much better when preserved than when eaten raw." This brought forth a shout of laughter.

Gibbon, Richards, and Jose Casas, their baggage again loaded on post-house mules, left La Paz on December 2, 1851, for Cochabamba on the eastern side of the Andes. They traversed high, barren, inhospitable country through the mining district of Potosi at 14,000 feet and past the head-waters of the Pilcomayo River, which ran south to Paraguay and La Plata basin. On December 9, they started down the eastern slopes of the Andes, and on December 10, they rode into "the beautiful city of Cochabamba."

Gaining the post-house we found a miserable woman and child its only inmates. Our baggage was piled up in one corner of the room. The child raised a terrible dust in sweeping the room and driving out the chickens, who laid eggs in the corners, and roosted on the centre table. Our postillions bade us farewell, and our mules were put in a yard close by. The woman cooked some chupe of mutton and potatoes. We were tired, sunburnt, and not a little disgusted with our situation.

On a platform, built of adobe, we spread our blankets. After an unsuccessful attempt to get to sleep upon this bed of sun-dried bricks, I got up and struck a light that I might see some rude, uninvited inmates of the posta, who were making themselves too familiar with us, and found them to be chicken lice, ticks, bed bugs, and fleas. It was difficult to tell which species predominated. There was no rest for the weary that night. Richards rolled and tossed in his sleep as though his bricks were baking. I generally watch Jose for information upon points which he has had some experience with. Looking out upon the bright starlight night, I found the old man sleeping soundly in the stable yard at the feet of the mules. He had shaken his cold blankets in the cold air and rolled himself in them, where the insects would not go.

After a long time daylight came to my relief; with an application of cold water and a change of clothes, the horrible little manteazers were gotten rid of.

After breakfast I walked through the city. The streets are laid off at right angles. On the south side of the main plaza stands a large cathedral, and opposite to it the palace occupies the whole side of the block. It is remarkable for its handsome appearance, being much superior to the palace in Lima. The ladies are also beautiful. In the centre of the plaza is a fountain fed by water from a snow peak on the ridge in sight. From the appearance of the houses and stores, there certainly must be wealth here for an inland town.

Strolling along looking at the people, I came to a corner where there was an unusually neat-looking store, and in the doorway stood an intelligent-looking gentleman, who seemed a stranger to this country. He was a German. The house belonged to a Frenchman, of whom I had heard. As soon as they found out I came to make an examination of the rivers, men were called to fetch our baggage and mules, and we were at once comfortably quartered. The French gentleman had been many years in Bolivia; was married to a Cochabambina, and surrounded by a beautiful young flock, who heartily laughed at our dislike to fleas.

The stream between the mountains and the town is a tributary of the Mamore. It flows around the town, and after creeping along the ridge some distance to the southward and eastward, it passes round the mountains, and enters northward into the Madeira.

While Gibbon was in Cochabamba, the President of Bolivia arrived; Gibbon sought his approval for a treaty giving U.S. citizens the right and privilege to navigate the rivers of Bolivia by steamboat or otherwise. The President listened to his proposition, but merely uttered polite generalities.

Gibbon, Richards, and Casas remained in Cochabamba nearly five months. During this period, Gibbon visited areas around the city, including the town of Tarija, containing a population of 5,129. Tarija was

situated on one of the tributaries of the river Bermejo, which flows through the Argentine confederation into the Paraguay. My impressions, from information, are that the Bermejo is a deeper and slower-motioned stream than the Pilcomayo, and that small sail-vessels may reach the town of Oran, a short distance south of the southern boundary of Bolivia. We are not, however, as certain of this as we are that the Pilcomayo has been reported not navigable in Bolivia. There is a wide field for exploration on La Plata.

When the party left Cochabamba on May 12, 1852, it included Gibbon, Richards, Casas, four arrieros, as well as 19 loaded mules following a white mare with a bell around her neck, and a dog named Mamore. For food, besides such staples as rice, they purchased a sheep in partnership with the arrieros to eat on the trip. They were able to purchase some food en route, and shot some wild turkeys.

On the evening of May 21, 1852, they reached the banks of the San Mateo, in the rain forest province of Yuracares, at a place called San Antonio,

composed of a single shed, very neatly built and thatched. Our hamacs were slung up and baggage put under cover. We bathed in the waters of the stream, and were refreshed by our suppers. We felt grateful we had crossed all the mountains in safety, as we look up at their heads among the clouds.

The evening is like that of spring. As we found everlasting winter on top, so perpetual summer is here. The flats are covered with a growth of forest trees, besides which there are cane-brakes, bamboo, and coarse grasses, sappy bushes, and plants that prove the soil to be of the richest kind. This is the place for the axe, the plough, and the hoe. The axe has never touched one of the trees, except when the Indian wanted its coat. The face of the country is a true picture of nature. The hand of civilization has not yet touched it, though probably it contains a soil and climate that would produce as well as the richest spot known, and would astonish the planter, not only by an enormous yield, but encourage him in planting a variety yet unexampled.

The next morning, with the help of four Indians and their canoe, baggage was ferried across the river. The mules were forced to swim. After a day to recuperate from this exertion the group reached the town of Vinchuta on May 23. Here Jose Casas left the expedition, and Gibbon and Richards gave up their mules. Gibbon parted very reluctantly with his saddle mule, Rose, who had carried him "nearly two thousand miles over the worst roads known to the white man, without having fallen once during the whole route."

On Tuesday, May 25, they prepared to embark in a canoe 40 feet long and 4 feet wide. Gibbon thought the craft was excellent, but the crew was deficient:

There were ten men here, four had been left along the banks of the river on their way up with the smallpox, and one of the ten men was taken sick here; therefore our crew was reduced to nine working men. The sick boy lay on the bank with this horrible disease, shaded by a few green leaves from the hot sun in the day, and partly protected from the rain during the night, without medical attention or any relief whatever. The poor creature seemed to bear the pain with patience, but his stare was sickening as he looked up from under the bushes.

Two of the crew were engaged with small iron axes cutting . . . wood [at] the ends on the inside of the canoe across the bottom, so as to leave an inch or two space under this flooring for any water to pass clear of the baggage. . . . Raw-hides were placed on the platforms, and on them the baggage was neatly laid . . . and . . . covered with raw-hide. As the bottom of our boxes were water-tight, we were satisfied that unless we upset or filled, the baggage would go perfectly dry—an important matter in a wet climate. . . .

Vines and creepers were bowed and fastened by the ends to the sides of the after-part of the canoe, and over them were spread raw-hides, hair side under, for the length of twelve feet. This was the cabin. Our gun was slung overhead, powder-flask and shotbag to the bows. The instrument box was safely stowed inside, so that we might get at the ruled paper, and chart the river. . . . Then, too, the schoolmaster and the disappointed ex-governor were to take passage in the same canoe; it was their only chance like ours, and as there was no telling when another canoe would be here, all claim a right to go. Of course I could not object, under such circumstances, although they would be very much in our way, as we were about to explore a critical part of navigation on the upper waters of the Madeira.

So our tent was pitched on the bank; it had been our house on the barren mountain-tops, and now it was put up in the wild woods. There the climate was cold, and the tent protected and kept us warm. Here the climate is hot, and when the tent is closed and the canvass became wet, we found the heat oppressive. . . . It was evident that the tent could not accommodate so many comfortably; we were therefore, driven out. . . . we all gathered round a large fire built by the Indians, and watched their mode of passing such a night.

The next day they were moving rapidly with the stream and soon entered the Chapare River, 100 yards wide and 12 feet deep. Taking soundings as often as possible, as well as meteorological observations, and camping on shore each night, the expedition reached the Mamore River on May 30, 1852. On June 1, 1852, they entered a channel leading to the Ybare River and went up an unnamed tributary to the city of Trinidad.

In Trinidad, Gibbon found many people sick of smallpox. It was almost impossible to arouse any enthusiasm in the population for a voyage down the Mamore to the Madeira and thence to the Amazon. He was told that the Madeira contained rapids, falls, and rocks capable of breaking an Indian canoe. Moreover, the Indians were unwilling to go so far from home that it might take them as much as seven months to return.

In Trinidad, Gibbon met a Brazilian trader named Don Antonio de Barras Cordoza. He told Gibbon that with two boats, he had "been seven months on his voyage here from Borba on the Madeira River; that he had dragged his boats over the land on rollers by several of the falls on the Madeira, unloading his cargo at the foot of each fall, and, after carrying it by the fall, launched his boat and embarked again."

Despite his trouble in getting to Trinidad, Don Antonio did not succeed as he had hoped in disposing of his goods; therefore, in August of 1852, he decided to leave, inviting Gibbon and Richards to accompany him. He agreed to their using the smaller of his two vessels, the *"Igarite,"* a little smaller than "a line of battle ship's launch built upon," with "a covered cabin, and a roof over the forward part of the hold," but without masts.

On August 14, 1852, their baggage was stowed on board the *"Igarite,"* over which the flag of the United States was hoisted. Don Antonio embarked his cargo on the *"Coberta,"* from which the flag of Brazil was suspended. Five Mojos Indians were employed in addition to the Brazilian crews. Two horses and two mules affected with pests were embarked in a canoe. Four dogs and one man crowded a small batteau. Four of the Brazilians had their wives with them. Just before the boat squadron got underway, there was trouble on board the *"Coberta"*—the men whipped their wives all around. After which they followed us down stream. The noise and activity in getting off was new to us. The Indians crowded the banks, while the Brazilian negroes seemed disposed to show their seamanship to advantage. We were delighted to get off.

Ten days later, the travellers reached Exaltacíon. Here Gibbon decided to temporarily leave Don Antonio's group. He obtained 14 Indians and a canoe for a trip to Forte do Principe da Beira on the Itenez (Guaporé) River in Brazil. Don Antonio gave them permission to exchange the canoe for a boat of his at Beira.

The boat's crew were mustered by the comisario, and in the presence of the correjidor, I paid them our passage money from Exaltacion to Forte do Principe da Beira, in Brazil, with the express understanding, that in case there were no men there for Don Antonio's boat to take me to the Amazon, they would continue with me to the town of Matto Grosso. It appeared very evident that the Indians disliked leaving the chacras, preferring much more to remain and gather their harvest than go on this voyage, which is seldom made by the Bolivians. They were fine, stout built men, and reported to be the very best crew belonging to the tribe. The correjidor gave them instructions to do whatever I desired of them, and to take good care of us, as we came down the mountains from where the President lived. He was also kind enough to give me the choice of all the canoes in port; the largest and best one measured thirty-nine feet long, by four feet three inches beam, and would carry, besides the crew, one thousand pounds weight; the paddles were five feet long.

The correjidor presented a raw-hide box filled with jerked beef—

charque, as it is called—some corn bread, and farinha. The superintendent of the mill sent a jug of molasses and some of his best white sugar. We had appointed the 30th of August as our day of sailing, when the crew came down, headed by their captain, to beg we would allow them to celebrate the Fiesta de Santa Rosa, when manana—next day—they would be ready to start. As there was dancing and an unusual encouragement of the chicha manufacturers in town, I saw there was no chance of getting off, and very unwillingly gave consent.

On September 1, 1852, Gibbon, Richards, and their Indians departed from Exaltaçion. By September 7, they had arrived at Forte do Principe da Beira. Don Antonio's boat was there, and the commandant agreed to have her put in order.

A few days later, Don Antonio arrived. He immediately confirmed the commandant's decision and even volunteered the services of one of his men, named Pedro, who had ascended the Madeira, as pilot. To help Pedro, the commandant assigned five soldiers as paddlers and steersman. The boat was 23 feet long and 4 feet 7 inches wide, with a one-piece bottom. The sides consisted of wood sections "calked with oakum and well pitched outside and in. The bow and stern, or two ends, were fastened up by a solid piece of wood, also made water-proof. She was more the shape of a barrel cut in half lengthwise, than a boat."

The expedition left the fort on September 14, 1852, with the soldiers paddling and steering, Pedro piloting, and Gibbon and Richards riding amidships. Because of the size of the craft and the number of people carried, baggage and provisions were reduced to a minimum, although the soldiers carried decent uniforms, muskets and ammunition, and a supply of farinha. The commandante gave Gibbon a passport for the soldiers as well as an "account of the public property in their charge."

As they travelled, Gibbon continued to take soundings and meteorological observations. By September 20, they reached the head of the first falls on the Mamore River. After unloading part of the baggage and portaging it past the falls, the boat was pulled through. During the next few days the same procedure was followed at other falls. Each time the task of getting the boat through became increasingly difficult.

The river flowed windingly; the baggage could be sent straight across; but the boat had to be dragged, towed, lifted, and pushed through the rough rocks and rushing waters for over a mile. This was trying work. The heat of the sun was very great; the negroes slipped, and it was with great difficulty at times they could hold the boat from being carried from them by the strength of the waters as they heavily passed through the choaked passages. The men stand easing down the boat up to their necks in water. The rocks are only a few feet above the water level; they are smoothed by the wearing of the water and drift wood. It is not easy for the men to keep their feet under water.

At that point Gibbon and Richards began to suspect the loyalty of their men and fear that they might be murdered at the first opportunity.

Somewhat worn out and harassed by anxiety, they reached the confluence of the Mamore and Beni rivers, the beginning of the Madeira River on September 22. Their problems with falls and rapids had not ended, however; in a few miles they encountered an area of precipitous falls and turbulence some three-quarters of a mile long called the "Madeira." The next day, September 23, they passed the "Miserecordia" rapids without much trouble, but encountered great difficulty in getting over an area of falls some two miles long called the "Ribeirao" falls.

> After descending some distance in the middle, we found the channels so large and dangerous, that we must gain the east side of the river; the only escape for us, besides retracing our steps, was to cross a wide channel with a furious cataract above, and another close below. We hugged the foot of the upper as close as possible, and the men pulled with such force that one of the paddles broke when we reached half the way. With the remaining three, we made a hairbreadth escape; the boat could not have lived an instant had we been carried over the lower fall. The rollers formed by the swiftness of the current are five feet high; large logs are carried down so fast they plough straight through the waves, and are out of sight in an instant. The men came near upsetting the boat in a dangerous pass. They seem to be giving out through pure exhaustion. They have very little to eat; farinha adds not much to their strength, and jerked beef spoils. No fish are to be found, nor birds; a monkey would be a treat. Night overtook us half way down the falls, and we came to, on a barren rock, where there were two small sticks of wood, of which we made a fire, boiled water, and gave the men coffee. I observed a southern star, and turning for another in the north, was glad to find it had passed the meridian, as sleep was much more necessary than latitude. On the west side of the falls stood three small hills; on the east side a large white-trunked forest tree. This was the largest tree we had yet seen, though not quite equal to a North American huge oak.

For six days they "crawled on" through a series of rapids and falls. Richards suffered from a severe pain in one ear and the crew suggested "woman's milk" as a remedy. When some Indian women with babies were met, Pedro milked one for the benefit of Richard's ear. The remedy did not help and soon "his under eye-lid hung down, the corner of his mouth became drawn up on one side, while he seemed to lose control of the muscles of his face; the pain was beyond endurance."

In the late afternoon of September 30, the party reached "Teotone" falls, with a drop of 15 feet, ten at a 45-degree angle, "the most terrific of them all." Here Gibbon was the victim of what he described as a "severe bilious fever, which brought me at once on my back. The pain in my left breast was somewhat like that described by those who have suffered with the 'chagres' fever. We were all worn out, then, and haggard."

On October 1, 1852, the baggage was carried round the falls while the boat was hauled out and transported around by rollers. This was all the men could accomplish in one day. The next day, the falls of "San Antonio," five miles below, were reached and passed without great difficulty. They were the last on the Madeira before its junction with the Amazon. On October 14, 1852, after almost 500 miles of additional travel, the group reached Borba and Gibbon, who by then could barely walk, "crawled up the steep bank to the house of Captain Diogo, father of my friend Don Antonio." The baggage was unlocked and the soldiers were put in charge of the chief of police. Gibbon and Richards set about recovering from their sicknesses. By the end of the month they were well enough to travel again. In a slightly larger boat, without Pedro but with the same crew of soldiers, they embarked on the Amazon and headed for Pará, following the route taken by Herndon some months before. Their journey was made more enjoyable by "two large cakes, with a jar of preserved oranges . . . sent to the boat by the wife of our friend Don Antonio, whose little child came to thank us for bringing letters from the father and husband."

Herndon returned to the United States in July 1852; the *New York Times* announced his arrival on Monday, July 5. It had already mentioned the expedition so this account was short and expressed anticipation for Herndon's report. Other newspapers and periodicals had also mentioned the expedition, partly due to Maury's public relations work, and partly because Herndon and Gibbon had sent letters to the United States when possible, so that Congress and the public were eager to read of their adventures.[10]

Herndon began his report immediately. It was finished by January 26, 1853, and sent to Secretary of the Navy John P. Kennedy, who in turn sent it to President Millard Fillmore on February 9. Fillmore sent it to Congress that same day; it was referred to the Senate's Committee on Naval Affairs, read, and ordered to be printed. By the end of the year it appeared as 32nd Congress, 2nd sess. *Senate Ex. Doc. No. 36,* and *House Ex. Doc. No. 43.*[11]

After this decision was made, Herndon proposed to the Secretary of the Navy, who agreed; that his report be considered Part 1 of a two-part work called *Exploration of the Valley of the Amazon* and that it contain everything, including all maps, as well as the drawings made by Gibbon before separation at Tarma, except Gibbon's account of his adventures from Tarma, Peru, to the mouth of the Madeira, which would appear as Part 2 of the total account.[12]

The first printing of Part 1 of *Exploration of the Valley of the Amazon* was a popular success. Most readers and reviewers in the United States considered it an excellent work in which the "gayety and bonhommie of the author" in face of great adversity was "a very appealing facet." British periodicals objected to what was considered an unnecessary expansionist tone.

Some British periodicals held that Herndon was unrealistic in his views on what western capital and colonization could do for Brazil and that he had not contributed anything new to geographical knowledge about the region.

The *Spectator,* for example, pointed out that Herndon followed generally the route taken in 1834 by Lieutenant William Smyth of the Royal Navy. Smyth's account was published in 1836 as Lowe, Frederick & Smyth, William, *Narrative of a Journey from Lima to Pará, across the Andes and down the Amazon: Undertaken with a View of Ascertaining the Practicability of a Navigable Communication with the Atlantic by the Rivers Pachitea, Ucayali, and Amazon,* (London, 1836). The best sections of Herndon's work, in the view of the *Spectator,* were those that shed light on mid-nineteenth-century politics in Latin America.[13]

Of great interest in this regard were Herndon's observations on the contemporary economic, political, and social situation in the areas through which he and Gibbon traveled in relation to the possibility of mutually advantageous cooperation between the United States and the states drained by the Amazon and its tributaries. He printed the text of a treaty made between Brazil and Peru dated October 23, 1851, for the navigation of the Amazon and its tributaries in which, in Herndon's opinion, Brazil had taken steps to effectively implement and thereby close the Amazon to foreigners. Then he noted that Bolivia and Peru were favorably disposed to having United States citizens and companies navigate the sections of the Amazon and its tributaries within their boundaries, and concluded:

> our citizens have a legal right, by express grant and decree, to trade upon the interior waters of Peru and Bolivia, and it is presumed that Brazil will not attempt to dispute the now well-settled doctrine, that no nation holding the mouth of a river has a right to bar the way to market of a nation holding higher up, or to prevent that nation's trade and intercourse with whom she will, by a great highway common to both.

From this point on, Chapter 19 is composed mainly of a very favorable summary about the economic and social potential of the region and how it could be realized through the competition of the world's great commercial nations. Herndon wrote:

> Such is the country whose destiny and the development of whose resources is in the hands of Brazil. It seems a pity that she should do all of the work alone; she is not strong enough; she should do what we are not too proud to do, stretch out her hands to the world at large, and say, "Come and help us to subdue the wilderness; here are homes, and broad lands, and protection for all who choose to come." She should break up her steamboat monopoly, and say to the sea-faring and commercial people of the world, "We are not a maritime people; we have no skill or practice in steam navigation; come and do our carrying, while we work the lands; bring your steamers laden with your manufactures, and take from the banks of our rivers the rich productions of our vast regions." With such a policy, and taking means to preserve her nationality, for which she is now abundantly strong, I have no hesitation in saying, that I believe in fifty

years Rio Janeiro, without losing a tittle of her wealth and greatness, will be but a village to Para, and Para will be what New Orleans would long ago have been but for the activity of New York and her own fatal climate, the greatest city of the New World; Santarem will be St. Louis, and Barra, Cincinnati.

The citizens of the United States are, of all foreign people, most interested in the free navigation of the Amazon. We, as in comparison with other foreigners, would reap the lion's share of the advantages to be derived from it. We would fear no competition. Our geographical position, the winds of Heaven, and the currents of the ocean, are our potential auxiliaries. Thanks to Maury's investigations of the winds and currents, we know that a chip flung into the sea at the mouth of the Amazon will float close by Cape Hatteras. We know that ships sailing from the mouth of the Amazon, for whatever port of the world are forced to our very doors by the SE. and NE. trade winds; that New York is the half-way house between Pará and Europe.

When Herndon's report was sent to the President, Gibbon was reported to be at Pará. He reached the United States in March, and within a few weeks he began to voice objections to the arrangement which made his report Part 2 of a larger whole and restricted it to the terminals of Tarma and the mouth of the Madeira. He contended that a separate report under his name alone should be written. The Secretary of the Navy and Herndon refused to accept this argument and, although their attitude was conciliatory, Gibbon was unwillingly forced to fit his report into the original scheme. On January 25, 1854, he submitted his report to Herndon, and eventually it was sent by the President to Congress on February 10, 1854.

By this time, Herndon's account was so popular that on January 6, 1854, the House voted to print 10,000 extra copies of the complete report. On April 13, 1854, it was resolved to print 20,000 more, "two-hundred and fifty copies for distribution by Lieutenant Herndon, and two hundred fifty copies by Lieutenant Gibbon, and the remainder for the use of the members of the House."

Thus, Gibbon's report was printed in conjunction with additional copies of Herndon's report. Like Herndon's, it contained illustrations and appendices of the meteorological and other observations made.[14]

However, Gibbon's report did not gain the same popularity, although Gibbon could and did claim that he and Richards were the first white men to descend the Madeira River from its source to the Amazon and to give a comprehensive report about that region.

In the publication of their report, the work of Herndon and Gibbon in collecting, preserving, and transporting specimens of all types to the United States was not accorded due appreciation. All such material was on deposit with the Patent Office, and early in 1854, Herndon asked that a description, with illustrations, of this collection be printed in connection with the official report. The Secretary of the Navy replied on February 14, 1854, that while the "Department highly appreciates the very interesting and instructive additions proposed to be made to the report already ordered to be printed by Congress it has under its control no appropriation which can be applied to the object; nor does it suppose your wishes can be attained except through the intervention, and of the legislature."[15] Between 1857 and 1862, all material on deposit at the Patent Office, including the Herndon-Gibbon specimens, was transferred to the National Museum of the Smithsonian Institution. Although the material caught the attention of Spencer Fullerton Baird and John Cassin, among others, no additional money was forthcoming, and no catalog of the Herndon-Gibbon collection was ever printed.[16]

After the submission of Gibbon's report, Herndon was ordered to the USS *San Jacinto,* where, he complained on October 2, 1854, that the Navy Register failed to credit him with the right amount of sea service since it did not list his Amazon trip in this category. He claimed that, as sea duty, he should be accorded the same privilege for his Amazon voyage from August 4, 1851, to July 1, 1852.[17]

In 1855, after being transferred to the USS *Potomac* and promoted to Commander, he applied for a leave of absence from the Navy in order to take command of a mail steamer, the *Central America,* carrying passengers and mail between Aspinwall (Colon) and New York. The ship was caught in a storm off Cape Hatteras and sunk on September 12, 1857; Herndon and 426 others went down with the ship. Maury wrote a eulogistic report to the Secretary of the Navy concerning Herndon's heroic behavior. In his memory, the "Herndon Monument" was later placed on the grounds of the United States Naval Academy.[18] A small historical marker on Cape Hatteras marks the spot where the ship sank.

The only monument to Gibbons was Volume 2 of the report on the *Exploration of the Valley of the Amazon.* He was promoted to Lieutenant on December 5, 1851, but resigned his commission on May 15, 1857. On May 2, 1861, he was commissioned a Captain in the Artillery Corps of the Confederate States Army. He resigned this commission on August 5, 1863, for unspecified reasons. The details of his subsequent career, and even the date of his death, have not been determined.[19]

# Chapter 6

# Naval Astronomical Expedition to the Southern Hemisphere, 1846-1852

On August 16, 1849, Lieutenant J. M. Gilliss, USN, left New York as a passenger on board the merchant steamer *Empire City*, bound for Chagres on the Isthmus of Panama. His ultimate destination was Chile by way of the Isthmus route and the port of Valparaiso, a journey that he expected to take 35 days.

Gilliss had orders from the Secretary of the Navy, dated November 16, 1848, to erect an observatory and other buildings necessary to conduct a series of observations on Mars and Venus in order to obtain a new, or to confirm the old, measurement of the solar parallax. He was also enjoined to obtain such data about geological, magnetic, meteorological, and other physical phenomena in Chile considered of importance to scientific societies and individual scientists in the United States and elsewhere. This expedition, authorized by Congress and for which that body had appropriated a total of $11,400,[1] had been in the planning stages as early as the winter of 1847.

Gilliss had been allowed three assistants; Passed Midshipmen Archibald MacRae and Henry C. Hunter, and a civilian "captain's clerk," Edmond Revel Smith. They had sailed from Baltimore on July 11, 1849, in the merchant ship *Luis Philippe*, bound around the Horn for Valparaiso. Gilliss expected them to arrive before he did; actually, he arrived on October 25 and his assistants and the equipment arrived five days later.

Born in Georgetown, D.C., in 1811, Gilliss entered the Navy as a Midshipman at the age of fifteen on March 1, 1827, was appointed Passed Midshipman in 1833 and Lieutenant on February 28, 1838. In 1833 he obtained a leave of absence to enter the University of Virginia. Too much study harmed his eyes, and he had to leave the University without completing his program of study. During 1835, he studied in Paris for six months. In 1836 he was attached to the Depot of Charts and Instruments in Washington. On June 14, 1837, he was placed in command of this agency.

As commanding officer of the Depot of Charts and Instruments, he made the observations necessary to evaluate the longitude observations of the Wilkes' expedition. In a "Report on the Erection of a Depot of Charts and Instruments," (*28th Cong., 2nd sess., Senate Ex. Doc. No. 114*) Gilliss wrote: "From that time till the return of the expedition in June, 1842, I observed every culmination of the moon, and every occultation visible at Washington, which occurred between two hours before sunset and two hours after sunrise."[2] Inbetween times, he observed 1,248 stars for the reason that "the mites which I could add to the data for more correctly locating 'the landmarks of the universe' would not be entirely unworthy of collection."[3]

In 1841, Gilliss reported to the Board of Naval Commissioners that existing facilities for astronomical research were inadequate. This report, with the recommendation of the Board and the approval of the Secretary of the Navy, was given to the President in December 1841. Congress appropriated money in August 1841 for the erection of a Naval Observatory in Washington, and Gilliss was ordered by the Secretary of the Navy to develop building plans and secure the necessary instruments. Gilliss visited Europe in 1842 to purchase equipment, and after he returned in March 1843, he set up the instruments he had purchased in the building erected for this purpose. By September 1844, the observatory was ready for operation. Gilliss, however, did not get the job of Superintendent; it was given to Lieutenant Matthew Fontaine Maury, USN, who had succeeded Gilliss as head of the Depot of Charts and Instruments in 1842.[4]

After the Naval Observatory had been established, Gilliss remained in Washington preparing his astronomical observations of 1838–42 for publication. They were printed in 1846 as "Astronomical Observations made at the Naval Observatory," the first such document to be published in the United States (Washington, D.C.; Gales and Seaton, Printers, 1846). He was then assigned to the Coast Survey in Washington, reducing for Coast Survey work the moon culminations previously observed and published by him.[5]

As part of his scientific interests, Gilliss corresponded with a German mathematician, Dr. C. L. Gerling, of Marburg, Germany. In April 1847, Gerling wrote a letter to Gilliss in which he said that a new and more accurate measurement of the solar parallax or a confirmation of the existing figure could be obtained by a series of observations on Venus carried out during approximately the same period in both the northern and southern hemispheres.

Gerling's idea as it was communicated to Gilliss did not involve any specific sites for the necessary observations. In considering Gerling's views, therefore, Gilliss concluded that if a site like Washington, D.C., was selected for the observations in the northern hemisphere and the Naval Observatory was able to do the corresponding work, a spot somewhere near Santiago, Chile, appeared to be appropriate for the observations in the southern hemisphere. Gilliss decided to try to do something about implementing Gerling's proposal along these lines, which meant sending a suitable expedition to Chile "to observe the planet near its stationary terms and opposition in 1849." Late in 1847, Gilliss set about trying to get such an expedition organized.[6]

One of his first moves involved gaining support from the American Philosophical Society in Philadelphia and the American Academy of Arts and Sciences in Boston. He wrote to both groups, enclosing Gerling's letter of April 17, 1847, and offered to try to organize an expedition to Chile if this way of implementing Gerling's proposal received encouragement from astronomers.

On January 7, 1848, a special committee of the American Philosophical Society reported to a meeting of the Society:

> That the method for determining more accurately the dimensions of the solar system by similar observations of Venus in the northern and southern hemispheres, at the conjunctions of that planet, proposed by Dr. Gerling in his letter to Lieut. Gilliss of April 17, 1847, is in their opinion practicable, and therefore worthy of attention and patronage. Also, that the plan of Lieut. Gilliss for carrying the views of Dr. Gerling into effect is well conceived, and if successfully accomplished, cannot fail to confer honor on our country and its naval service.
>
> ... as our country had hitherto contributed but little, comparatively with the other principal nations, to astronomy and navigation, and as the plan of Lieut. Gilliss is so American, your committee suggest that the Society should commend it earnestly to the attention and patronage of the Navy Department; ... And they therefore propose the following resolutions:
>
> "*Resolved,*" That the proposed method of Dr. Gerling, of Marburg, for determining the solar parallax by observations of the planet Venus, when stationary and at the conjunctions, and the plan of Lieut. Gilliss for its accomplishment by means of similar observations at the Naval Observatory at Washington and in South America, would, if successfully carried out under the direction of the Navy Department, furnish valuable astronomical data, and confer honor upon our country.[7]

A few days later, the American Academy of Arts and Sciences adopted a similar resolution. Both of these expressions of opinion on the part of these groups were sent to Gilliss for transmittal to the Secretary of the Navy.[8]

On February 10, 1848, Gilliss wrote to the Secretary of the Navy, John Y. Mason, forwarding the resolutions of the American Philosophical Society as well as the American Academy of Arts and Sciences. In this letter he proposed that if he was furnished with instruments already within the department; assigned an officer as his assistant; and given authority to embark for Valparaiso, or other port in Chile, to make observations there from February 1849 until April 1851, he would pledge "that the expenses of every kind, exclusive of instruments, should not exceed five thousand dollars."

At the end of March, Secretary Mason sent this more comprehensive proposal to the Naval Committee of the House of Representatives, with a request for an appropriation of $5,000. The Secretary of the Navy included with his communication copies of the letters which had passed between Gilliss and Gerling on the subject as well as favorable opinions of the proposed action by the American Academy of Arts and Sciences and the American Philosophical Society. He also enclosed letters from Sears C. Walker and Alexander Dallas Bache of the Coast Survey, Professor Benjamin Pierce of Harvard University, and R. W. Patterson, written in answer to letters sent them by Gilliss.

The Naval Committee solicited the view of Matthew Fontaine Maury, Superintendent of the Naval Observatory. Maury did not favor the project, saying "from the best reflection that I have been enabled to give the subject, that the proposed expedition, notwithstanding it would possess interest in many points of view, would not be likely to set aside, or invalidate by its re-sults, the value of the sun's parallax, as at present received."

After a period of discussion, and despite Maury's objections, the com-mittee reported to the House of Representatives:

> It is proposed to set on foot an expedition to the most southern available position on the Western Continent, for the purpose of making observations on the planet Venus, during the period of her retrograde motion, in con-junction with similar observations to be made at the observatory in this city, with a view to the more accurate determination of the solar parallax, which involves not only the distance of our own planet from the sun, but the dimensions of the orbits of all the bodies of the solar system. These ob-servations, if successfully made in the manner proposed, will present data *solely American* for a new and independent determination of this most im-portant element. . . .
>
> . . . And the various other observations he will be able to make during the two years he proposes to devote to this work, will furnish a rich and valuable series; for which alone, entirely apart from the consideration of the main design, astronomers and scientific men in other spheres, as ap-pears from the accompanying correspondence, have applauded and warmly commended his purpose.
>
> . . . the committee are fully impressed with the importance of the object in view; and as the sum required will not exceed $5,000 they report an amendment to the naval appropriation bill to enable the Secretary to ac-complish it. . . . [9]

On August 3, 1848, President James K. Polk signed an act authorizing the Secretary of the Navy to spend $5,000, or so much thereof as might be necessary, "to cause the observations which have been recently recom-mended to him by the 'American Philosophical Society' and the 'Academy of Arts and Sciences'." [10] The report of the Naval Committee of the House of Representatives and the tenor of the debate in Congress, however, called for more to be accomplished than had been contemplated in Gilliss' proposal of February 10, 1848, and put him in a situation of being responsible for a task for the accomplishment of which $5,000 was inadequate.

Faced with this problem, Gilliss, on August 4, 1848, asked the Secretary of the Navy for orders to consult with the representatives of the two societies in Philadelphia and Boston for the development of a plan of operations as well as a determination of what additional instruments, if any, would be needed and how this possible additional expense could be handled within the $5,000 appropriated by Congress. On August 29, he received such permission, and was told by the Secretary of the Navy to hold himself "in readiness to perform the special service authorized by the act of Congress referred to by you." [11]

For about the next month, Gilliss spent his time conferring with representatives of the American Philosophical Society in Boston, and the American Academy of Arts and Sciences in Philadelphia, and scientists in Washington and elsewhere for the purpose of determining a plan of operation for the expedition acceptable to these two societies. On September 25, Gilliss submitted his report to Secretary Mason. [12]

During the following weeks, Gilliss seems to have talked with Secretary Mason about his report and to have received verbal approval to order some instruments and materials to be paid for out of the $5,000 appropriation and to seek private financing for others. One instrument needed due to the enlarged scope of the proposed expedition was a 3-foot meridian circle. With the permission of the Secretary of the Navy and the concurrence of the two societies, Gilliss ordered it from the firm of Piston and Martins, in Berlin.

At the same time, Gilliss sought the aid of the Smithsonian Institution in the acquisition of an $8\frac{1}{2}$-foot equatorial telescope. The Navy possessed a 5-foot telescope purchased for the Wilkes expedition, but the work to be done in Chile required a larger instrument. In November of 1848, the Smithsonian Institution agreed to purchase such a telescope, to be paid for in three years, but asked that Gilliss conduct a series of observations concerned with earthquake phenomena with a seismometer they would furnish. The telescope and seismometer were ordered from William G. Young of Philadelphia; the telescope was to cost $2,100.00. Because of lack of time and necessary credit arrangements, Gilliss could not obtain a lens for this instrument from Germany, and ordered one from W. Henry Fitz, an optician in New York. This was the first order for an American-made lens of considerable size. [13]

Gilliss also wrote to instrument-makers, merchants, and scientists in the United States, in England, and on the continent for advice and counsel concerning the preparations he was making for the expedition, and his requests for help did not go unanswered. One person who gave him assistance was Admiral Sir Francis Beaufort, Hydrographer of the Royal Navy; [14] another,

Lieutenant Colonel Edward Sabine of the Royal Society in England. In a letter to Sabine, Gilliss described the various observations planned and listed some of the expedition's equipment:

> The Observations I propose are:—Mars on the meridian and extra-meridian during the oppositions (apparitions) of 1849 and 1852, and Venus under analogous conditions at the inferior conjunctions and stationary terms of 1850 and 1852. These observations are to be differential, and, as the grant of Congress implies, are the paramount objects of the expedition: but as they will occupy only a portion of our time, the following series have also been decided on. 1st: With a view to improvement in the constant of lunar parallax, Burckhardt's semidiameter and the local longitude, the moon and culminating stars on the meridian:—both . . . at opposition and near conjunction. 2nd: The smaller planets on the meridian. 3rd: A catalogue of stars to the 8th magnitude inclusive with 60° of the south pole. Three hours of every suitable night will be given to this work, and the arrangement is such that we shall observe every star three times and yet sweep the whole 60° within the proposed term of residence . . .
> 4th–8th . . .
> 9th: Earthquakes. The registrations of a Seismometer.
> The astronomical equipment will consist of a meridian circle with a telescope of 52 lines aperture, ordered from Piston and Martins;—a 6 inches (French) Equatorial with clock motion which (I have just learned,) the Smithsonian Institution will purchase and lend me;—a 48 lines equatorial of Fraunhofer's make;—a clock and one or two portable instruments.

He asked for advice about where he could obtain a good seismometer and other instruments needed to test magnetism and gather meteorological data. Sabine volunteered to procure magnetic instruments and a part of the meteorological equipment.[15]

In addition to planning the observations and instruments necessary for a successful expedition, Gilliss also arranged for buildings in which to house the equipment; these were erected, then broken into sections for shipment to Chile.[16]

Even with the help of the Smithsonian and other groups and individuals, by the late fall of 1848 it became apparent that $5,000 was not enough to outfit the expedition and operate it in the manner intended by Congress when it appropriated this sum.

Many of the instruments expected from the Navy had either been loaned to other expeditions, needed repair, or were inadequate for the task at hand. In this situation, Gilliss decided that Congress should be asked for a grant to cover the cost of instruments, reserving the $5,000 for operational expenses. On December 13, 1848, Gilliss wrote to F. P. Stanton, Chairman of the Naval Committee in the House of Representatives, requesting an additional appropriation of $6,400. Just before this he had written to Professor Benjamin Pierce at Cambridge, Massachusetts, telling him that members of the American Philosophical Society and the American Academy of Arts and Sciences should use their influence to get Congress to vote an additional sum if they wanted to see the expedition operate as they had envisioned it. In particular, Pierce was told to flatter Stanton as a friend of science if the two societies wanted to get enough money to pay for the services of a naturalist with the expedition and to remember, in this connection, the words of scripture that "soft words turneth away anger." [17]

After bitter debate during which charges of duplicity were leveled against the promoters of the expedition, Congress voted $6,400 to pay for instruments, including the 8½-foot equatorial telescope. This enabled Gilliss to pay for his instruments without completely depleting his operational funds and without having to rely upon the Smithsonian Institution or other private sources. In a letter to the Secretary of the Navy, Gilliss expressed his displeasure at what he considered to be misstatements in Congress about his original position in the matter, but he accepted the result of the debate.[18]

On November 1, 1848, Smith, then a student, was officially appointed a Captain's Clerk in the United States Navy as of May 1, 1849, at $500 per year. He was told that it would be advantageous if he could spend some time in suitable study, and he therefore spent some months at Yale studying botany, zoology, mineralogy, and Spanish. He also learned to operate a daguerreotype apparatus.

No money was obtained for a naturalist, however, and materials and instruments for the collection of specimens were obtained only after the expedition arrived in Chile.[19]

During the first six months of 1848, Gilliss encouraged observatories in the United States and elsewhere to make observations in the northern hemisphere necessary for the complete success of the expedition. In June 1849, a circular prepared under the direction of Lieutenant Maury and addressed "To The Friends of Astronomical Science," explained in part:

> The series of astronomical observations, in which the co-operation of other observers is more especially invited, will consist of differential measurements during certain portions of the years 1849, '50, '51, and '52 upon Venus and Mars, with certain stars along their paths.
>
> Those astronomers who are disposed to forward the objects of the Expedition so far as to co-operate with it in conducting an auxiliary series of observations, will perceive that the results of their labors will be enhanced by using, whenever practicable, the stars of comparison which Lieut. Gilliss has selected . . . and by following generally the plan of observations proposed by him, and herein explained.
>
> Each co-laborer is requested to send annually to the Superintendent of the National Observatory at Washington his observations, with an account of the instruments with which they were made, together with such other information in relation thereto as is necessary to a full understanding and appreciation of them, and the results arising therefrom.[20]

The first task after Gilliss and his assistants reached Chile was to find a suitable location for the observatory.[21] With the help of the Chilean government, a site near Santiago was selected. The first building was erected and the equatorial telescope set up by December 6, and observations of Mars commenced on the night of December 10. During the next 52 nights (except on six times when atmospheric conditions prevented) more than 13,000 different measures were made.

The meridian circle arrived from Berlin at the end of December, but the stone piers of the building in which it was placed had to be altered in order for it to function properly. These adjustments were completed in February, after which Gilliss and MacRae, working on alternate nights, started a systematic search of the heavens, "beginning at the south pole and working toward the zenith in belts 24' wide." Their purpose was to fix the position of stars through the 10th magnitude inclusive up to 65° 50' south declination. The first series of these observations was made on 72 nights between February 4 and April 21, 1850.

On January 21, 1850, Hunter was thrown from a horse and seriously injured and had to be sent home. His replacement, Midshipman S. L. Phelps, did not arrive until September 1850. Phelps and MacRae then took charge of the meridian circle for another series of astronomical sweeps, but Gilliss also used it to conduct an examination of stars in the 1742 catalog of N. L. La Caille between "the zenith of Santiago (35° 26') and the upper zone (65° 50' Dec) which never had been re-observed." When the work of astronomical observations ended in 1852, 23,000 stars had been positioned within 24 1/5° of the south pole in addition to those in the 1742 catalog of La Caille which had been reexamined and, in some cases, corrected.

Observations on Venus were begun on October 19, 1850. The first of 992 differential measures lasted until February 10, 1851. A second series of 336 observations was made in 1852. During both periods, the meridian passage of Venus was observed 119 times. A second series of more than 2,000 observations of Mars extended from December 10, 1851 to March 15, 1852.

In addition to working with the meridian circle, rechecking La Caille's catalog, and observing Mars and Venus, the expedition also observed the stars of the southern hemisphere listed in the Nautical Almanac, and the moon, planets, and the ephemerides, which could be observed from the station for the appointed periods of Mars and Venus. Excluding the differential measures made on Mars and Venus, 42,600 observations were made in all.

On the first, eleventh, and last day of each month (except when such days fell on Sunday in which case they worked on Monday), magnetic observations were made uniformly "in a garden near Santa Lucia." Whenever assistance was offered by the Chilean students studying with Gilliss, "observations for declination were continued at intervals of 5 minutes through 24 hours." The number of magnetic observations, excluding the observations made at five-minute intervals of the day, came to above 600.

Starting in November 1849, and continuing to September 14, 1852, meteorological observations were made every three hours from 6 a.m. until midnight with hourly observations being made on the twenty-first day of each month. This duty was assigned exclusively to Smith, who was excused from taking readings at 3 a.m. to prevent possible injury to his health. In his report to the Secretary of the Navy dated November 15, 1852, Gilliss also said that:

> During the winter of the southern hemisphere in 1851 the magnetical instruments, a chronometer and Barometer[s] were conveyed to the provinces of Coquimbo, and Atacama and observations made at Valparaiso, Coquimbo, Caldera, Copiapo and the silver district of Chanarcillo, the last having been made at an elevation of 3,000 feet above the ocean.

In May of 1852, in between his observations of Mars and Venus, Gilliss journeyed as far south as Talca; "descending the river Maule to the sea and visiting the battle field of Loncomilla."

As Gilliss had noted in his reports and letters, the astronomical and other observations did not occupy all of the time of the staff. Gilliss also gave instructions in practical astronomy to three young Chileans named by the Chilean government. The entire staff collected birds, mammals, fish, reptiles, shells, fossils, minerals, botanical specimens, and artifacts of various sorts. Gilliss spent some $650 of his own money for such specimens since he believed that the government funds would not cover the expense of operation and collecting.[22]

Some of the specimens sent to the United States were displayed in the Patent Office building. They were seen by Spencer Fullerton Baird, Assistant Secretary of the Smithsonian Institution, who wrote to Gilliss that he had seen the specimens and asked him to send material to the Smithsonian. Later, Baird told Gilliss the Smithsonian would pay thirty or forty dollars for a natural history collection and would be glad to exchange items with appropriate institutions in Chile.[23]

From these letters a long and fruitful relationship was established that benefited the collections of the Smithsonian, and the scientists associated with it, as well as the data presented to the public through the printed reports of the expedition.

Gilliss also corresponded with and sent specimens to William D. Brackenridge, who kept the greenhouse containing plants brought to Washington by the Wilkes' Expedition, under the supervision of the Patent Office.

In Panama, Gilliss had sent some bulbs to Brackenridge, and soon after arriving in Chile, he sent two boxes of Araucarian pine seeds to the Secretary of the Navy with the recommendation that they be turned over to Brackenridge. More of the same seeds were sent five months later. In addition, Gilliss persuaded Luis Sada, director of the National Agricultural School of Chile, to prepare a collection of 133 indigenous plants which was sent to Brackenridge. Strawberry seeds were also sent to Washington.

In return, Brackenridge sent Gilliss a package of flower and tree seeds which he distributed among three or four friends, the main portion going to the director of the National Botanic Garden in Santiago. Brackenridge, however, in a letter to Gilliss dated June 27, 1850, which Gilliss received on January 23, 1851, said that he would try to collect another package of seeds in the fall for dispatch to Chile. This irritated Gilliss somewhat, for he hoped the seed packages would be sent at shorter intervals. He told Brackenridge: "Seed, and good seed of American trees and plants I will have and if you Washington botanists won't send them, my parcels shall go to the New Yorkers who will." [24]

By July of 1852 the expedition began preparations for returning to the United States. Gilliss had authority to dispose of his astronomical equipment to the Chilean government at original cost; since Chile wanted to continue the observatory as a national project, it was so agreed.

The buildings were purchased by Chile at an independently appraised price. A graduate of the University of Marburg, Carlos Moesta, was appointed director of the observatory and two of the students trained by Gilliss were selected as his assistants.

After the Chilean government purchased the astronomical instruments, Gilliss ordered Archibald MacRae (then serving in the rank of Lieutenant) to return to the United States by crossing the Andes and traversing the pampas area of Argentina to Buenos Aires. MacRae was to make magnetic and meteorological observations and to collect information on geography, natural resources, agricultural, and mineral products en route.

MacRae waited for the snow to melt in the mountain passes and then left Santiago on November 8, 1852. Soon afterward, he had an accident with his horse, and his instruments were damaged to the extent that their accuracy was doubtful. Some sixty days after he left Santiago, he reached Buenos Aires. Upon his return to the United States in April 1853, MacRae volunteered to retrace his route at his own expense if he was issued a new set of instruments. With the approval of the Navy, MacRae returned to Chile in August 1853 to do so. He was back in the United States in March 1854. [26]

Gilliss and Phelps left Santiago on October 1, 1852, reaching New York in November. Smith resigned and remained in Chile to visit and study the Araucarian Indians.

In Washington, Gilliss found that the series of observations on Mars and Venus that were supposed to have been made by the Naval Observatory in conjunction with the work in Chile had not been performed properly. Moreover, data submitted by other observatories was very meager. Nothing conclusive about the solar parallax could be drawn from the Chilean data alone; from this point of view the mission had not been successful. However,

Gilliss and his officers had made a great number of astronomical observations of independent value and obtained much magnetic and meteorological data, in addition to collecting valuable natural history specimens. Although the attempt to measure the solar parallax was not as successful as Gilliss might have wished, there seemed to be no great obstacle to preparing and publishing a worthwhile report on the scientific data and specimens collected.

Accordingly, Gilliss was allowed to work at the Naval Observatory and placed under the immediate command of the Chief of the Bureau of Ordnance and Hydrography, Commander Charles Morris. By December 1852, Gilliss began preparing his report. Later that month he asked Commander Morris to provide additional personnel, including a porter, and stationery and forms needed for the notation of mathematical data. On January 17, 1853, he advised the Secretary of the Navy that the specimens were being deposited at the Smithsonian Institution and that he was prepared to accept $650 if the Navy Department wanted to reimburse him for his expense and make the collection government property. A month later he advised the Secretary that it would cost an estimated $3,000 more for proper classification and exhibition of the collection.[27]

In informing the new Secretary of the Navy, John P. Kennedy, that additional money was involved, Gilliss ran into a little trouble. In 1849, he had been given $4,159.51 for the operating expenses of the expedition. Expenditures for the expedition, including the cost of the specimen collection, came to $4,262.64. As more than $5,000 had been realized from the sale of the instruments and buildings to Chile, Gilliss felt that such money should be allocated to cover the cost of illustrating, classifying, and analyzing the specimen collection, and to reimburse him for the expense of making the collection and preparing his report.[28]

On the basis of available records, it appears that Secretary Kennedy was favorably disposed to reimbursing Gilliss for the cost of the specimens, but was not inclined to spend any appreciable sum for illustrating, classifying, and analyzing the collection. Kennedy wished to use a sizeable portion of the money obtained from the sale of the expedition's instruments to purchase a private collection of minerals for the Naval Academy. On February 26, 1853, Kennedy wrote to Gilliss:

I have received your letter of the 17th ins. enclosing a copy of one from Professor Henry of the Smithsonian Institution, relative to certain specimens of Natural History sent by you to the Institute. The estimate offered by you as made by Professor Baird of the expenses which will be incurred in the examination and description of the Specimens referred to so far exceeds what was supposed would be necessary that I at once decline that arrangement.—It is absolutely necessary that of the appropriations made for astronomical observations in Chile, $3,500.00 should be reserved, and all expenses for Extra Computers, Office furniture, stationery, etc. must be curtailed to secure the amount to be reserved.[29]

In order to divert the money to pay for this collection, Kennedy needed Congressional approval, which, in the end, was not forthcoming. However, for a period of some weeks Gilliss was doubtful that he would get his $650, and even more important to his way of thinking, whether the specimen collection would be properly illustrated, classified, and analyzed for his report.

In March 1853, J. C. Dobbin became Secretary of the Navy, and on March 18, 1853, Gilliss wrote him requesting reimbursement for the specimen collection.[30] On May 9, 1853, he again wrote to Dobbin:

> Had Congress given this authority in accordance with a recommendation from the Senate Naval Committee there would not have remained to the credit of the Astronomical Expedition a sum sufficiently great to cover this expense, and the Honorable Secretary considering himself pledged to the owner of the minerals referred to, declined authorizing the expenditure for properly illustrating the collection which we had brought home.
>
> But Congress did not sanction the diversion of those funds and there is an ample amount to cover all expenses. The collection is pronounced as most interesting and more complete in some of its branches than is to be found in any Cabinet of the world. I therefore most earnestly and respectfully ask, that it may be properly made known.[31]

Dobbin's first response was to order Gilliss to loan a collection of ores brought home from Chile to Professor B. Silliman for exhibition at the Industry of all Nations Exhibition in New York City. Gilliss, with the help of Spencer Fullerton Baird, selected specimens "especially meriting exhibition."[32]

In June, Dobbin gave verbal permission to Gilliss to allow the Smithsonian to handle the illustration and classification of the specimen collection. On July 5, 1853, Gilliss advised Dobbin that he had instructed "officers of the Smithsonian Institution" to prepare proper illustrations and reports on the specimens brought from Chile, and subsequently to have them prepared for exhibition. The expenses for all these purposes were not to exceed $3,000.[33]

With this problem settled, Gilliss began the preparation of his report. He had to press continually for recognition that his work was important for the Navy and that, therefore, his assistant junior officers should not be transferred away from him. He also continued to correspond with and send helpful material to his friends in Chile for their new observatory. By July 1854, the first part of his report had been completed. He also noted that:

> should Congress be pleased to direct the printing of the Report and observations, as the latter can only be arranged for quarto pages, I would

most respectfully suggest the propriety of printing the volumes of a uniform size. To secure faithful copies of the maps and illustrations, it is particularly desirable that the Department have supervisory control over their execution, and I beg leave to suggest that such recommendations be made the Honbl. House of Representatives, where the Expedition was originated.[34]

Congress authorized printing the report, and two volumes were published in 1855. The first dealing with Gilliss's observations on Chile, supplemented with information gathered from other works, was titled *Chile: Its Geography, Climate, Earthquakes, Government, Social Conditions, Minerals and Agricultural Resources, etc.* The first part of the second volume contained MacRae's *Report of a Journey Across the Andes and Pampas of the Argentine Provinces* and for the most part described the route he traveled and the towns he visited. The second part contained scientific reports on the specimens in natural history as well as Indian antiquities brought to the United States by Gilliss.

The Smithsonian Institution had been allowed to name the scientists to work on Gilliss's specimens. Asa Gray, America's leading botanist, had been selected to handle dried plants, and was able to identify and list 103 plants from Chile and 9 from the Andes and Buenos Aires, although in 18 instances there was still a question about one aspect or another. Gray's work was printed in part II of the second volume, as well as Spencer Fullerton Baird's report on the mammals brought back from Chile.

The second volume also contained William D. Brackenridge's identification and listing of 64 varieties of living plants—flowering plants, grains, and alfalfa. He noted that there were more than 200 Araucarian pine seedlings in the greenhouse of the Patent Office and that there were 60 to 80 bulbs that had not yet been identified. Many of the plants had been distributed by the time the report was published.[35]

In 1856, the third volume was printed. The first part was subtitled *"Origin and Operations of the U.S. Naval Astronomical Expedition."* It contained a brief account of the work of the Expedition, useful for gaining knowledge of its history. The volume also contained a description of the equipment used in Chile, explanatory material and computations dealing with the determination of the solar parallax based on the observations of the Astronomical Expedition in Chile in relation to the inadequate number of observations made in the United States, and a table of observations of Mars and Venus.

A fourth volume, with the designation of volume 6, was given a publication date of 1856, but was printed actually in 1857. It carried the sub-title "Magnetical and Meteorological Observations under the Direction of Lieut. J. M. Gilliss, LL.D. Superintendent," The general title of all four volumes is *The U.S. Astronomical Expedition to the Southern Hemisphere, During the Years 1849-'50-'51-'52.*[36]

The first two volumes generally were received favorably. In the *American Journal of Science and Arts* for January 1856, Gilliss's account of Chile was recommended for the general reader, historian, geographer, and political economist as a worthwhile work. The *Canadian Journal of Industry, Science, and Art* for May 1857 especially pointed out what it called the pleasing and spirited style of the volumes. *Putnam's Monthly* for September 1856 observed that the narratives could have been cut down and the accounts of social, civil, and religious customs, with disapproving comment, might well have been omitted. The *Journal of the Franklin Institute (3rd Series., vol. 37, 1859)* also contained an article dealing with the expedition which disclosed the fact that the Naval Observatory and other observatories in the northern hemisphere had not responded to the problem as well as they should have.[37]

In 1858, the same year that the first two volumes of his report were published, Gilliss was placed on the "reserved list" by the Naval Retiring Board on the ground that he had not seen sea service for twenty years. This humiliated him, and he wrote a long letter to the Secretary of the Navy complaining that he had been ordered to perform duties of a scientific nature not involving sea service, that he had taken great pains to carry out his duties satisfactorily, and that it was an injustice to penalize him for obeying both the letter and spirit of his orders. The Secretary ordered him retained on full pay to complete his report of the Astronomical Expedition, and he so continued until Maury resigned from the Navy in 1861, when he became Superintendent of the Naval Observatory.[38]

During the period between the publication of the first part of volume III of his report, and the outbreak of the Civil War, Gilliss continued to take an interest in Chile's astronomical work and participated in scientific investigation on his own. Early in 1853, Professor Gerling of Marburg, Germany, wrote to him about the possibility of using U.S. naval vessels off the coast of Peru to observe a total eclipse of the sun on November 30 of that year. Gilliss could not encourage this idea, but he urged the Chilean observatory to send a representative with appropriate instruments to Peru. He informed Gerling that the Chilean students he had trained were not working out well as assistants at the Chilean observatory. It is interesting to note that the National Observatory of Chile did participate in observing the eclipse and that Gilliss received a detailed report on this accomplishment.[39]

In January 1854, Gilliss sent a large package of books, including copies of the 1853 report of the Patent Office on agriculture, to Andres Bello, rector of the University of Chile, with a request that Bello distribute them to individuals he designated. That year and later, he continued to send books and other materials to Chile and helped procure instruments for Chile's observatory. This arrangement was formalized somewhat in the late 1850s when Gilliss undertook to have books and related items sent to Chile as part of the annual Smithsonian Institution exchange shipment. His attitude in this endeavor is expressed in a letter to Bello dated June 3, 1854, in which he said in part: "If I succeed in inspiring greater kind sentiment between our countrymen, or in affording information on any branch of knowledge or art, I shall be amply repaid for the little trouble and expense which these shipments occasion."[40]

In 1858, Gilliss again went to South America, crossed the Peruvian desert to Olmos, and between bouts of intermittent fever observed a solar eclipse. Two years later he observed another eclipse in the Washington Territory.[41]

During the Civil War, he worked hard to equip U.S. Navy vessels with appropriate charts and instruments, incidentally stimulating the production of American instruments and lenses. He put the instruments of the Observatory in good condition, added astronomers to the staff, and began a cooperative program with other astronomical institutions for the rapid publication of data accumulated at the Observatory and elsewhere over the previous 14 years. While so engaged, on February 9, 1865, Gilliss died suddenly of apoplexy.

# Chapter 7

# Page Expedition to the Rio de la Plata and Rio Paraguay, 1853-1856

On January 19, 1853, the USS *Water Witch,* a 150-foot-long paddle wheel steamer under the command of Lieutenant Thomas J. Page, left Baltimore and headed down the Chesapeake Bay for Norfolk, Virginia. The 378-ton ship carried seven line officers, an assistant surgeon, four engineers, and 50 men, and her mission was to "explore and survey the river La Plata and its tributaries."

After time-consuming repairs and voyage preparations, the ship sailed from Norfolk on February 8, and making an uncertain 10 knots, took her way south. She finally reached Buenos Aires, at the mouth of the La Plata, on May 25, 1853. Various official and diplomatic problems having little direct bearing on exploration delayed the expedition in Buenos Aires, so it was not until early September that Page finally took his ship up the Paraná River and began the work for which his expedition had been organized.[1]

The U.S. Navy's expedition to explore the La Plata resulted from a combination of several events. One was the formation of the United States and Paraguay Navigation Company, financed by about $100,000, largely from investors in the state of Rhode Island, and chartered by the legislators of Rhode Island, with Edward Augustus Hopkins, a U.S. citizen, one of the principal organizers. Hopkins had also arranged to have himself named as vice-consul in Asunción, the capital of Paraguay. Having spent much time in the La Plata region and being well acquainted with its possibilities as well as with South American leaders, Hopkins actively sought to persuade people in the United States of the value of the area for American trade and enterprise as well as the need for more accurate and comprehensive information about it. In May 1852, his speech to the American Geographical and Statistical Society resulted in a memorial to Secretary of the Navy William A. Graham, requesting "the scientific exploration of the River Plata and its tributaries."[2]

Almost at the same time, conditions in Argentina suddenly favored such exploration. General Justo José de Urquiza, the governor of the province of Entre Rios, became the political leader of Argentina as "Provisional Director of the Argentine Confederation," and soon after assuming power, issued a decree proclaiming free navigation of Argentina's rivers.

Accordingly, when John P. Kennedy became Secretary of the Navy in July 1852, the time seemed appropriate for a surveying and exploring expedition to the La Plata and its tributaries.[3]

Kennedy decided that he would not have to ask Congress for special permission or earmarked funds, since sending a ship to Argentinian waters to engage in surveying work seemed within his power as Secretary of the Navy. The ship selected for the expedition, the *Water Witch*, had been recently completed at the Washington Navy Yard. Her paddle wheels were 19 feet in diameter, 5 feet wide, and dipped 42 inches beneath the surface. She had an extreme beam of 23 feet, draft of 9 feet, and carried a 24-pounder and two 12-pound howitzers.

Exploration appealed to Lieutenant Page, selected to command the expedition, who had served in the Navy for 25 years, during which time he had sailed in the West Indies, Mediterranean, South Atlantic, and Far East. While in command of the *Dolphin* in the Far East, he had discussed with R. B. Forbes, a Boston merchant, shipbuilder, ship owner, and former captain in the China trade, who was then in China on business, the need for a surveying expedition to be sent to the China seas for the benefit of United States whalers and commerce. When Page returned to the United States, he proposed such an expedition to the Secretary of the Navy, and the Secretary replied that the Department hoped to do it some day. However, the idea became reality sooner than expected, and the area to be covered was enlarged to include the Bering Sea and the North Pacific. This included a larger expedition than that proposed by Page, one that needed a more senior officer in command. Commander Cadwallader Ringgold was chosen for that duty. Page was offered the position of second in command but declined because he thought the North Pacific expedition had been his idea in the first place.[4]

After taking command of the *Water Witch*, Page worked to outfit the expedition and to secure the necessary officers, men, and equipment, some of which was especially selected. In particular, Lieutenant Daniel Ammen was ordered to New York to select "a Daguerrean apparatus," the camera invented by L. V. M. Daguerre in 1839.

Page obtained permission from the Department to purchase books not ordinarily found on naval vessels, such as Castelnau's *Histoire du Voyage, dans les Parties Centrales de l'Amerique du Sud*. The *Water Witch* also carried weapons, powder and shot, tools, camping equipment, and a variety of instruments and materials for preserving and collecting natural history specimens.

In outfitting, Page was helped by Lieutenant Matthew Fontaine Maury, Superintendent of the Naval Observatory, and by Assistant Secretary of the Smithsonian Institution, Spencer F. Baird. The subsequent record indicated that Page planned well, but was not able always to utilize his equipment in the most advantageous way.

In addition to the equipment carried in the *Water Witch,* Page arranged to have other material shipped ahead. This included a steam engine, two boilers, and a supply of oak and pine lumber, with which Page intended to build a small steamer in Paraguay for use in rivers too shallow for the *Water Witch.* He also sent ahead two metallic lifeboats, for use in streams where the small steamer could not go, or if it broke down.[5] Even before the *Water Witch* left Norfolk, her engineers had to repair the engine, which induced Page to hope that "... the difficulties under which the Engine previously labored will soon be removed."[6] The engine, a noncondensing type built at the Washington Navy Yard, had cylinders 37.6" in diameter and a 72" stroke, and was eight years old then, having come out of the previous *Water Witch.* Despite Page's hopes, the engine did not improve with age.

Page faced other problems. The passed midshipmen attached to the expedition submitted a petition requesting that they be given, while with the expedition, appointments as acting lieutenants with all the privileges of that rank. They claimed that the Secretary of the Navy had the power to do this since they were attached to an expedition and expeditions need not follow usual complement regulations. Page forwarded it to the Secretary with the comment, "I take pleasure in doing so and ask your favorable consideration of the request contained therein." The Secretary of the Navy replied that since the expedition "is fitted out in accordance with the ordinary powers of the Department—having no special fund, nor authority of Congress," the passed midshipmen would be "subject to all the conditions of usual and ordinary service." Petition denied.[7]

Subsequently, when opportunity presented, Page on his own initiative promoted them to the rank of acting lieutenant and acting master, and then asked for approval. Since there was a complete turnover in lieutenants during the cruise, with only one bona fide lieutenant on board at one time, Page had ample pretexts for such action. His actions were not always approved by the Department, but in much of his writing the new titles were used without explaining that they were unconfirmed "field" promotions.[8] Thus, Passed Midshipman Murdaugh is referred to variously as passed midshipman, acting master, and acting lieutenant. When quoting from Page's reports, such "acting" ranks have been used; otherwise, ranks used were those in effect before the *Water Witch* left Norfolk.

After being named to command the expedition, Page was called to Washington to consult with Secretary of the Navy Kennedy. This meeting took place on January 12, 1853, a few days before the *Water Witch* sailed from Baltimore to Norfolk. While in Norfolk, on January 29, 1853, Page received his final instructions.

The expedition was to test the navigability of the rivers of the regions, to chart their courses, indicating the channels which should be used for passage, and to report upon the environmental aspects of the area. The collection of specimens was also covered. In addition to commanding the expedition, Page was commissioned to act with the United States Consul at Rio de Janeiro and the United States chargé d'affaires at Buenos Aires in negotiating a treaty with Paraguay for the free navigation of the rivers there, and received from the Secretary of State, Edward Everett, instructions on what he had been empowered to do by President Millard Fillmore.

To defray the expenses of the expedition after the *Water Witch* left the United States, Page was authorized to act as his own purser and to draw bills on Baring Brothers, London, or, with proper notice, directly upon the Navy Department.[9]

On February 4, 1853, Lieutenant Matthew Fontaine Maury wrote to Page enclosing an incomplete draft of instructions which Maury said had not been completed or sent earlier because the Secretary of the Navy, John P. Kennedy, had written his own instructions and had sent these to Page first. Maury's instructions departed somewhat from Kennedy's in their emphasis on the collection of data relating to the possible connection of the Amazon valley with the Rio de la Plata system. That possibility had been raised by Maury in his November 1850 memorandum to the Secretary of the Navy, William Graham, advocating an exploration of the Amazon. It would appear from Page's instructions to his officers, the log of the *Water Witch*, and notebooks kept by Page's officers, that Page tried to carry out Maury's instructions and that he wrote Maury subsequently about his work. Unfortunately, some of his letters from South America to Maury seem not to have received a personal reply since Maury was in Europe at that time.

Ten days out of Norfolk, on February 18, the *Water Witch* reached St. Thomas, in the Virgin Islands, where she spent a few days to load coal and overhaul the engines.[10] Her next stop, on March 4, was at Demerara, British Guiana, where it took nine days to find and load coal. Then she went on to Maranhao, Brazil, where she arrived on March 24, to again load coal and to overhaul the engines. There had been some skepticism at home about the performance of the ship's engines and paddle wheels "amounting to a certainty of their failure," but Page felt they had proved successful.

On April 7, 1853, the *Water Witch* reached Rio de Janeiro, as the USS *Vandalia* was leaving. Commander Pope of the *Vandalia* sent a note to Page directing him "if it can be done without inconvenience" to exchange one of the *Water Witch's* chronometers for one aboard the *Vandalia*. This Page declined to do, unless he received a positive and unconditional order. Commander Pope responded with a positive and unconditional order to make the exchange. Page had no alternative but to comply, but complained bitterly of Pope's action and suggested that it was detrimental to and might impair the success of the expedition. He also advised the Bureau of Construction, Equipment, and Repair of repairs required before the *Water Witch* could make a sea cruise or return home, although, he added, "I consider her nevertheless—at this time—fully capable of performing such service as the nature of the Expedition may demand."

Finally, on May 25, 1853, the ship reached Buenos Aires, and Page was presented to Urquiza, the "Provisional Director of the Argentine Confederation," by Mr. John Pendleton, United States chargé d'affaires.

General Urquiza's favorable attitude toward the expedition, plus the fact that low water season in the Paraná River seemed to be approaching, induced Page to plan to sail for Paraguay on the last day of June, and he so advised Captain Samuel W. Downing, Senior Officer in Command of the Brazil Station, on board the *Jamestown*. Much to Page's surprise, Downing ordered him not to leave and to be prepared to tow the *Jamestown* over the harbor bar on July 2. Page protested that in view of his orders from the Secretary of the Navy, the *Water Witch* should not be subjected to such orders, but Downing remained firm and again Page obeyed. He then reported to the Secretary that he considered Downing's orders to be unfavorable and capricious, with little relevance to the public welfare. In the same report he announced that he would try to leave on July 6.

The arrival of the *Water Witch* at Buenos Aires coincided with General Urquiza's attempt to induce the city to join his government. Buenos Aires had revolted against his authority and General Urquiza was besieging it. Page and the *Water Witch* became involved in this conflict, somewhat to Page's consternation, when the *Jamestown* sailed for Rio, ostensibly to be caulked, without informing the chargé d'affaires and left the *Water Witch* the only United States man-of-war in the harbor. Page was requested to remain to assist the U.S. citizens in case fighting broke out. As matters turned out, violence was avoided and peace was brought about between the city authorities and General Urquiza's forces. However, Mr. Pendleton requested that the *Water Witch* transport General Urquiza and his suite from their headquarters on the outskirts of the city to the province of Entre Rios. Page consented to this, and on July 13, 1853, "General Urquiza, his Suit both civil and military, together with a portion of his Guard—85 in all—were received on board." They were disembarked in Entre Rios at the port of Gualequaychi, on July 18.

This service engendered good relations between the United States and General Urquiza's government that in turn helped Page's mission, but the 85 passengers devoured the financial stability of the officer's mess, and Page requested the Navy Department to grant

> . . . such remuneration . . . for the subsisting of those persons, as the Honorable Secretary of the Navy may consider proper and just. . . .
>
> As this service is of somewhat a novel character, the application may appear to the Department in the same light, but in the British Navy it is quite common and remuneration is always made.

Page's expectation of remuneration was also based on the fact that willingness to accommodate General Urquiza was a factor in inducing him to sign treaties with the United States, France, and Great Britain, for formally recognizing the free navigation of the Parana and Uruguay rivers within the boundaries of the Argentine Confederation, which had been proclaimed previously by decree. There was no remuneration; the Secretary of the Navy felt that Congress should appropriate a sum especially for this purpose, which Congress refused to do. However, the HMS *Trident* did receive extra compensation for transporting a portion of Urquiza's army from the area of Buenos Aires to Entre Rios at the same time.

On August 3, the *Water Witch* sailed for Montevideo to load coal from the barque *St. Andrews,* and to tow smaller vessels loaded with the coal to Paraguay or Corrientes.

While loading coal, Page reported to the Secretary of the Navy a dispute which had arisen between him and the enterprising Mr. Hopkins, recently appointed U.S. Vice Consul in Paraguay. Hopkins had obtained the services of a Buenos Aires steamer, manned by members of the Buenos Aires Navy, to convey his personal belongings, as well as equipment to be used by the United States and Paraguay Navigation Company, which he had organized, to operate in Paraguay. Page objected to the Buenos Aires ship flying the American flag, since Hopkins could produce no documents authorizing it, and the U.S. Consul at Montevideo held that Hopkins had no legal right to do so. It was finally agreed that the steamer could proceed to Buenos Aires under the flag of the United States where the flag would be hauled down, and the matter was placed in the hands of Mr. Pendleton.

On August 31, 1853, the *Water Witch* finally got underway for Asunción, the capital of Paraguay. En route, Page supervised the construction of a chart of the Paraná River to Asunción, and gathered material for a lengthy report on the trip:

> In ascending the river Parana up to the confluence of the Paraguay, the territory on both sides belongs to the Argentine Confederation, with the exception of a portion of the right bank—about 145 miles in extent—which pertains to the State of Buenos Ayres. The provinces bordering the river are, Entre Rios and Corrientes on the left, and Santa Fe on the right bank, the northern portion of this latter province extending into "El Gran Chaco"—the home, and almost boundless domain of various tribes of inhospitable Indians. This is an extent of country embracing not less than 200,000 square miles; and notwithstanding it has been partitioned out by imaginary limits among the different states surrounding it—the Argentine Confederation, Bolivia, Paraguay, and Brazil—the Indian yet roams that vast domain in undisturbed possession. He sallies forth at times to rob the white man, and when pursued finds refuge in the immensity of this region, which he calls his own. This extent of pampa country—similar to our prairie—is well watered by streams, whose navigability in part, has been

proved, and whose banks are well studded with timber and wood for fuel. The fertility of the soil is unsurpassed, and the grass, in luxuriance unequalled, affords rich pasture for innumerable herds of cattle, horses, sheep, etc.

On the opposite bank, in the provinces of Entre Rios and Corrientes, we find a sparse, but hospitable population, inhabiting a country rich in natural resources—save those of minerals—soil fertile, and susceptible of producing in great abundance the various grain crops, cotton, tobacco, and every variety of vegetable. From the interior of these provinces small rivers empty into the Parana, whose navigability, at certain seasons of the year, would afford the medium of easy transportation to market for all the products of the country.

The city of Parana, the seat of government, is one of the most important towns of Entre Rios, although not the most populous. In Sante Fe, the province immediately opposite, the chief towns are Sante Fe and Rosario—the latter being the principal port of entry of the confederation. The population of this place has increased, within the past three years, in a ratio truly surprising, showing the effect of confidence in the recently established popular form of government.

There are many points in which the Parana and Paraguay assimulate to our western waters. Their course is from north to south. They have their periodical rise and fall, caused not by the melting of snow and ice which influence the latter, but by the rainy and dry seasons of the tropical region of Brazil, in which they take their rise. The average rise of the Parana is 12 feet, which begins in December, reaches its maximum in February and March, and will be found at its lowest state in August and September. In the month of October there is a partial rise of six feet, called the *repunta,* which continues no longer than one month, when it subsides again to its low state.

The *Water Witch,* with a draught varying from 8 to 9 feet, ascended the river during the month of September, when it was at its lowest state, and experienced no difficulty from the want of a sufficient depth of water. Its channel is subject to changes during the season of increase. This, however, occasions no difficulty in the navigation of the river, because the vigilant pilot soon learns, from experience in river navigation, to discern, by inspection, the course of the main channel. The velocity of the current averages $2\frac{1}{2}$ miles the hour. Owing to the almost numberless islands with which this river is studded, some of them many miles in extent, its width, in parts, from mainland to mainland, is as much as 15 miles; but the width of the river proper varies from one-fourth to one mile. Its banks, at the distance of 300 miles from its mouth, towards its source, are well covered with the best quality of wood for steamers; and they maintain this character throughout. Many of the islands are sufficiently elevated to escape inundation, and offer an inexhaustibly fertile soil for cultivation, especially in rice.

On entering the Paraguay river, at the point spoken of, we have Paraguay on the left bank, and still "El Gran Chaco" on the right. This river differs from the Parana in several particulars. Its period of rising is generally the reverse; it contains but few islands; is confined between narrow limits; is more easy of navigation, because less obstructed by shoals; and the course of its channel is less variable; its width from one-eighth to three-fourths of a mile; its velocity two miles per hour; and its rise is from twelve to fifteen feet. In October it attains its maximum, and in February its minimum state. From its mouth to Asuncion, (the capital) a distance of 250 miles, there were found no less than twenty feet of water.

The *Water Witch* reached Asuncion on October 1, 1853. Page called upon the Minister of Foreign Relations with the letter of credence that had been given him by the Secretary of State. Afterwards, he was presented to the President, Señor Don Carlos Antonio López, for a cordial interview during which Page showed López his commission and discussed with him the object of the expedition.

The chargé d'affaires at Buenos Aires, in conjunction with the representatives of Great Britain, France, and Sardinia, had already concluded a treaty of commerce and navigation with Paraguay, so their talk centered around the exploration work of the *Water Witch*. Page sensed that Lopez, despite his expressed willingness to cooperate, was reluctant to have the Paraguay explored. The Argentine Confederation, Brazil, Paraguay, and Bolivia were involved in territorial disputes with one another, and free navigation of the Paraguay River might strengthen Bolivia and Brazil at Paraguay's expense.

Because of this fear, Paraguay had recently prohibited Brazilian vessels from ascending the Paraguay River through Paraguay and had prohibited navigation on an important branch of the river, the Vermejo.

Page resigned himself to using diplomacy to get permission from López to explore the rivers within Paraguay, and as a start, Page wrote to the Secretary of the Navy:

> As I have good reason to know that the President would be pleased to receive the small steamboat—I hope to construct here—after the operations of the Expedition shall have been concluded I take the liberty of suggesting to the Honorable Secretary of the Navy that it would tend much to the success of my operations if I were instructed to present her to the President after the work shall have been accomplished; and I ask permission to do so.

The small steamer, named the *Pilcomayo,* was assembled under the direction of Lieutenant Ammen and Assistant Engineer Lamdin. She was

> built of the cedar of Paraguay, sixty-five feet in length, fourteen feet beam, twenty-three inches draught, flat bottom, depth of hold three feet, deck laid in hatches, sides of deck house of half-inch cedar boards to the height of five feet, and covered with painted canvas. Upon this deck the officers and men slept. A table, four feet by two and a half, on movable legs, served on one side as a drawing-board, while on the other we took our meals. The

seats, which were boxes fourteen inches square, served as lockers for clothes. Two small high-pressure engines of six-inch cylinders, eighteen inches stroke, with two locomotive boilers, which proved worthless, and wheels of twelve feet diameter, constituted the propelling power.

Paraguay refused payment for the materials supplied to Page. On October 20, 1853, Page reported that President López had given him permission "to ascend the river Paraguay, to the extent of this country's territories; notwithstanding the President's previously settled purpose to prohibit the navigation of the river to the vessels of every nation, until the questions of boundary between Paraguay and Brazil shall have been settled."

By the end of November, the *Water Witch* had ascended the Paraguay River as far as possible, and on December 1, Page wrote from Corumba, Brazil:

> I have now arrived at the point beyond which I do not deem it advisable to proceed, at this time; inasmuch as the river is falling fast; and I have already passed over shoal parts of it,—having only one foot more water than the vessel draws. My ascending the river, beyond this point, is therefore arrested not by the authorities of Brazil, but by the shoaliness of the water: inasmuch as I am informed by the Commander of this post, that my arrival in the Exploration of this River, is looked for in Cuyaba by the President of Matto Grosso—a province of Brazil. This I hope to accomplish at some future time in the small steamer.
>
> The *Water Witch* has ascended the River Paraguay, about seven hundred miles above Asuncion, about two thousand from the Ocean, and about six hundred, beyond the point, above which no other vessel, of any Nation, has ever gone. In no part of the River have I found less than 10 feet of water. . . .

Subsequently, Page learned that Brazil did not want him to travel further than Corumba, and if he had indicated a desire to do so he would have been stopped.

The next day, Page started the return trip to Asunción, where he arrived on December 23, 1853. There he found President López in ill humor because the Expedition had gone beyond what he considered to be the boundaries of Paraguay, but hoped to be able to quiet the President's displeasure. In the meantime he stated that he would

> send the *Water Witch* to Montevideo in a few days, for provisions for the crew and to have certain repairs made to the engines of pressing importance, which cannot be done here. In the meantime, I shall proceed with my work in the small steamer, she being so far finished, as to induce me to believe we will be ready to work in ten days or two weeks.

While the small steamer neared completion, the expedition prepared specimens for delivery to Washington. On January 26, 1854, Page wrote that he had

> ordered Lieutenant Donaldson to proceed to the United States in charge of Specimens in Natural History—and to report himself in person to the Honorable the Secretary of the Navy; and, at the same time, to deliver over to the Navy Department the Specimens under his charge.
>
> The animals are the Tapir, the Capinda or Capabara, the Quaty [Coati], and the Micuna [Kinkaju]—and a young deer. The birds are four Motus [Mitū], and one Taha [Jaja]. . . .
>
> . . . The Botanical Specimens, and those of fish, reptiles, etc. which are preserved in alcohol are not so numerous as I would have desired; but it is important that I should send them home for better preservation. . . .
>
> I send a paper containing the letters of reference, with the positions. On each specimen (regardless of the kingdom to which it may belong) is attached a letter of reference; and on examining this register of the letters— the corresponding letter therein found will indicate the point at which the specimen was collected. This Register of Letters should be sent to whomsoever the Department may entrust the specimens. In the boxes of preserved birds, skins and Botanical Specimens, there will be found a descriptive list of each specimen. The animals and birds alive are from Paraguay.

While Page was trying to appease President López, he also had to handle a quarrel between Lieutenant Ammen and Assistant Engineer Lamdin. Ammen was in charge of constructing the small steamer, while Lamdin was supposed to install its engine.

Unfortunately, the engine would not operate successfully. In trying to find the solution to this problem, both Ammen and Lamdin grew testy toward each other and finally, after work was completed in January, 1854, each complained in writing to Page that the other had interfered in his assigned duties. Ammen even went to the extent of arranging a hearing before Vice Consul Hopkins, at which Page was not present, for the purpose of officially recording his side of the case as well as the views of Lamdin. Page was able to contain this quarrel to the degree that the work of the *Water Witch* did not suffer and, at Lieutenant Ammen's request, he sent copies of the written complaints and record to the Department without commenting on the merits of the case. Subsequently, Ammen requested to be detached from the expedition, and his request was approved by Page and the Navy Department.

All of Page's time was not spent placating President López or patching up quarrels among his officers. Between February 6 and March 10, he and some of his officers rode to Encarnación and back, a distance of about 600 miles, when he reported:

> Before leaving the waters of the Paraguay river, a very thorough exploration of the country of Paraguay was made. This was performed principally by the aid of Lieutenants Powell and Henry, who by means of the

sextant, pocket chronometer and artificial horizon, determined the position in latitude and longitude of many important points. By this work, we are enabled to contribute to geographical science a degree of accuracy in position which this country does not enjoy at the present time. The agricultural districts, as well as those of the natural products, the "yerba," etc. were explored, and the mode of gathering and curing the "tea of Paraguay" accurately observed and noted by Lieut. Powell. The interesting establishments of the Jesuits, under whose benignant rule the "Guarany Indians were redeemed from a state of barbarism to civilization and Christianity," were visited, and their geographical positions determined. These establishments still retain in remarkable preservation evidences of the wonderful zeal, perseverance, skill and ability of their founders, in the structure, carving and painting of their churches. When it is remembered what the condition of the country was at the period of the erection of these buildings, with all that pertained to them; that it was a wilderness; that its inhabitants were savages; that out of this wilderness, and by these savages, these truly magnificent edifices were erected, and at such a distance from any civilized nation, one is lost in wonder and admiration at the will, the nerve, the zeal to attempt, and the intellect and skill to achieve such master works.

Page felt that the country's potential was not being fully developed to raise the standard of living for its inhabitants, and that "so long as their absolute wants can be supplied by the natural products of the soil, combined with the smallest possible degree of labor, enterprise cannot be expected of them."

Meanwhile, Passed Midshipman Murdaugh took the *Pilcomayo* up the Paraguay for about 60 miles to examine its right bank in a futile search for the mouth of a river reported by some natives. He did, however, ascend a small stream which entered the Paraguay about 12 miles from Asunción. He traveled only about 25 miles before returning to Asunción. It was Page's opinion that "this little river is another mouth . . . of the river Pilcomayo . . . whose importance will be more strikingly exemplified should I succeed in establishing its navigability. . . . The Pilcomayo extends into Bolivia and would give an exit for (her) produce."

The *Water Witch* was detained in Montevideo for wheel repair while Page, Henry, and Powell explored Paraguay on land and Murdaugh sailed the *Pilcomayo* on the rivers. When the *Water Witch* arrived in Asunción, Page found that further extensive repairs had to be made, with such materials as they had on board. How effective these repairs would be was questionable, for Page noted: "In justice to myself, I must nevertheless assure the Department, that my movements have been much embarrassed by the constant accidents which have occurred to the wheels of the *Water Witch* and the loss of time consumed in their repair."

On May 22, 1845, while the *Water Witch* was being repaired, Page left with the *Pilcomayo* and a crew of 23 officers and men, to explore the Bermejo River. In 32 days, steaming against the three to four knot current, they covered only 130 miles. Page was very disappointed at the failure of the *Pilcomayo* to go faster, and returned to Asunción to modify her.

> This river has *never been ascended* [italicized by Page] by any species of boat; its navigability is presumed from the vague accounts given of it, by two persons, who descended it, one in 1790, the other in 1836. All that has been written relative to the Vermejo and all that one will hear said are simply calculated to mislead. Trusting to the information I had gained from every source, I attempted its navigation, without sufficient means. The boat, in her draught and construction was given in charge to Lieutenant Ammen; to whom, in a previous communication to the Department I had given all the credit. He constructed her, no doubt, in his judgment after the best model: but it proved the very worst, for the violent current of the Vermejo. I confidently hope that the changes which will be made in her now, will enable me to succeed in the next attempt.

During Page's absence exploring the Bermejo, Lieutenant Powell was instructed by Page to visit a part of Paraguay called the "Yerbales" where the production of yerba was especially important and to note the cultivation and general resources of that region.

While the small steamer was being modified, Page sent Passed Midshipman G.P. Welsh to Washington with five boxes of specimens—birds, botanical items, seeds and medicinal plants, reptiles, and geological items. [11] The botanical specimens were also named in the "Guarani" language—"the language of the aboriginal tribe of Indians of Paraguay." In an accompanying letter Page wrote that he was sending

> ... some of the seed of the Yerba Mate, (the tea of Paraguay) but I have some doubt of their vegetating; because it is said in Paraguay, that the seed will not vegetate, unless they be planted within a very short time—some say ten days—after they have been gathered from the tree. I shall take measures to procure seed, at the next season, directly from the tree; and protecting them from the atmosphere, in the best manner forward them to the Navy Department, by the earliest opportunity; or to the Commissioner of Patents; he having requested me to do so. . . .
>
> There are eighteen varieties of Beans and Peas. . . . There are some specimens of earth—showing the soil in different localities; and the character of the different state of the banks of the river Vermejo—up to the extent, I have as yet gone. A close analysis of these might possibly develop some interesting truths. Lieutenant Maury having taken great interest in the analyzing of earths; it is possible that they could not fall into better hands.

Page next visited the country around the town of Corrientes, where he reported on August 13, 1854, that in a southerly direction

> a vast extent of this Province is represented as marsh and swamp. It is pe-

culiarly so in the vicinity of this town. The Estancias produce nothing for sale but oranges. The soil is not cultivated because laboring men are not to be had: the population is spare, but still there are some who could if they would labor. Much of this absence of cultivation is owning to the natural apathy and want of energy of the landholders themselves: and until the introduction of a foreign, laboring population, the resources of the country must remain dormant.

At Corrientes, Page learned of the outbreak in Asuncion of a dispute between President López and E. A. Hopkins, the Vice-Consul of the United States, concerning the work and property of the United States and Paraguay Navigation Company. Page's comment on this quarrel at this stage was that there was error on both sides; that he did not feel he should become involved and jeopardize the success of the expedition, but he stood ready, if need be, to protect the lives and property of U.S. citizens.

By the middle of September, Page was back in Asunción. The quarrel between the Paraguayan Government and Hopkins had not abated, but in terms of good news Page found a letter from the United States Consul at Rio de Janeiro informing him that the Brazilian government had given permission for the *Water Witch* to ascend the Paraguay River as far as she could. In addition to modifying the *Pilcomayo,* Page now faced the problem of what to do in case he became involved in the dispute between Hopkins and López, and Paraguay prohibited him from sailing in its territory.

On September 25, he asked the Secretary of the Navy for advice in a letter which reached that official on January 10, 1855; a week later he recommended that violence not be used. He suggested that if Page could not accomplish his mission peacefully, he should sell the small steamer and return to the United States with the *Water Witch,* and added that Page was so "remote from the Department that I am compelled to rely largely on your prudence and sound discretion which this far I have had no reason to distrust." There is no record as to when Page received this letter.

In the midst of these worries, Page and his officers completed the hydrographic chart and report of the Paraná River up to the confluence of the Paraguay, and sent it to Washington on September 28, 1854. The next day Page reported that Lieutenant James H. Moore was bringing home a small box containing gum (resin) of the "Palo Santo" for the President of the United States. It was "a present from Señor Antonio Tachena, an old gentleman of Consepcion (sic)." The term "Palo Santo," or holy stick, refers to the Guayacan tree found in Argentina. It produces an aromatic gum, or resin, that was used either alone or in a mixture with the sawdust of Guayacan bark as a medicine for syphilis, skin disease, and rheumatism, and as a perfume.[12]

Page also informed the Secretary of the Navy that the quarrel between the Paraguayan Government and Hopkins had deteriorated to the extent that he felt it his duty to receive Hopkins, the other citizens of the United States associated with him, and their possessions aboard the *Water Witch* in order to give them safe passage out of the country.

On September 29, 1854, these people boarded the *Water Witch* with their personal belongings and the ship sailed for Corrientes in the Argentine Confederation. Page reported his feelings in the matter:

> The tyrannical course of this government, can scarcely be imagined, by those who are not familiar with its acts. I cannot but indulge the hope and express the wish to the Honorable the Secretary that our Government may take some steps to assure this government that its acts of oppression and tyranny will not be submitted to when exercised on American Citizens.
>
> My course has been dictated by the most anxious desire to maintain good relations; and such was the case until the conduct of this government resolved itself into *persecution* of those Americans who are in the country. Annoyances and the ill will of the people have begun to manifest themselves even towards the Officers of the *Water Witch;* who have most studiously avoided connecting themselves, in any way, with the difficulties of Mr. Hopkins; and these are sure indications of the feelings of the government.
>
> I shall move my work to Corrientes—complete the repairs of the little steamer and go on with the work, in obedience to my instructions, in those waters over which Paraguay has no control. The Parana above Corrientes is a very important river, of which there seems to be nothing known, notwithstanding it is wide and extensive. The Vermejo, in my opinion is open to navigation or exploration under the permit of the President of the Argentine Confederation. . . . I desire nevertheless the views of the Department before I attempt it: assuring the Honorable the Secretary that if he sanctioned my attempting the navigation I will do so, the will of Paraguay to the contrary notwithstanding. . . . The waters of the Uruguay and Salado rivers are streams of deep interest to commerce and geographical knowledge.
>
> I should be most happy to carry out any instructions of the Honorable the Secretary in relation to demanding indemnification for the losses the American Company has sustained should he not think it a matter of sufficient importance to instruct the Commodore about: To make a demand with the *Water Witch* alone, would be fruitless. The *Water Witch* could tow up the Brig, and they two would be sufficient. We could take possession of what is called their Navy—and thus induce suitable terms.

The *Water Witch* reached Corrientes on October 2. The next day Page forwarded a complaint from her engineers, addressed to the Secretary of the Navy, which he said represented a combination "against the order and discipline of the service," exceeding "anything of the kind I have ever witnessed." The paper, complaining of being assigned to duty not considered legitimate, was signed by R. C. Potts, Senior Engineer; Wm. J. Lamdin, 2nd Assistant Engineer; T. B. C. Stump, 3rd Assistant Engineer; P. Henry Taylor, 3rd Assistant Engineer.

> We, the undersigned, Engineers of the U.S. Navy, now attached to this vessel, respectfully represent: that for many months past we have been performing, at one and the same time, our legitimate duties together with those of a deck officer, in direct violation of article first of the regulation of 26 Feb., 1845, respecting the Engineer's Corps of the Navy, whilst the officers of the vessel to whom these latter duties properly belong have been residing on shore:—and that we have protested to the Commander of the vessel against this imposition, when instead of relief we received a restoration of the order.
>
> Feeling that this state of affairs is becoming intolerable, and seeing no prospect of its termination, we appeal to you for protection.
>
> At the present time two of the Engineers being engaged in reconstructing the steamer *"Pilcomayo,"* but two remain on board this vessel to be loaded with the discharge of its multifarious duties.

Page's reaction to this document and its accompanying explanatory statements, was one of condemnation of its spirit and denial of its allegations. He pointed out that when the *Water Witch* returned to Asunción from Montevideo the engineers had volunteered to stand watch since only one deck officer, Lieutenant Moore, was on board, and he was in command of the vessel. Page asserted that he had received no protests from the engineers on this situation. Furthermore, he noted that at times most of the deck officers were ashore simply because they were working on the hydrographic reports and charts. He asserted that the only order he gave to the engineers that might be connected with their protest about "multifarious duties" was to order them to record thermometer and barometer readings at certain times during the day. In conclusion Page quoted an extract from his instructions that said:

> No special directions are thought necessary in regard to the mode of conducting the researches and experiments which you are enjoined to prosecute, nor is it intended to limit the officers, who accompany you each to a particular sphere, all are expected to cooperate harmoniously in all the duties of the Expedition.

The fact of the matter was that the engineers seemingly had performed "deck officer" duties simply because they had to "volunteer" for the work; their services in this connection seem to have been taken for granted subsequently to the extent that their protest came as a surprise and shock to Page. Accordingly, Page reacted in a hurt fashion, but he recovered his equilibrium fairly quickly and this incident did not seriously hamper the expedition. It is noteworthy that the engineers subsequently performed "deck officer" duties, although at least three of them—Lamdin, Potts, and

Stump—asked to be transferred. The Secretary of the Navy did not grant their requests and seemingly took no action on their complaint.[13]

On October 17, 1854, Page notified the Department that he had received "at the hands of Mr. C. R. Buckalew" the treaty between the United States and Paraguay with a Commission and power from the President—accompanied by instructions from the Secretary of State—to "effect the Exchange of Ratification with such person, as may be duly authorized by the latter government." This proved impossible to accomplish. After the *Water Witch* had transported Hopkins and his associates to Montevideo, President Lopez issued a decree closing the Paraguay River to foreign warships. Page could not reach Asunción in the *Water Witch*. He sent Passed Midshipman Murdaugh to Asunción with a letter informing the Paraguay government that the United States desired to exchange ratifications. The letter was in English, and the Paraguayan government refused to receive it, as it had refused to receive letters in English at the time of the Hopkins crisis. Page refused to have his epistle translated into Spanish, and in a letter to the Department dated November 5, 1854, which arrived in Washington on February 7, 1855, he suggested that

> the Honorable the Secretary of State address a letter to the Ministry of Foreign Relations of Paraguay informing him that I have been commissioned by the President of the United States to exchange the ratification of the treaty; and give me orders to proceed to Asuncion in the *Water Witch* and deliver that letter . . . I neither design or desire to make war upon Paraguay; but that the United States shall assume such a position—as will hence-forward, secure to her, the respect not only of Paraguay, but of the whole of these South American States, I must anxiously desire and sanguinely hope.

There is no evidence that the Secretary of State ever acted as Page suggested, and there is no record of any corresponding orders being issued to him.

In the midst of this impasse, on November 11, 1854, and again on January 1, 1855, Page sent home reports, charts, and specimens relative to the expedition's work. By that time, he was anxious to start exploring the Salado River. Efforts to increase the power and speed of the *Pilcomayo* had failed. Page wrote on January 3, 1855, that he intended

> to explore the river "Salado" which empties into the Parana through the Province of Santa Fe. I shall make this attempt, because it is the belief, although there seems to be but little knowledge on the subject, that there is not much current in the Salado River. Should the boat prove here, inefficient, it is my intention to see what can be done in the two iron life boats [the two metallic life boats shipped to Page by private merchant vessel from Norfolk]. The disappointment I have experienced in the failure of this boat is greater than I can express.

In the meantime, I shall send the *Water Witch,* under charge of Lieutenant Jeffers to explore the Parana above this port so far as she can safely go: This portion of the Parana River is the common boundary between the Argentine Confederation and Paraguay.

Page left Corrientes on January 31, 1855, on the *Pilcomayo* with the two boats, three officers, including 2nd Assistant Engineer Stump, and 16 men. The next day, Lieutenant Jeffers took the *Water Witch* from Corrientes and got about three to four miles into the Parana River before the ship grounded near the Argentine shore. Jeffers refloated the ship and tried to follow a channel near the Paraguay shore. When the fort of Itapura fired on her, the *Water Witch* returned the fire. Helmsman Samuel Chaney, quartermaster, was killed, several men were wounded slightly, and the ship was "hulled" 10 times, but not dangerously. Once past the fort, the pilot warned Jeffers that they were in danger of grounding again, so Jeffers stopped the ship and backed past the fort. Again the ship was fired upon, but it did not return the fire, and returned to Corrientes. In view of the troubles with the engineers, it is interesting to note that in his report, Jeffers wrote:

> In conclusion I must fulfill an agreeable duty in bearing witness to the zealous manner in which the Engineers of this ship supported me on this occasion. Mr. Potts was in charge of the deck: Mr. Lamdin of a division of guns, and the latter assisted personally in loading after some of his men had deserted from their quarters. The Engine was worked by Mr. Taylor with as much promptitude as on ordinary occasions.

When Page heard of this incident, he returned immediately to Corrientes, and on February 5, 1855, advised the Secretary of the Navy that he was taking the ship to Montevideo

> with the hope of obtaining from the Commodore or Senior Officer, two or three guns of suitable calibre, and an addition of a few men. With this force, I shall feel confident of the ability of the *Water Witch* to avenge the outrage which has been perpetrated on the Flag of the United States.
>
> I indulge the sanguine hope that the Commodore will act in this matter with all the promptness which the exigencies of the case require; and that such a course will receive the approval of the Department.

En route, Page diverted to Buenos Aires, where he reported on February 11 that no ships of the Brazil Squadron were in the La Plata area. He requested permission to try to gain possession of a small steamer, 90 feet in length and with a draft of 26 inches, available from the United States and Paraguay Navigation Company, to replace the *Pilcomayo*.

For several weeks Page journeyed between Buenos Aires and Montevideo, trying to convince the commander of the Brazil Squadron and the Department to take action against Paraguay. The commander of the Brazil Squadron, Commodore William D. Salter, refused to give Page any additional guns and declined to engage his ships in a fight with Paraguay. Salter's decision was not reversed by the Navy Department.

While hoping for this opportunity for a contest with Paraguayan guns, Page continued the exploration work as best he could. From Montevideo he sent to Washington on April 8, 1855, a cedar box containing geological specimens, some reptiles, butterflies, and insects.

He reported that the Bureau of Construction, Equipment, and Repairs requested the wood and that the specimens were identified by appropriate indigenous names.

After repairing the engine and wheels of the *Water Witch,* Page sailed her to Buenos Aires to check chronometers and then up the Uruguay River to an area of rapids before returning to Montevideo and Buenos Aires.

> Since my last communication of April 16th, I have made an exploration of the Rio Uruguay as far as the "Salto Grande." This is the head of navigation of the river, at all seasons of the year, save the months September and October; when in consequence of the rains in Brazil, its tributaries become very much swollen and the water rises in the Uruguay at this point (Salto Grande) to the height of 32 feet: thus making the navigation over and above the fall or rapid, practicable, for the distance of three or four hundred miles, with no other obstacle save a rapid. . . . At the season of high water, I hope to be able to push the exploration of this river to its extent of navigation, at that season.

On June 18, 1855, the crosshead of the engine broke. Repairs would necessitate time, so Page arranged a two-month charter of the small steamer previously mentioned in order to explore the Salado River, and paid her owners for the charter by giving them the *Pilcomayo.*

On July 13, 1855, Page took the steamer into the Salado River with Passed Midshipman William H. Murdaugh, Lieutenant William L. Powell, Assistant Surgeon Robert Carter, Assistant Engineer T. B. C. Stump, and a crew of 32 men. They had ascended the river some 360 miles by July 26 when the depth of the water decreased to about two and half feet. At this point, the steamer returned to Santa Fe while Page, with Murdaugh and a sailor named only as Cornelius, went by land to "the upper waters of the Salado." In five days they rode 600 miles to the town of Santiago, where the Governor helped them obtain a small boat. This they hauled, by ox-drawn wagon, about 40 miles to the Salado. Starting on September 13, 1855, they floated down that river for some distance, then walked to a point a few miles above the area reached by the steamer. On October 22, 1855, Page wrote: "I have now the very pleasing satisfaction to inform the Department, that from this exploration of this river, the navigability for the distance of 800 miles, is established. Strange though it may seem, it is nevertheless a fact, that the Salado has flowed on through a country settled for centuries past by the Spanish race and never, until now, has it been known to be navigable."

Two months later he reported further:

In the farther examination of the river Salado, its navigability has been found to extend up to a place called San Miguel in the Province of Salta, a distance by land of about 130 miles above the point at which we commenced the descent of the river on the 13th of September; of which the Department has been informed. This gives to the Provinces Salta, Jujuy, and Catamaraca the benefit of a still nearer approach to navigable waters.

The enthusiasm of the authorities and people of the different Provinces through which we passed (Santa Fe, Santiago, Tucaman and Salta) on the discovery of the navigability of the Salado, is greater than I can describe.

The determination that the Salado was navigable for 800 miles from its mouth to Santiago and about 130 miles beyond was not an easy feat for Page and his men.

After his return to the United States, Page reported to the Secretary of the Navy:

While descending the Salado we encountered hostile Indians at two different points. They were attacked by our escort, and, considering the odds so much in our favor, they defended themselves most gallantly, and at times, after their usual mode of fighting, would make a dash with considerable effect. They were mounted and armed with the lance. Their expertness with this weapon, and their management of the horse, are scarcely equalled by the "Gaucho," their civilized enemy. There were recovered from them two or three hundred head of cattle and as many horses, which they had stolen but a few days previously from the "estancias" and poor people living along the Salado.

The privation and exposure we experienced throughout this exploration, not only of the Salado, but of the country, somewhat in the interior of the provinces, were calculated to try our physical endurance, and test our zeal and energies even in a cause of such deep interest and importance. We nevertheless found ourselves relieved from the fatigues of the day, after a night spent upon the soft grass of the pampa, with the canopy of heaven our vaulted roof. The rain would descend with tropical force, but our India-rubber ponchos seldom failed to secure us refreshing sleep. The dawn would find us, though wet, prepared for the toils of the day. The life was one of health and vigor. Never were our physical energies more nerved to meet and overcome toil and privation. Weeks and months thus passed away; and had the time been doubled, and the exposure greater, so happy a termination of our labors would have amply compensated all such endurance.

While Page, Murdaugh, and the rest of their group explored the Salado, Lieutenant Jeffers and the remaining officers and crew surveyed the confluence of the Paraná and Uruguay rivers. They discovered a new channel into La Plata, two feet deeper than the old channel and more easily entered. Moreover, it had a political significance, for the Island Martin Garcia, now in the possession of Buenos Aires commands the old channel most effectually; through the new channel a vessel may pass at the distance of one and a quarter miles from the Island. The new channel passes between Martin Garcia and the Banda Oriental—whereas the old channel passes between Martin Garcia and Buenos Aires; —and the Island being claimed and now in the possession of Buenos Aires, that asserts the right—though who has not attempted the exercise of that right by force—to control the navigation of that channel.

By the end of January 1856, the work of the expedition was nearly completed. The rivers above Asunción were closed to the Americans by López's action; they could not ascend the Pilcomayo because of revolutionary turmoil in Bolivia. The enlistments of many of the men had expired. On his return from the Salado, Page received orders to return to the United States. On February 3, 1856, the *Water Witch* left Rio de Janeiro; on May 7, 1856, she reached the Washington Navy Yard. The next day Page sent the Navy Department his report on the ship along with the senior engineer's report on the engine, boilers, and paddle wheels.

In the next few weeks, the crew was discharged and Page put his financial accounts in order. After paying off the officers and crew, he still had $2,608.57, which was deposited in the Navy Yard Treasury. The total cost of the expedition came to an estimated $122,000.[14]

The instruments obtained for the expedition were sent to the Naval Observatory, and the rest of the material was stored at the Navy Yard. A Brazilian tiger and nutria were, at the direction of the Secretary of State, placed in a rather odd substitute for a zoo, the Government Asylum for the Insane.[15]

While Page was in South America, the *New York Herald* on February 1, 1855, printed a letter criticizing him for paying more attention to President López of Paraguay than to Vice Consul Hopkins. The letter, from Lieutenant Charles G. Hunter, who had commanded the United States Brig *Bainbridge* on the Brazil station a few months previously, complained that Page was not treating Hopkins with due respect, even to the extent of ordering the officers sent home not to carry Hopkins' despatches. Not evident in the letter was the fact that Hunter had, three days earlier, been dismissed from the Navy by direct presidential order for leaving his station and sailing the *Bainbridge* back to the United States without orders.[16]

Hunter's accusations were denied by Page in a letter to the Secretary of the Navy dated March 21, 1855, which reached the Department about the middle of May 1855. Moreover, the press printed favorable accounts of his exploration work as well as of his response to the expulsion of Hopkins from Paraguay and the shelling of the *Water Witch,* which more than counterbalanced Hunter's criticism.

When Congress convened in December 1856, the atmosphere seemed favorable for the Secretary of the Navy to request an appropriation for printing the expedition's charts. Congress was also asked to appropriate enough money for an exploration of the Paraguay beyond the point Page had reached in the first expedition and for an investigation of other rivers like the Bermejo and the Pilcomayo which had not been studied adequately during the previous voyage. The 1857–58 appropriations bill for the Navy contained $6,700 for publishing the charts of both the La Plata and the Bering Seas expeditions plus $25,000 to continue the exploration of the La Plata and its tributaries.[17]

Even before Congress passed this bill, Page was busy preparing charts for the printers. By the end of 1857, four charts were completed. The naval appropriations bill for 1858–59 contained $5,000 for "completing the publication of the charts of the late expedition for the exploration of the river La Plata and its tributaries."[18] Eventually, at least 19 different sectional charts plus a general reference chart of the surveys made between 1853 and 1854 were produced.

While engaged in chart preparation for publication, Page also began to organize the second La Plata expedition, which he was to command. In May 1857, the Secretary of the Navy wrote to him that in organizing and implementing this second expedition, as its commander, he was to follow the orders of 1853 pertaining to the first La Plata expedition. It appears that no other formal orders appointing him as commander of the second expedition were issued previous to this letter.[19]

Under authority of this letter and as part of his organizing effort, he corresponded with Spencer Fullerton Baird of the Smithsonian about the specimens he should collect as well as the type of men and equipment.[20]

After Page returned from his first expedition to the La Plata region, he again consulted R. B. Forbes of Boston about his hopes for a second trip, just as he had done in the Far East years earlier. When Congress voted only $25,000 for another expedition, Forbes volunteered to build a suitable steamer and charter it to the Navy according to certain terms. He did this in order to help Page get as much for the money as he could, since a comparison of costs indicated that if a government ship was used, $25,000 would probably not cover the cost of a second expedition.

Consequently the Secretary of the Navy entered into an arrangement with Forbes for the construction, at Forbes' expense, of a steamer 98 feet in length, 16 feet in beam, drawing 4 feet, which was to be delivered to a convenient point on the La Plata and chartered from there by the Government at $300 per month exclusive of crew, fuel, provisions, and armament necessary for exploration work.

This steamer, named the *Argentina,* and described as a "three masted merchant ship," was sailed to Montevideo under command of Captain J. B. Breck, arriving there in March 1858 after a passage of about 70 days.[21] By April 19 the ship was at Buenos Aires. The officers attached to the expedition were Lieutenants Jonathan Carter, Ralph Chandler, Oscar Johnston, and Charles McGary, Assistant Surgeon Dunigan, and 3rd Assistant Engineer Lyman. They sailed in February, 1858, in merchant vessels, and arrived in Buenos Aires on March 29.

In a letter to Secretary of the Navy Isaac Toucey, dated April 22, 1858, Lieutenant McGary reported that they planned to take the *Argentina* from Buenos Aires to Rosario in the Argentine Confederation to wait for Page and to begin surveying and hydrographic work.[22] This was confirmed in the Secretary's Annual Report, dated December 6, 1858. Page did not leave the United States with his officers because he was still preparing the La Plata charts for publication.

In December of 1857, the Secretary of the Navy informed Page that the commandant of the Washington Navy Yard had been ordered to enlist 16 landsmen for the second expedition. There is no record of whether they were actually enlisted, or if and how they reached the La Plata estuary. A muster roll for the *Argentina* dated March 31, 1860, listed 10 men, only two of whom were landsmen. Date and place of enlistment were not shown, but it would appear that some men were enlisted after Page took command of the *Argentina* in Buenos Aires.[23]

In June 1858, Congress voted $10,000 to pay the expenses of an expedition to arrange a satisfactory solution to the differences between the United States and Paraguay arising out of the shelling of the *Water Witch,* the expulsion of Hopkins, and the refusal of Paraguay to ratify the 1853 treaty. In his message to Congress of December 1857 President Buchanan mentioned these matters and requested authority and money to deal firmly with Paraguay.

With the money voted by Congress and under the authorization of the President, the Navy Department assembled a fleet of 19 ships under the command of Flag Officer William B. Shubrick, to carry James B. Bowlin as a commissioner of the United States to treat with President Carlos Antonio López. The fleet, which included the *Water Witch,* carried 2,500 men and 200 guns. Page was given command of the flagship, the frigate *Salinas,* with the rank of Fleet Captain. The expedition sailed from New York in October 1858.

While most of the fleet waited at various places in the La Plata estuary, Shubrick and Bowlin took the *Water Witch* and a few other vessels to Asunción. Soon after their arrival on January 26, 1859, Lopez adopted a conciliatory attitude and agreed to pay $10,000 to the heirs of Quartermaster Chaney, killed during the Itapura incident. He also agreed to arbitrate the claims of the United States and Paraguay Navigation Company. Of more immediate importance to Page was a treaty, signed on February 4, 1859, granting the United States freedom of navigation on the Paraguay River.[24]

After obtaining these agreements, Bowlin, Shubrick, and most of the expeditionary force returned to the United States. Page was detached from the *Salinas* and took command of the *Argentina* at Buenos Aires in March 1859. Between the time the *Argentina* reached Montevideo and Page's arrival aboard the *Salinas,* it was found that the *Argentina's* boiler was defective and that she drew more water than existed in some of the tributaries Page wanted to explore. While the *Argentina* waited at Montevideo, Forbes sent out a new boiler, and built for Page's use a 22-ton iron paddle wheel steamer called the *Alpha,* which drew a little over two feet of water. She was sent to Montevideo as deck cargo on the 260-ton *Nankin,* bound for China. The *Alpha* was stowed on deck "diagonally, the bow resting against the topgallant forecastle on the port side, while the stern rested in chocks, near the half-poop, on the other side. The boiler was stowed on deck; one of the paddle-wheels and its box was stowed over the stern of the brig, on skids, and the other on the main deck."

The *Nankin* left Boston on November 18, 1858, and arrived at Montevideo on January 12, 1859. When she reached Montevideo, the *Salinas* was present with Page still aboard as Fleet Captain. Forbes sailed from Boston with the *Nankin* and at Montevideo, with the help of Page, he decided to try to deliver the *Alpha* without having to pay customs on her as cargo. Accordingly, Page obtained the use of the storeship *Supply* to lift the *Alpha* into the water, and the boiler, paddle wheels, smoke stack, and other devices were fixed in their proper place, Then the *Alpha* raised steam, proceeded to the custom house and was entered as a recent arrival by sea from Boston. The collector asked Forbes some pertinent questions as to

> how a steamer of twenty-two tons, with only two men, had come from Boston; how much fuel she had consumed, how many ports she had visited on the way, and whether she used steam or sail? All of which questions I answered truly: that she came in fifty four days; put into no port; that she was under steam many times (making fresh water); that she had her fires going every day; never shipped a sea, and brought two men in her cabin as passengers (Mr. Tremens and the second mate)! The collector made some remark as to the indomitable energy and ingenuity of the Americanos, and requested his deputy to make note of the facts stated, in the custom-house archives. It will be readily seen by my readers, that the *Alpha* could not have been brought out and entered as cargo without subjecting me to heavy expenses, nor could she have been permitted to navigate the waters of the La Plata and its tributaries in any other way.[25]

Since Page was still engaged in his duties as Fleet Captain, Forbes, with a private crew, sailed the *Alpha* up the Uruguay River and Rio Negro before turning her over to Page during the first week of March, then headed back to Boston.[26]

Page's first objective after he took command of the *Argentina* and *Alpha* was to ascend the Paraguay to the San Lorenzo River, go up the San Lorenzo to the Cuiba River, and then take the Cuiba River to the town of Cuiba, the capital of the Brazilian province of Mato Grasso. Because it was the season of low water, the *Argentina* could not leave the San Lorenzo River and remained there to explore while Page took the *Alpha* to Cuiba. After experiencing some trouble in obtaining coal in Paraguay, he reached Cuiba in July 1859. He explored the Cuiba as far as the *Alpha* could go and then, late in July, continued the exploration of the Paraguay. By November 6, 1859, Page and the *Argentina* were at Corrientes, within the boundaries of the Argentine Confederation. On that date, Page reported that he had sent to Buenos Aires five boxes and a keg of specimens, for the Smithsonian Institution. He requested permission (eventually denied by the Secretary) to present a field howitzer, with its carriage and ammunition, which was part of the equipment of the *Argentina,* to the President of the Argentine Confederation.

Page also reported that after leaving Cuiba, he had ascended the Paraguay River to latitude 15°49″, about forty miles above the town of Villa Maria. The *Argentina* had steamed up the San Lorenzo River 50 miles from its confluence with the Cuiba, and the "Lakes Oberoba, Gaiba and Mandiori" had been explored. He characterized the knowledge he had gained as not only of interest to geographical science, "but important in the settlement of the adjacent country, and the consequent extension of commerce."

From Corrientes, the *Argentina* went to Buenos Aires to provision while Page, with the *Alpha,* explored the Bermejo and Paraná rivers. By the first week in March 1860, he had completed this work and was beginning to anticipate returning to the United States; he thought all work would be finished by the autumn of 1860. By May, he sent Lieutenant Chandler home, and the following month Lieutenant McGary was allowed to return to the United States.

In October, after having explored the Uruguay River again to "Uruguayana," Page felt he had accomplished the objectives of the second La Plata expedition. On October 6, 1860 in Buenos Aires, he reported that all possible work under his instructions had been completed and that he had turned the *Argentina* and *Alpha* over to the representative of R. B. Forbes. Some days later, with his remaining two lieutenants, the assistant surgeon, the engineer, and three men, Page took passage to the United States on the barque *La Plata* which reached New York on December 9. There Page wrote to the Secretary of the Navy to request leaves of absence for the officers, submitted requisitions for pay, and prepared to send specimens to the Smithsonian Institution.[27]

By January 1, 1861, Page was engaged in putting his accounts in order, writing his report, and preparing charts for publication. As late as the second week of April, he was still involved in this work, but it was never finished. As the United States moved into the Civil War, Virginia seceded from the Union and Page went with it—dismissed from the U.S. Navy as of April 22, 1861.[28]

Page's desire for a comprehensive publication containing a scientific evaluation of the specimens sent to the Smithsonian Institution by the two La Plata expeditions was never realized. Baird, of the Smithsonian, thought highly of Page's work in specimen collection, even to the extent of comparing it with collections made by Europeans, and told Page he hoped to obtain financial support for its proper classification and presentation. Despite Baird's approbation and Page's attempts, no money could be secured from the government or other sources, before Page left for the La Plata in 1859. When he returned to the United States and began his report on the second expedition, the general situation was too troubled for anything to be done, and after the end of the Civil War nothing was done to correct this situation.

Fortunately, Page's scientific endeavors did not go unnoticed by Baird of the Smithsonian, who used his position to bring them to the attention of appropriate scientists.[29]

In 1859, Harper and Brothers published Page's account of the first expedition under the title *La Plata, The Argentine Confederation, and Paraguay. Being a Narrative of the Exploration of the River La Plata and Adjacent Countries, during the years 1853, '54, and '56, under the orders of the United States Government.* Two appendices contained an evaluation by John Cassin of Page's bird collection and another by Charles Girard of the fishes and reptiles sent home by the first expedition.

In other respects, Page's work also found favor. *Harper's New Monthly Magazine* for February 1859 carried a very favorable account of the expedition and told how "Lieutenant Page performed the duties entrusted to him with rare tact, fidelity, and intelligence." Littell's *The Living Age* for October 1859, printed an extract from *The Critic* in which Page's book was described as being "freely and unostentatiously told, relating the facts of the expedition in a quiet, business-like manner; the social sketches of life and manners in the different countries visited are lightly, and sometimes wittingly sketched; and the notes upon natural history, the geology, flora, and fauna of those countries, with which the volume is plentifully stored, are evidently the work of a well-informed, cultivated mind."[30]

Lieutenant Thomas Jefferson Page, in leading two expeditions to explore the La Plata and its tributaries, accomplished a feat of reporting on the geographical features and economic resources of the region superior to that of any other nineteenth-century expedition to South America. The public gained knowledge of previously little-known regions, and travel to and between these points was made easier. Even though published descriptions were limited, the Page expeditions produced the best natural history collection of that region available for scientific study. Despite difficulties with the dictator of Paraguay, Page's expeditions improved relations with the Argentine Confederation under Urquiza and with Brazil. This development, along with the opening of the Paraná, Paraguay, and various tributaries, to United States merchant ships within the Argentine Confederation and Paraguay led to a better climate for commerce. The charts of hitherto uncharted areas of the La Plata estuary and its tributaries provided new navigational help to ship captains, thereby allowing increased commerce to flow smoothly and advantageously for the benefit of all.

Page, his officers, and his men, on both expeditions, accomplished the task of making the La Plata and its tributaries known to the people who lived there as well as to the United States in a way and with a quality and amount of information hitherto unknown. From this point of view their effort can be looked upon as a pioneer effort, as well as a lasting achievement.

During the Civil War, Page served in the Confederate Navy. He first commanded coastal defense batteries; later he spent a year as a Confederate secret service agent in Florence, Italy. In the fall of 1864, he went to Denmark and took command of a powerful ironclad, named the *Stonewall*. The ship was in Havana, Cuba, when the Civil War ended, and Page turned it over to the Spanish authorities. Subsequently, Page went to Argentina. For a time he resided on a cattle ranch in Entre Rios. Later he was employed by the government of Argentina to superintend the construction of four ironclads in England. About 1880, Page went to Italy. He died in Rome at the age of 92 years.

# Chapter 8

# Perry Expedition to the China Sea and First Mission to Japan, 1852-1856

On November 24, 1852, the USS *Mississippi* departed from Norfolk, Virginia, on a voyage to Japan that would last nearly 30 months. She carried Commodore Matthew C. Perry, who had been selected to command the East India Squadron. Perry had orders from the President and the Secretary of the Navy to visit Japan for the purpose of opening commercial intercourse with the United States and securing better treatment for American seamen shipwrecked on Japanese shores. These orders climaxed U.S. agitation for such action that began when the *Essex* sailed to the Pacific during the War of 1812.

On the basis of his experience in the Pacific during that cruise in the *Essex,* her commanding officer, Captain David Porter, considered that it would be advantageous for the United States to enter into commerce with Japan. He wrote to President James Madison, "The time may be favorable, and it would be a glory beyond that acquired by any other nation for us, a nation of only forty years standing, to beat down their rooted prejudices, secure to ourselves a valuable trade, and make that people known to the world."[2] This suggestion was not taken up immediately. In 1835, Edwin Roberts, who had performed missions to Siam and to the Sultanate of Muscat in previous years, was given a letter from President Jackson to the Emperor of Japan, but Roberts died en route and the letter was not delivered. Two years later an American businessman in Canton, C. W. King, organized a voyage to Japan to return to that country seven Japanese seamen, picked up in various parts of the Pacific, who had found their way to Canton. This undertaking was contrary to Japanese law. So, even though the peaceful nature of his voyage was made perfectly clear, his ship, the *Morrison,* was not allowed to stop in Japan and was driven away by gun fire.

In 1845, another American vessel, the *Manhattan,* reached Tokyo Bay with some Japanese picked up at sea. That time, the Japanese allowed the men to land and provided for the needs of the ship. Great precautions, however, were taken to see that no Americans went ashore, and the captain of the vessel was warned that he would not be welcomed again except at the port of Nagasaki.[3] In the United States these rebuffs were played up very widely and brought pleas for government action on the part of various merchant interests. Added to a case of what seemed like an insult to American good will was the fact that shipwrecked American seamen who found their way to Japan were treated very harshly. Foremost among those demanding action by the government to rectify this situation was Aaron H. Palmer, a director of the American and Foreign Agency, who made a series of proposals for a mission to Japan. In 1845, the same year that the *Manhattan* visited Japan, pressure from commercial, whaling, religious, humanitarian, and other interests in the United States succeeded in getting before the House of Representatives a resolution calling for "immediate measures for effecting commercial arrangements with the Empire of Japan and the Kingdom of Korea."

This resolution was tabled, but in the same year Alexander H. Everett was sent by the United States to replace Caleb Cushing as United States Commissioner to China and to exchange with China ratifications of the Treaty of Wang Hiya. Everett was also given full power to negotiate a treaty with Japan. Two ships were detailed as a special squadron, under the command of Commodore James Biddle, to take Everett to China; ship-of-the-line *Columbus,* and sloop-of-war *Vincennes.*

In his orders to Biddle, Secretary of the Navy George Bancroft stated that in the event Everett could not or chose not to go to Japan, Biddle could sail his ships there to "ascertain if the ports of Japan are accessible." If he did go to Japan, Biddle was also instructed not to excite hostile feelings since the policy of the United States was "avowedly pacific."

On the way to the Far East, Everett became ill and left the squadron at Rio de Janeiro. Biddle assumed Everett's diplomatic powers, took his ships to China, and exchanged ratifications of the Treaty of Wanghia with the Chinese on December 31, 1845. Then he decided to sail to Japan.

Biddle's ships anchored at the entrance to Tokyo Bay in July 1846. The Japanese demanded that all negotiations be conducted through the Dutch established at Nagasaki. They enforced their demands by having guard boats swarm around Biddle's ships and tricking him into thinking that he was negotiating with high officials when, in fact, he was talking only with subordinates. Biddle felt that he should not take strong measures against the Japanese and lost control of the situation. In the end, he thought he was receiving a letter from the emperor, but it was only a common document without address, seal, or date. At one point, he stepped aboard a patrol boat, mistaking it for an official vessel, and a Japanese guard gave him a "blow or push, which threw me back into the boat." The Commodore asked that the man be seized and then returned to his ship. When the Japanese expressed great sorrow over what had happened and wanted to punish the culprit, Biddle did nothing except leave the manner of punishment to the laws of Japan. He accomplished very little except to ascertain that the ports were not accessible, and sailed away with a letter that said, "The Emperor positively refuses the permission that you desire. He earnestly advises you to depart immediately and to consult your own safety and not appear again upon our coast."[4]

Biddle's failure seems to have made the U.S. Navy the laughing stock of the Japanese.

In 1849, Commander James Glynn went to Nagasaki in the USS *Preble* to claim 15 seamen who had deserted their ship on the coast of Japan. These men had been in prison in Japan for many years and had been treated severely, some of them having been put in cages where they could not stand erect. The Japanese tried to prevent Commander Glynn from carrying out his mission by massing soldiers near the anchorage and training some sixty guns on his ship. In the beginning stages, they refused every demand for the release of the prisoners. Commander Glynn, not to be dissuaded, answered threat with threat. Finally, he obtained release of all the survivors (one had died and one had committed suicide), plus an American adventurer named MacDonald, who had somehow found his way ashore in a small boat. When Glynn returned to the United States in 1851, he visited Washington, talked with President Millard Fillmore, and submitted suggestions on what the United States should do about Japan. His suggestions were reinforced by independent advice from Americans in the Far East.

That same year the U.S. found a pretext for action—17 shipwrecked Japanese were rescued by American vessels in the spring of 1851 and taken to San Francisco. It was decided to entrust the commander of the East India Squadron to return them to Japan and to "beef up" his force so as to give the expedition more chance of success. The squadron then under the command of Commodore John Aulick consisted of the bark-rigged steam frigate, the USS *Susquehanna* (the first American steam vessel of war to visit the Far East), and the sloops-of-war *Plymouth* and *Saratoga*. It sailed from the U.S. in June of 1851. As passengers to Rio de Janeiro, Brazil, Aulick had on board the *Susquehanna* the Chevalier S. de Macedo, minister of Brazil to the United States, Mr. Robert C. Schenck, U.S. minister to Brazil, and Mr. J. S. Pendleton, chargé d'affaires to the Argentine Confederation.

After the *Susquehanna* reached Rio de Janeiro, Schenck wrote to the State Department accusing Aulick of having led Macedo to believe that he was traveling to Rio de Janeiro at Aulick's expense when in fact he was traveling at the expense of the United States government. Schenck's letter reached the State Department about the middle of November. On November 18, 1851, the President decided to recall Aulick in anticipation of any protestations that might be made by Brazil. On that same day, Secretary of the Navy William Graham wrote to Aulick, directing him to remain at Hong Kong or Macao as commander of the East India Squadron until a relief arrived.

Graham's letter reached Aulick after the *Susquehanna* had arrived on station. Aulick replied to Schenck's charges by letter and then waited until March 1853, before returning to the United States, where he asked for an official investigation of the affair. This was denied by the Secretary of the Navy on the grounds that Aulick's explanation was satisfactory. Aulick was relieved by Commodore Matthew Calbraith Perry, who received orders to command the East India Squadron on March 24, 1852. For the next six months, Perry busied himself in preparing to assume command and conduct the proposed mission to Japan. He studied information supplied by American businessmen, the letter of Commander Glynn, documents and maps purchased from the Dutch, and other sources. He obtained items of American manufacture as presents for the Emperor, and carefully selected men for what he considered to be "key" positions. One such person was Lieutenant Silas Bent, who had served with Glynn in the *Preble* and was acquainted with the waters off Japan. No civilians as such were included, but two artists and an agricultural expert were given temporary commissions for the duration of the expedition.[5]

In a letter dated November 5, 1852, acting Secretary of State C. M. Conrad sent the Secretary of the Navy, John P. Kennedy, diplomatic instructions for Perry, which Perry himself had helped to formulate. On November 13, 1852, the Secretary gave Perry his sailing instructions. Perry also carried a letter from the President of the United States to the Emperor of Japan and a commission authorizing him to act as the special envoy of the United States to Japan.[6]

After leaving the Chesapeake, the *Mississippi* headed for Madeira for "refreshments" and coal—a 17-day voyage.[7] While she took on supplies and coal, and some of the officers and men investigated the island, Commodore Perry reported to the Secretary of the Navy:

Sir:
    Since leaving the United States, I have had leisure to reflect more fully upon the probable result of my visit to Japan, and though there is still some doubt in my mind as to the chances of meeting success in bringing a strange government to any practical negotiation, yet I feel confident that in the end the great object in view will be effected.

    As a preliminary step, and one of the easier accomplishments, one or more ports of refuge and supply to our whaling and other ships must at once be secured; and should the Japanese government object to the granting of such ports from the mainland, and if they cannot be occupied without resort to force and bloodshed, then it will be desirable in the beginning, and indeed, necessary, that the squadron should establish places of rendezvous at one or two of the islands south of Japan, having a good harbor, and possessing facilities for obtaining water and supplies, and seek by kindness and gentle treatment to conciliate the inhabitants so as to bring about their familiar intercourse.

    The islands called the Lew Chew Group are said to be dependencies of

Japan as conquered by that power centuries ago, but their actual sovereignty is disputed by the government of China.

These islands come within the jurisdiction of the Prince of Satsuma, the most powerful of Princes of the Empire. . . . He exercises his rights more from the influence of the fear of the simple islanders than from any power to coerce their obedience. . . .

Now, it strikes me, that the occupation of the principal ports of those islands for the accommodation of our ships of war, and for the safe resort of merchant vessels of whatever nation, would be a measure not only justified by the strictest rules of moral law, but which is also to be considered, by the laws of stern necessity. . . .

. . . When we look at the possessions in the East of our great maritime rival, England, and at the constant and rapid increase of their fortified force, we should be admonished of the necessity of prompt measures on our part. By reference to the map of the world, it will be seen that Great Britain is already in possession of the most important points in the East India and China Seas, especially in reference to the China Seas.

With Singapore commanding the Southwestern, while Hong Kong covers the Northeastern entrance, and with the Island of Labuan on the Eastern coast of Borneo, an intermediate point, she will have the power of shutting up at will and controlling the enormous trade of those seas, amounting, it is said in value to 300,000 tons of shipping, carrying cargo certainly not under £15,000,000 sterling.

Fortunately the Japanese and many other islands of the Pacific are still left untouched by this "Annexing" government; and, as some of them lay in the route of commerce which is destined to become of great importance to the United States, no time should be lost in adopting active measures to secure sufficient number of ports of refuge. And hence I shall look with much anxiety for the arrival of the *Powhatan* and the other vessels to be sent to me.

I have thus exhibited, in this crude and informal communication, my views upon a subject which is exciting extraordinary tension throughout the world, and I trust that the department will approve the course I propose to pursue.

This letter was dated December 14, 1852. On February 15, 1853, Secretary of State Edward Everett answered Perry:

Sir:

Your dispatch of the 14th of December has been referred by the Secretary of the Navy to this Department, and by me submitted to the President. The President concurs with you in the opinion that it is highly desirable, probably necessary for the safety for the expedition under your command, that you should secure one or more ports of refuge of easy access. If you find that these cannot be obtained in the Japanese Islands without resort to force, it will be necessary that you should seek them elsewhere. The President agrees with you in thinking that you are most likely to succeed in this object in the Lew Chew Islands. They are, from their position, well adapted to the purpose; and the friendly and peaceful character of the natives encourages the hope that your visit will be welcomed by them.

In establishing yourself at one or two convenient points in those islands, with the consent of the natives, you will yourself pursue the most friendly and conciliatory course, and enjoin the same conduct in all under your command. Take no supplies from them except by fair purchase, or satisfactory consideration. Forbid, and at all hazards prevent blunder and acts of violence on the part of your men toward the simple and unwarlike people, for such they are described to be. Let them from the first see that you are coming among them as a benefit, not an evil to them. Make no use of force, except in the last resort for defense if attacked, and self-preservation. The President approved the idea suggested by you encouraging natives to turn their attention to agriculture, and has given orders to have the implements of husbandry mentioned by you, sent out by the *Vermont*. He has also directed a small printing press, with type and materials for printing of all kinds, to be sent out by the *Vermont*. The President is gratified to perceive that you are impressed with the importance of the enterprise confided to your direction, the success of which will mainly depend upon your prudence and interest. It will attract a large share of the attention of the civilized world; and the President feels great confidence that the measures adopted by you will effect credit on your own wisdom and discretion and do honor to your country.

On Wednesday evening, December 15, the *Mississippi* left Madeira. On December 22, Commodore Perry issued a general order forbidding communications to the public at home touching the movements of the expedition, and prohibiting such information to the medium of private letters. It was also required that all private journals and notes kept by any member of the expedition be considered as belonging to the government until their publication should be permitted expressly by the Department of the Navy. The next day a second general order was issued:

Entertaining the opinion that the talents and acquirements of the officers of the squadron, if properly directed and brought into action, will be found equal to a plain and practical examination and illucidation of various objects pertaining to the arts and sciences that may come under their observation during the present cruise, and being aware of the limited accommodation of the vessels under my command, I have invariably objected to the employment of persons drawn from civil life to conduct those departments more immediately connected with science.

Therefore, I have to request and direct, that each officer of the respective ships will employ such portions of his time as can be spared from his regular duties and proper hours of relaxation, in contributing to the general mass of information which is desirable to collect; and in order to simplify and methodize these researches, a paper is self-joined particularizing the various departments in reference to which information is more especially wanted; so that each officer may select one or more of those departments most congenial to his tastes and inclinations.

All captains and commanders are required to render every facility consistent with the proper duties of their respective vessels to those officers who may manifest a zealous cooperation in the pursuits herein specified; and it is to be plainly understood that I do not officially require the officers to perform any involuntary duty. I shall exact that only which may come within the legitimate sphere of my authority, leaving to the officers themselves to engage as far as they may see fit only, in those investigations which, in an official point of view, may be considered as on their part gratuitous.

It would always give the greatest pleasure to have to notice the labors of each and every individual who may contribute to the general work.

The subjects suggested by Commodore Perry in the paper attached to this general order included hydrography, meteorology, naval architecture in its adaptation to war and commerce, military affairs, geology, geography, terrestrial magnetism, philology and ethnology, artistic matters, costumes and related material, religion, diseases and sanitary laws, agriculture, statistics of supplies, botany, ontomology, ornithology, zoology, conchology, ichthyology, and the magnetic telegraph.

The *Mississippi* took on coal at the Cape of Good Hope, and again at Mauritius. She made Point de Galle, in Ceylon, on March 13, 1853. There it was learned that

> ... the United States commercial agent, a native of Scotland, was confined to his premises under an execution for debt. Various accounts of the circumstances connected with this unfortunate condition of affairs were communicated to the Commodore, but he studiously avoided any interference with the matter. It was no part of his business or duty to interpose; and as humiliating as was the state of things he could not but feel that the fault was in the former consular system of the United States. Our country had no right to expect our consuls and commercial agents, many of whom were unfitted in every respect for their station, to aid and represent us and sustain the commercial interest of the nation so long as the system then existing was followed. . . . The recent action of Congress has shown the sense entertained by that body of the correctness of these views and of the need for reform; and it is hoped the measures adopted will guarantee for the future a dignified representative of our commercial interests wherever we have a consul.

The ship began provisioning, and Perry attempted, in connection with the presence of a Siamese war ship in the harbor, to open up new connections with the government of Siam. After a visit to the *Mississippi* by the Siamese commander and an exchange of presents and letters, Perry began to think of going to Siam. In the official report of the expedition to Japan, published after Perry's return to the United States, it is stated that "uncontrollable circumstances prevented" him, but they were not explained.

On March 15, the *Mississippi* sailed for the Strait of Malacca. She anchored at Singapore on March 25, for a short stay.

Perry exchanged visits and salutes as required, and transacted some business with the United States consul. Many officers from the *Mississippi* formed an agreeable association with a Chinese merchant named Whampoa. These officers, including Commodore Perry, dined and spent at least one night at the country residence of this merchant, which, in his narrative of the expedition, Perry described as the "most beautiful on the island."

At Singapore, the ship again took on supplies, water, and 230 tons of coal from the Oriental and Pacific Company. Commodore Perry promised to return that amount at Hong Kong as the company was running short of coal there.

The *Mississippi* left Singapore on March 29, 1853. During the morning of April 6, large numbers of fishing boats were seen as far as the eye could reach. Some 269 of them were counted at one time, "sailing in couples, about 19 fathoms apart, before the wind, with a net extended between each two. They were curiously rigged, having square sails set upon two or three masts, which had, at a distance, some of the appearance of courses of topsails which they hoisted and lowered as they desired to graduate the rate of sailing, in order to keep way with their consorts. The vessels were engaged in taking small fish similar to the sardine of the Mediterranean, and the same mode of netting them is pursued in both localities."

On April 7, the *Mississippi* anchored off Hong Kong, where the sloops-of-war *Plymouth* and *Saratoga* and the storeship *Supply* were present. The *Susquehanna,* a steam frigate, had sailed a fortnight before for Shanghai, carrying the United States commissioner to China, the honorable Mr. Marshall; Dr. Parker, the secretary of Legation; and Mr. Paul S. Forbes,[8] the United States consul to Canton. Perry particularly desired to see these gentlemen before sailing for Japan, so he dispatched the *Plymouth* to Shanghai with instructions to the captain of the *Susquehanna,* Commodore Franklin Buchanan, to wait for the arrival of the *Mississippi.* On April 8, the customary salutes were exchanged with foreign vessels at Hong Kong, followed by an exchange of personal courtesies among the officers of the various nations represented. Later, Commodore Perry said, "In no instance, during long service in foreign countries, have I experienced any want of hospitable attention; and, in fact, the governments of all nations with the exception of that of the United States, have furnished the means for public entertainments by ample allowance of 'table money' and it thus becomes a duty as it is doubtless a pleasure, of these officers to extend it hospitably."

From Hong Kong, the *Mississippi* sailed to Macao and from Macao to

Whampoa on the Canton River. Perry visited Canton on business, and with some of his officers, was accommodated at the house of "Mr. Forbes, the consul of the United States and the head of the firm of Russell and Company."

> ... Mr. Forbes was absent at the time, but the hospitalities of his establishment were most freely dispensed by one of his partners, Mr. Spooner. So well known was this establishment, and so highly appreciated were his proprieters by the Chinese, that all that was necessary in making a purchase in the city, was simply to direct the shopkeeper to send the article to the house of Mr. Forbes, and there was never any hesitation in assenting at once. The same may be said indeed of all the American houses, with respect both to hospitality and the confidence of the Chinese.

On Perry's return to Macao, he was again accommodated by Russell and Company in a magnificent residence belonging to that firm, placed at his disposal by Mr. Spooner. On April 28, he departed with the *Mississippi*, leaving the *Saratoga* to take on board Dr. S. W. Williams of Canton who had been appointed interpreter to the expedition, an exception to Perry's policy of not employing civilians.

> On leaving, the pilot became confused and the ship got out of the channel, but by good fortune did not stop, though she ran into 19 foot water, one foot less than her drafts, on the South Sand. The power of her engines proved her salvation. The wealthy foreign merchants established at Shanghai, who were gathering plentiful harvests from the increasing trade of the place, should contribute some of their thousands toward rendering the navigation less dangerous. It is but justice to say that a willingness has been expressed by some of these gentlemen to subscribe liberally toward the accomplishment of the desired object, and, in fact, a boat had been ordered to be built in the United States, for the purpose of towing vessels up and down the river. The Commodore himself was convinced after the incident of the *Mississippi* that until proper landmarks and beacons were established to indicate how to get into the port, it would be an unfit resort for any but the smaller vessels of the squadron and consequently an unfit place for a naval depot.

At Shanghai, Commodore Perry was again the guest of the American firm of Russell and Company, and visited Chinese officials of the city who afterward visited the *Mississippi*. He was pressured by American business firms to provide them some naval protection because of the T'ai P'ing Rebellion. With their property valued at about $1,200,000, they considered themselves fairly entitled to such protection. Commodore Perry resolved to leave the *Plymouth* at Shanghai to protect his countrymen, but not otherwise to interfere with the internal problems of China. "The request of the American commissioner to have the vessel of war to convey him to the mouth of the Peiho, in order to secure a recognition on the part of the Chinese government of his official presence, was not complied with by the Commodore, who declined not only on the score of policy, but from the necessity of concentrating all the naval force he could to the naval expedition to Japan."

Between May 4 and 17, Perry and his staff transferred to the *Susquehanna* and the ships were provisioned. Supplies included five tons of Chinese "cash"—small copper coins worth about 1,200 to the dollar, for use in trading. The *Susquehanna* sailed on May 23, followed by the *Mississippi* with the *Supply* in tow, bound for Naha, the capital port of the Great Lew Chew Island (Okinawa).

> During the passage, the crew were regularly called to quarters and exercised in all the usual maneuvers necessary for preparation for action, and on the morning of the 25th of May, after quarters, general orders 11 and 12 were read; the former related to the discipline to be observed on board ship during the visit to the Lew Chew Islands, and the latter enjoined the necessity of keeping up the most friendly relations with the Japanese inhabitants wherever found, and also stated that the expedition was ordered to use all possible friendly means, not to resort to force but from the sternest necessity.

Naha was reached on the evening of May 26, and the ships entered the harbor. Lieutenant Bent, an officer aboard the *Mississippi*, who had visited Naha earlier in the *Preble*, piloted the ships in.

Two native officials soon approached in a small boat, to present a red card on which formal greetings were written. Commodore Perry refused to accept it, or to receive the officials; he would receive no one but a dignitary of the highest rank in accordance with the previous plans.

Next day four boats came alongside the *Susquehanna*, with the same officials who had visited the ship before, and a variety of presents. Again, they were not received and their presents were not accepted.

Perry then sent his interpreter, Dr. Williams, and Flag Lieutenant Contee ashore to tell the mayor of Naha that the Americans would receive no presents until a person of the highest rank had met with the Commodore.

The next afternoon, the Regent of the island made a visit of state. He was received by Perry, who announced that he would return the visit on June 6 by traveling to the Regent's palace at Shuri. This proved very distasteful to the Regent and he tried unsuccessfully to change Perry's mind. On the appointed day the Regent tried to divert Perry to other buildings before he arrived at the palace. But Perry was not to be denied, and sitting in an elaborate sedan chair, followed by some of his officers also in sedan chairs, and accompanied by a company of marines, band, two pieces of brass artillery and natives bearing presents, he was carried two miles to the palace at Shuri. The meeting went well, and after a feast, everyone was aboard ship again by mid-afternoon.

After this, the authorities of Lew Chew put into effect a policy of what might be called passive resistance. They dogged the footsteps of Americans who went ashore in an effort to restrict their movements; they made contacts with the inhabitants difficult; and they prevented any presents being given by the Americans to the inhabitants.

To this situation Commodore Perry objected. He declared that the members of his force who went ashore would act as if they had a right to freedom of movement and to meet and converse with the inhabitants. Once more, he demanded the right to a house to be used by the members of his expedition, which was given to him before the end of his stay in Naha. To show his determination in these matters, on May 30, Perry had dispatched a party to explore the region around Naha, and especially to look for coal and to make scientific observations. They found the natives helpless, with no force to oppose them. On June 4, they returned to the ships.

On June 9, 1853, the *Susquehanna* sailed for the Bonin Islands with the *Saratoga* in tow. The *Mississippi* and the *Supply* remained at Naha under the command of Commander Lee, the senior officer. En route, the crews were exercised at quarters. Once after dark

> night signals were made to the *Saratoga* by means of lanterns and blue lights, and to those who were not "old salts" enough to have seen such sights before, the effect was alike novel and exciting. The blue lights illuminating the broad sails, with their full tension under the influence of the monsoon, the men at their several stations all brought out in the glare of an artificial light, which, though bright as daylight, yet was an unearthly aspect, gave to the scene somewhat of a startling effect, and forceably impressed the imagination with the peculiar features of the night engagement.

On June 14, the *Susquehanna* and the *Saratoga* anchored off the entrance of Port Lloyd, on Peel Island, about which Perry was interested in obtaining all possible information. The next day he sent two exploring parties ashore and dispatched an officer to report on the general condition of the island of Stapleton. On both islands there were cats, hogs, and goats running wild, and dogs and sheep that were more domesticated. There seemed to be no cattle, and a deficiency in garden produce. Perry landed "two bulls and two cows, with a hope to their increase," and distributed garden seeds to the white settlers.

He hoped thus to provide a store of provisions for future steamers stopping there en route to China and Japan. Accordingly, a site was selected for the erection of offices, wharves, coal sheds and other depot buildings, and title to the land was obtained. Later, Perry recommended to the Secretary of the Navy that Peel Island be considered for a depot site.

On June 18, 1853, the *Susquehanna,* with the *Saratoga* still in tow, began the return trip to Naha. En route, they passed the Island of Disappointment and determined its location. Next they headed for the Borodinos, which were sighted on June 22, and determined their position. On the evening of June 23, the ships reached Naha, where they found the *Mississippi, Plymouth,* and *Supply.*

A new Regent had been installed at Naha, so another round of ceremonial visits began, to confirm the position Perry had established previously. Meanwhile, some of the officers examined the island and its inhabitants. "The general impression left on the minds of the gentlemen of the expedition was that Lew Chew was a beautiful island, abundantly supplied, and needed but a good government to form, so far as bodily comfort is concerned, as pleasant a residence as could be desired."

Early on July 2, 1853, the *Susquehanna,* the *Mississippi,* the *Saratoga* and the *Plymouth* sailed for Japan. The *Supply* was left behind; the *Caprice* was sent to Shanghai. The Fourth of July, 1853, the seventy-seventh anniversary of the founding of the United States, was celebrated by all ships firing a 17-gun salute and by "the serving of an additional ration of grog to Jack, while the officers brought the barrels of the resources of various messes, give due enjoyment and impressiveness to the day." The crews were allowed to feel that it was a holiday, and were excused from the usual muster at general quarters and from the drill, "which had been kept up during the passage with great strictness and regularity, in order that the squadron might be prepared for any event at its arrival in Japan."

On the afternoon of July 8, the squadron anchored off Uraga, on the western side of the Bay of Tokyo.[9] Numerous guard boats came from all directions, trying to take up stations around the ships.

> The Commodore, however, had fully determined beforehand that they should not thus surround the ships. They made several attempts to get alongside and on board the *Saratoga;* the tow lines with which they made fast to any part of the ships were unceremoniously cast off. They attempted to climb up by the chains, but the crew was ordered to prevent them, and the sight of pikes, cutlasses, and pistols, checked them, and when they found that their officers were very much in earnest, they desisted from their attempts to board.

Finally, a boat carrying the vice-governor of Uraga came alongside the *Susquehanna,* and Perry detailed his aide, Flag Lieutenant Contee, to meet this official. The vice-governor, and another Japanese official who spoke Dutch, came on board and were received by Contee in the Captain's cabin. The Commodore stayed in his own quarters in accordance with his determination to follow the same policy in Japan as he had followed on the Island of Lew Chew; to talk with no one except a dignitary of the highest rank.

The Japanese tried to convince the Americans that they should conduct their business in Nagasaki; they claimed that all foreign business was done there. Lieutenant Contee repeated Commodore Perry's view that he would not go to Nagasaki, that he had a letter from the President of the United

States to the Emperor which he expected to be delivered to the Emperor at Tokyo. The Americans did not understand that the Emperor was in Kyoto, not Tokyo, and the Japanese did not tell them that the Shogun ruled Japan from Tokyo. Finding that they could not budge the American position, the Japanese officials left, promising that in the morning a higher official would come to answer their demands.

Next day, a man calling himself the governor of Uraga arrived and was allowed on board. Commodore Perry again refused to conduct negotiations personally, and talks with the governor were conducted through the medium of another officer. This discussion ended with the Japanese asking for instructions from a still higher level and the Americans agreeing not to go ashore. The Commodore allowed three days for an answer to his demand that the letter be received on shore by an official of high rank, perhaps next to the Emperor. No Japanese official was to be welcome aboard the *Susquehanna* unless he brought a satisfactory reply.

While the talks with the "governor" were going on, surveying boats under the command of Lieutenant Silas Bent of the *Mississippi* worked the waters around Uraga, and approached close enough to shore to see fortifications—mere earthwork, and barracks and magazines built of wood. The Japanese seemed in no position to challenge the might of the American ships. On July 11, 1853, the survey boats were sent further into the Bay of Tokyo; the *Mississippi* followed to protect them. In his subsequent report to Washington, Perry wrote that he "had done enough to work upon the fears of the Emperor without going too far." That same day the "governor" of Uraga boarded the *Susquehanna* to say that the American letter would be received the following day and to find out what the *Mississippi* and the survey boats were doing. Perry directed that he be told that unless a satisfactory reply was received to the demands for their visit, the ships would have to return in the spring and would need an anchorage nearer to Tokyo so that they could communicate with the shore more conveniently.

On the last day allowed by Perry for an answer to his demands, the "governor" came on board to conduct additional negotiations. Again there was no face-to-face meeting with Perry. It was agreed that another meeting would take place the following day. In that meeting it was agreed that the letter from President Fillmore would be accepted on shore by a high official the day following. On both days, the survey boats continued their observations.

On the morning of July 14, 1853, the ceremony of handing President Fillmore's letter to the appropriate Japanese official was conducted in a building erected for that ceremony near the village of Kurihama. Perry, with his officers and men, presented all the pomp and show that was possible. The Japanese also conducted their affairs with an eye to pageantry. In accepting the letter the Japanese official gave a written reply: "The letter of the President of the United States of North America, and copy, I hereby

receive and it will be delivered to the Emperor. It has been many times intimated that business related to foreign countries cannot be transacted here
in Uraga, but at Nagasaki: nevertheless it has been observed that the Admiral in his quality of ambassador of the President, would feel himself in-
sulted by a refusal to receive the letter at this place, the justice of which
having been acknowledged, the above mentioned letter is hereby received in
opposition to the Japanese laws. As this is not the place wherein to negotiate
with foreigners, so neither can conferences nor entertainment be held.
Therefore, after the letter has been received, you can depart."

When the document was received there was a few moments of silence
while Commodore Perry digested its content. Finally he replied that the
ships would leave in two or three days, but that he would return in the
spring, in April or May, to get the answer to the questions raised in the
President's letter. When the ceremony ended, the Americans marched back
to the beach and returned to their ships.

At the end of the day, Commodore Perry's interpreter, Williams, wrote:
"Thus closed this eventful day on which the key was put into the lock and
the beginning made to do away with the long seclusion of this nation."[10] All
in all, as Williams had indicated, the day had gone well for Commodore
Perry; the Americans were leaving the scene in good order, and their Commodore had made much "face." Perry, however, was not completely
satisfied. In particular, he felt somewhat unhappy about the last sentence of
the Japanese letter, which suggested that the Americans should leave. Upon
rejoining the *Susquehanna,* he determined to take his ships further up the
bay before sailing. They moved about ten miles to a small bay near two islands which had been surveyed earlier by Lieutenant Bent. Perry called this
spot American Anchorage.

Finally, on Sunday, July 17, the steamers took the sloops in tow and put
to sea. On the morning of July 25, after a period of extremely unfavorable
weather, the ships entered Naha harbor where the *Supply* was waiting. The
steam frigate *Powhatan,* which was supposed to have come out to China,
had not arrived. Perry again opened negotiations with the authorities for
further concessions by sending Commander Henry Adams of the *Saratoga*
and Dr. Williams ashore with the following instructions:

> Establish rate of pay for rent of house for one year. State that I wish a
> suitable and convenient building for the storage of coal, say to hold 600
> tons. If they have no such building, I desire to employ native workmen to
> erect one after the fashion of the island, or if the Lew Chewian government
> prefers, it can be done under the inspection of the mayor at government ex-
> pense and I will agree to pay an annual rent for it. Either one or the other
> arrangement must be made.
>
> Speak about the spies, and say if they continue to follow the officers
> about, it may lead to serious consequences, and perhaps to bloodshed,
> which I should deplore, as I wish to continue on the most friendly terms

with the authorities. And should any disturbances ensue, it will be the fault of the Lew Chewians, who have no right to set spys upon American citizens who may be about their own lawful business.

We must have a free trade in the market, and the right to purchase articles for the ships.

It will be wise, therefore, for the Lew Chewians to abrogate those thoughts and customs which are not suited to the present age, and which they have no power to enforce, *and by* a persistence in which they will surely involve themselves in trouble.

Let the mayor clearly understand that this port is to be one of rendezvous, probably for years, and that the authorities better come to an understanding at once.

Thank the mayor for the kind act of the authorities of putting a tombstone of the remains of the boy buried from the *Susquehanna* and ask the privilege of paying the costs of the same.

Require prompt and orderly replies to all these propositions and demands.[11]

When Adams discussed these propositions with the mayor of Naha, he was told that all the demands had to be referred to the Regent. Adams then told the mayor that Commodore Perry wanted to have a meeting with the Regent, either the next day or the day after. The next morning, it was learned that the Regent had appointed the following day, July 28, as the time for the interview. The meeting was not entirely satisfactory because the Regent attempted to evade Perry's demands. Perry, not to be put off with evasions, stated that unless satisfactory answers to all demands were received by noon the next day, he would land some 200 men, take possession of the palace, and hold it until the matter was settled. He then returned to the *Susquehanna*. He had no intention of landing a force, but it was clear that only such a resolute declaration would achieve the desired results. Whether or not he was right in this respect, the fact was that the next day the mayor of Naha came on board to say all of Perry's demands had been met. The local authorities would start building a coal shed, and a bazaar, or market, would be held on Monday, August 1, 1853, from 6:00 a.m. to 9:00 a.m., as Perry planned to leave at the latter hour.

In the last days of their stay at Naha, the officers and artists of the ships explored the island and visited old ruins. No unpleasant incidents occurred.

On Monday, August 1, after parties from the ships made their final purchases, the squadron sailed for Hong Kong and Canton. The *Plymouth*, under command of Commander Kelly, remained at Naha to "keep alive the friendly interest and good feeling then subsisting between the Americans and the islanders."

Two days out of Naha, the squadron met the *Vandalia;* she reported that the *Powhatan* had arrived at Hong Kong and was preparing to steam to Naha. They reached Hong Kong on Sunday, August 7, 1853. The *Powhatan* had sailed the day before, and did not return until August 25. The *Vandalia* arrived on August 14.

In Hong Kong there was great anxiety over the T'ai P'ing Rebellion; the American community asked earnestly for the protection of American ships.

Perry located his ships where they could refit, and at the same time offer the desired protection, and haven of retreat if necessary, and landed Marines to guard American property in Canton. Plans were drawn to meet various contingencies. The Commodore then moved to a house in Macao to complete his reports. Here, members of the expedition brought their notes to deal with their work. A hospital was established in the town; "... the work on the expedition was not allowed any remission."[12]

When the USS *Lexington* arrived in Hong Kong as a reinforcement, Commodore Perry decided not to wait until spring to return to Japan. Accordingly, on January 14, 1854, he sailed the squadron—*Susquehanna, Powhatan, Mississippi, Lexington,* and *Southampton*—for Lew Chew. The *Macedonian, Supply,* and *Vandalia* were already en route; the *Plymouth* was at Shanghai, and the *Saratoga* would join them at Lew Chew.

Their route lay along the east coast of Formosa to Naha. The steamships arrived on January 20, 1854, followed a few days later by the sailing vessels. There they spent about two weeks getting ready for the return trip to Tokyo Bay. Finally, on February 7, 1854, the sailing ships left for Japan, with the exception of the *Supply,* which returned to Shanghai to load coal and provisions for the ships in Tokyo Bay. The steamers left Naha a few days later. By February 12, all ships assembled at the anchorage.

Almost immediately the Americans and Japanese began discussion about the place and manner in which talks between the Commodore and an appropriate high Japanese official would take place.[13] During these discussions, and despite Japanese protests, survey parties were active, one group within four miles of Tokyo. After some days of discussion, with the Japanese insisting on negotiations taking place at Uraga and Perry wanting a spot closer to Tokyo, the ships were moved to an anchorage off Kanagawa close enough to hear the bells of Tokyo, on February 25, 1854. This broke the stalemate, and the Japanese agreed to treat with Perry at a spot just north of Yokohama. The ships then moved to a suitable position commanding the treaty spot and anchored in line-of-battle about a mile offshore.

Marines armed with musket, sword, pistols and extra cartridges escorted Commodore Perry ashore on March 8, 1854. The boat guns were mounted and supplied with ammunition; even the bandsmen carried swords and pistols. The ships too were ready for action. However, as in the previous year, the only bombastic aspect of the meeting and negotiations was the color and pageantry within which formality ruled.

When serious business commenced, the Japanese, represented by a high commissioner and four other commissioners, gave Commodore Perry an unsigned scroll containing an answer to President Fillmore's letter. They agreed to provide better treatment for shipwrecked sailors and to allow ships that needed them to obtain supplies in Japan. As for a commercial port, they offered only one where coal could be secured.

After reading the document, the Commodore returned it with the request that it be signed by the Japanese commissioners and delivered to him the next day. He then began talking about a subject that had been uppermost in his mind for quite some time, a treaty between Japan and the United States. He said that he had been sent by the United States to make a treaty, and if he was not successful, the United States would probably send additional ships for this purpose. He added that he hoped everything could be settled between him and the Japanese in an amicable manner, enabling him to send two ships to the United States to prevent others from coming. To the Japanese he gave a copy of the recent Sino-American Treaty, written in English, Chinese, and Dutch, along with two notes and a letter.

Next they discussed a suitable burial for a Marine who had died two days previous to the conference. Perry wanted to buy a piece of ground for interment of the body and for any other American who might die while the ships were in Japanese waters. The Japanese replied that a temple had been set apart at Nagasaki for the burial of strangers and the body should be sent there. After considerable discussion, it was agreed that the body would be buried near a temple in Yokohama in view of the American ships. With this decided, Perry departed, "followed by his suite and procession of officers as before, and marching down, to the music of the bands, between the files of marines on either side, embarked in his barge and pulled for the ship. The other boats soon followed, filled with numerous officers, sailors, marines, and others who had shared in the ceremonies of the day."

Early the next morning, the Marine was buried and negotiations continued, this time by written communication over the points and propositions presented by Perry the previous day. The Japanese reply to President Fillmore's letter, duly certified and signed by four Japanese commissioners, was delivered. In addition, Monday, March 13, was agreed upon for the reception of presents from the United States. On that day, presents were sent ashore in several boats

which left the ship, escorted by a number of officers, and a company of marines, and a band of music, all under the superintendence of Captain Abbott, who was delegated to deliver the presents, with proper ceremony, to the Japanese high commissioners. A building adjoining the treaty house had been suitably constructed for the purpose, and on landing, Captain Abbott was met by Yezaiman, the governor of Uraga, and several subordinate officials, and conducted to the treaty house.

While Captain Abbott talked to the Japanese, officers and men unpacked and arranged the presents for exhibition. The Japanese authorities helped in every way they could. Finally, a piece of ground was selected

for laying down the circular track of the little locomotive, and posts were brought and erected for the extension of the telegraph wires, the Japanese taking a very great part in all the labors, and watching results arranging and putting together of the machinery with an innocent and child-like delight. The telegraphic apparatus, under the direction of Mssrs. Draper and Williams, was soon in working order, the wires extending nearly a mile, in a direct line, one end being at the treaty house and another at a building expressly allotted for the purpose. When communication was opened up between the operators at either extremity, the Japanese watched with intent curiosity the *modus operandi,* and were greatly amazed to find that in an instant of time messages were conveyed in the English, Dutch and Japanese languages from building to building. Day after day, the dignitaries and many of the people would gather, and eagerly beseeching the operators to work the telegraph, watch with great interest the sending and receiving of messages.

Nor did the railway, under the direction of engineers Gay and Dandy, with its Lilliputian locomotive car and tender excite less interest. All the parts of the mechanism were perfect, and the car was a most tasteful specimen of workmanship, but so small that it could hardly carry a child of six years of age. The Japanese, however, were not to be cheated out of a ride, and, as they were unable to reduce themselves to the capacity inside the carriage, they betook themselves to the roof. It was a spectacle not a little ludicrous to behold a dignified mandarin whirling around the circular road at the rate of 20 miles per hour, with his loose robes flying in the wind. As he clung with a desperate hold to the edge of the roof, grinning with intense interest, and his huddled body shook convulsively with a kind of laughing timidity, while the car spun rapidly around the circle, you might have supposed that the movement, somehow or other, was dependent rather upon the enormous exertions of the uneasy mandarin than upon the power of the little puffing locomotive which was so easily performing its work. While the Japanese were enjoying these specimens of American workmanship, as well as many others, Captain Abbott secured the agreement from the Japanese that on Thursday, March 16, there would be another interview with Commodore Perry at the treaty house on shore.

Because of a storm, the conference for Thursday, March 16, was postponed until the next morning. On Friday, March 17, the Commodore, accompanied by interpreters, secretaries, and two or three of his officers, met the commissioners at the treaty house without the usual military display and ceremony of the former visit. At this meeting, it was agreed that a possible treaty port in lieu of Nagasaki could be the port of Simoda. The Japanese agreed that the Commodore should dispatch one or more vessels to that port, and Japanese of high rank would meet them there, in order to examine the harbor and see if it might be fit for the purpose required. It was agreed that if the port was not suitable, another one somewhere in the southern part of the Japanese empire would be substituted. Accordingly, on March 20, the *Vandalia* and *Southampton* were sent to Simoda to investigate these facilities.

That was the only clear-cut agreement that came out of the conference. However, the Japanese said that they would give a definite answer on Thursday, March 23, to the opening up of another port.

That day, a deputation of Japanese visited the *Powhatan* to suggest that Hakodate be used, to which Perry acceded. His concession offered "a favorable prospect for successful issues of the great purpose of the expedition; and the Commodore now looked forward with sanguine expectations to an early consummation of his labors in the formation of a satisfactory treaty."

On Friday, March 24, 1854, Perry went ashore to receive gifts which had been ordered by the Emperor as a return to the courtesy of the United States. Perry, himself, was given two complete sets of Japanese coins, three matchlocks, and two swords. "These gifts, though of no great intrinsic value, were very significant evidences of the desire of the Japanese to express their respect for the representative of the United States. The mere bestowal of the coins, in direct opposition to the Japanese laws, which forbid absolutely all issuance of money beyond the kingdom was an act of marked favor."

As the Commodore prepared to depart, the commissioner said that there was one article intended for the President that had not yet been exhibited, and showed him one or two hundred sacks of rice that were ready to be sent on board the ships. As that immense supply of substantial food seemed to excite some wonder on the part of the Americans, Yenoske, the interpreter, remarked that it was always customary with the Japanese when bestowing royal presents, to include a certain quantity of rice, although he did not say whether that quantity was always so great.

After a feast, and a series of Japanese wrestling demonstrations, Perry returned to the *Powhatan*. On Monday, March 27, the Japanese commissioners came on board, to be entertained at an uproarious and jovial banquet.

The following day the Commodore recommended once again a conference regarding remaining points of the treaty that was being hammered out.

As soon as the Commodore had taken his seat, a letter was handed to him which, the Japanese stated, they had just received from Simoda. It was from Commander Pope, and had been transmitted through the authorities over land. Its contents gave a satisfactory report of Simoda, and the Commodore said at once that he accepted that port, and declared that it must be opened without delay. Hakodadi, . . . , would do for the other, and Naha, in Lew Chew could be retained for the third. In regard to the other two he was willing he said, to postpone their consideration until some other time.

The Commodore now proposed to sign an agreement in regard to the three ports, and directed his interpreter to read it in Dutch. When the document had been read, and carefully perused by the Japanese, they stated that they were prepared to concur in everything except immediate opening of Hakodate. After discussion, it was finally settled that though the port might be opened, the Japanese would address a note to the Commodore, stating that everything that might be wanted by ships could not be furnished there before the expiration of 10 months, but that wood and water, and whatever else the place possessed, would be supplied immediately. To this note the Commodore promised a reply, and expressed satisfaction with such an arrangement.

During the next several days notes passed between the Commodore and the Japanese commissioner, by which various questions were considered and settled. On March 29, the *Vandalia* and *Southampton* arrived from Simoda with a confirmation of the letter that Commodore Perry had already read. All seemed in readiness for the signing of the treaty.

Friday, March 31, 1854, was selected as the day for the ceremony. At the treaty house, Perry signed three drafts of the treaty "written in the English language, and delivered them to the commissioners, together with three copies of the same in the Dutch and Chinese languages, certified by the interpreters, Mssrs. Williams and Portland, for the United States. At the same time, the Japanese commissioners, on behalf of their government, handed the Commodore three drafts of the treaty written respectively in the Japanese, Chinese, and Dutch languages, signed by the official of their body, especially delegated by the emperor for that purpose." Commodore Perry then presented the Japanese with various gifts and the Japanese commissioners invited the Commodore and his officers to a feast prepared especially for the occasion.

The feast did not impress the Americans. "The dinner given to commissioners on board the *Powhatan* would have made, in quantity, at least a score of that offered by the Japanese on this occasion. To dispose of the subject in one word, the entertainments of the Japanese, generally, while full of hospitality, left an unfavorable impression of their skill in cookery. Lew Chewians evidently excelled them in good living."

On the morning of April 4, 1854, the *Saratoga* sailed, via the Hawaiian Islands, for the United States. Two days later, Commodore Perry went ashore with some of his officers and walked into the country to meet some Japanese. On April 9, notwithstanding a protest from the Japanese, Perry sent word that he would, on the following day, take his steamers as near to Tokyo as the depth of water would allow. Next day, the whole squadron got underway and moved up the bay. After coming within sight of Tokyo, the

Commodore decided not to anchor in front of the city and took his ships back to the "American Anchorage."

After this trip, Commodore Perry concluded that there was no longer any reason to remain so near to Tokyo and began sending his ships away, mostly to Simoda. On April 18, the last ships to leave, the *Powhatan* and the *Mississippi,* made the short trip and joined the *Southampton, Supply,* and *Lexington* there.

During the stay at Simoda, a surveying party made a complete examination of the harbor and recorded items of interest to the navigator. On April 21, the Commodore, with a small number of officers, landed and paid an official visit to the prefect. On his return to the ship he was accompanied by several Japanese officials who made arrangements for the supplies and provisions required by the squadron. On subsequent days, some of the officers began to stroll about the town and neighboring country. They were followed by a squad of soldiers, to which they often objected. The Japanese authorities then agreed that officers would not be followed by soldiers, that they would disperse Japanese whom the sailors might meet, and that houses should not be ordered to close upon the approach of foreigners.

On May 2, the *Macedonian* arrived from the Bonin Islands with a welcome supply of fine turtles.

> The market of Simoda was not well supplied with fresh meats; for, because of the prevailing Buddhism, and the simple habits of the people, there were but few animals which could be obtained for food. Poultry was very scarce, and the few cattle in the place were too much valued as beasts of burden to be readily offered for sacrifice to the carnivorous propensities of strangers; so the arrival of the turtles was very gratefully welcome by those on board ship who, with the exception of supplies of fish and vegetables, had been so long confined to a sea diet of biscuit and salt-junk.

The *Lexington* had sailed for Lew Chew on April 20, and on May 6 the *Macedonian, Vandalia,* and *Southampton* sailed for Hakodate followed a few days later by the *Powhatan* and the *Mississippi.* Perry agreed to return to Simoda to talk with the Japanese again before he left Japan, and the storeship *Supply* was left there. "On leaving the outer harbor, Oho-Sima and other islands of the cluster lying at the entrance of the Gulf of Yedo came in full sight. For the sake of examining the former, and observing more closely the volcano, the steamers were steered so as to pass near its southern end."

After examining the shores of Oshima, they encountered the influence of the ocean current the Japanese called Kuro-Siwo. Lieutenant Silas Bent took particular interest in studying the current and later prepared a report on it. Apparently the current started south of Formosa and divided into two parts upon hitting this island, one part going into the China Sea and the other traveling along the eastern coast of Formosa and the southeastern coastlines of the Japanese islands to the Straits of Sangar. From the south end of Formosa to the Straits of Sangar, its average speed was found to be 35 to 40 miles per day; its width was not ascertained precisely.

> In the latitude of 40° N. and to the eastward of the meridian 143° E. the stream turns more to the eastward, and thus allows a cold counter-current to intervene between it and the southern coast of the island of Yesso. Our hydrographers could not positively ascertain the fact, but they believed that this hyperborean current, found on the coast of Yesso, passes to the westward through the Straits of Sangar down through the Japan sea, between Corea and the Japanese islands, finding an outlet through the Formosa channel into the China sea. The data they had, together with the known fact that a strong southwardly current prevails between Formosa and the coast of China, particularly during the northeast monsoon, when the northwardly current along the east coast of Formosa continues unimpeded, would seem to give probability to this conjecture of the gentlemen. ... The *Vandalia* was ordered from Hakodati, to pass westward through the Straits of Sangar and proceed to China, on the western side of Japan. One object of this was to make observations on current and temperature; but, unfortunately, the Commodore left China before the report was made, and it has never reached him.

The *Powhatan* and *Mississippi* anchored at Hakodate the morning of May 17 and in a few hours several Japanese officials went aboard her. They were presented with a letter the Commodore bore from the Japanese commissioners who had signed the treaty plus the copy of the treaty in the Chinese language. These officials stated that the officers from Tokyo who had been delegated to meet the Americans had not yet come and that the people of the town were greatly alarmed at the arrival of the ships since they had had no previous intimation of the visit and had not even heard of the treaty or the opening of Simoda. Commodore Perry told them that the next day he would send officers ashore to talk with them.

At the time of these talks, preparations were being made for a survey of the harbor that was completed during their stay. After the visit of the Americans on shore, the highest dignitary of the local governing class at Hakodate was received on board the *Mississippi,* where the Commodore temporarily had shifted his flag. Everything seemed to be auspicious for the opening of the port, except for some matters over which the Japanese said that they had no local authority and had to have instructions from the authorities at Tokyo.

On subsequent days, additional meetings took place, either on shore or aboard ship. So smoothly did affairs seem to be going, that on the morning of May 31, the *Macedonian* sailed for Simoda and the *Vandalia* for Shanghai. The next day the delegation from Tokyo arrived. The Commodore, accordingly, sent his flag lieutenant, Bent (Contee having resigned his commission on the return of the squadron to Hong Kong after the first visit to Japan),[14] to meet the Japanese delegates and to make arrangements for them to visit him aboard the *Powhatan*. After some problems in getting the Japanese to meet the Commodore at the time he desired, the meeting was finally held.

The conference went off reasonably well; however, the delegates said that they could not establish the boundaries of Hakodate as far as American interests were concerned. The Commodore decided not to press the matter, but to postpone all negotiations until he could meet the imperial commissioners at Simoda, as the time appointed for such a meeting was rapidly approaching.

> After a farewell visit of ceremony on the shore, and an interchange of courtesies and presents, (among which was a block of granite for the Washington Monument), the *Powhatan* and the *Mississippi,* which were the only vessels of the squadron left, took their departure for Simoda on the 3rd of June 1854. The steamers, however, had hardly got underway at an early sunrise when they were forced to anchor again at the mouth of the bay, because of the onset of a dense fog. It was providential that the weather had remained clear for sufficient time to enable the ships to obtain a safe anchorage. As the day advanced the fog was dissipated, and the two steamers, weighing again, cleared the straits before night.

At Simoda, Commodore Perry settled to his satisfaction all the outstanding matters relative to the opening of the treaty ports at Simoda and Hakodate in a document of additional regulations entitled, "Additional Regulations, Agreed to Between Commodore Matthew C. Perry, special envoy to Japan for the United States of America . . ."[15]

> On the morning of the 28th of June, 1854, the whole squadron got under way; but the wind shifting to the Southward, the *Macedonian* and *Supply* were obliged to anchor again. The Commodore, accordingly, ordered these vessels to warp into a safe berth, and sail when the wind and weather should permit, and to keep company, if possible, to Kelung and Formosa, where they were bound. There seemed no occasion to wait for them, as their destination was different, and any further delay on the part of the steamers would only result in an unnecessary consumption of coal; so the *Mississippi* and the *Powhatan,* with the *Southampton* in tow, stood out to sea and shaped a course to the southward and westward.

Once clear of Simoda, the *Mississippi,* with the *Powhatan* towing *Southampton,* headed for the island of Oshima, which was sighted the next morning. After determining the positions of prominent headlands, a party in charge of Lieutenants Maury and Webb went ashore to investigate a little bay. They met some poorly clad but very civil inhabitants armed with "clubs, stones, and one old firelock" who exchanged fowls and vegetables for bread and pork.

After leaving Oshima, a British ship was encountered, which delayed their entering Naha until July 1. Before entering the harbor, the *Southampton* was released to sail directly to Hong Kong.

At Naha, the captain of the *Lexington* informed Perry that two master's mates in charge of the coal depot at Tumai had been involved in petty incidents. The authorities there did not take them seriously, so relations were not marred.

Another more serious incident was made the subject of an inquiry. A drunk American sailor had attempted to rape a Japanese woman; he was accosted by a group of natives, stoned, chased into the sea, and drowned. The authorities of Naha sentenced one of the natives to banishment for life and five others to banishment for a shorter time. Two other sailors who had gotten drunk with the drowned man were court-martialed, and the case was closed.[16]

Commodore Perry next proceeded to make a treaty with the leaders of Lew Chew, called the "Compact between the United States and the kingdom of Lew Chew," along the same lines as the agreements with the Japanese. In the meantime, while the judicial proceedings in the case of the sailor's death were still underway, all of the coal ashore was transported to the steamers and the coal shed was placed in charge of the local authorities for future use.

On July 12, 1854, the Regent sent Perry a large bell as a gift.* With this on board, plus a stone from Lew Chew for the Washington Monument, the *Powhatan* and *Mississippi* left Naha on July 17, 1854; the *Lexington* had left for Hong Kong on July 15.

When the *Mississippi* arrived in Hong Kong, Commodore Perry found a letter there from the Secretary of the Navy ordering him home, either on the *Mississippi* or as a passenger on a British mail steamer, as he might choose. He selected the latter and arrived in New York via London on January 12, 1855, after an absence of two years and two months.[17]

The expedition terminated officially on April 23, 1855, when ". . . the *Mississippi* reached the Navy yard at Brooklyn, and on the next day the Commodore, repairing on board, and formally hauling down his flag, thus consummated the final act in the story of the United States expedition to Japan."

After hauling down his flag, Perry and a staff spent months in Washington, preparing official reports from all the obtainable records kept by members of the party, and completing work on the charts and other navigational data that were to be presented to the government and the public. The presents received from the Japanese were checked and properly distributed. The report was completed with the help of the Reverend Francis L. Hawks, rector of Perry's church in New York, and some former members

---

*The bell now stands in front of Bancroft Hall at the U.S. Naval Academy.

of the expedition. It included much of the charts and other navigational work in three volumes, costing about $360,000 to prepare, which were printed by the government in 1856.

The first two volumes were titled *Narrative of the Expedition of an American Squadron to the China Seas and Japan, performed in the years 1852, 1853 and 1854, under the Command of Commodore M. C. Perry, United States Navy.* The first volume contained the narrative portion of the report with observations on the economic, political, religious and social situation in Japan with some comparisons with conditions in China. The second volume contained scientific papers written by expedition members, miscellaneous material, and descriptions by John Cassin, Asa Gray, and others of the natural history specimens collected. Both were illustrated. The third volume was titled *United States Japan Expedition Observations on the Zodiacal Light from April 2, 1853, to April 22, 1855. Made Chiefly on Board The United States Steam-Frigate Mississippi During Her Late Cruise in Eastern Seas, and Her Voyage Homeward: With Conclusions From the Data Thus Obtained,* by Rev. George Jones, A.M., Chaplain, United States Navy, volume 3 (Washington, D.C.: Beverley Tucker, Senate Printer, 1856). The same year a smaller-sized volume 1, without many of the illustrations contained in the larger version, was published for Perry in New York by D. Appleton and Company. In 1855, the Senate printed the Official Correspondence as *Senate Ex. Doc. No. 34,* serial no. 751, and in the same year sailing directions for Tokyo, Simoda, Hakodate, Naha, and Lloyd's Harbor in the Bonin Islands, based on the expedition's work appeared in Matthew Fontaine Maury's *"Sailing Directions."* Within a few years, articles began to appear in scholarly journals such as the *Bulletin of the American Geographical and Statistical Society,* which in 1856 printed "The Japanese Gulf Stream," by Lieutenant Silas Bent. Later some private accounts by members of the expedition were printed, but many such sources remained in manuscript until recent years. Excepting all personal gifts, the bulk of the presents were deposited with the Smithsonian Institution.[18]

When it became known in the United States that the expedition to the China Seas and Japan had completed its mission successfully, newspapers and periodicals printed many laudatory and boastful articles. Perry was publicly congratulated and feted at social functions, including a formal state dinner in Washington, and was granted a bonus of $20,000 by Congress. Such honors were not long enjoyed. Soon after his receiving orders to command the Mediterranean Squadron, Perry died, on March 4, 1858.

By that time, nine citizens of the United States had visited Japan under the protection of the treaty he had made. Townshend Harris, the first American Consul in Japan, had negotiated a commercial treaty which provided the basis, to 1941, for Japanese-American relations in Japan. In 1860, the Japanese 292-ton steamer of war *Kanrin Maru,* carrying 57 men, 10 guns, and coal for nine days of steaming, reached San Francisco.[19] The successful expedition to Japan commanded by Commodore Matthew C. Perry had provided the wedge for Japanese entry onto the world stage in a part that was destined to become more important and forceful in subsequent years.

# Various Expeditions to Explore the Isthmus of Darien, 1854-1857

On the morning of January 17, 1854, the USS *Cyane* anchored in Caledonia Bay, on the Atlantic coast of the Isthmus of Darien. There she was to land an exploring party with orders to investigate the region between Caledonia Bay and Darien Harbor on the Pacific coast and determine whether the region was suitable for the construction of an inter-oceanic canal.[1]

Almost immediately the ship was boarded by Indians of the Cuna tribe. As they controlled the route between Caledonia Bay and Darien Harbor, and were known not to welcome foreign travelers, Captain George Nichols Hollins requested a meeting with the local Indians and others from the interior for the purpose of getting permission to explore their territory.

On January 18, Captain Hollins and Lieutenant Isaac G. Strain met with the Indians to argue for unmolested passage across Cuna territory. The party, under Strain, was to include volunteers from the *Cyane* as well as men specifically ordered to the expedition and consisted of 12 officers* and 13 seamen, plus two delegates from the government of New Granada.

The Indians, from all available evidence, acted fearlessly and were intelligent and observant; some of them spoke broken English or Spanish. They all opposed the expedition. For about 18 hours, they presented a number of arguments in support of their position. One was that if God had wanted an exploration of their territory to be made for the purpose of determining whether a canal could be built there, the facilities for such a journey and such a construction project would have been provided. Since this had not been done, the Indians felt that they should not be disturbed in the quiet possession of the land that God had given to them. Finally, concluding that the exploring party would land, with or without their permission, they gave their consent, since it seemed to be the will of God; they stipulated only that

---

*Passed Midshipman William T. Truxtun, Midshipman H. M. Garland, First Assistant Engineer J. M. Maury, Assistant Engineers A. T. Boggs, S. H. Kettlewell, J. Sterret Hollis, George U. Mayo and three other civilian volunteers (assistant engineers) Theodore Winthrop, Frederick Avery, and a Mr. Holcomb, plus Dr. J. C. Bird, of Wilmington, Delaware (surgeon). Maury was appointed astronomer and secretary. Truxtun was appointed acting master and executive officer. Passed Midshipman Charles Latimer received orders, but did not join due to illness.

their property was not to be disturbed and their women were not to be harmed. This agreement was celebrated by a hearty meal, during which the Indians indulged freely but not immoderately in alcoholic beverages.

On January 19, 1854, Strain and his group disembarked. Their equipment, averaging about 50 pounds per individual, included provisions for 10 days, blankets, clothing and toilet articles, and a variety of arms and ammunition: a Sharp's rifle, a fowling piece, carbines, muskets with 40 rounds of ball cartridges, and revolvers with 50 rounds of ammunition for each. The amount of provisions and equipment was as much as a man could carry through the wilderness and tropical climate that they would encounter and was considered to be more than adequate. Even when one boat capsized in the surf with the loss of some food, Strain did not feel that the safety of his mission was jeopardized.

Despite the mishap of the overturned boat, the exploring party landed with confident spirits and marched to an abandoned Indian fishing village at the mouth of the Caledonia River. Here they found good water and spent the night. Four armed sentinels were posted, and the others tried to sleep despite the incessant booming of the surf.

So began Lieutenant Isaac Strain's mission to the Isthmus of Darien. Born on March 4, 1821, Strain entered the Navy as a Midshipman on December 11, 1837. He had served in the *Erie* in the West Indies and in the *Concord* and *Marion* off the Brazilian Coast. In 1842, he entered the Naval School at Philadelphia, where he remained for a year. He volunteered in 1843 for command of a private exploration expedition, partly financed by the Academy of Natural Sciences of Philadelphia, to explore the interior of South America. For this purpose, he obtained a two years' leave of absence.

The party of six people, including a civil engineer, two naturalists, and a man with some knowledge of law, was sent to Rio de Janeiro in the USS *Levant*. Strain went to some personal expense to help outfit the expedition and induced the Navy Department to loan instruments for determining positions and making magnetic observations. He achieved some official standing for his expedition by obtaining Navy Department orders to make magnetic observations. On December 8, 1843, in Rio de Janeiro, Strain advised the Navy Department that the party would leave the next day for the interior. What happened after the journey began remains somewhat of a mystery. Evidently, the men who accompanied Strain lacked the stamina and fortitude necessary for travel and life in the interior of Brazil, and one by one they deserted from the expedition. Since the other members of the group were civilians and the expedition was not under official orders from the Navy Department, Strain could not count on naval discipline to keep his party together. It might also be surmised that at this early stage in his career Strain lacked the leadership and command qualities necessary to control a party of this sort. His subsequent career gave him the opportunity to develop the characteristics of an expedition leader, and his later successes indicate that his failure to keep the 1844 expedition together was not due to any intrinsic weakness in leadership ability, but rather to lack of experience as well as the absence of naval discipline.

Whatever the problem, on September 3, 1844, Captain John Percival of the *Constitution* found Passed Midshipman Strain in Rio. Strain's expedition had failed through the desertion of all his companions, except one. Percival had a vacancy for a Passed Midshipman, took Strain aboard, and asked the Navy Department to approve his action.

For the next four years, Strain served in the *Constitution* in the East Indies, in the *Columbia* on the coast of Brazil, and in the *Ohio* on the Pacific station. While the *Ohio* lay at La Paz, Baja California, Strain landed and explored the peninsula as far as time would allow. He then requested permission to spend six months in South America and to return to the United States at his own expense. In 1849, he was detached from the Pacific Squadron, proceeded to Valparaiso, Chile, and crossed the continent to Buenos Aires. His observations of this trip were published in 1853 under the title *Cordillera and Pampa, Mountain and Plain: Sketches of the Journey in Chile and the Argentine Provinces in 1849.*[2]

In 1850, Strain was lent by the Navy Department to the Interior Department to serve on the Mexican Boundary Commission. Then he was ordered to the African Squadron. On February 6, 1851, Strain wrote to the Navy Department from the *John Adams* at Norfolk, requesting permission to test an instrument he had developed for ascertaining whether a ship was trimmed by the head or stern, or whether it was on an even keel. He stated that his device had been recommended by the Chiefs of the Bureaus of the Navy Department to whom it had been referred. There is no evidence to indicate that Strain tested this instrument or that the test was successful.[3]

After a year in the African Squadron, Strain returned to the United States. In Washington, he furnished the Secretary of the Navy a highly commendatory letter from Commodore E. A. F. Lavalette, Commander in Chief of the African Squadron, relative to his work on that station, in support of his application for orders to lead an exploring party to survey the Isthmus of Darien relative to the possibility of constructing an inter-oceanic canal there.

Strain's desire to explore the Isthmus of Darien had been aroused by events in England, where in 1850, an Irish doctor, Edward Cullen, had created a sensation with the announcement that he had found a short and easy canal route between Caledonia Bay and the junctions of the Lara and the Sabana rivers. Cullen based his announcement on the supposed discovery of a gap no more than 150 feet above sea level in the mountains traversing that region. Cullen insisted that in 1849 he had journeyed across the Isthmus several times without any great difficulty, and that each journey took only a few hours.

Cullen's confident announcement convinced three fairly distinguished engineers—Charles Fox, John Henderson, and Thomas Brassey—who formed a syndicate to finance a preliminary survey of Cullen's route and hired an engineer of excellent reputation, Lionel Gisborne, to carry out the exploration. In 1852, Gisborne, with an assistant, H. C. Forde, began their survey. They were unable to locate Cullen's pass, and soon became lost. Finally a band of Cuna Indians very forcefully told them to return to their starting point and threatened them with death if they did not. Mistakenly thinking that they had already crossed the main mountain range and that anything further would not be very productive, the engineers returned to Caledonia Bay.

From Aspinwall, they crossed to Panama, and began a fresh start from the Pacific side, through Darien Harbor and up the Sabana river. A few miles above the point where the Lara and Sabana rivers come together they set out on foot overland. They soon came to water that they thought flowed east with a gradual trend to the northeast, and came to the conclusion that because of the topography it must flow into the Atlantic. This conclusion was erroneous; the dense forest prevented any sort of a clear view for more than a few yards, and they could not see high mountains that still barred their way to the Atlantic Ocean.

Gisborne and Forde reached Panama again on July 30, and returned to England. All in all they had spent about 40 days in Central America and about eight days in actual exploration of the Darien Isthmus. Although they had seen almost nothing of the country and had done no detailed surveying, Forde presented a very optimistic report and recommended the construction of a sea level canal to cost $60,000,000.

On the basis of this recommendation, Fox, Henderson, and Brassey reorganized themselves as the Atlantic and Pacific Junction Company. They issued a prospectus inviting the public to subscribe $375,000 for the purchase of a concession across the Isthmus and the execution of a more detailed survey, supervision of which was entrusted to Gisborne and Forde.

Because this new company hoped to dispose of stock in countries other than England, they asked the governments of Great Britain, France, the United States, and New Granada to participate officially in the explorations. France detailed one ship. New Granada assigned a Colonel Codazzi, head of the National Topographical Commission, with two special delegates and furnished a large corps of laborers, including many convicts, to the project. Great Britain made the brig *Espiegle* and schooner *Scorpion* available on the Atlantic side and the steam-sloop *Virago* on the Pacific side. The United States Navy Department was at first loath to participate. Lieutenant Strain learned of the cooperative project when he returned to Washington in 1853, and made very earnest pleas to lead a naval exploring party in the venture. Reluctantly, the Department agreed. On December 12, 1853, Secretary of the Navy James C. Dobbin issued orders to Captain Hollins of the *Cyane* that indicated nothing more than grudging acquiescence: "You are sent on this expedition because it is within the limits of the cruising grounds of the home squadron and it can add but little to the ordinary expenses; the results may prove beneficial to the commerce of the world."[4] In separate instructions, Strain was cautioned to act in cooperation with the other expeditions.

The British were the first to begin the exploration of the Isthmus. On December 19, 1853, a group from the *Virago* ascended the Sabana River as far as possible in small boats and then began to walk in what they considered to be the direction of Puerto Escoces on the Atlantic coast. For 15 days they struggled through the jungle, to cover about 26 miles. On January 2, the commander divided the expedition, leaving four seamen to guard their provisions while the rest pushed on for two more days. Even then they had not attained the main divide, although they had reached an altitude of at least 800 feet, and had not started down toward the Atlantic. Fearing Indian attack, they decided to return, only to find the four seamen and provisions gone. They finally found three men dead of gunshot wounds. The fourth man was never found, and it was presumed that he was either killed or taken prisoner. Afraid that they would be attacked, the party left the bodies where they lay, hurried to their boats, and returned to their ship.[5]

When the *Cyane* party arrived at Caledonia Bay on January 17, 1854, the only indication that they were part of an international operation was the presence of the two delegates of New Granada. Hollins and Strain, moreover, were unaware of the difficulties encountered by the exploring party from the *Virago*. They decided that there was no compelling reason to wait for the ships from France or Great Britain, or for Gisborne, Forde, and the rest of the New Granada contingent. Strain, now in his fourth expedition, considered himself an experienced traveler. On the basis of the reports by Cullen, Gisborne, and Forde, he did not expect any problems that he could not solve in less than ten days. He especially minimized the Indian danger. On January 10, 1854, he had written to the Secretary of the Navy: "We have many rumors in regard to the hostility of the Darien Indians. . . . All I believe to be exaggerated. . . ."[6]

After spending their first night ashore in the Indian village, the party moved into the interior on January 20. Officers and men wore blue flannel shirts, blue trousers and belts, with a white star on their shirt collars. The seamen wore blue caps with visors, while the officers wore Panama hats. Everyone, except Kettlewell, the draftsman, was armed. Strain carried a spy glass. Machetes were used to help clear the way.

For the first few days, they followed the bed of the Caledonia River. Several abandoned Indian campsites were found, producing a measure of uneasiness because they had apparently been abandoned in haste at the approach of the white men. In his instructions to Captain Hollins, Secretary of the Navy Dobbin had ordered him to instruct Strain "that should unfortunately any obstacle be interposed by the Indian tribes," Strain was to "retire from the undertaking unless it can be accomplished without un-friendly collision and . . . hazard of human life. . . ." The refusal of the In-dians to meet the white men was not a good augury of cooperation. Strain hoped for the best and carefully watched that no one disturb Indian property and thereby give the Indians a pretext for an attack.

At night, the seamen ate separately, although they all had the same menu of salt pork, coffee or tea, plus whatever extras they had picked up along the way. Sentinels were posted, and the officers and seamen sat around their respective fires smoking, telling stories, or singing until they turned in, in pairs, with one blanket beneath and the other above them under the open sky.

At the break of day, the boatswain's call "heave round" brought every man to his feet. Usually the next call was "saddle up," and the men got in line ready to march. Breakfast came only after the camp was some distance behind. During the first two days, the men sang such songs as "Caledonia is a hard stream to travel" to the tune of "Jordan is a hard road to travel."

On January 22, Strain decided to leave the river since it seemed to be heading too far southward toward a very high range of mountains. They were at a place where the river banks were high and steep, making the ascent out of the river very difficult. As the party climbed out of the river bed, Strain found a well-defined path leading over the mountains to the southward and westward that he thought was the Indian route to the Pacific. He decided to follow this route, but then found that Assistant-Engineer Hollis, Dr. Bird, and three seamen were missing. They had im-patiently climbed to the top of the river bank by a different route and be-come separated from the main party. Strain fired three shots—the agreed upon signal to close immediately. Answering shots were heard, but despite a wait of some minutes, the missing men did not show up. More shots were fired and were answered, but the responses became more and more faint and distant. Finally Strain decided to continue on in the hope that the missing men were ahead of the party. They failed to come into camp that night. The next morning, search parties found no trace of them, so Strain gave the order to go forward again since he felt that further delay might endanger those still under his command as well as the success of the expedition. Luckily, the five missing men found their way back to Caledonia Bay and re-joined the *Cyane*.

The Strain party soon came to the Sucubti River, which on the maps made public by Cullen and Gisborne, looked as if it flowed into the Sabana, but which actually drained into the tortuous and twisting Chucunaque River. Strain, believing that he had found a river road to the Sabana, directed his group to walk along the stream, the bed of which was covered with huge boulders and masses of stone rolled together that made passage very difficult. At 5 o'clock, tired and hungry, they camped at the mouth of a small tributary stream, having walked only eight or nine miles.

The next day, January 24, about 11 a.m., they found some Indian huts recently abandoned and burning. This looked ominous, and Strain repeated his orders that nothing belonging to the Indians, even food from their plantations and storehouses, was to be touched.

On this day the group walked about ten miles, and at 6 p.m., finding what they considered to be a defensible position, pitched their camp. For the first time there was no song or laughter; they were too tired. To help enliven their spirits, all hands shared a bottle of medicinal brandy. Because of the rough going, they feared the bottle would soon be broken in any case.

Next day they again found the river bed very difficult to follow; the banks were almost closed by dense undergrowth. By noon they had covered only three miles. Soon they came to some plantain fields and heard the distant barking of a dog. A halt was called while they consulted about their next move. Their position was dangerous, the Indians could attack almost unseen from the river banks, and there was very little cover. They decided to press ahead until they were out of the vicinity or until the banks provided the possibility of leaving the river and taking cover in case of an attack. They followed a narrow ledge, two feet wide, until it ended and they had to take to the river again. Next they came to several abandoned houses situated amidst plantain and other fruit trees, and the remains of seven canoes which had just been destroyed. At this point Strain decided to try marching on land again, so they crossed the river, entered a path which seemed to follow the right bank, and met five Indians approaching rapidly.

After but a moment's reflection, Strain decided to try to convince them that he and his group were friendly. He handed his carbine to the man behind him and advanced toward the Indians calling out in Spanish that he came in friendship.

When Strain came close enough he recognized two of the Indians as having been on board the *Cyane* on January 18. One of them spoke a little English, one spoke Spanish intelligibly, and the others used the Sucubti dialect. They all shook hands with Strain and the leader told them they were on the Chucunaque instead of the Sabana, and offered to lead them to the Sabana.

Strain was beginning to doubt the wisdom of continuing on the river that they had followed for some days. He asked the Indian leader how long it would take to get to the Sabana, and when he was told three days, Strain decided to accept the offer, but took the precaution of detailing Truxtun to act as rear-guard and ordered him to blaze a trail with a machete as they proceeded.

That night they camped in a deep ravine through which a rivulet flowed. The Indians left, promising to return in the morning with some plantains. After a supper of pork and biscuits, the watch was set and officers and men bedded down where the bank of the rivulet gave a certain barrier against attack from the rear. Fires were lit some distance away so as to mislead any surprise attackers.

The next morning the Indians returned with two new companions but no plantains. The Indians advised the party to supply themselves with water from the rivulet since future supplies might be scarce, and the march would be severe. Strain and his men filled their bottles and flasks, drank deeply from the rivulet, and began walking along a path going westward over a very steep hill some 800 feet in height. Reaching the summit, they saw many higher ranges and peaks to the northward and, resting for only a short time, began the descent.

Most of the time they went up and down hills, climbed and slid over boulders, and generally floundered over one of the most broken countries imaginable. During one ascent, seaman Edward Lombard, who carried the boatswain's whistle, was stung on the hand by a scorpion. Strain asked Lombard to drink a little brandy, but Lombard was a "temperance man" and declined to do so until given a direct order. After drinking the brandy and putting wet tobacco on his wound, he rallied and became as active and energetic as before.

At another point the group met a number of new Indians, the chief of whom gave a speech of some vehemence that Strain's guide refused to interpret. When the march started again some of these new Indians accompanied the exploring party.

That night, after walking 12 miles, they camped by a small stream in front of plantain groves. Both officers and men were dead tired, and, to add to their problems, the English-speaking Indian announced that he had to leave them, but that friends of his would take them on to the Sabana, a march of about a day and a half.

At this point, Strain estimated that they were at least seven days' hard march from the *Cyane,* with less than one day's provisions and very doubtful guides, a position not pleasant to contemplate.

The next morning, as the group fixed breakfast, about forty Indians were seen watching the camp, and some of them strolled in to investigate more closely. Among them was the old guide who said again that he could not accompany Strain, but who also reaffirmed that the Sabana was a day and a half away and that new guides would take the exploring party there. From the point at which they would reach the Sabana it was only two and a half days' journey by canoe to Darien Harbor.

Strain attempted to buy provisions but the Indians would neither give nor sell. Strain then said that if they would neither give nor sell the fruit from their trees, he might have to take it to avoid starvation. He received no response.

There seemed to be no choice but to follow the new guides, who took position about 100 yards ahead and walked very rapidly. They appeared determined to allow no time for rest, and when the exploring party began to slow down the Indians disappeared. Strain halted, shouted for the Indians, and receiving no answer, gave the order to countermarch. Disappointed and frustrated, the group slowly and with difficulty returned to the camp they had just left.

Here all the officers, the New Granadian delegates, and the engineers held a council of war. As Strain interpreted their maps, they were on the banks of the River Iglesias that flowed into the Sabana near the mouth of the larger river. It was possible, however, that they were in the upper reaches of the winding, long, and fantastically tortuous Chucunaque, along the lower reaches of which there were white settlements. The question was whether they should strike out on their own across the mountains in an attempt to reach the Sabana by the path traveled that morning, or whether they should follow the river. It was decided unanimously to take the river route. No proposition was made to return to the ship.

This was a tragic decision, for only five or six miles westward was the trail cut by the party from HMS *Virago* which would have led them to the Sabana and Darien Harbor. Strain and his men, knowing nothing of the HMS *Virago's* exploring efforts nor of the existence of such a trail, chose to follow the river to the coast, or a settled area, rather than enter unknown country where even water might not be available.

Actually, the river they voted to follow was indeed the Chucunaque, a river so crooked that "it would be almost impossible to double up a stream so as to get more length in the same space." On the morning of January 29, the exploring party left camp at 9 a.m., "many of the party with legs and hands much swollen from the bites of mosquitos and sand-flies, and one of the engineers completely speckled with their bites and badly swollen." For the next 15 days as they attempted to follow the twists and turns of the river, their physical condition deteriorated under the bites of insects, the hardships of the terrain, and the lack of food. Several times they took to the river on makeshift rafts, but were soon stopped by obstructions in the river. They ate iguanas, hawks, cranes, a few "turkeys," as well as plantains, bananas, palmetto leaves, and various seeds of trees resembling nuts. Eventually, they made most use of a palm nut covered with an acid pulp. This food helped to meet the pangs of hunger, but the acid covering attacked the enamel of the teeth and interfered with the digestive processes to the extent that vomiting and stomach pains became common.

In the first few days the men kept up their discipline and spirits with stories and songs. "One man, named Wilson, had a superb voice, and he made the woods echo with Negro songs—'Ole Virginny' and 'Jim Crow;' and often during the day his comic songs would bring peals of laughter from the party, and discordant choruses would burst forth on every side. Another had made a fife out of a reed, which he played on with considerable skill, and made the camp merry with its music."

By February 12, Strain concluded that if they were to survive they needed help more quickly than the pace of the whole group was likely to provide. The undergrowth was so thick that two men at a time had to take turns cutting a path while the others waited. It took hours to advance even a half mile. Food was so scarce they killed a buzzard and tried to prepare it for eating. The smell made them decide otherwise, but the mere attempt, plus the diminishment of song and merriment as the physical condition of the group deteriorated, convinced Strain that he should take a few of the strongest men ahead as rapidly as possible for help. His journal noted:

> Proceeded down stream about a quarter of a mile, when finding a place to camp, built a fire and spread our blankets in the mild moonlight. We all felt downhearted tonight, being without anything to eat, and not having eaten enough each man for the six or eight days to make one good meal; our clothes all in pieces, and nearly all almost shoeless and bootless. Have no idea where we are, nor, of course, when we shall reach the Pacific. The sick almost discouraged, and ready to be left in the woods to take their chances. I would freely give twenty dollars for a pound of meat, but money is of no use here.

Early the next morning, Strain announced that he had decided to leave the party and by forced marches reach the settlements he believed to be down river. He called for three volunteers to go with him and chose the three men he considered to be in best physical condition. The rest he placed under the command of Truxtun, with orders to continue along the river in easy stages. Strain and his party carried two machetes, a small pocket-compass, blankets, the Sharp's rifle, two carbines, two Colt's revolvers, and their empty haversacks. The best compass was left with the main party to take the bearings of the river and direct their course, as was a double-barreled fowling piece.

Without breakfast, but with hope, Strain and his volunteers set out from the main party at a good pace. That day they traveled about 15 miles without food. The next day, February 14, they started at dawn, again without breakfast. Soon they had to cut a path through dense undergrowth, and later an impassable swamp forced them to retrace their steps. Discouraged by the difficulties of walking along the river banks, Strain decided to build another raft and try floating down the river again. With great difficulty they succeeded in constructing a raft, and after eating some acid nuts they fell asleep on a hard clay bank beside the river.

The next day, in spite of obstacles in the river, they were able to float downstream for a time. At one point, they had to take the raft apart and float each log over a shallow stretch in the river and then assemble it again. They were compensated for this effort, however, by the discovery of some 120 clams "said to be nearly identical with the 'Little Neck Clams' of New York—which they eagerly devoured."

The raft was caught by a swift current the next day, and two men were pushed off by overhanging branches. One of them had the matches, and since it was impossible to strike fire by other means, the camp that night was damp and dark.

On February 17, the day after the wetting incident, Strain decided to abandon the raft and try walking again. Painfully marching "around swamps, through thickets, still on, toward an ocean that seemed infinitely removed—the half-naked, half-starved group cut their toilsome, disheartening way," subsisting mostly on acid nuts, with a few birds, fish, and a monkey for a change in diet.

On Saturday, February 25, Strain's journal recorded that they

Slept well last night, the camp being free from mosquitoes. Set out at eight a.m., and found bad walking all day, both in the forest and on the beaches which we met. In the former we had to cut our way, while the beaches were so steep that we had sometimes to cut steps to crawl along, and even then we were in constant danger of falling into the river, which I did on one occasion.

Encamped about six p.m. on a mud bank, having made about six miles. During the day's march we found about thirty-two clams, which, divided, gave us something to support life, as the acid nut-skins are less ripe than some miles above, while their kernels are so hard as to be almost inedible in the existing state of our teeth, which have been deprived of their enamel by the use of the acid.

Saw several turkeys, but could obtain none, owing to the state of our fire arms, which had become almost useless. My carbine, which was the best in the party, being loaded with difficulty, and requiring two men to fire it, one to take aim and pull the trigger, and the other to pull the cock back, and let it go at the word, invariably destroying the aim; under these circumstances I am not ashamed to say that I fired several times at turkeys without success.

About sunset we saw a wild hog, weighing some 300 pounds, which came rushing toward us as if intending to attack, but paused about twenty yards distant. Considering the ferocity of this animal, and the state of our firearms, I should have hesitated in attacking him had we not been so pressed for food; but it was a matter of life and death in either case. I took deliberate aim at his body behind his shoulders, and with the assistance of Wilson fired my carbine, wounding him severely. I feared firing at his head, lest I should miss him altogether. After receiving the ball he paused a moment, as if uncertain whether to attack, after which he rushed off rapidly some fifty yards; when he was seized with a coughing fit, and slackened his pace to a walk. Handing my carbine to Wilson to reload, I followed him into the jungle, but soon lost him in the darkness of the forest. I am inclined to believe that this animal was not the peccary or wild hog of tropical climates, but one of the domesticated species, which, either in his own generation or that of his progenitors had become wild, because I do not think the peccary ever grow so large. His color was black with white spots. I passed an almost sleepless night in regretting that we had not obtained him, for at this time food was our only thought, except to push through and obtain assistance for those behind.

On March 1 or 2, they built a two-man raft, and for the next few days Strain and another man floated down river on the raft while the two who objected to using it walked. On March 9, Strain went into the forest away from the river to look for food. When he returned, the men who had been left with the raft were gone. He concluded from the fact that there was no evidence of violence that they had been picked up by friendly natives. He floated downstream on the raft and soon met two canoes paddled by friendly Indians. Strain immediately borrowed a pipe and tobacco and "for the first time since the 4th of February, enjoyed the luxury of a smoke."

The Indians brought Strain to the village of Yavisa where his companions were waiting. Here they were fed, and Strain learned that the HMS *Virago* was at Darien Harbor but was due to sail in a few days for Panama. He decided to try to reach her to obtain provisions, while at the same time sending the healthiest of his three companions up river with provisions and canoes on the assumption that the main party must have followed for some distance and would not be too far away.

Deciding upon a course of action was one thing, but implementing it was another. The Indians were reluctant to go up river; canoes were difficult to obtain, and provisions had to be purchased. Luckily Strain had retained enough money so he was just barely able to purchase provisions for the main party. By dint of persistence and cajolery, canoes and men were obtained. Strain himself obtained a ride to Darien Harbor, thanks to a white man, Mr. Lucre, who lived in Santa Maria de Real, a village just below Yavisa, and who told Strain to use his canoe beyond that point.

Strain arrived at Darien Harbor on March 12, and to his disappointment learned that the *Virago* had sailed two days before and was not due back until March 17. He also was told of a supply depot of the Atlantic and Pacific Junction Company on the Sabana River, in charge of W. C. Bennett. Strain decided to go there for help, and set out the next morning. He arrived in the early afternoon, was received with warmth and given provisions, and later the same day started back for Yavisa, where he arrived on March 15.

Two days later the party which Strain had sent up river returned, bringing with them only one man from the main group, a seaman named Parks. When Strain and his volunteers left the main party on February 13, Truxtun and his men had obeyed orders and slowly followed down the river, making fewer miles each day as they grew weaker and more despondent. Food was so scarce no one thought of turning away from buzzard. Once they killed an 18-pound wild pig, which gave them a fairly substantial meal.

After 19 days some of the men were near death. On Saturday, March 4, a seaman named Holmes did die. The next day Parks wandered away from the main party. He was the first man brought back to Yavisa by Strain's rescue party. Twenty-one days after Strain's departure, a council was held and it was decided to try to retrace their steps in order to reach the Indian plantain and banana fields that they had passed. If Strain had not been able to bring relief in 21 days, to continue following him seemed madness, for death had in all likelihood taken him. Thus, to the strains of "Up anchor for home" on the boatswain's pipe, the group started back and Truxtun left the following letter in a detonating cap-pouch, hung on a cross over Holmes' grave:

> Dear Strain—This is Holmes's grave. He died yesterday, March 4, partly from disease and partly from starvation. The rapidly failing strength of my party, combined with the earnest solicitation of the officers and men, and your long-continued absence, have induced me to turn back to the ship. If you can come up with provisions soon, for God's sake try to overtake us, for we are nearly starving. I have, however, no doubt of reaching the plantain patches if the party be able to hold out on slow marches and reaching them, I intend to recruit. Since you left I have been detained in camp eighteen days by the sickness of Holmes and the Spaniards [representatives of New Granada].
>
> I trust I am right in going back and that when you know all more fully, you will approve of my conduct in the course, the more particularly as even the palm-nuts and palmetto are no longer sufficiently abundant as we advance for our sustenance, and as I am now convinced that something most serious has happened to yourself and party to prevent your return to us. After long and serious deliberation with the officers, I have come to the conclusion that the only means of securing the safety of the party, of saving the lives of several, if not all, is at once to return in the way and to the place of provisions.
>
> With the kindest remembrances and best wishes of the party for your safe return to the *Cyane* and a happy meeting aboard, I am, yours truly,— W. T. Truxtun.

From March 6 to 22, the party struggled along the banks of the river, passing and sometimes stopping in the camps that had been made on the way down. During this time one of the New Granadian delegates died, another stayed behind because he could not keep up, and later died, and Lombard, the seaman who carried the boatswain's whistle was left behind, at his own request, to die. On Thursday, March 23, it seemed clear that three more men would have to be left behind to die, and the camp that night might justly be described as despondently forlorn. It was then that Strain and his rescue party arrived, and Truxtun and the main party were brought "up the steeps of despair to hope and life once more."

When Strain's first rescue party had come down the river with only the seaman, Parks, who had wandered away from the main group, Strain decided to go for help to the *Virago,* which returned to Darien Harbor that same day. The next morning, as he was organizing a new rescue attempt, Parks died. Strain arranged for his burial and then set out again for Darien Harbor.

After travelling all day—some sixteen or eighteen miles—Strain met a boat party from the *Virago* commanded by Lieutenant W. C. Forsyth, RN, and accompanied by W. C. Bennett, of the Atlantic and Pacific Junction Company's station. When Bennett had heard the *Virago's* guns at the mouth of the Sabana, he had traveled by canoe to report Strain's predicament. It was due to this action that assistance from the *Virago* was dispatched so promptly.

Strain transferred to the *Virago* boat and they all traveled to Yavisa. The next morning, after they had "partly by entreaties and partly force" obtained the services of three canoes and native rowers, the party set out in search of Truxtun and his men. In three days they reached a point beyond which the boat could not go. Here they were joined by two more canoes with Indian rowers, and leaving the *Virago's* boat with eight men, the rest started off in the canoes. The seamen from the *Virago* proved to be very dexterous with the canoes, which was "accounted for by the fact that the *Virago* had been for some time under repair in Puget Sound, on the northwest coast of America where the sailors had frequent opportunities of amusing themselves with the canoes of the Indians, which are much less stable even than those of the Isthmus." This skill proved invaluable in meeting obstacles, such as fallen trees, that Strain and his men had encountered on the way down.

As the rescue party struggled up the river, they found the graves of the two men who had died, and the body of the New Granadian delegate who had been left behind by the main party. This filled them with great anxiety, and it was with almost indescribable joy that Strain again met Truxtun and the survivors on March 23.

The rest of the account of the expedition is anti-climactic, yet it includes dramatic as well as tragic incidents. The American flag taken ashore from the *Cyane* had been carried to the last by a seaman named M'Guiness. He had wrapped it around his body, and though almost everything else had been thrown away, he would not part with it. On the journey back to Yavisa after the rescue party had found Truxtun and his men, Strain, without thinking, ordered M'Guiness to place his flag in Strain's canoe. M'Guiness did not obey the order immediately, and

> cast such an appealing look to Strain, that the latter asked him what was the matter. His eyes instantly filled with tears, and he replied: "Captain, I have never parted with this ensign a single instant since you trusted it to my care on the Atlantic coast, and don't take it from me now." Touched by the noble devotion of the man, he replied: "By no means, my brave fellow, shall it be taken from you; display it yourself!" His face beamed a smile of

thankfulness, and unbinding it with his skeleton hand from the rags that but hardly covered him, he gave it, tattered and torn, to the wind, and three cheers went up from the little fleet. There is a whole poem in this little incident. That flag had been displayed when they marched from the beach at Caledonia Bay, it was now unrolled to announce their deliverance. Once more only was it used, and then to shroud the coffin of one of their number.

Soon after the arrival of Strain and his rescue party, Philip Vermilyea, seaman, died. He was buried at Yavisa before they left for Darien Harbor, which they reached on March 29. Here Strain chartered a 40-foot open boat, and left the group behind as he sailed for Panama, 90 miles away. At Panama he hired mules for the journey across the Isthmus to Colon and the *Cyane.* Since he and his men had long been given up as dead, Strain's reunion with Captain Hollins and others aboard the *Cyane* was a lively and touching affair.

Strain did not stop long enough to enjoy the attention he got, for after obtaining some money from Captain Hollins, he returned to Panama, chartered a sloop, and sailed back to Darien Harbor. The officers and seamen left there were well except Assistant Engineer Boggs. It was hoped that Boggs would rally when they brought him to Panama, but the day after they arrived in Panama, Boggs died and was buried there. The others hastened across the Isthmus and on April 25, 1854, boarded the *Cyane.* The ship at once hoisted sail and got underway for home, arriving at the Brooklyn Navy Yard, New York, on May 18, 1854.

When it became known in the United States that Strain with most of his officers and seamen had not perished in the wilderness of the Darien Isthmus, newspapers printed expressions of surprise—for the exploring party had been given up for dead—and of joy. At the same time some periodicals and newspapers such as *Harpers New Monthly Magazine* and *Littell's Living Age* called for an end to the exploration of the Caledonia Bay–Darien Harbor area as a proposed inter-oceanic canal route since Strain's experience had shown such a project to be impracticable.[7]

This attitude did not indicate lack of interest in the story of the Darien exploring party's adventures. On the contrary, Strain was ordered to Washington to report in person to the Navy Department, and subsequently he was asked to talk before various organizations and otherwise relate the details of the journey from Caledonia Bay to Darien Harbor. Strain addressed the New York Historical Society and his remarks were reported in various newspapers there, especially the *New York Times.*[8] On October 25, 1854, Strain presented his full report of the exploring party's march across the Isthmus of Darien to the Secretary of the Navy. This report declared the Caledonia Bay–Darien Harbor route to be "utterly impracticable" for the purpose of an interoceanic canal. At the same time, it included recognition of the spirit and discipline of Strain's officers and men while paying due credit to the crew of HMS *Virago* and others who had helped rescue Truxtun and his men. Strain concluded his report as follows:

... I would most respectfully call your attention to the subordination and general good conduct of those employed upon the expedition. Greater difficulties, more intense physical suffering, and more discouraging circumstances, have seldom been encountered, and have never, I am assured, been met with greater equanimity, good-nature, and quiet endurance. Although suffering for long periods from scarcity of food, and even perishing for want of it, there was, I am happy to state, developed none of those humiliating instances of selfishness which have so frequently distinguished periods of great distress. I am also happy in being able to report to you that the officers and seamen under my command adopted, and with apparent willingness, a principle of action which was suggested to them at an early period in the journey of the expedition, and that those who survived have nothing to regret or blush for.

In having the services of passed midshipman W. T. Truxtun, 1st assistant-engineer, Mr. Maury, and midshipman H. M. Garland, I was especially fortunate, and to these officers I would respectfully direct the attention of the Department.

Mr. Truxtun, while I was present, was an able and cheerful assistant, and while I was absent he sustained nobly the responsibility which his fearful position imposed upon him. Mr. Maury, owing to his physical endurance, which surpassed that of any member of the party, was enabled to render to the weak and debilitated assistance which entitles him to their and my gratitude, and I feel assured that, even in a profession where chivalry and generosity are characteristic, that few would have deserved so much the high compliment which was paid to him by Mr. Truxtun, when making to me his verbal report of the events which occurred in the main body of the party during my absence.

"Maury," he said, "is the only man in the whole circle of my acquaintance, who could have endured so much privation, and passed through so many trials, without displaying a single instance of selfishness." For my own part, acquainted as I am with all the circumstances, I am at a loss which to prefer, the magnanimity of Mr. Truxtun, or the deportment of Mr. Maury, who richly deserved this handsome compliment from his immediate commanding officer, whose own conduct was so deserving of eulogium.

Mr. Garland suffered exceedingly in his own person, but was at all times ready and willing to afford every assistance compatible with his own state of health, as I can testify, and as is fully set forth in the report of Mr. Truxtun, which will be found in the appendix.

You, Sir, are already aware of the assistance rendered to my party by the officers and crew of Her Britannic Majesty's steamsloop *Virago*, which, pending the action of the Government, I recognized in a letter to Commander Edward Marshal, R.N., which has already been published.

You, Sir, have already informed me that the thanks of the Navy Department have been communicated to those officers and seamen, and any additional national action which might be taken to call the attention of H.B. Majesty's Government to the generous and chivalrous conduct of Lieutenant W. C. Forsyth, Assistant-Surgeon William Ross, Paymaster W. H. Hills (R. Navy), and Mr. W. C. Bennett, Civil Engineer, will be most gratefully received by my party and myself. The foregoing narrative will explain the extent of service which those gentlemen, and certain seamen of the *Virago*, rendered us at no small personal risk.

I would also respectfully call the attention of the Department to the fact that my entire party were transported on the Panama Railroad free of charge, I having crossed the Isthmus at that point three times, and that upon all occasions we received from the Colonel Totten, the Superintendent, Messrs. Monroe, Green, Baldwin, and the various other employes of that Company the kindest possible attention.[9]

The heroic nature of the march across the Isthmus of Darien by personnel of the United States Navy was described in a three-part article by J. T. Headley, published in *Harper's Magazine* in 1855.

In this article it was asserted that the American expedition under Strain was the first to accomplish a passage across the Isthmus of Darien since 1788. Records of the British Admiralty, however, indicate that the English engineer, Lionel Gisborne, debarking from the British ship on February 1, 1854 crossed the Isthmus alone with the help of a native guide in five days. This feat seems not to have been known to Strain or to the writer of the article(s) in *Harper's*.

The heroic nature of Strain's march was also challenged by an article in the *Algemeine Zeitung* written by an Italian engineer in the service of New Granada, Colonel Codazzi, who arrived at Darien with a party of convict laborers after Strain had departed into the interior with his party. Codazzi's thesis was that rather than being called heroes, the Americans should be classified as lucky blunderers who should have planned better, waited for the arrival of the men and ships of France, Great Britain and New Granada before starting into the interior, and whose conduct on the march was not as exemplary as reported. Strain replied to this criticism in a speech to the New York Historical Society, June 17, 1856, later printed under the title, *A Paper on the History and Prospects of Interoceanic Communication By the American Isthmus* (New York: Charles Vinten, Printer, 1856).[10]

Because of the hardship he encountered as the leader of the Darien exploration project, Strain remained ashore for some time recovering his health. On November 8, 1856, he was ordered to the Coast Survey steamer *Vixen* under the command of Lieutenant Otway H. Berryman, USN, and helped make soundings for a possible submarine telegraph cable route between the United States and Great Britain. On April 29, 1857, he was detached from the *Vixen* and ordered to report to the *Cyane* at Aspinwall.

Strain arrived at Aspinwall on May 14, 1857, on the mail steamer *Illinois*. He left the steamer and went to a local hotel where he died suddenly that evening. Commodore Hiram Paulding, commanding the Home Squadron, reported his death to the Navy Department the next day. It was commonly accepted, by Commodore Paulding as well as others, that Strain had not really recovered from the effects of the Darien expedition and that, even after an interval of three years, his death was due basically to the hardships encountered on the exploration trip. It appears that Strain fell ill with an undescribed fever and that his weakened constitution succumbed to this disturbance, however minor in nature.

No autopsy was made and there is no record of his burial, but presumably it was at Aspinwall. In a letter dated May 19, 1857, Commodore Paulding informed the Department that Strain's effects had been returned to the United States by the *Illinois* and that the bill of lading had been sent to the Commandant of the Navy Yard at New York.[11]

Lieutenant Isaac Strain died before he ever commanded a ship. He was ambitious, however, and his interest in exploration won the recognition of his superiors while his ability to maintain the morale and discipline of his men brought him admiration from foreign officers. In his Report of the Secretary of the Navy, 1854, James Cochran Dobbin called him "an accomplished and enterprising officer." Nine lives were lost in the Darien expedition, but Strain met catastrophe with unflinching courage, leading English naval officers at Panama to consider the conduct of his command as the "perfection of military discipline." At the time of his death, Strain was also a corresponding member of the Historical and Geographical Institute of Brazil, the American Ethnological Society of New York, and the Academy of Natural Sciences of Philadelphia.

The experiences of Strain and his men on their passage from Caledonia Bay to Yavisa and Darien Harbor, and Strain's conclusion that an interoceanic canal could not successfully be built in the area he explored, did not extinguish interest in the Caledonia Bay-Darien Harbor route as the location for an inter-oceanic canal.

Soon after Strain's observations and conclusions became known to the public Dr. Edward Cullen interjected himself into the question with a letter to the *New York Times* in which he maintained that Strain's report had not disproved his claim that a route not over 150 feet above sea level existed between Caledonia Bay and Darien Harbor, but rather had confirmed some of the natural advantages of the area for a canal. Furthermore, he said that his claim to have discovered a pass no higher than 150 feet would be verified some day.[12]

In 1857, an assistant surgeon from the *Independence,* Dr. W. C. Caldwell, submitted a report to the Secretary of the Navy, in which he supported Cullen's position by claiming to have easily, with only a seaman named W. H. Parker as a companion, traveled from Darien Harbor to a point about five miles from the northern part of Caledonia Bay. Caldwell related in his report that after obtaining leave from his ship for the purpose of testing Cullen's claim and securing the services of Parker, he bought provisions and hired canoes and native helpers at his own expense for his exploring venture. Then he and his party ascended the Sabana River to the village of Principe where they started overland in a northeasterly direction. After only a few miles of walking, the native helpers deserted, but Caldwell and the seaman continued their march over what Caldwell said was unforested country covered with dense undergrowth not over 150 feet above sea level. After five days on the trail they began to suffer from lack of water and to feel very tired. When Parker climbed a tree and said he could see the Atlantic Ocean from a place Caldwell estimated to be about five miles from the Atlantic coast, Caldwell decided to go back since they seemed to have accomplished their task. (Caldwell was unable to climb the tree and did not see the Atlantic himself.)

The gist of Caldwell's report appeared in newspapers such as the *New York Times,* and some interest was expressed for the dispatch of a new official Darien expedition to reconcile the Strain and Caldwell reports.

In 1859, Commander Thornton Jenkins, captain of the USS *Preble,* was ordered by the Secretary of the Navy to make the preparations necessary for a party of volunteers from the *Preble* and four civilians again to explore the area between Caledonia Bay and San Miguel on the Pacific for the purpose of reporting upon its suitability for a canal. The members of the civilian group were Frederick Avery, William A. Harris, Dr. Sutton Hayes, and William C. Gritzner. All four were taken into the Navy as Master's Mates and the evidence indicates that Avery was to be the guide for the reconnaissance.

Unfortunately, Avery did not behave as well as was expected of an expedition leader. Jenkins secured volunteers for the trip, and made other preparations, but while the *Preble* was at Aspinwall, Avery became drunk. This led to his dismissal from the Navy and the cancelling of the expedition. Moreover, the four civilians were supposed to defray all the extraordinary expenses of the expedition and even before the drunken incident it was discovered that they had insufficient money for the purpose so the expedition probably would have been cancelled anyway for that reason.[13]

During the Civil War the search for a Darien inter-oceanic canal was suspended. After the war ended there was renewed official interest in an inter-oceanic canal across Central America. On March 19, 1866, the United States Senate passed a resolution asking the Secretary of the Navy to submit all available information about the various routes proposed up to that time with a comparison of their merits. Rear Admiral Charles H. Davis was ordered by the Secretary of the Navy to prepare this report. After presenting what was known on the subject of possible ship canal routes through Tehuantepec, Nicaragua, Panama, the Isthmus of Darien, as well as the San Blas and Atrato river regions, Davis concluded with the assertion that

> . . . there does not exist in the libraries of the world the means of deter-
> mining, even approximately, the most practicable route for a ship
> canal. . . . It may be thought premature to say that the time has arrived
> for its execution. But it will not be denied that the present opportunity is
> the most favorable that could possibly arise for conducting, on our part,
> the preliminary surveys without interruption, interference, or unwelcome
> participation [by foreign governments].[14]

The suggestion by Davis was not acted upon immediately, but in 1869, Commodore Daniel Ammen, chief of the Bureau of Navigation, was ordered to organize a series of surveying expeditions in Central America. The result was that between 1870 and 1875, that region was explored in a full and meticulous fashion by the United States Navy for the purpose of determining the best route for an interoceanic ship canal. The experiences of previous expeditions were taken into account in outfitting parties engaged in the work. The results of these endeavors came under the review and evaluation of the Interoceanic Canal Commission appointed by President Grant on March 15, 1872, to consist of Admiral Ammen, Brigadier General Andrew H. Humphreys, the Army's Chief of Engineers, and C. P. Patterson, superintendent of the Coast Survey.

As part of this work of surveying, an expedition under Commander Thomas Oliver Selfridge, which consisted of Commander Edward Phelps Lull, 33 other officers and technicians, and about 250 sailors and Marines, explored the Caledonia Bay-Darien Harbor route for two months early in 1870. They found no indication of Cullen's pass or any place in the mountain less than 1,000 feet above sea level; neither could they discover anywhere a water supply sufficient to flood a large canal.[15]

After studying the data submitted to it, the Interoceanic Canal Commission dismissed the Caledonia Bay-Darien Harbor route as impracticable and declared that they favored a canal across Nicaragua. This pronouncement, however, did not exclude the Caledonia Bay-Darien Harbor route forever from further consideration. In 1898, Thomas Wright Hurst of Chicago petitioned Congress to authorize the organization of a Darien Ship Canal Company to dig a canal connecting Darien Harbor and Caledonia Bay, but the project received no encouragement. On March 3, 1899, Congress authorized a new investigation of the Caledonia Bay-Darien Harbor route in connection with new surveys to be made of the Panama, Nicaragua, and San Blas routes. The body brought into being to do this work, the Isthmian Canal Commission, usually referred to as the second Walker commission, formulated plans for three alternative routes between Caledonia Bay and Darien Harbor, each one to tunnel through high elevations between the Atlantic and Pacific Oceans. The cost estimates of all of these possible ways were larger by far than those for either Panama or Nicaragua and the commission advised the elimination of the Darien Harbor-Caledonia Bay route from further consideration.

In January 1902, the second Walker commission declared itself in favor of a canal across Panama. Six months later in June, Congress passed legislation authorizing the President to purchase for not more than $40,000,000 the rights and property of the Compagnie Nouvelle, the private French firm which had tried to construct a canal and had failed and to obtain from Colombia "perpetual control of a canal strip not less than 6 miles wide." On June 28, 1902, President Theodore Roosevelt signed the bill into law. Negotiations were opened immediately with Colombia, but Colombia refused to be hurried into an agreement. Stalemate on the issue was avoided when Panama revolted in 1903 and gained its independence from Colombia. A treaty designed for the construction of a canal under U.S. ownership and protection was quickly made with the newly independent country, and in 1907, after three years of preparatory work, construction began on the Panama Canal.[16] The Canal opened for seagoing traffic in 1914, sixty years after Lieutenant Isaac Strain first landed in Darien.

# Chapter 10

# Arctic Exploration and the Search for Sir John Franklin, 1850-1855

On May 19, 1845, HMS *Erebus* and HMS *Terror* left England under the command of Sir John Franklin to search for the North West Passage. It was the seventh expedition the Admiralty had sent to the Arctic for such a purpose since 1816. Two expeditions had been sent out in 1818, one under Captain John Ross, RN, and the other under Captain Alexander Buchan, RN. Between 1819 and 1827 Captain William Edward Parry, RN, had led five expeditions into the Arctic. Franklin's expedition represented a resumption of the Admiralty's interest in finding a Northwest Passage that had been dormant since Parry's last voyage in 1827.

Franklin's orders read, in part:

> ... You will not stop to examine any openings either to the northward or the southward in Barrow Strait, but continue to push to the westward without loss of time, in the latitude of 74° ½'N., till you have reached that portion of land on which Cape Walker is situated, or about 98° (North Somerset). From that point we desire that every effort be used to penetrate to the southward and westward in a course as direct towards Behring Strait as the position and extent of the ice or the existence of land, at present unknown may admit. . . .[1]

Franklin's ships were observed in Baffin Bay on July 24, 1845. Then, it appears that instead of following his instructions, Franklin sailed north to explore the Wellington Channel. During the winter season of 1845–46 the ships were beset by ice near Beechey Island at the entrance to the channel. They were called steamships, but their 20-horsepower engines were of little use in ice.

When melting of the ice in the summer of 1846 made travel again possible, Franklin took his ships south out of Barrow Strait to a point southwest of the Boothia Peninsula off the shores of King William Island. Here they were caught in the ice again, and were still beset by ice when Franklin died on June 11, 1847.

The ships had been provisioned for three years, so they waited out almost another year off King William Island. On April 22, 1848, Captain F.R.M. Crozier, RN, of the *Terror,* and Captain James Fitzjames, RN, of the *Erebus,* with 103 officers and men abandoned their ships and marched south in an attempt to reach the northernmost posts of the Hudson's Bay Company. Every one of these men died before reaching their destination.

Fairly definite proof of what had happened to the Franklin party was not obtained until some years later. In 1854, Dr. John Rae, Chief Factor of the Hudson's Bay Company, heard from a group of Eskimos that at least one of their number had climbed aboard the deserted ships, that some of them had seen many corpses, and that about forty white men had been encountered some indefinite number of months after April 1848, pulling heavy sledges. The Eskimos claimed they had traded some meat to these men and then left, never to see them again.

In 1858, Captain Leopold McClintock, RN, in command of a 177-ton screw yacht, the *Fox,* sent to the Arctic by Lady Jane Franklin on her own account, found a piece of paper in a tin cylinder in a cairn on King William Island. It was a brief record of the Franklin expedition to May 28, 1847, signed by Sir John Franklin, and a note dated April 25, 1848, signed by Crozier and Fitzjames, saying that they had abandoned their ships three days before. The note said that their ships had been beset in the ice since September 1846, in a location "5 leagues N.N.W. of this," and that "the total loss of deaths in the expedition has been to this date 9 officers and 15 men." McClintock found skeletons along Crozier's presumed march as well as abandoned clothing, stores, and quantities of other materials. The Eskimos said the *Erebus* and *Terror* had been crushed by the ice and sank after they had been abandoned. After gathering as much evidence as he could transport (but no corpses), McClintock returned to England in 1859. He published an account of his discoveries in a book called *Voyage of the Fox* and his evidence was accepted as proof that Franklin, his officers and men, as well as the *Erebus* and *Terror,* had all perished.

Long before McClintock's expedition, the Admiralty had sent out its own searching parties. In 1848, three such expeditions were dispatched, but all returned to England without any word of the Franklin party. This resulted in a rash of public interest, both in England and the United States, that made new efforts on a large scale almost inevitable.[2]

One of those most active in seeking new search efforts was Lady Jane Franklin, who wrote many letters to important and influential people soliciting their help and support. During 1849, she made two appeals to the President of the United States, Zachary Taylor. On January 4, 1850, the President sent her letters to the Congress for whatever action it deemed appropriate; the Congress turned the material over to its Committee on Naval Affairs.[3]

It is somewhat doubtful if anything concrete in the way of an American expedition would have materialized if a wealthy New York merchant, Henry Grinnell, had not become interested in Franklin's fate. Grinnell offered privately to furnish and outfit two ships, the brigs *Advance* and *Rescue,* for a rescue attempt. The *Advance,* built in 1847, was an 88-foot hermaphrodite brig of approximately 144 tons displacement with a 21-foot beam. The *Rescue,* a 65-foot, 90-ton craft, built as a schooner but re-rigged as a brig, was virtually new; her only voyage had been from the building yard in Maine to Grinnell's dock in New York. With the help of Lieutenant Matthew Fontaine Maury and the support of Senator Henry Clay, Grinnell managed to get Congress to make the expedition an official Navy Department operation, and subject to naval discipline. On May 2, at Clay's urging, Congress authorized the President to provide officers and men to conduct the proposed search.[4]

Under this authority, Secretary of the Navy William B. Preston issued the appropriate instructions. At the suggestion of Lieutenant Maury, Lieutenant Edwin J. DeHaven was designated commander of the expedition and given command of the *Advance.* Passed Midshipman S. P. Griffin was chosen as second-in-command and given command of the *Rescue.* A total of 8 officers and 23 men were assigned.[5] Dr. Elisha Kent Kane was ordered to the *Advance* as Assistant Surgeon.[6] This was a fortunate choice; Kane produced an excellent account of the rescue venture, later went on to lead his own expedition into the Arctic, and became a noted authority and writer on many scientific aspects of arctic exploration.

On May 22, 1850, the *Advance* and *Rescue* left New York.[7] Both ships had been strengthened at the Brooklyn Navy Yard for arctic operation. Bay into Barrow Strait. Once through Barrow Strait, DeHaven was to afford relief to Sir John Franklin of the Royal Navy and his companions." He was to first explore Lancaster Sound, extending westward from Baffin Bay into Barrow Straits. Once through Barrow Straits, DeHaven was to sail northward to Wellington Channel and westward to Cape Walker. If he found it expedient, he was to push through the Arctic into the Pacific Ocean and contact any United States naval forces there for assistance. That DeHaven might be able to make this northwest passage was at least indirectly supported by statements in his orders that called his attention to the very probable existence of an open polar sea with a warmer climate than its surrounding ice belt. If, on the other hand, Lancaster Sound and Barrow Strait were blocked by ice, DeHaven was instructed to attempt an exploration northward to Jones Sound and Smith Sound if necessary. He was instructed to avoid, if at all possible, becoming icebound and having to winter over.

DeHaven also had official approval to carry out, if possible, a request by Lieutenant Matthew Fontaine Maury to obtain data of value to work on his theories about an open polar sea. To this end, Maury sent DeHaven detailed instructions and tried to see to it that DeHaven carried all the necessary equipment. In the matter of equipment, however, he was not completely successful. Nevertheless, from this point on, the expedition had a scientific as well as a humane mission.[8]

The ships skirted the western coast of Greenland and then headed northward through Baffin Bay to Lancaster Sound. There, on August 23, 1851, they met the 90-ton schooner *Prince Albert,* under the command of Commander Charles C. Forsyth, RN. The ship had been equipped and sent out as a private venture by Lady Franklin to search for her husband. For awhile they traveled together. On August 27, at Beechey Island, they met the Hudson's Bay Company schooner *Felix* under the command of Sir John Ross, and the brigs *Lady Franklin* and the *Sophia,* commanded by a whaling captain, William Penny. The next day HBM *Resolute,* commanded by Captain Horatio Austin, arrived, accompanied by a screw steam tender, the *Pioneer.*[9]

On Beechey Island, one of Captain Penny's men located the graves of three of Franklin's party, identified on painted headboards as:

> . . . W. Braine, R.M., H.M.S. 'Erebus.' Died April 3rd, 1846, aged 32 years.
> . . . Jno. Hartwell, A.B., H.M.S. 'Erebus,' aged 23 years.
> . . . Jn. Torrington, who departed this life January 1st, AD 1846, on board H.M.S. 'Terror,' aged 20.

There was nothing to show what direction Franklin had taken from Beechey Island. At this point, DeHaven decided to leave the company of the British ships and sail north into Wellington Channel, but after a short distance, an impenetrable ice-barrier forced them to retreat. They then tried Barrow Strait, but turned back again because of ice. Kane vividly described their trials.

> September 10. Unaccountable, most unaccountable, the caprices of this ice-locked region! Here we are . . . again, all together, all anchored . . . to the 'fasts' off Griffith's Island. The way to the west completely shut out.
> September 11. Snow . . . covering the decks and carried by our clothes into our little cabin. . . . We are still alongside of the fixed ice . . .
> September 12. . . . the heavy snow . . . changed to a drifting drift. . . . At three the *Rescue* parted her cable's hold and was carried out to sea, leaving two men, her boat, and her anchors behind. We snapped our stern cable, lost our anchor, swung out, but fortunately held by the forward line. . . . I have seldom seen a night of greater trial. The wind roared over the snow floes and everything about the vessel froze into heavy ice. . . . The *Rescue* was last seen beating to windward against the gale . . .
> September 12. 10 p.m. Just from deck. How very dismal everything seems! The snow is driven like sand upon a level reach. . . . The wind, too, is howling in a shrill minor, singing across the hummock ridges. . . . The thermometer stands at 14°. At this temperature the young ice forms in spite of the increasing movement of the waves, stretching out from the floe in long, zigzag lines of smoothness resembling watered silk. . . . Now when you remember that we are in open sea, attached to precarious ice, and surrounded by floating streams; that the coast is unknown and the ice forming

inshore so as to make harbors, if we knew them, inaccessible, you may suppose our position is far from pleasant.

September 13. ... at about three this morning the squadron commenced getting under way. The rimecoated rigging was cleared; the hawsers thrashed; the ice-clogged boats hauled in; the streamers steamed, and off went the rest of us as we might. The *Rescue* is now the object of our search. Could she be found the captain has determined to turn his steps homeward. We are literally running for our lives, surrounded by the imminent hazards of sudden consolidation in an open sea. All minor perils, nips, bumps, and sunken bergs are discarded; we are staggering along under full sail, forcing our way while we can.

Our captain who was at his usual post, conning the ship from the foretop-sail yard, made out [the *Rescue*] and immediately determined upon boring the intervening ice. This was done successfully, the brig bearing the hard knocks nobly. ... We were no sooner through, than signal was made to the *Rescue* to "cast off," and our ensign was run up from the peak; the captain had determined upon attempting a return to the United States.

As the ships worked their way eastward on a homeward course, they were caught in ice forming over open water and frozen into a large drifting ice field. By an odd turn of events, this ice pack took them north again in Wellington Channel as far as latitude 75° 24′. All hands anxiously searched the horizon for any sign of open water. Cornwallis Island, forming the western side of the channel, lay on their port side; to the north there appeared to be a strip of land with mountain tops above the clouds, to which the name of Grinnell was given; westward, between Cornwallis Island and Grinnell Island there seemed to be a wide channel of open water with a dark cloud of frost smoke over it. DeHaven named the area for Maury, "whose theory with regard to an open sea to the north is likely to be realized through this channel."

Nothing could be done to explore this channel since for the next nine months both the *Advance* and *Rescue* were fast in the drifting ice and at the mercy of its movements. During this period, arrangements were made to ensure at least a modicum of comfort in the ships for the officers and men.

A housing of thick felt was drawn completely over the deck, resting on a sort of ridge-pole running fore and aft, and coming down close at the sides. The rime and snow-drift in an hour or two made it nearly impervious to the weather. The cook's galley stood on the keelson, under the main hatch; its stove-pipe rising through the housing above, and its funnel-shaped apparatus for melting snow attached below. The bulkheads between cabin and forecastle had been removed; and two stoves, one at each end of the berth-deck, distributed their heat among officers and seamen alike. We had of course a community of all manner of odors; and as our only direct ventilation was by the gangway, we had the certainty of a sufficient diversity of temperatures.

Kane gave careful attention to diet and hygiene while the thick ice provided a surface for occasional exercise. His lectures on scientific subjects helped the men keep their minds occupied. Theater parties were held, and the one for Christmas Day was described by Kane:

*December* 25. "Ye Christmas of ye Arctic cruisers!" Our Christmas passed without a lack of the good things of this life. "Goodies" we had galore; but that best of earthly blessings, the communion of loved sympathies, these Arctic cruisers had not. It was curious to observe the depressing influences of each man's home thoughts, and absolutely saddening the effort of each man to impose upon his neighbor and be very boon and jolly. We joked incessantly, but badly, and laughed incessantly, but badly too; ate of good things, and drank up a moiety of our Heidsiek; and then we sang negro songs, wanting only tune, measure, and harmony, but abounding in noise; and after a closing bumper to Mr. Grinnell, adjourned with creditable jollity from table to the theatre.

It was on deck, of course, but veiled from the sky by our felt covering. A large ship's ensign, stretched from the caboose to the bulwarks, was understood to hide the stage, and certain meat-casks and candle-boxes represented the parquet. The thermometer gave us −6° at first; but the favoring elements soon changed this to the more comfortable temperature of −4°.

Never had I enjoyed the tawdry quackery of the stage half so much. The theatre has always been to me a wretched simulation of realities; and I have too little sympathy with the unreal to find pleasure in it long. Not so our Arctic theatre: it was one continual frolic from beginning to end.

The "*Blue Devils:*" God bless us! but it was very, very funny. None knew their parts, and the prompter could not read glibly enough to do his office . . .

After this followed the Star Spangled Banner; then a complicated Marseillaise by our French cook, Henri; then a sailor's hornpipe by the diversely-talented Bruce; the orchestra—Stewart, playing out the intervals on the Jews-harp from the top of a lard-cask. In fact, we were very happy fellows. We had had a footrace in the morning over the midnight ice for three purses of a flannel shirt each, and a splicing of the main-brace. The day was night, the stars shining feebly through the mist.

But even here that kindly custom of Christmas-gifting was not forgotten. I found in my morning stocking a jack-knife, symbolical of my altered looks, a piece of Castile soap—this last article in great request—a Jews-harp, and a string of beads! On the other hand, I prescribed from the medical stores two bottles of Cognac, to protect the mess from indigestion. So passed Christmas. Thermometer, minimum, −16°; maximum, −7°. Wind west.

These events, however, could not completely compensate for the tedium of the long winter. As Kane recorded it, each day seemed almost without meaning:

*February* 11, Wednesday. Day very hazy, and nothing to interrupt its monotony. It requires an effort to bear up against this solemn transit of unvarying time.

I will show you how I spend one of these days—that is, all of them. It is the only palliation I can offer for my meagreness of incident. As for the study we used to talk about—even you, terrible worker as you are, could not study in the Arctic regions.

Within a little area, whose cubic contents are less than father's library, you have the entire abiding-place of thirty-three heavily-clad men. Of these I am one. Three stoves and a cooking galley, four Argand and three bear-fat lamps burn with the constancy of a vestal shrine. Damp furs, soiled woolens, cast-off boots, sick men, cookery, tobacco-smoke, and digestion are compounding their effluvia around and within me. Hour by hour, and day after day, without even a bunk to retire to or a blanket-curtain to hide me, this and these make up the reality of my home.

Outside, grim death, in the shape of −40°, is trying—most foolishly, I think—to chill the energy of these his allies. My bedding lies upon the bare deck, right under the hatch. A thermometer, placed at the head of my cot, gives a mean temperature of 64°; at my feet, under the hatchway, +16° to −4°—ice at my feet, vapor at my head. The sleeping-bunks aft range from 70° to 93°; those forward, regulated by the medical officer, from 60° to 65°.

We rise, the crew at six bells, seven o'clock, and the officers at seven bells, half an hour later. Thus comports himself your brother. He sits up in the midst of his blankets, and drinks a glass of cold water; eyes, nose, and mouth chippy with lampblack and undue evaporation. Oh! how comforting this water is! That over, a tin-basin in its turn, is brought round by Morton, mush-like with snow; and in this mixture by the aid of a hard towel, with a daily regularity that knows no intermission, he goes over his entire skeleton, frictionizing.

This done, comes the dressing—the two pairs of stockings, the three under-shirts, the fur outer robing, and the seal-skin boots; and then, with a hurried cough of disgust and semi-suffocation, he is on deck. There the air, pure and sharply cold, now about 26° or 30°, last week 40° below zero, braces you up like peach and honey in a Virginia fog, or a tass of mountain dew in the Highlands. Then to breakfast. Here are the mess, with the fresh smell of overnight undisturbed, and on our table griddle cakes of Indian meal, hominy, and mackerel: with hot coffee and good appetites, we fall to manfully.

Breakfast over, on go the furs again; and we escape from the accumulating fumes of "servants' hall," walking the floes, or climbing to the tops, till we are frozen enough to go below again. One hour spent now in an attempt to study—vainly enough, poor devil! But he does try, and what little he does is done then. By half past ten our entire little band of officers are out upon the floes for a bout at anti-scorbutic exercise, a game of romps: first foot-ball, at which we kick till our legs ache; next sliding, at which we slide until we can slide no more: then off, with carbine on shoulder, and Henri as satellite, on an ice-tramp.

Coming back, dinner lags at two. Then for the afternoon—God spare the man who can with unscathed nose stand the effluvium. But night follows soon, and with it the saddening question, What has the day achieved? And then we stretch ourselves out under the hatches, and sleep to the music of our thirty odd room-mates.

On June 6, 1851, the ice field finally broke up and the ships headed for the Whalefish Islands off the coast of Greenland. On June 9, 1851, they were separated in a dense fog and the *Advance* arrived first at the Whalefish Islands on June 16. Soon after arriving, DeHaven decided to proceed to Lievely on Disco Island, and left orders for the *Rescue* to follow. The *Advance* reached Lievely on June 17; the *Rescue* arrived the next day.

For the next five days, the "crews were indulged with a run on shore every day that we remained, which they enjoyed exceedingly after their tedious winter confinement. This recreation, together with a few vegetables of an antiscorbutic character which were obtained, was of much benefit to them." Unfortunately, quantities of fresh provisions could not be obtained, but the *Advance* and *Rescue* did get a few articles from a Danish supply ship from Copenhagen that arrived at Lievely while they were there. June 22 saw them sailing north again, but ice prevented their entering Lancaster Sound and on August 19, DeHaven decided to return to the United States. En route, the ships were separated by a storm; the *Advance* reached New York on the last of September and the *Rescue* arrived a week later.[10]

As Kane recorded it, the 16-month voyage ended as "our noble friend, Henry Grinnell, was the first to welcome us on the pier-head."

For DeHaven and Griffin this concluded their role in the search for Sir John Franklin. DeHaven turned in a short report, and after a period of rest was assigned to the Coast Survey. Besides his official report, a chart of his geographical work printed by the Naval Observatory, some notices in popular periodicals, and two relatively short scientific papers dealing with a few botanical specimens brought back to the United States by the expedition were the only other results of his hazardous venture into the Arctic.[11] DeHaven resigned his commission in 1857 because of near blindness and died in 1865. Griffin, evidently, returned to the anonymity from which he came.

Dr. Kane found it impossible to forget about Franklin and polar exploration. As soon as he recovered from the effects of the trip, he sought to raise money for another expedition to search for some trace of Franklin and to confirm the existence of an open polar sea.

Grinnell again offered the *Advance* for another expedition, and during the winter of 1852–53, Kane worked hard to get the financial backing. He wrote an engaging account of the adventures of the *Advance* and the *Rescue: The U.S. Grinnell Expedition in Search of Sir John Franklin; A Personal Narrative,* in which he printed DeHaven's report as well as the meteorological data and other scientific observations made on that expedition. With the approval of Matthew Fontaine Maury and the political assistance of Hamilton Field, he convinced Secretary of the Navy John P. Kennedy and his successor, James C. Dobbin, to order him and 9 volunteers on special duty at "duty-rate" pay. The Navy was also to furnish him with medical supplies, rations, daguerreotype equipment and some but not all of the scientific instruments he needed, selected with Maury's advice.

He lectured before and corresponded with groups likely to help him, such as the American Geographical and Statistical Society, the American Philosophical Society and others; and he solicited and received valuable information about arctic travel from prominent British arctic explorers. But he could not convince the administration of Millard Fillmore, who became President in March 1853, to back him, nor could he get Congress to vote an appropriation for the expedition.

Finally, through private contributions from men such as George Peabody, an international financier of London, the American Geographical and Statistical Society and the American Philosophical Society, and the generosity of Grinnell, the *Advance* was ready for sea. She sailed from New York on May 30, 1853, with Kane, seven "officers," and 10 men.[12] The orders issued by Secretary of the Navy Kennedy on November 27, 1852, and February 9, 1853, were still in force. Under the first date, Kennedy wrote:

> SIR:—Lady Franklin having urged you to undertake a search for her husband, Sir John Franklin, and his companions, and a vessel, the *Advance,* having been placed at your disposition by Mr. Grinnell, you are hereby assigned to special duty for the purpose of conducting an overland journey from the upper waters of Baffin's Bay to the shores of the Polar Seas.
>
> Relying upon your zeal and discretion, the Department sends you forth upon an undertaking which will be attended with great peril and exposure. Trusting that you will be sustained by the laudable object in view, and wishing you success and a safe return to your friends, I am, respectfully, your obedient servant,
>
> John P. Kennedy.

Some two months later he modified his original order by saying:

> SIR:—In connection with the special duty assigned to you by the order of this Department bearing date November 27, 1852, your attention is invited to objects of scientific inquiry; particularly to such as relate to the existence of an open Polar Sea, terrestrial magnetism, general meteorology, and subjects of importance in connection with natural history.
>
> You will transmit to the Department, when opportunities offer, reports of your progress and the results of your search, and, on your return to the United States, a full and detailed narrative of the incidents and discoveries of your exploration by land and sea, as matters of the scientific observations herein referred to.

Repeating my best wishes for your success, I am, very respectfully, &c.[13]

Thus, like the DeHaven expedition, Kane's expedition had a scientific as well as a humane objective. Kane was conscious of the value of naval discipline that the "special duty" orders made possible,[14] but since his was not a regular naval expedition and eight of the men were not members of the U.S. Navy, he established only three rules: absolute obedience to the leader, no use of liquor, and no profanity.

As the *Advance* sailed up the coast of Greenland, sled dogs and two additional men were added to Kane's party. At Fishernaes, Hans Christian, an Eskimo raised by Moravian missionaries, was enrolled as hunter and dog-keeper and at the Danish settlement of Upernavik, Kane secured the services of John C. C. Petersen, then acting as vice-governor of Upernavik. Petersen knew the Eskimo language, he had a vast amount of experience in polar travel, and he was much more used to the climate of the polar region than Kane or his crew. Then Kane began to purchase dogs at the different settlements, until he had a total of about 60.[15]

On July 27, 1853, the *Advance* arrived off Melville Bay and a week later passed Cape York. Next she entered a stretch of water leading to Smith Sound called the North Water. There was little or no ice, so the ship made good progress, and on August 6, she passed between Cape Alexander on the Greenland side and Cape Isabella, on Ellesmere Island, and headed into Smith Sound. Sailing cautiously into Smith Sound, the *Advance* reached Littleton Island. There they left a cache of supplies and a lifeboat. On August 7, 1853, they went beyond the highest latitude, 78°28', reached by a British explorer, Commander Edward A. Inglefield, RN, the year before and reached latitude 78°45'N. There, facing what seemed to be an impenetrable ice pack and difficult weather, Kane put into a small bay he named Refuge Inlet. Later the brig was moored to an islet, but the wind and ice broke the lines.

> Our six-inch hawser had parted, and we were swinging by the two others; the gale roaring like a lion to the southward.
>
> Half a minute more and "twang, twang!" came a second report. I knew it was the whale-line by the shrillness of the ring. Our noble ten-inch manila still held on.
>
> The manila cable was proving its excellence when I reached the deck. We could hear its deep Eolian chant, swelling through all the rattle of the running-gear and moaning of the shrouds. It was the death song! The strands gave way with the noise of a shotted gun; and in the smoke that followed their recoil, we were dragged out by the wild [ice] at its mercy.
>
> We steadied and did some petty warping, and got the brig a good bed in the rushing drift; but it all came to nothing. . . .
>
> There was but one thing left for us—to keep in some sort of command of the helm by going freely where we must otherwise be driven. We allowed

her to scud under a reefed foretopsail; all hands watching the enemy, as we closed, in silence. . . . We dropped our heaviest anchor with the desperate hope of winding the brig; but there was no withstanding the ice-torrent that followed us. We had only time to fasten a spar as a buoy to the chain, and let her slip. . . . I had seen such ice only once before, and never in such rapid motion. One upturned mass rose above our gunwale, smashing in our bulwarks, and depositing half a ton of ice in a lump upon our decks. Our staunch little brig bore herself through all this wild adventure as if she had a charmed life.

When the gale subsided, the only way for the *Advance* to continue northward was to follow a narrow stretch of comparatively open water between the shore and the ice pack. Kane decided to take this perilous way:

The effort occupied us until the 1st September. It was attended by the usual dangers of ice penetration. We were on our beam-ends whenever the receding tides left us in deficient soundings; and on two of such occasions, it was impossible to secure our stoves so as to prevent the brig from taking fire. We reached latitude 78° 43′ on the 29th August, having lost a part of our starboard bulwarks, a quarter boat, our jib-boom, our best bower anchor, and about 600 fathoms of hawser; but with our brig in all essentials uninjured.

At this point, the other officers advised Kane, in writing, to return to a more southerly harbor for the winter. He did not agree, and decided to send a reconnaissance party northward, first by whaleboat and then by sledge and on foot, to see if there was any chance of the *Advance's* going further north. After covering 74 miles in about 5 days, Kane reached a headland, 1,100 feet high, that

commanded a prospect of the ice to the north and west, as high as latitude 80°. A black ridge running nearby due north, which we found afterwards to be a glacier, terminated our view along the Greenland coast to the eastward. Numerous icebergs were crowded in masses throughout the axes of the channel; and as our vision extended, the entire surface was a frozen sea. The island named Louis Napoleon, on the charts of Captain Inglefield, does not exist. The resemblance of ice to land will readily explain the misapprehension.

This journey convinced Kane the brig would have to winter where he had left her. On September 10, 1853, he announced this decision to his officers and crew. The ship was towed to a fairly deep spot sheltered from outside ice named Rensselaer Harbor and preparations began for wintering in. The ship was arranged to provide the men a maximum amount of warmth, and a routine was established to keep them active. Until November 20, 1853, when darkness prevented further such work, provision depots were established northward to facilitate sledging operations to be carried out in the spring. The largest of these was located at 79° 12′7″, or 35′ north of Rensselaer

Harbor. An astronomical observatory was erected in which a "transit" and theodolite were mounted

upon pedestals of stone, cemented by ice. Great care was taken by Mr. Sontag, the astronomer to the expedition, in determining our geographical position. The results for the determination of longitude, as based upon moon culminations, are in every respect satisfactory; they are corroborated by occultations of planets and the late solar eclipse of May, 1855. An occultation of Saturn simultaneously observed by Mr. Sontag and myself at temperatures of 60° and 53°, differed but two seconds. This is the lowest temperature at which such an observation has ever been taken.

The position of our observatory may be stated as in latitude 78° 37', longitude, 70° 40'6".

A room artificially heated was attached to the observatory as a magnetic station. The observations were both absolute and relative, and were sustained by a corps of volunteers among the officers.

This activity, with proper attention to diet and general hygiene kept the men in fairly good health, but for some unknown cause 57 of the dogs died before March 1854. This forced Kane to reconsider his plans for the spring. Without the dogs, they could not make the planned long marches along the coast of Greenland. The only hope of ever reaching the polar sea lay in crossing the ice toward Ellesmere Island, and then "through or over the great ice-fields to the north."

Toward the middle of March an advance party set out to establish a supply depot at "ten days' journey from the brig." Bad weather forced them to turn back after 50 miles, and Jefferson Baker and Peter Schubert died from exposure to the cold. Their bodies were placed in pine coffins and buried on "Observatory Island."

Nevertheless, as soon as the health of his men seemed to justify, Kane resumed plans for exploration northward. One party, under William Morton, reached 80° 10'N latitude, establishing a new "far north" record. At that point Morton reported seeing open water to the north and northwest. Dr. Isaac I. Hayes, the surgeon of the expedition, and a companion, William Godfrey, were the first explorers to reach the northern half of Ellesmere Island, or Grinnell Land.[16] In April, Kane's hopes were given a new lift when some Eskimos visited the ship and he obtained four dogs, which with the three left, "formed a slender team." During the next four months, they traveled nearly 3,000 miles, and accomplished

1. The survey and delineation of the north coast of Greenland to its termination by a great glacier.

2. The survey of this glacial mass and its extension northward into the new land named Washington.

3. The discovery of a large channel to the northwest, free from ice, and leading into an open and expanding area equally free. The whole embraces an iceless area of four thousand two hundred miles.

4. The discovery and delineation of a large tract of land forming the extension northward of the American continent.

5. The completed survey of the American coast to the south and west as far as Cape Sabine, thus connecting our survey with the last-determined position of Captain Inglefield, and completing the circuit of the straits and bay heretofore known at their southernmost opening as Smith's Sound.[17]

By July, Kane was becoming concerned over the failure of the ice to break up. He decided to leave the ship and set out on July 12, in a whaleboat with five volunteers for Beechey Island where he thought he might meet some British ships searching for Franklin. This attempt was not successful, and by August it began to be apparent that they would have to spend another winter in Rensselaer Harbor, a forbidding prospect as their physical condition was poorer and their supplies diminished. Because of this situation, half of the men under the leadership of Hayes and August Sontag, the astronomer, decided to try to reach civilization again by boat, and Kane allowed them to do so. On August 28, 1854, the Hayes-Sontag party set out on a futile journey; after months of wandering and miserable camp life, they made their way back to the *Advance* in December.

With their return, Kane's anxieties were somewhat diminished, but such was not the case with the physical and psychological condition of his men. By that time they had established a working relationship with the Eskimos that contributed to their survival. After several occasions of vandalism and pilfering by visiting Eskimos, Kane decided to seek redress, and sent two men after the culprits. At an Eskimo hut about 30 miles away they found the wives of two Eskimos decked out in some of the items taken from the *Advance*. The women were tied and marched back to the brig. Five days later the chief of the nearest Eskimo village at Etah came to ransom the women with a load of material taken from the *Advance* on previous visits by members of his group. At this time a treaty was made between Kane and the Eskimos. The Eskimos promised "that we will not steal. We promise we will bring you fresh meat. We promise we will sell or lend you dogs. We will keep you company whenever you want us and show you where to find game."

For his part, Kane promised: "that we will not visit you with death or sorcery, nor do you any hurt or mischief whatsoever. We will shoot for you on our hunts. You shall be made welcome aboard ship. We will give you presents of needles, pins, two kinds of knife, a hoop, three bits of hard wood, some fat, an awl, and some sewing thread; and we will trade with these and everything else you want for walrus and seal-meat of the first quality. We the high contracting parties, pledge ourselves now and forever, brothers and friends."

The date of this agreement was September 6, 1854; winter was fast approaching, and as the group became debilitated from lack of a proper diet and activity, they settled down to wait out the end of the cold season.

In the spring of 1855, as soon as the majority of the men were able to move, Kane decided to abandon the *Advance* and try to reach the Danish settlement of Upernavik, over 500 miles south on the Greenland coast. Four sledges were constructed of timber from the *Advance*. Three of them had cradles designed to carry two 24-foot whaleboats and a smaller dinghy. A fourth was to carry the invalids and most of the provisions to the hut where the Eskimo women had been captured some months before. This was to "serve as an entrepot of stores and a wayside shelter for those of the party who were already broken down, or might yield to the first trials of the journey."

While Kane was busy between the hut and the brig, the other men, under Boatswain Henry Brooks, started southward, pulling the sledges across the still firm ice. Travel proved difficult and in order to lighten the sledges, a theodolite of the Coast Survey, a self-registering barometer of the American Philosophical Society, books, daguerreotype equipment and natural history specimens were abandoned. Kane saved expedition records, chronometers, magnetic devices, and various astronomical instruments with which he continued to make observations.

As they proceeded slowly southward, misfortune dogged their steps, relieved only by the help of the Etah Eskimos. On June 12, "Acting Carpenter Ohlsen" died as a result of an internal injury suffered while trying to rescue a sledge which had broken through the ice. He was buried on Littleton Island. By June 18, they had reached the southern limit of the solid ice and went on by "alternate movements over ice and water. So protracted and arduous were these, that between the 20th of June and 6th of July we had advanced but one hundred miles."

On July 21, 1855, the party arrived at Melville Bay. Then they traveled by boat to Horse Head, which they reached on August 3. Three days later they were at Upernavik, "eighty-three days after having left the *Advance*. We did not intermit our observations by sextant and artificial horizon as we came down the bay, and succeeded in adding to our meteorological and magnetic registers."

The Americans received a hospitable welcome from Danish authorities, and when the Danish brig *Marianne* arrived on her annual visit, Kane secured passage for his party to the Shetland Islands. But when the *Marianne* anchored at Disco for a few days, they were met by the USS *Release* and the USS *Arctic* comprising the "Expedition for Relief of Dr. Kane and Companions," commanded by Lieutenant Henry J. Hartstene.

The expedition commanded by Hartstene was the result of public and governmental anxiety over the failure to receive any news from Kane after his arrival at Upernavik in July 1853. Much pressure was exerted in political circles to do something about breaking this silence, and on February 3, 1855, Congress approved a resolution authorizing the Secretary of the Navy "to provide and dispatch a suitable naval or other steamer, and, if necessary, a tender, to the Arctic seas, for the purpose of rescuing or affording relief to Passed Assistant Surgeon E. K. Kane, of the United States Navy, and the officers and men under his command."[18]

In accordance with this resolution, the Secretary of the Navy on March 21, 1855, ordered Hartstene to report to the Commandant of the Brooklyn Navy Yard "for special duty in connection with the equipment and outfit" of the ship purchased for the expedition.[19] Eventually the USS *Release*, a bark, and the *Arctic*, a small propeller steamer, were selected and work started to prepare them for arctic service, while Hartstene assembled a crew, equipment, and provisions.[20]

In orders dated May 25, 1855, Hartstene was told:

It is understood from reliable sources that you can renew your supply of coal at Waigat Island, at which point it would seem to be advisable that you should touch, unless unforeseen circumstances admonish you to do otherwise, or some more practicable point should be ascertained by you. I will endeavor to procure and forward to you letters of introduction from the representative of Denmark to the governor of the Danish settlements, at which it may be useful and prudent that you should touch, for the purpose of making inquiry and procuring information. . . .

The Department has every confidence in your judgment, and relies implicitly upon your sound discretion. You are aware of the generous considerations which prompted Congress to authorize this mission of humanity. I have determined to trust you with its execution, *untrammeled by stringent directions, which might embarrass you and conflict with the suggestions of circumstances and developments of the future.* Judge Kane, the father of the doctor, is in possession of much important information left by his son, to be used in the event of a search for him. This will aid you much. I would suggest, however, that you should, unless constrained by strong hopes of future success, avoid passing a winter in the Arctic regions, and on no account uselessly hazard the safety of the vessels under your command, or, what is of more importance, unnecessarily expose to danger the officers and men committed to your charge. Your attention is also especially directed to the care and preservation of their health, for which hygienics have been abundantly furnished..

I transmit herewith, for your information and guidance, a copy of the instructions to Dr. Kane, dated November 27, 1852, as also copies of a series of letters from Sir Edward Parry, Sir Francis Beaufort, and other Arctic authorities, written by command of the British Admiralty, and kindly furnished to Dr. Kane, with the object of advancing the interests of the expedition to which he had been assigned by the Department. . . .[21]

While Hartstene continued his passage northward, Kane had reached Upernavik. On September 8, 1855, the *Release* and *Arctic* met a British whaler, and Hartstene gave that ship a letter to be forwarded to the Secretary of the Navy. He told of meeting the Eskimos who had made the treaty with Kane and learning from them they had helped Kane's party in their march southward. With this evidence in hand, Hartstene turned south in an attempt to catch up with the Kane group, which he did at Disco. On October 11, 1855, Hartstene and his ships arrived in New York. Of the 17 officers and men who had sailed from New York with Kane, only 14 returned as passengers aboard Hartstene's ships. No official report by Hartstene was ever published, but his letters to the Secretary of the Navy were reproduced as an Appendix in Kane's book as well as supplementary material to the *Report of the Secretary of the Navy* for 1855. Dr. John K. Kane, a brother of Elisha Kane, also wrote an account of Hartstene's mission, "The Kane Relief Expedition," in *Putnam's Magazine* for May 1856.[22]

Kane's return to New York was accompanied by great excitement and an outpouring of admiration; he became the hero of the moment. In that atmosphere, he began a book about his expedition which appeared in 1856 in two volumes under the title *Arctic Explorations in the Years 1853, '54, '55*. Almost immediately it became a popular work, 65,000 copies being sold within a few months. It went through a number of editions, especially in Germany where a ninth edition appeared at Leipzig in 1909.[23] Another narrative was written by William C. Godfrey as *Godfrey's Narrative of the Last Grinnell Arctic Exploring Expedition, in Search of Sir John Franklin, 1853-4-5* (Philadelphia, 1857).

Dr. Isaac I. Hayes, the surgeon of the group, also published an *Arctic Boat Journey* (Boston, 1860), dealing with the attempt he and eight others made to reach civilization in the summer and fall of 1854.[24]

Other accounts and summaries of the Kane expedition appeared in journals and newspapers throughout the United States.[25] Of perhaps more lasting publication importance in addition to Kane's volumes were the reports on the scientific value of his work. After a careful analysis of Kane's astronomical data, the map published with his two-volume book was redrawn by the Coast Survey. This correction was reported in the American Association for the Advancement of Science *Proceedings,* Volume 14, for 1860 (pp. 9–16) by Alexander Dallas Bache as "Abstract of the Principal Results of the Astronomical Observations at Van Rensselaer Harbor . . . during 1853, 1854, 1855 . . ." Kane's surveying work covered the Greenland coast, and his party was the first to map almost the entire eastern coast of Ellesmere Island. With the revisions reported by Bache, the general accuracy of the surveying work was attested to by later expeditions.

At about the same time that Bache's article on Kane's astronomical data appeared, and in subsequent years, other discussions of Kane's work in such areas as measurement of tides, meteorological observations, and the recording of magnetic data, were published. In 1859, Volume 11 of the *Smithsonian Contributions to Knowledge* carried an article by Elisha Kent Kane, "Meteorological Observations in the Arctic Seas" . . . reduced and discussed by Charles A. Schott. Schott and Alexander Dallas Bache had already reported separately on Kane's data dealing with atmospheric pressure and wind in the *Proceedings* of the American Association for the Advancement of Science; these reports, in connection with Schott's more general and comprehensive treatment, were very influential in their day and were used by scholars of later years in such areas as the study of atmospheric circulation and climatology in general.

In a like manner, the data on magnetism gathered by the Kane party was also collated and used by scientists. In volume 10 of the *Smithsonian Contributions to Knowledge,* published in 1858, Schott reduced and discussed this magnetic data. In 1872, Sir Edward Sabine, the British expert on magnetism who had sent advice to Kane, used this material in a fundamental compilation of declination, dip, and force in the latitudes of the far north. This work appeared as "Contributions to Terrestrial Magnetism, No. XIII," Royal Society of London, *Philosophical Transactions,* 162 (1872). In this form, Kane's scientific work encouraged subsequent theorizing and data gathering concerning the effect of magnetism on navigation instruments and communications.

Kane died in 1857 before this process was well underway, but would have been pleased to know that the great inconveniences that he and his party suffered in order to gather appropriate magnetic data had such results. In this regard, it is instructive to read Kane's own words about the hardships of magnetic data gathering in the far north:

March 7, Tuesday.—I have said very little in this business journal about our daily Arctic life. I have had no time to draw pictures.

But we have some trials which might make up a day's adventures. Our Arctic observatory is cold beyond any of its class, Kesan, Pulkowa, Toronto, or even its shifting predecessors, Bossetop and Melville Island. Imagine it a term-day, a magnetic term-day.

The observer, if he were only at home, would be the "observed of all observers." He is clad in a pair of seal-skin pants, a dog-skin cap, a reindeer jumper, and walrus boots. He sits upon a box that once held a transit instrument. A stove, glowing with at least a bucketful of anthracite, represents pictorially a heating apparatus, and reduces the thermometer as near as may be to ten degrees below zero. One hand holds a chronometer, and is left bare to warm it; the other luxuriates in a fox-skin mitten. The right hand and the left take it "watch and watch about." As one burns with cold, the chronometer shifts to the other, and the mitten takes its place.

Perched on a pedestal of frozen gravel is a magnetometer; stretching out from it, a telescope: and, bending down to this, an abject human eye. Every six minutes, said eye takes cognizance of a finely-divided arc, and notes the result in a cold memorandum-book. This process continues for twenty-four hours, two sets of eyes taking it by turns; and, when twenty-four hours are over, term-day is over too.

We have such frolics every week. I have just been relieved from one, and after a few hours am to be called out of bed in the night to watch and dot again. I have been engaged in this way when the thermometer gave 20°

above zero at the instrument, 20° below at two feet above the floor, and 43° below at the floor itself: on my person, facing the little lobster-red fury of a stove, 94° above; on my person, away from the stove, 10° below zero. "A grateful country" will of course appreciate the value of these labors, and, as it cons over hereafter the four hundred and eighty results which go to make up our record for each week, will never think of asking "*Cui bono* all this?"

But this is no adventure. The adventure is the travel to and fro. We have night *now* only half the time; and half the time can go and come with eyes to help us. It was not so a little while since.

Although Kane had to abandon his natural history collections, he did bring back a small plant collection. Appendix 18, pp. 442–67, to his two-volume work contains an account of the collection by Elias Durand. Durand also published an article on Kane's botanical work in the *Journal of the Academy of Natural Sciences* 3, sec. 2, (Philadelphia, 1856): 179–204, which was widely cited in subsequent years. By 1909, a note of warning about its accuracy was sounded by H. G. Simmons in his *A Revised List of the Flowering Plants and Ferns of North Western Greenland* (Report of the Second Norwegian Arctic Expedition in the *Fram,* 1898–1902, No. 16, Kristrania, 1909), pp. 11–12.

In addition to his works of scientific import, Kane's theories about an open polar sea, his observations about the Eskimos, as well as other matters, were also given attention by subsequent writers.[26]

On the basis of the feats accomplished, dangers surmounted, and scientific results achieved, Kane's expedition was a landmark in arctic exploration conducted with the help of the United States Navy. Such military-civilian cooperation was not repeated for many years. Between 1855 and the late 1870s the Arctic was explored, without much help from the Navy, by Dr. Isaac Israel Hayes, the surgeon of the Kane expedition, and Charles Francis Hall; it was not until Lieutenant George Washington DeLong, USN, explored the Arctic in the 1870s on "Special Service" that the United States Navy again became a meaningful participant in the work of arctic exploration.

# Chapter 11

# Interest in Western Africa and the Reconnaissance of Liberia, 1852-1853

On November 13, 1852, Captain William F. Lynch, USN, departed from New York aboard a merchant ship bound for Liberia on the west coast of Africa. He had orders from the Secretary of the Navy, John P. Kennedy, dated October 25, 1852, assigning him to the African Squadron under special instructions to explore the west coast of Africa from approximately 15° to 5° N, (the length of Liberia to the Gaboon River), for the purpose of recommending one or more points of entry for a large-scale expedition of exploration into that area of Africa directly eastward of Liberia.

He was also instructed to report on the best way of traveling into the area, either overland or by water, how an expedition into the interior should be supplied, whether hostility from the inhabitants of the region could be expected, as well as other information that would be useful for the organizing and implementation of a large scale U.S. naval exploration effort. The small steamer, USS *Vixen,* was to be attached to the African Squadron in case Lynch needed the help of such a vessel, and a small sum of money was placed at his disposal to meet any contingencies he might encounter on his trip. The Secretary of State had granted approval for him to travel as far south as the Gaboon River.

Lynch's mission had been prompted by the favorable reception given by Secretary of the Navy John P. Kennedy to a request from the Colonization Society of Pennsylvania for aid in the exploration of the interior of Africa to the east of Liberia, where it was hoped to discover land suitable for the colonization of former black slaves similar to that which had taken place already in Liberia. Kennedy was sympathetic to the work of the society and believed that whenever possible the ships and men of the US Navy should be utilized for such work. He did not have the money to launch a full-scale expedition, nor did he want to wait for a congressional appropriation. In his report to the President in December 1852, he suggested that

> by the employment of such means as have been provided for the ordinary exigencies of the service, I might profitably prepare the way for such an expedition as Congress might hereafter think fit to authorize. I have accordingly directed a preliminary investigation to be made by an officer of the navy whom I have attached to the African squadron, with orders to

devote the months of the coming winter to an examination of necessary conditions which this undertaking may require.

Kennedy urged that Congress vote:

a liberal appropriation of money, and an enlarged discretion to be confided to the Navy Department for the organization and arrangement of a plan of operations which must embrace the employment of a number of men, the supply of boats, armaments and tools, and the enlistment of such scientific aid as a long and laborious inland exploration, beset with many dangers and difficulties, will suggest.[1]

When the ship stopped at Teneriffe Lynch took the opportunity to obtain information and purchase charts and various instruments. On January 13, 1853, Cape Verde was sighted and a few hours later the ship arrived at the French settlement of Goree. Lynch sailed 80 miles further to the Gambia by coasting vessel. There he found the *John Adams:*

Her presence relieved me from the necessity, for which I had prepared by the purchase of charts and instruments, for making my reconnaissance in a small coasting vessel manned by Africans. It was with infinite satisfaction, therefore, that I grasped the hand of her manly and most excellent commander, and exchanged greetings with her intelligent officers, and looked upon her snow-white decks, her splendid battery, and clean, cheerful, and well-disciplined crew.

To the captain of the *John Adams,* Commander Samuel Barron, USN, Lynch presented his orders to explore the coast of Liberia and also the permission of the Secretary of State to expand the reconnaissance to the Gaboon River if time permitted. Barron's response was to offer Lynch a choice; the ship could take him along the coast of Liberia, stopping as he desired, or directly to the Gaboon and from thence return to Porto Praya, but the state of her provisions would not permit doing both. Lynch expected that the steamer *Vixen* would meet him soon, so he accepted the first proposition.

Leaving the Gambia, the *John Adams* set a course for Sierra Leone, on a slow passage occasioned by light winds and calms.

After a short stay at Sierra Leone the *John Adams* headed for Monrovia.[2] On January 31, 1853,

we made Cape Mesurado, dimly visible through a thin white mist which shrouded the horizon.

As we slowly sailed along, the mist rising with the sun, the surrounding scenery, feature by feature, was unveiled, and by the time we cast our anchor in the bay the whole was distinctly revealed.

Abreast of us was a lofty promontory; a little beyond, and partly hidden by it, was the town of Monrovia; and to the east and north a densely wooded country, its sandy shore interrupted only in two places, where the rivers Mesurado and St. Paul's find outlets to the sea—those outlets marked by the foam of breakers flashing in the sunlight.

Soon after his arrival at Monrovia, Lynch set out to explore the St. Paul's River. In a canoe manned by natives, he traveled up a channel called Stockton Creek, "a wide and shallow stream, with a low mangrove swamp on each side," for the first six miles. After passing the settlement of Caldwell, Lynch entered the St. Paul's, a "swift-flowing river, three-fourths of a mile in width, with banks 10 to 30 feet high, dotted with farm-houses, few of them a quarter of a mile apart," which did not narrow any less than one fourth of a mile in width for 14 miles from its mouth. Lynch characterized it as a magnificent stream, pouring down a great volume of water, and speculated that its sources resided far in the interior.

As he proceeded, Lynch landed at four or five places to see the dwellings of the inhabitants and observe the products they were cultivating. Lynch described Millsburg, at the head of navigation, and the farthest inland settlement in Liberia, as flourishing, comparatively healthy, and beautiful.

About 70 miles from Millsburg, Lynch reported, there was a large native town called Boporah reached by a path through a dense forest in which there were elephants "and many other wild animals. For the first fifty miles there are no villages, and the only natives met with are the elephant-hunters, who are numerous, and represented as friendly. The St. Paul's passes within 25 miles of the town, winding, in its course, among many islands."

From Monrovia, the *John Adams* took Lynch to the mouth of the Junk River. Here Lynch waited to go ashore for nearly two days, "in consequence of heavy breakers on the bar." When they did go in for a landing, the wind and huge waves almost swamped their boat. They were able to stay right side up, however, and landed just below Bassa Point near the dwelling of a colonist. With his help and that of his laborers, the boat was dragged to the South Junk, a stream running parallel to the coast, which united with the Junk inside the bar. Traveling on the South Junk, Lynch reached the town of Marshall on Sunday, February 7, 1852. After attending church services with the inhabitants, he set out to explore the Red Junk, which near its source was connected to the Mesurado by a narrow portage, and the main river, the Junk itself, navigable "by boats for thirteen miles; and twelve miles further there is a ridge of high land, east of which is an extensive lake, from whence the river issues. Twenty miles beyond the first ridge is a second and loftier one, from which the blue crest of a mountain is visible to the southward and eastward."

From all he could learn, Lynch concluded that there was much camwood (used for dye) and many elephants in the interior. He speculated that exports could be much increased, for "it needs only a glance in any direction to see the numerous palm-trees, bearing aloft thick clusters of fruit, which only require the hand of industry to gather and express from them the valuable oil; the demand for which, now that it can be deprived of its stearine, increases with every successive year."

The nearby settlement of Marshall, Lynch thought, was badly situated. He decided that if it could be moved near to the confluence of the Red Junk and the Junk, and if the ratio of men to women could be increased, it could raise enough for subsistence and "by means of a direct intercourse with the interior up one stream, and with Monrovia by another, unaffected by the weather on the coast, would, doubtless, carry on a thriving business."

The *John Adams* next moved to the mouth of the St. John's. Just inside the bar, the waters of three rivers came together, the Mechlin flowing from the north, the Benson River from the east, and the St. John's from the northeast. Between the Mechlin and the sea the village of Edina was situated, while on the west side of the Benson stood the town of Buchanan, founded by the New York and Pennsylvania Colonization Societies in 1835. Both settlements seemed to Lynch to present a "dingy, semi-dilapidated appearance."

Lynch found the St. John's itself to be about half a mile wide at the estuary and only 200 yards wide 7 miles from its mouth near a farming settlement called Bexley. The scenery was much the same as on the Junk and, including Bexley, there were 250 colonists on the St. John's above Buchanan. Canoes navigated the St. Paul's for about six miles beyond Bexley, or a total of 13 miles from the sea. About 30 to 50 miles from the sea was an uninterrupted camwood forest, and Lynch observed that "the whole world might be supplied with camwood rafted down the St. John's."

After a perilous reembarkation because of the heavy surf, Lynch and the *John Adams* traveled eighty miles further down the coast to Sinoe.

> Between the St. John's and the Sinoe river there are several streams coming down from the interior, but all are shallow and mostly difficult of access. First, the "New Cess" where was the last slave mart between Cape Mount and Cape Palmas. There are here masses of sienite upon the beach and a range of hills stretching inland. Next, the "Little Culloh," south of the highland peak, and accessible to boats in fair weather, and with a good landing just below it. Then follows the "Grand Culloh" river, with its entrance barred up at this season; and the "Tembo," which has a good landing on its southern beach; "Sestos" river, where a slave factory was long established; the "New" river, coming in by "Diabolito rock"; the "Broom" river, at the mouth of which is Bahyah rock, sixty feet above the sea; and the "Sangwin" and the "Grand Bouton" rivers, the latter having a bluff 260 feet on its southern shore, and the "Yulee" shoal before it.
>
> There are many rivulets besides these streams, all pouring down, even in this dry season, immense volumes of water, but none of them admitting vessels drawing more than six feet water, except the "Sangwin," which at the flood had upwards of ten feet water upon its bar, within which it is spread out and is navigable but for a short distance.

The Sinoe River was fairly deep just within the bar, but navigable for only 17 miles. After that it ran "shallow and obstructed, through the same belt of wilderness which lies behind the colony inland throughout its entire length. . . ." A settlement called Greenville was located on the right bank just above the river's mouth; upstream were the smaller settlements of Rossville and Readville.

Between the Sinoe and the Garaway, "the southern line of the republic," Lynch reported the existence of three streams, the "Dehvoeh," "Coroo," and "Teeroroah." From the Garaway to Cape Palmas was the coast territory settled by the Maryland Colonization Society. Lynch landed at Cape Palmas to visit the settlements of the area, principally those of Harper and Latrobe. On the day he visited, there was an election, which he described as follows:

> In the two colonial settlements there are 122 voters and about 800 inhabitants. I was there on an election day, and the place was quite lively. The people were in their best attire. The men gathered in groups near the building where the poll was held, while the women stood about in the shade, principally near the stands, where some of their sex displayed, on long tables, cakes, fruit, etc., for sale.
>
> A short time ago it was unanimously decided to declare the independence of the colony, and this day the voters were assembled to elect commissioners, to proceed to the United States and confer with the Maryland Colonization Society on the subject. At the same time, delegates were to be elected to a convention for forming a State constitution. This act, seemingly premature, is, I believe, the offspring of necessity. I am inclined to think so from what I see around me, and am convinced of it by the concurrence of the Society at home, which in most respects has heretofore so wisely directed the affairs of the colony. The election was conducted in a quiet and orderly manner, and I am satisfied that in its climate, soil, geographical position, and the general character of its settlers, this colony possesses the elements of undeveloped prosperity. The settlement has heretofore been retarded in its growth by the number of emigrants sent out, who were either infirm in health, feeble from age, or indolent in their habits and of listless characters—too many recently emancipated from slavery, with no idea of freedom beyond exemption from labor. A better time is approaching; and when the colony becomes an independent State, it will compete with its sister republic to the north, in the advantages it presents to the enterprising settler.

On February 16, 1853, in company with Commander Barron and Surgeon Sinclair of the *John Adams,* Lynch called upon Bishop Payne of the Episcopal Church at his mission headquarters, Half Cavally. This place was located on Shepherd's Lake, which lies parallel to the sea but is separated from it by a high and narrow strip of sand. As a result of information obtained at Half Cavally, Lynch decided not to ask Commander Barron to take him to the Cavally River. Lynch was told he could not take a boat across its bar at that season, and even though it was only 15 miles to the river it might take the *John Adams* weeks to return against the current to Cape Palmas. He decided to visit the Cape Palmas area for a few more days in the hope that the steamer *Vixen* might arrive. In the course of his extended visit, Lynch fell ill with fever and had to end his reconnaissance. The *John Adams* took him to Monrovia and then to Sierra Leone, where he boarded a ship to New York. He arrived there on May 1, 1853.

In his report, Lynch recommended that any exploring party planning to march into the interior should land at Monrovia, rendezvous at Millsburg, and make Boporah the "pivot of operations for advancing inland, and keeping up a communication with the sea-shore." From Boporah, Lynch suggested that the march be regulated by the nature of the country as well as the distance and direction of the nearest mountain range, "which must form the water shed between the tributary streams of the Niger and those which flow into the Atlantic." Once the mountain range was reached, Lynch further suggested that it might be followed to the parallel of Cape Palmas, "with a particular eye to the country on its Atlantic slope," and then the expedition might descend and make its way to the sea.

> The party should consist of as few whites as possible. The commander; an officer to take his place, should he perish; a physician, who should also be a naturalist; and some twelve or fifteen colonists, would perhaps be sufficient.
>
> The energy of the white man is indispensable for such an undertaking; but, from the hostility of the climate to his race, as few as possible should embark in it. The main body, therefore, should be citizens of Liberia; but as no man of resolution and judgment would undertake to head them unless they were under military organization, and bound to follow as long as he led the way, I suggest that if an expedition be organized, the government of Liberia consent to its citizens enlisting under the flag of the United States, and thereby subject themselves to its martial code. All ought to possess physical stamina, and the whites, especially, should be in the vigor of life, and, if possible, natives of our southern States.

In his report Lynch also included as much commercial information as possible and recommended that the United States make treaties "with the principal independent tribes along the coast," primarily in order to be in a position to use a ship of war to collect debts. He advocated that steamers replace sailing ships in the African Squadron and that naval officers in the African Squadron attaining a higher grade by the death of their superiors retain that rank permanently.

Another aspect of Lynch's report deserves mention: the observations about the natives and their way of life. The report devoted space to discussions of the Kroos, or Kroomen, "Grebos," "Jaloffs," "Mandingoes," and "Bassa" tribes, with material about other natives on every page. Lynch obtained his information, for the most part, from missionaries, merchants, and natives, although some of it was based on personal observation.

The information gathered by Lynch and his recommendations regarding the entry, organization, and work of an exploring party did not result in a full-scale expedition. Through the efforts of Senator J. W. Miller of New Jersey, the Senate on March 3, 1853, was presented with an amendment to the naval appropriation bill which read:

> For equipment, maintenance, and supply of an expedition for the exploration of the interior of Africa eastward of Liberia, and the ascertaining of the resources of that region, and for the colonization of the free blacks of the United States, to be expended under the direction of the Secretary of the Navy, $125,000.

Senator Miller said such an expedition was needed to help develop the untapped resources of Africa for the benefit of the world, to ensure for the United States a fair share of the increasing commercial activity that was bound to develop with Africa, and to aid "in the colonization of free persons of color from the United States into Africa." Counter arguments were offered against these points. In the end the amendment was defeated by a very close vote. Two former Secretaries of the Navy, John Y. Mason and Isaac Toucey, voted against it. The House of Representatives failed to take any action in the matter, and African exploration on the part of the United States went into limbo until after the Civil War.[3]

# Chapter 12

# Expedition to the North Pacific, Bering Straits and China Sea, 1852-1863

In August 1852, Congress appropriated $125,000 "for prosecuting a survey and reconnaissance for naval and commercial purposes, of such parts of Behrings Straits, of the North Pacific Ocean and of the China Seas, as are frequented by American whaleships and by trading vessels in their routes between the United States and China." To help carry out this task, Secretary of the Navy John P. Kennedy authorized five ships to act as a squadron for special duty. The ships selected were the sloop-of-war *Vincennes* (flag ship), the brig *Porpoise,* the schooner *Fenimore Cooper,* the steamer *John Hancock,* and the storeship *John P. Kennedy.* Commander Cadwallader Ringgold, USN, was named to command the expedition.[1]

Ringgold, in the fall of 1852, began to organize and equip his squadron. The charts, surveys, and factual reports on the Japanese archipelago that the United States government had purchased from the Netherlands to help the Perry expedition were available for study by Ringgold and his officers. Ringgold was supplied with the account of commercial and scientific problems of the Far East written by Aaron H. Palmer, a commission merchant and a promoter of New York. He also received a copy of the letter, written in 1850 by Commander James Glynn (p. 136) on the desirability of exploring Japanese waters, after his ship, the USS *Preble,* had rescued some American whalingmen stranded in Japan. Information about the region to be surveyed was requested from the navies of England, France, and Russia. Charts based on available but incomplete data were prepared for the expedition's use by the Depot of Charts and Instruments under the direction of Lieutenant Matthew Fontaine Maury.[2]

All such material, however, was not enough to satisfy the questions raised about the preparation of the expedition, nor did it seem complete enough to handle questions that in all probability would arise after it left the United States. Ringgold then requested the Secretary of the Navy to furnish additional material of this sort.

On March 2, 1853, the Secretary replied:

> . . . Professor Baird of the Smithsonian Institution is authorized to procure, and forward to you when attained, one or more copies of such Books, as in his opinion may be of interest.

The expenses attending such purchases to be paid out of the Special fund for expenditures under his supervision.[3]

Baird prepared a long list of books that, in his opinion, were essential to the mission of the expedition. It is uncertain as to how many of his suggestions were both available and consulted, but it appears that the narratives of previous explorers such as Krusenstern, Golovnin, Broughton and La Perouse were used.

Baird's part in the preparation of this expedition was not limited to procuring books. Congress had declared that the expedition was for "naval and commercial purposes;" the Secretary of the Navy interpreted this to mean that scientific interests in the United States were to be served as well, and at his request Baird prepared a plan for the organization and implementation of the scientific part of the expedition. He also arranged with the Secretary to have specimens collected by the expedition sent directly to the Smithsonian Institution and for the Navy Department to pay for their transportation, care and preservation.[4] When Kennedy left office in July, 1853, the new Secretary of the Navy, James C. Dobbin, attempted to alter these arrangements. Baird then induced Kennedy to write a long letter to Dobbin asking that the role of the Smithsonian in the expedition be allowed to remain unchanged. This letter, dated December 26, 1853, is worthy of being quoted, at least in part, to show the extent to which Kennedy valued the scientific possibilities of the expedition and the lengths to which he had gone in cooperation with the Smithsonian:

> The general organization of the expedition will show you that it was my purpose to combine with its primary nautical aspect as much exploration in the field of natural History as the opportunities of the cruise might allow. The former voyage of Exploration under Commodore Wilkes had amply demonstrated the value of such an organization, and had also suggested many improvements in the character of the equipment. Commodore Ringgold's squadron, accordingly, possess a more complete scientific corps and more effective apparatus for this particular service. In forming this corps I had . . . recourse to the advice of Prof. Henry and Baird of the Smithsonian Institute, and found in these gentlemen the most efficient and valuable aid.

Kennedy then went on to say that he had ordered Ringgold to send natural history specimens to the Smithsonian Institution that would be preserved, classified and made available for scientific study and presentation to the public. He voiced the hope that this situation could be continued.

The letter evidently convinced Dobbin, for somewhat later Baird wrote Kennedy that the affair had been settled and that the Smithsonian Institution would get the specimens collected by the expedition—and it did.[5]

It is noteworthy in this respect that, under the authorization of the Secretary of the Navy, Matthew Fontaine Maury corresponded with scientists such as Louis Agassiz, Joseph Henry, Jacob Whitman Bailey, and the Royal Geographical Society and the American Geographical and Statistical Society, soliciting suggestions about the scientific program that should be followed by the expedition. Maury recommended that the responses he received be incorporated in Ringgold's official instructions. The Secretary of the Navy saw fit to accept this recommendation and noted in his orders to Ringgold that the suggestions so received were to be "regarded as forming a part of your instructions. . . ."[6]

To implement the scientific portion of the expedition's work, as noted in Kennedy's letter to Baird as well as in relation to the suggestions offered by the groups and persons to whom Maury wrote, a number of civilians were appointed for special tasks, including William Stimpson and Charles Wright as naturalists at $1,000 per year and "one ration per day, while attached to a vessel for sea Service." Wright was ordered to Cambridge, Massachusetts, to confer with Professor Asa Gray and "to procure various outfits necessary in the Botanical departments. . . ."

The materials Wright and Stimpson wanted were purchased by the Navy Department. In a similar way, Edward M. Kern, the artist, was appointed "to take charge of the Photographic apparatus of the expedition as a masters' mate at $800 per annum."

A. A. Ames was given the job of "collector or assistant naturalist to serve on board the *John Hancock* as master's mate with a salary of $600 per annum," but at Capetown he left the expedition and returned to the United States. When the ship reached the East Indies his place was taken by L. M. Squires, assistant naturalist and translator. Ringgold also received authorization to employ "two assistant Draughtsmen" as well as one "mathematical instrument maker and repairer" at $500 per year.

It is noteworthy that Ringgold felt he needed a "mathematical instrument maker and repairer," because Kennedy's scientific plans for the expedition made various astronomical instruments a part of the equipment. These included a "zenith, and equal altitude telescope," a "transit and sideral clock," and an unspecified number of sextants, chronometers, and other instruments. To help with the astronomical work, Sidney Coolidge, a Harvard graduate, was appointed at $800 per year.[7]

Ringgold took great care to see that the ships were properly provisioned and manned. Much of his correspondence with the Secretary of the Navy concerned personnel. His recommendations on numbers and types of officers he wanted were approved, but he was not always able to have his way in filling the positions, despite being given much latitude in the matter.

Acting Master John M. Brooke, who was then under orders to the USS *Powhatan,* was ordered to the New York Navy Yard for "duty as a Lieutenant on board the Tender *Fenimore Cooper.*" Four days later, at Ringgold's request, the orders were suspended and Brooke was told to remain in Washington and to follow Ringgold's instructions in testing chronometers and other instruments to be used by the expedition. In March, he was ordered to the *Vincennes.*

Brooke had had experience with survey work in the Coast Survey, was the inventor of an innovative deep sea sounding lead called the Brooke lead, and had had a tour of duty at the Naval Observatory where he had earned the support and friendship of Matthew F. Maury. Ringgold's request for his services was probably made at the instigation of Maury. As part of its scientific mission the expedition was expected to gather data about the make-up of the oceans on which it traveled. Maury was interested in such data, especially that which might be obtained from the Bering Strait area, to help him further his own scientific endeavors. Brooke's membership in the expedition was looked upon by Maury as added assurance that this part of the expedition's objectives would be carried out in a manner useful to Maury. Brooke was given the status of senior astronomer and hydrographer with the expedition.

On March 3, 1853, the Secretary wrote that the "Comt. at New York has been authorized to enlist a master of the Band, and four musicians in place of five seamen for the U.S. Ship *Vincennes.*"[8] The sound and pageantry of a naval band was considered important for morale and the maintenance of a satisfactory diplomatic position in strange lands with regard to such possible events as land marches and meetings.

The Secretary's operational instructions to Ringgold, dated February 28, 1853, stated that:

> Although the primary object of the Expedition is the promotion of the great interests of Commerce and navigation, yet you will on all occasions not incompatible with the great purpose of your undertaking extend the bounds of science and promote the acquisition of knowledge.
>
> The Hydrography and biography of the various Seas and countries you may visit . . . will occupy your special attention, and all the researches connected with them as well as with astronomy, terrestrial magnetism, and meteorology will be confined to the officer under your command in whose zeal and talents the Department confidently relies for such results as will enable future navigators to pass over the route covered by your vessels without fear and without danger. . . .
>
> You will adopt the most efficient measures to prepare all specimens of natural history that may be collected . . . forwarding as frequently as may be done with safety, details of your voyages and doings. . . .
>
> You will therefore use your best endeavors wherever you may go to leave behind a favorable impression of your country and countrymen. The expedition is not for conquest but discovery. Its objects are all peaceful. They are to extend the empire of commerce and of science; to diminish the hazards of the ocean and point out to future navigators a course by which they may avoid dangers and find safety. . . .

A second letter, the same day, detailed the routes and procedures Ringgold was to use in carrying out his mission.[9]

On June 11, 1853, the squadron sailed from Hampton Roads, Virginia, en route to Madeira and the Cape of Good Hope. They reached Simon's Bay, at the Cape, by September 20. A severe storm did considerable damage to the ships, and repairs prevented them from leaving until the second week in November.

On leaving the Cape of Good Hope, the expedition split up. The *Hancock, Cooper,* and the *Kennedy* made for Batavia. En route, they charted the Gaspar and Karimata strait and the archipelagos between Singapore and Java. Around the end of May, the *Hancock* and *Kennedy* arrived in Hong Kong. The *Cooper* arrived later after a side trip to Singapore and some charting in the South China Sea.

The *Vincennes* and the *Porpoise* crossed the Indian Ocean, rounded the southern tip of Australia, and reached Sydney on December 26, 1853. They then sailed through the Coral Sea, near the Solomon and Caroline Islands, and to Guam. From Guam they sailed past the Bashee Islands (Batan Islands), and reached Hong Kong on March 19, 1854.[10]

Stimpson, the naturalist aboard the *Vincennes,* kept a journal during the cruise that indicated that the civilian scientists, at least, were not happy with the way it was being conducted. On February 24, 1854, he recorded the position of the *Vincennes* at latitude 6°47' N, longitude 158°30' E, and noted:

> In the morning we found ourselves close off the South side of the verdant island of Bornabi [on the basis of the location he gives this probably was Ponape], which appears covered with vegetation in all the luxuriance of the tropics. Its aspect is tempting indeed, and as we sailed along the coral reefs, we members of the Scientific Corps, viewing it from the tops did most heartily lament our hard fate in not being allowed to land for the purpose of making observations. Many of us feel quite discouraged at our situation: our hopes of exploring in unknown regions being greatly dampened when we find we can have chances to land and collect only in the sea ports which have been searched for years by collectors in all departments. We remained nearly all day off the island. A whale-ship passed us going in to a capacious harbor on the S. W. side in which two or three others were lying at anchor. A boat (in which were Capt. Rolando and Mr. Stewart) was sent to communicate with them, and returned bringing a variety of delicious tropical fruits, with yams, taro, bread fruit, cocoanuts etc. A whale boat, and two or three large canoes, manned by natives and commanded by renegade whalers residing on the island, came off to us at different times offering their services to pilot us in, which Capt. Ringgold refused.[11]

Ringgold found Hong Kong in considerable turmoil due to the T'ai P'ing Rebellion. The situation was considered dangerous to United States interests, especially in the Canton area where Americans had much property, and Ringgold decided to defer his plans and to remain in Hong Kong to protect United States citizens. As part of this resolution, the *Kennedy* was turned over to the U.S. East India Squadron and was sent to Canton.[12]

While at Hong Kong, the health and readiness of the expedition deteriorated alarmingly. Ringgold seems to have suffered a temporary mental breakdown; liquor and disease affected officers and enlisted men. When Commodore Matthew Perry returned to Hong Kong from his expedition to Japan, he convened a board of naval physicians to investigate Ringgold's condition.

As Ringgold was found unfit for service, Perry removed him from command of the expedition and replaced him with Lieutenant John Rodgers, the commanding officer of the *Hancock*. Rodgers assumed duties aboard the *Vincennes* during the second week of August 1854, and then ordered Lieutenant Henry Stevens, USN, to take command of the *Hancock,* and Acting Lieutenant William Gibson, the *Fenimore Cooper*. On September 4, 1854, Ringgold left for the United States on board the USS *Susquehanna*.[13]

In a letter dated August 1854, Rodgers wrote to the Secretary of the Navy, James C. Dobbin, about his actions and plans with regard to the expedition:

> In consequence of the illness of Captain Cadwallader Ringgold and his condemnation by a board of medical officers, the command of the Surveying Expedition, which had been entrusted to him, had devolved upon myself.
>
> From causes various in their nature and which it would not be interesting for me to relate, many changes had become necessary. While I am abundantly able, I think, to show full cause for the somewhat sweeping hand with which I have carried out these changes, I hope that I may be spared the pain of narrating them, since I flatter myself, no complaint will be made of my action from the gentlemen concerned.
>
> The Store Ship *John P. Kennedy,* even after the extensive repairs put upon her by order of Captain Ringgold, remains too much decayed for general sea service—still less fit is she for the peculiarly exposed duty to which surveying vessels are liable. To have repaired the *Kennedy* fully would have cost no less perhaps than to build a new vessel, while the hull, when finished, would have been patch-work. . . .
>
> Coming as I did into a command which had fallen into a state of disorganization, my position has been one of trial and difficulty. Very fortunately, I have been able in many things to throw myself upon the experience, judgment and good officers of Commodore Perry, who has been most kind to me. . . . I have every thing to hope from the zeal and intelligence of the officers who are to cooperate with me. The work to be done is plain, and the rest is easy.
>
> I deem that the field of the work of the American Surveying Expedition lies principally in the North Pacific Ocean, and its bays and inlets. The route between Australia and the British possessions in the East is more particularly a British interest. No one but ourselves has any desire to

survey the particular fields of our commercial enterprise. Our ships from San Francisco to China and our Whalers in the Pacific, and waters which empty into it, whiten the Ocean. For them, if I judge rightly, was this expedition fitted out.

While the field then, which I think allotted to me, is broad, it is also well defined, and nothing, unknown which I can take up in this vast theatre is without value and significance to our commercial career. . . .

The plan which I have selected is the one which upon mature consideration appears to offer the gratest results. While it seems bold, it will escape the imputation of rashness. The season at present is too advanced for us to penetrate far north. We shall however find employment in surveying islands in temperate regions, until the middle of next February. We shall then return to this place, fill up with provisions and repair the vessels. I propose then to start about the first day of March, to carry out the work sketched on the accompanying piece of tracing paper, giving to each vessel the portion which is there allotted to her. The plan is large enough to embrace two seasons. Full justice can scarcely be done to it in one; much however can certainly be accomplished, but I may have to leave to some more fortunate man the honor of perfecting what we have drawn hastily.[14]

In a letter to Rodgers dated November 18, 1854, Secretary of the Navy James C. Dobbin gave his confirmation to the change in command of the squadron and to the plans of Rodgers. The new state of affairs was also approved by the scientists with the expedition such as Stimpson.[15] Before Rodgers had left the United States as commanding officer of the *Hancock,* he had corresponded with Maury concerning data he desired to be obtained, especially in the Bering Strait region. He continued to correspond with Maury after he took command of the squadron and this aspect of the expedition's work, although not as complete as Maury desired, was continued much to his satisfaction and the profit of science.[16]

During the troubled period when Rodgers relieved Ringgold, some officers and men of the expedition did manage to interest themselves in the sights and everyday life in China. One of these was Lieutenant A. W. Habersham, who, on his return to the United States, recorded his observations of the Hong Kong area in a book called *My Last Cruise or Where We Went and What We Saw*[17] which was illustrated by Edward Kern. This account and a German language work by Wilhelm Heine are the main published contemporary narratives of the expedition.

In his book, published in Philadelphia in 1857, Habersham noted that "the view of Whampoa is beautiful from an upper point of the river;" that "Macao is remarkable for its pure air, cool temperature, fine summer retreats, and as the residence of Portugal's great epic poet,—the second Milton,—Camoens the beautiful;" and that "the most attractive (?) object in Canton is the execution-ground or slaughter-yard." He also recorded a situation that in one form or another has been part of the literature of children for a long time.

We were now running along the edge of an extensive ricefield, and the pilot called my attention to a queer-looking boat that was fastened to the bank. "That is a duck-boat," he said: "did you ever see one before?"

I replied in the negative, and he then pointed out hundreds of ducks working their clumsy way through the half-grown rice.

"They live in that boat," he continued, "with the man and his family who own them,—the people in the middle and the ducks in those side-pens. They are let out to feed whenever the boat drifts by a good place, and when the man whistles they get back as fast as they can. The last one that gets back is whipped."

"Whipped?" I exclaimed.

"Yes; he slaps him hard, and then the next time he doesn't come last."

I give the above as it was given to me, and as it is given to almost every one visiting China, and must add, in confirmation of it, something of the kind which I witnessed myself.

We had left this first duck-boat well astern and were approaching a second. The man of this second had apparently "whistled," for his ducks were returning in an awful hurry.

They were apparently making the most desperate efforts to regain the boat. Some of them were half flying, half swimming through the mud, weeds, and water of the field; others striking out like good fellows across a little creek that separated them from their home. All seemed anxious to arrive first; and, as they gained the boat's side, they tumbled in, heels over head, without the least apparent regard to life or limb. I watched, with the pilot, to see one of them slapped; but, to his evident chagrin, there seemed to be no "last duck" that time.[17]

While at Hong Kong, a long report on botanical specimens, the specimens, and various charts and journals, had been sent to the Secretary of the Navy. With the reorganization of the squadron completed, the ships sailed on September 9, 1854.

The *Hancock*, often towing the *Cooper*, sailed to Shanghai to embark Robert M. McLane, Commissioner of the United States, and Dr. Peter Parker, Secretary of the United States Legation, for a trip to North China. Their objective was to treat with the central government of China, along with British and French representatives, for revision of the treaties signed with China in the period 1842–44. On October 15, the *Hancock* and *Cooper* anchored at the mouth of the Peiho River for a few days until the envoys were received officially. While negotiations were in progress, the Americans surveyed the mouths of the Min, Huangp'u, Yangtze, Hwang Hai, and Pei rivers and investigated the Gulf of Pechihli.

After McLane, Parker, and the British and French representatives had concluded their negotiations, which were unsuccessful, the ships returned to

Shanghai with the American envoys. Then they sailed to northern Formosa where they examined sections of the island's eastern coast, especially some coal mines in the region, and returned again to Hong Kong on February 13, 1855.

The *Vincennes* and the *Porpoise* sailed at the same time, through the Strait of Taiwan to a point north and west of the Pescadores Islands. There, on September 21, 1854, both ships were laboring against northeast monsoons, with the *Vincennes* trying for the Bashee Passage, when the *Porpoise* disappeared.

The *Vincennes* put into Port Lloyd in the Bonin Islands on October 19, and waited for the *Porpoise* until November 6, when she sailed to continue surveys and soundings. She anchored at Naha on the Greal Lew Chew Island (Okinawa) on November 16. The *Vincennes* surveyed around Okinawa for the next few weeks, during which time there was no trace of the *Porpoise*. The ship evidently went down in a typhoon, soon after she was last seen on September 21.[18]

In his journal, Stimpson recorded that a scientific station was also established on shore for the time at a small village, which he called Tusui, a half mile north of Naha. There they landed

> Brooke and Kern, with Astronomical and Daguerrotype instruments, and a small party of men to attend the tidegauge and assist the officers of the Scientific Corps generally. Among the men was Pelkey, my assistant, who devoted his attention to stuffing birds etc. when other duties permitted, which, in his opinion at least, was not often. Mr. Wright and myself remained on board, visiting the shore daily for a few hours (10h to 4h) to make collections.[19]

While surveying off Okinawa, Rodgers decided that the islanders were not being attentive and civil enough, so he determined to persuade them to do better. First, he obtained an interview with the Regent. Taking with him all the men who could be spared from the *Vincennes,* he confronted the Regent with the propositions that the United States did not agree with the failure of the Japanese to furnish pilots, and that the reefs around the island should be buoyed permanently. (Both of these were part of the Japanese agreement with Perry.) To the second proposition the Regent agreed to comply while he recognized the first. With this agreement, boats from the *Vincennes* put buoys in positions Rodgers designated as a guide to the Japanese when they put down permanent ones.

Once this was accomplished, however, Rodgers began to experience difficulties in procuring supplies. He wrote to the Secretary after the *Vincennes* returned to Hong Kong that

> Wood and water were sent in insufficient quantities. Of water there is of course plenty, wood I really believe is scarce enough to make it dear; but we saw large piles, such as would serve an American wood merchant for

his stock. It was clear that the supply of wood on hand was abundant. They wished to know how many pounds of wood we wanted. When told they said they could not furnish so much. Finding that I was more pertinacious in requiring about six cords to complete our quantity than I had been with other things, the government interpreter reported to Mr. Moreton for my information that "if they furnished the wood we demanded it would take every stick on the island, that none would be left for them to cook their food, that they would all die of starvation and finally all Loo-Choo would become one vast sepulcher."

This very pretty figure of speech had less effect than they had hoped, first, because we had seen fifty times the quantity we required, cut, piled, and ready for sale; next, because the wood was necessary for the ship. Their making use of so bold a figure shows that they believed we were simple credulous people, easily imposed upon, and very soft hearted.

I deemed a display of energy absolutely required; we had endured a long course of evasion, of subterfuge, of practical refusal to abide by the treaty; they had forced us at last to take a stand, and I was glad it should be upon wood rather than food. This I deemed the more important as I fancied it was an experiment upon our forebearance, a trial of how far they might practically evade their convention at only the expense of a few untruths. I believed that my acquiescence would be taken for a precedent, and their subterfuges were part of a systematic attempt to make the convention waste paper. I thought it important to show that we regarded it as law.

I replied that if the wood were not furnished in twenty-four hours, I should take an armed force with a field piece up to the palace, and learn from the Regent why he infringed the convention of his government with the United States.

They apparently took me too for an Oriental, and supposed I did not necessarily mean what I said.

The wood did not come, and I accordingly landed about 100 men, officers, sailors, and Marines, all armed, and with one of Dahlgren's field pieces, marched up to the palace at Sheudi [Shui or Shuri].

They said the young king would die of fright at the sight of so many armed men; the reply was obvious; that it was to be hoped he would learn to make his mandarins observe the treaty. The heir apparent is said to be about 14 years old. Before we set out I-cher-a-chi-chi wished to know whether I would receive the Regent on the beach, and have our conference there. I said no, I should do as I had threatened, go to the palace.

When in Sheudi they told me the Regent was waiting to receive me at a house by the road side. We marched steadily on. They then said a feast was prepared for us. We still marched on. At last they requested that I would not take the men inside the walls running around the grounds of the palace. I readily said that I would not.

The people thronged the wayside, they filled all the cross streets in dense crowds. Their expression was, however, that of curiosity and pleasure. They took it for an honor, for a tributary offering possibly.

The clank of the wheels of the fieldpiece on the stone-pavement, and the tread of the men were the only noise.

Evidently they had calculated on our stopping by the wayside, for as I rejected the feast by saying that I had come to complain of their conduct, not to a feast, a number of men started at full speed toward the palace, and when we arrived there the gates were wide open. Two stone lions guarded the portal. I entered, accompanied by some of the officers, leaving some of them in charge of the men. They went in with pistols in their belts; I was unarmed. The grouping and stage effect were striking. I regarded the whole matter as a trial of skill. An Asiatic race had been trying to carry their point by Asiatic weapons; we were pleading the treaty, and endeavoring to show that we expected compliance with it. They had been using evasion, subterfuge, and all manners of disingenuousness to avoid giving us supplies, and so to induce us to leave, and never to come back again; to render their port worthless to passing ships. We were trying to convert their harbor into a useful stopping place, and with our humble means to expound in the only way which could reach their conviction that the treaty was law, and insisted upon under a penalty.

I-cher-a-chi-chi said that the Regent had gone about twenty miles into the country the evening before, and that he could not receive me; that the Pu-ching kwan next in rank to him would do so with the Tafung-kwan, governor of Napa. He had just before said that the Regent was waiting for me at a feast.

I did not appear to notice the discrepancy, but said that I wished to complain to the government, and I did not care whom it was said to if they would learn by it.

Chairs and tables were brought into the building, and the officers were all seated. Sacki, tea, and cakes were offered.

I had written a paper commenting upon their disingenuousness in language, which though deserved I found I had not the heart to use to timid and helpless old gentlemen. I contented myself with recapitulating the instances in which they had broken their engagements, that their whole conduct had been a course of evasion, that I was grieved that they had forced me to take other than a courteous manner toward them: that we wanted wood.

They replied that the inferiors were to blame, and that, if I wished it, they would punish them. I answered to this that I had nothing to do with the disobedience of inferiors, that I looked to them. The high officers evidently wished to make a peace-offering of innocent victims.

I finally said that it appeared they were unable to carry out in good faith what they agreed to do, that I should recommend my government to appoint a consul. At this both the Loo-Choo officers rose and bowed in a supplicating manner. "Loo Choo man no want a consul," said I-cher-a-chi-chi, and this closed the conference.

As we went out, chairs and tables were borne before by runners, who were disfurnishing the palace to furnish the house where we had been invited to accept a feast as we came up, and which invitation was now repeated.

They gave us an entertainment, and to the sailors and marines they gave tea. I presented to the Pu-ching kwan and Tafung-kwan each a carbine, with the hope that when they saw them, they would remember the treaty. We returned to the vessel about sunset.

Long strings of men were bringing down wood in their arms to the waterside all night, and at daylight the boats came alongside. About ten o'clock we had turned off two large junk loads of fuel: we had refused two bullocks and a quantity of other provisions, the bills were paid, a pilot was lying ahead of the vessel with an American flag in his boat on a long pole, ready to precede us; and we got underway.[20]

Near the end of December, 1854, the *Vincennes* anchored in Kagoshima Bay, off the island of Kyushu. The hostile attitude of the natives made the Americans feel unwelcome and indicated that the *Vincennes* should leave at once. But the ship needed water, so Rodgers made another show of force and got the 10,000 gallons he wanted.

The ship sailed on January 6, 1855, and after a brief time put into a little bay at the northern end of Tanegashima. There the people were more at ease with strangers and offered no opposition when a party went ashore from the ship for sightseeing.

Next the ship made soundings in the vicinity of the Alemene and Pacifique Islands in the Yokara Strait. On January 18 she anchored at Kago-Sima. A party landed to observe and procure provisions, but the people were reluctant to deal with the Americans, and supplies could not be obtained. Nothing seemed to be gained by remaining there, so the ship moved on to the bay of Sima-u off Oshima. Again the inhabitants proved unfriendly, so Rodgers decided to sail for Hong Kong where the *Vincennes* arrived on January 29, 1855.[21]

With the squadron assembled again, plans were made for the final stages of the expedition. The *Cooper* and the *Hancock* were to sail to Okinawa and survey until the *Vincennes* arrived, then the three vessels would proceed northward along the island chain of Japan, surveying as they went. At Simoda, Rodgers planned to stop and confer with the Japanese government, on problems expected en route, such as those met at Yama Gawa, in Kago-Sima Bay.

Rodgers expected his ships to be at Hakodate, Island of Ezo (Hokkaido), about May 15, to take on provisions from the brig *Greta,* of Hamburg, which he chartered for $5,000. After reprovisioning, the *Cooper* would survey in the Aleutian Islands and search for the crew of the whaling ship *Monongahela,* a search ordered by the Secretary of the Navy in a letter dated December 9, 1854. The *Hancock* and the *Vincennes* would make for the Arctic Ocean; all ships were to meet in San Francisco during October 1855.[22]

While engaged in preparing these plans, Rodgers sent home various scientific collections; among them were seeds and natural history specimens including 3,000 zoological items belonging to 1,153 species. The shipment included the following charts prepared up to that time:

South Extreme of Japan and the islands toward Loo-Choo
Asses Ears and Vincennes Rocks
Ousima & Kakirouma
Bay of Kago Sima and on Kiushu
Bay of Sima-u in Ou-sima
Lloyd's Harbor in the Bonin Islands, (unfinished)
Sketch of Lot's Wife [an island]
Reconnaissance of Borodino Islands
Reconnaissance of Rosario Island
Bullocks Harbor
Bar and Mouth of the Teen Tsin Ho [Peiho].[23]

Late in March, the *Cooper* and the *Hancock* departed from Hong Kong followed a little later by the *Vincennes*. On April 9, 1855, the *Vincennes* joined the *Cooper* and the *Hancock* in Naha. On April 27, 1855, the three ships sailed for a two-week survey of the Amakirima group. The *Cooper* then went north along the western coast of Kyushu, charting as she traveled, through the Tsushima Strait, and reached Hakodate on June 6, 1855.

After surveying the Amakirma group, the *Hancock* and the *Vincennes* passed the north end of the island of Okinawa, and then along the west side of Okiu and Kakirouma. Next they surveyed the southern side of Oshima and on May 8, 1855, they reached Yakono-shima. On May 12, Fujiyama was sighted, and the next day they anchored in the treaty port of Simoda.[24]

At Shimoda, Rodgers decided to try to chart the coast from Yedo Bay (Tokyo Bay) to the northeastward by means of a launch working off the coastline. He requested permission from the local authority for this trip but his request was denied. An appeal to the authorities at Yedo received no response. Finally, he decided to do the work without Japanese approval, using the launch, *"Vincennes Jr,"* under Lieutenant John M. Brooke. With the launch went Edward M. Kern, the artist, and 13 crewmen. They carried water, a 12-lb. howitzer, 40 rounds of ammunition, carbines, cutlasses, pistols, and pikes. Considering that Japanese approval had not been secured; that there were no treaty provisions for providing shore landings that would be necessary in view of the size of the launch; that Brooke and his men faced unknown navigational hazards; and that they sailed along a previously uncharted coast to produce a chart of valuable aid to mariners, it was a daring and profitable voyage that deserves recounting at least in part.

*218*

The launch sailed from Simoda on May 28, 1855, in headwinds and a rough sea. Rain obscured the land. That evening they anchored in the small harbor of Sino Hama, 10 or 12 miles north of Simoda. Some of the men slept on the beach. At dawn they were visited by Japanese officials. Brooke explained why they were there and the Japanese offered to supply fresh provisions. The Americans accepted the offer but when the Japanese left they did not wait to see it fulfilled.

On May 29, 1855, the launch headed toward the volcanic Island of Oshima against a continuing north wind. Around noon they encountered a powerful current that swept them to the north and east. About the same time, the wind changed to the south and they ran toward the entrance of the Bay of Yedo (Edo) in company with 30 large junks. That night the launch "anchored North of the larger of two islands shown in Siebolds chart."

In the morning the Bay of Susaki near the entrance to the Bay of Yedo was examined. Brooke found this bay to be "capacious with good holding ground and easy of access, open to the West but more safe than the port of Simoda." At night they found

shelter in a rocky basin frequented by fishermen and adjoining a shallow bay formed by a reef, and in which were moored several small junks: a village named Simo Hama, literally white beach, stood upon the shore, and a temple upon the promontory separating the two harbors. The inhabitants to the number of five or six hundred covered the sides of the basin in which we were lying and so dense was the throng that we could with difficulty find a footing upon the shore. We landed and walked a short distance into the country, entered their houses and were kindly received. The harvest was being gathered in and the heaps of yellow grain gave an agricultural air of plenty to the place. The young men are employed in fishing and the females manage the farms, usually of small extent. There were but three sword wearing officials seen and they did not appear to be inclined to limit our rambles or our intercourse with the people. At night we slept in the boat but before the dawn were awakened by the voices of our friends, who at that early hour resumed their stations upon the rocks. There were men women and children, many of the latter at the breast. So inquisitive were these people that we and our apparel were subjected to the closest scrutiny. Indeed, the beats of our pulses were numbered, the temperature of our hands tried. Nor were the females less forward than the men in these investigations; it seemed that they would not have hesitated to admit us as members of their families. The young girls were engaging in their manners and some of them were singularly beautiful, but the married women were disfigured in our estimation by the blackening of their teeth to which we were not yet accustomed.

At this port we first saw a portion of the fishing fleet engaged off the SE extremity of Nippon where the Sea affords abundance. Their large boats, double the length of our launch, were propelled with great velocity by twelve men, and in the management of their powerful sculling oars they exhibit the most perfect specimens of athletic and graceful men that I have ever seen. A single stripe of cloth about their loins left to view their persons, and in leaving the port many of them threw into their action an air of pride.

Leaving this hospitable port we rounded Cape King and entered the bight upon which Siebold places several villages and anchorages. As the evening approached we sought in vain for some shelter, two villages were visited in succession but the ports were hardly worthy of the name, for a few rocks breaking the rollers permitted their flat and light boats by dexterous management to land upon the beach where they were hauled beyond the reach of the waves.

The barometer slowly falling and clouds forming to the S West it was thought expedient to leave the lee land for the open sea.

As we stood out, a sea without warning broke with great violence near the boat, but only once, rain fell and fitful gusts swept over us. In the morning standing in to examine a port which appeared little better than those seen the preceding evening, we were overhauled by eighty fishing boats, manned by more than a thousand men; the press was tremendous and to avoid carrying away our jib boom it was rigged in. We were upon our guard, but from these unceremonious people we experienced only kindness; they threw into our boat fish of various species, rice, tobacco and wood; each boat thus offered a tribute which was always accepted, returning them fishing hooks, lead, buttons &c. Finally we were so hemmed in that we lost steerage way and got out our oars upon which they made more room for us, but still heedless of our remonstrances pressing by us and ahead we intimated our desires more clearly by discharging a revolver athwart their bows, which they took in good part and laughing left us to pursue our course.

It became necessary to replenish our water barrels and we therefore entered a deep but small bay, formed by a reef, bare at low water, upon which were some hundreds of the Japanese collecting sea weed apparently for exportation. Three large junks were lying in the harbor which opens to the South and is not inviting to ships of large size. We were visited by officials and supplied with wood and water; remuneration was declined and no persuasion induced them to receive it. We were permitted to land but not to visit the town. There is a spring of excellent water, at the foot of a verdant hill surmounted by a temple, and within a stone cast of the anchorage. We left an hour or two after anchoring, examining the most important portions of the bay and its entrance. In accomplishing the survey we employed our oars, and the weather cloth being down, the rollers at the entrance of the harbor rendered the operation somewhat hazardous.[25]

On June 3, 1855, the launch was off the Cape of Daiho Saki. There seemed to be a fine harbor on the north shore, but that time and weather conditions prevented a close examination. The next day the weather was rainy and foggy with the wind ahead. After a while the barometer fell and the waves began to run very high in generally threatening weather. They took the launch into deeper water and prepared for a heavy gale.

> The square sail and whole mainsail were set, and we then had an opportunity of admiring the good qualities of our boat; with her true gunwale often eighteen inches below the water, and her cloth to its edge, she yet answered her helm and attained a surprising swiftness. We desired to leave the rollers, over which we sailed as over hills, before they should break, when the safety of even a larger vessel would become doubtful. We were rapidly clearing the land when a sea was observed to break about two points on our weather bow, a column of white foam high in the air. The helm put down, the sails lowered and the main quickly reefed to weather it, we were relieved in seeing the jet of a spouting whale in the hollow of the sea: it was upon his back that the sea had broken and not upon a rock.
>
> So admirably did the boat head the waves which now began to curl, that we laid her by the wind under balanced reefed mainsail and foresail for the night. There were indications of Cirro cumuli in the haze of the sky, the sun broke faintly through and at midnight the clouds were going, the moon was up, the sea moderating, and a cast of the lead gave thirty-nine fathoms.
>
> We were pleased indeed, for the rain had drenched us and we were chilled by the N East wind.[26]

During the next two days, the launch proceeded up the coast until on the morning of June 9, 1855, she was off the Bay of Sendai. Brooke was charmed by this bay and brought the *Vincennes Jr.* over the bar, entered the river Tomigawa and anchored at the town of Isokona. The officials and people of the town gave the Americans a warm and very inquisitive reception. The Japanese hardly left the men of the *Vincennes* alone for a minute in their desire to examine the strangers and their equipment as well as to give them all sorts of supplies. From this, Brooke concluded that no European had entered the Tomigawa River before. The only request that Brooke made that was refused outright was that he be permitted to walk in the town.

From Sendai, the *Vincennes Jr.* coasted northward surveying as it went. On the morning of June 16, 1855, the boat entered the Strait of Sangar and at 10 p.m. reached the anchorage of Hakodate, having spent 21 days in traveling about 450 miles.[27]

Meanwhile the *Cooper, Hancock,* and *Vincennes* arrived in Hakodate, where Rodgers experienced difficulty with the local officials over the interpretation of the rights of the United States with respect to Perry's treaty. However, they continued their survey and purchased coal, food, and souvenirs in preparation for their final departure.[28]

Between June 26–28, 1855, the ships left Hakodate. The *Cooper* and *Vincennes* sailed first, to survey along the Kurile Islands and then head for Petropavlovsk, which they reached on July 8, 1855. The *Cooper* sailed from Petropavlovsk a week later, surveyed among the Aleutian Islands, visited in

Sitka, Alaska, and then commenced a survey of the North American coast south to San Francisco, where she arrived on October 11, 1855.[29]

After leaving Hakodate, the *Hancock* investigated the coastlines of the Sea of Okhotsk. She surveyed Kamchatka, Penjinsk, the Gulf of Yamsk, Ayan, the Shantar Islands, and the Gulf of Sakhalin. The season was too late to risk a visit to the Amur River. At various points on the coast, parties landed to gain information about the flora, fauna, geology, and inhabitants of the area and make astronomical observations. On the Kamchatka coast at 61° 15′N and 161° 31′E, a deposit of coal was discovered and the *Hancock* filled her bunkers. Digging and loading the coal aboard ship proved to be a very difficult task. As soon as a sufficient quantity of coal had been dug, all hands and the ship's boats were employed in getting it aboard ship. As Habersham later wrote:

> . . . We soon found it to be any thing but a pleasant job, however; for, having to carry the boats to the very foot of the coal-stratum in order to fill them, and then to pull back over the mud-flat to deep water, the ebb-tide often got the start of us, and left us sprinkled about over said flat, sometimes with full boats, sometimes with empty ones, and always with the pleasant alternative of remaining in the boats to be half frozen, or of walking through the cold mud to the distant fire.

As an alternative to this situation, it was determined to move the *Hancock* each day to a spot that would enable the loaded boats to get to the steamer and return to shore without grounding. Since high tide occurred at night, this operation had to take place then, so each night for five nights the steamer was moved close to shore—sometimes in only three fathoms—and each morning it returned to deeper water. In five nights of hard work the steamer took on a full load, some 100 tons of coal.

The coal had to be loaded if the survey was to be completed successfully, since it could not be done under sail. Habersham later recorded that as they surveyed:

> . . . we took good care to obtain and preserve not only specimens from the hills and beach, but from the bottom of the sea also. We had two species of "patent leads" for this latter work, and they both acted admirably. One of them was intended for bringing up specimens off the bottom when the depth of water exceeded two or three hundred fathoms, and did actually once bring up a thimbleful of sand and mud from the enormous depth of three thousand five hundred fathoms. That was in the North Pacific. The other was intended to be used in from one fathom to one or two hundred, and it often brought up a pint or more at a single haul. It was curious to wash out these specimens in a bucket of water and hunt for shells and other "wonders of the deep" in mud and sand that had existed at the bottom of the ocean for centuries in their undisturbed seclusion.

It is also worthy of remark that both of these admirable inventions sprang from the brains of two of our own officers,—the shoal-water one having been made in Hong-Kong, under the immediate direction of Commander Rodgers, while the "deep-sea explorer" was got up by Passed Midshipman (now Lieutenant) John M. Brooke, the able astronomer of the expedition, and who is even now trying to bring it before the notice of Congress.

In anticipation of these leads "working well," we had provided ourselves with several hundred small vials, in which every thing worth preserving was stowed away, after which it was sealed up and labelled carefully, for future examination.[30]

The *Vincennes* sailed from Petropavlovsk on July 14, 1855, and for the next few days hugged the Siberian coast, passing between St. Lawrence Island and Cape Tchaplin on August 1. Fog then obscured the shore, so Rodgers changed course and headed for the harbor of Glassenappe on the Asiatic side of the Bering Strait. Almost as soon as the ship anchored, she was greeted by a party of about 75 Chuckchi men, women, and children.

At Glassenappe Rodgers issued orders to Brooke instructing him to take command of a party consisting of Kern, Stimpson, and Wright, three sailors, three marines, and a Siberian interpreter who spoke no English, for the purpose of making scientific observations ashore while the *Vincennes* sailed further north. Rodgers went ashore with Brooke on August 4 to select a site for their work and help the party get established. Two boats were to be left for their use.

On August 5, Brooke and his men moved into camp on a peninsula on the headland of Kayne Island. The natives proved very helpful, even to the extent of carrying howitzer ammunition to the camp, which "was fortified as well as our means and time allowed. Empty provision barrels, filled with earth were placed close together around their sleeping place, and a trench dug, throwing the earth upon the barrels. Over these, a house was made of spare spars and canvass, and tents for instruments were pitched."[31]

After the detachment was settled, the *Vincennes* got underway, and crossed the Arctic Circle. Two days later, on August 13, she passed Herald Island. Between the parallels of 71° and 72° north latitude, temperature and specific gravity readings were taken at the surface, somewhat below the surface, and near the bottom with the thermometer and hydrometer.[32] After reaching 72° latitude and 175° W longitude without sighting land, Rodgers took the ship back to Herald Island. The log of the *Vincennes* for August 15, 1855 reads:

At 1 A.M., fog lifting made Herald Island. The bay of Middle Point covered with ice, which extended to N.W. by N. different portions of the island covered with snow and ice. Depth of water at 4 A.M., twenty-four fathoms. Two boats left the ship to land on Herald Island to take observations. No other land in sight. Small floes of ice drifting to the north. The boats returned, bringing specimens of plants and minerals and of birds, which were exceedingly numerous and so tame as to be caught by the hand. At noon Herald Island about three miles distant. No other land in sight from royal yard, with a clear horizon to north and northwest. Latitude observed 71° 21′36″N.

After leaving Herald Island, Rodgers set the *Vincennes* on a course for the supposed location of an island reported seen by Commodore Kellett, RN, called Plover Island. This island could not be found, however, and Rodgers decided that Commodore Kellett had been deceived and the island did not exist. Next the *Vincennes* sailed for Wrangel Island, but when the ship encountered a heavy barrier of ice at latitude 70°41′, longitude 177°21′W, and scurvy broke out among the crew, Rodgers turned back to the Semiavine Strait (Glassenappe) where the ship arrived on September 5.[33]

Meanwhile, Brooke's shore party continued their observations. In the beginning, the weather was pleasant. There was an abundance of plants and shrubs, most of them dwarf varieties. The Chuckchis proved to be very curious about the activities of Brooke's detachment from dawn to sundown. and since they were not belligerent, but showed a willingness to be friends, they contributed to the pleasant nature of the situation, rather than otherwise.

In the *San Francisco Herald* for October 19, 1855, the following description of this people appeared:

> They depend almost entirely upon the hard-earned fruits of the chase for subsistence, seemingly having but little taste or desire for the luxuries that might be obtained from the Russians in exchange for furs. . . . They live in communities usually consisting of four men and their families. Having no means of warming their habitations, they sleep in hammocks of sufficient capacity to accommodate a whole family. . . . Their government consists of two chieftains—a military and a civil chief. During a season when the weather will not permit of the chase, the war chief, who is also the chief of the hunt, assembles his warriors for exercise, and sitting on the ground, he directs their movements, which according to the description given by our informant, resembles, in every particular, the outdoor performances of the San Francisco Turn-Verein Society. . . . The dress of the men is made to fit quite close, and from sketches in water color, executed by Mr. Kern, they appear to display a commendable degree of taste in the fashion of their apparel. . . .[34]

Brooke also described the Chuckchis as being large people, generally with black hair and large cheek bones that stuck out on flat faces. Some women had facial tattoos. When the *Vincennes* was in the harbor, the men were not hesitant about boarding her. Later, the account of the expedition by Wilhelm Heine quoted, from Brooke's journal, an incident describing Kern's interest in the women and girls:

They remained in the baidars [canoes] since their party did not permit them to come aboard, until a Mr. Kern asked to draw them. He invited them to come on deck. We all were surprised to find women of such pleasing and gentle looks in such a country under such circumstances as surround their existence. Our sailors gave gifts of needles, tobacco . . . to the women, who were allowed to go down between decks. The women were most pleased. . . . While the women were on board, in vain Mr. Kern attempted to induce one of the girls to wash, but she shuddered from the contact with the cold water. Then he daubed the cheeks of several children with a cinnabar red, which delighted them greatly. He did this also to the noses of several men. Then, he gave a big, blue glass pearl to the prettiest of the girls, which seemed to delight her no end.[35]

On August 9, the chieftain, Ih-ack-til-ha (Ih-ak for short), brought his people together to entertain the Americans. After some opening ceremonies, the young men put on a lengthy display of wrestling skill. When the entertainment ended, the Americans served hot punch. Brooke rationalized this action: "Since they already know about brandy, at least it is desirable that they learn to drink it like civilized peoples." The next day Brooke went to the Chukchi camp to return the visit. That evening, he noted,

a young woman with a boy came to the camp and entertained us a long time with dancing. The dance at first consisted of various slow arm movements, after which, her body shook back and forth and contorted itself in other indescribably odd ways, whereupon she leered and gave out a half-suppressed gutteral sound like the heavy breathing of one in a deep sleep.[36]

On August 20, a group of natives from a neighboring village arrived in two large canoes. Some of them were allowed to enter the enclosure about the encampment even though they acted almost overbearingly haughty and were very demanding. After a while, Brooke ordered them to leave the confines of the camp. One of the men at first refused, but after some moments of waiting, Brooke had him ejected without further ceremony. As this was being done, Brooke and Kern had their arms ready, but no violence occurred and after the tension subsided the newcomers acted in a more cooperative manner.[37]

Collecting and observing birds, shells, and plants kept Stimpson and Wright busy during the stay on the island. They already had an abundant collection, but continued to make additions to it. Kern also participated in this work and added the duties of observing and recording the habits of the natives as well, particularly in their acquisition of food and ways of getting clothing.[38]

This interest sometimes occasioned great excitement with regard to the possibility of making an unusual discovery. One such incident happened when Kern and Brooke saw some natives hastening toward the shore line, two of whom fired their guns at something in the water. About the time the guns were fired, Brooke and Kern

> ... saw in the water three white objects ... which immediately after the shooting, disappeared. Our curiosity was aroused and Mr. Kern exclaimed, "A whale, a whale!" But I said, "It couldn't have been a whale, because it didn't spout," ... and then added in jest, "I wouldn't be surprised if it had been the big sea serpent." When we approached the camp we met Mr. Stimpson in great excitement. He asked if we had seen the big sea serpent and he said that he "would stake his reputation as a naturalist that he had seen it with his own eyes." We immediately pushed our boat into the water and started a chase with telescope and arms to try and get a glimpse of the monster again, if possible. But it was only once more visible in the far distance, and this time I could see through the glass that it had fins. After we returned to camp, everybody noisily voiced his opinion that it had been a serpent, a whale. ... In order to conciliate the various views and to be able to draw a safe conclusion, each of us made a drawing of the form in which he had observed the strange apparition. What we had thought to be a sea serpent was just three whales. ...[39]

Bad weather, including fog and rain, greeted the return of the *Vincennes* to Glassenappe. Scurvy broke out and it became necessary to find fresh provisions. Brooke was dispatched in the largest launch to look for food, but obtained only enough caribou meat to last for a few days. Others searched for berries as an addition to their limited food supply. Despite the precarious nature of their provision situation, Brooke's detachment was not very anxious to depart, and managed to remain on shore until just before the ship sailed. They had enjoyed their stay on land and were reluctant to exchange their shore billet for the limited confines of the ship.

On September 12, Brooke and Kern visited aboard the *Vincennes*. Rodgers was in bed with a bullet wound in his foot—his pistol had fallen from its holster and discharged accidentally. After a brief visit, Brooke and Kern went ashore and began breaking camp. The natives seemed sad to see them go, for some pleasant friendships had been formed.

The *Vincennes* got underway on September 17, cleared Amoukta Pass in the Aleutian chain a week later, and crossed the North Pacific. She reached Cape Mendocino on October 11 and arrived in San Francisco two days later.

By October 19, all the ships of the expedition had reached San Francisco. On October 25th the *Vincennes* moved to Mare Island for docking and repairs. To meet the similar needs of the *Cooper,* the ship was towed to Benica by the *Hancock.*[40]

As the *Cooper* arrived in San Francisco before the *Vincennes,* her commanding officer, Acting Lieutenant William Gibson, sent a report of his activities since leaving Hakodate directly to the Secretary of the Navy on October 11, 1855. Rodger's report on the activities of the *Vincennes* since leaving Petropavlovsk was dated October 19, 1855; he also forwarded to the Secretary of the Navy a list of charts in preparation or ready to be sent to Washington, and other reports, by Lieutenant H. K. Stevens of the *Hancock,* and Charles Wright, botanist, William Stimpson, zoologist, and James Small, on a botanical collection.[41]

In a letter to the Secretary of State dated June 23, 1855, at Hakodate, Rodgers had written: "I propose from San Francisco to survey the Southern route to Shanghai, through the trades in the three belts to Shanghai, because interesting points lie on the route, and because opinion points to that as the Chinese Emporium of American Commerce. From Shanghai to Hong Kong, and Caroline Islands, to Valparaiso. Thence to Rio de Janeiro, thence home."[42]

On December 5, 1855, Secretary Dobbin wrote Rodgers that funds were not available for continuing the expedition on to Shanghai as he had proposed. He ordered him to turn the *Cooper* over to the Navy Yard at Mare Island, and to transfer her officers and crew to the *Vincennes,* which was then to proceed to New York by such a route as Rodgers might deem advisable. Rodgers acknowledged receipt of these orders on January 26, 1856. The *Hancock* remained on the Pacific coast and was later used for pacification of Indians in the Northwest.[43]

The *Vincennes* left San Francisco on February 2, 1856. She sailed about 1,500 miles due west to investigate an island reported by some mariners, turned toward the Hawaiian Islands, and anchored at Hilo on March 11, for a three-day stop to procure wood and water. The ship then sailed to Tahiti, followed the great circle route to the Horn which was rounded on May 24, and reached the Brooklyn Navy Yard on July 13, 1856.

The results obtained by the expedition under Rodgers, from the standpoint of shipping and commerce, were extremely valuable. Many navigational hazards had been accurately charted, information about winds and currents had been secured, and depth soundings had been taken around the world. The scientific achievements were considered to be quite significant by the scientists of the day. The Smithsonian Institution reported that the natural history results were of great magnitude, and that very many new species of animals had been obtained. There were 5,211 species of animals in the collection; the plants, not yet classified, would be as numerous. All collections were stowed in the Smithsonian building, waiting for Congress to take some action which would permit publishing the results to the world.[44]

The 3rd session of the 34th Congress in 1857 appropriated the sum of $15,000 for "preparing, arranging, classifying, and labeling the specimens brought home by the North Pacific exploring and surveying expedition, and for reporting the same to Congress, with the appropriate drawings and catalogues. . . ."[45] Scientists were engaged to accomplish this objective, but little was accomplished before the Civil War and afterward nothing was done to produce a comprehensive scientific report for publication. In the late 1850s William Stimpson published a number of short Latin descriptions (prodromi) of the specimens he had collected in the *Proceedings* of the Academy of Natural Sciences in Philadelphia, and also wrote some additional articles for the *Proceedings* of the Boston Academy of Natural History.

Soon after the expedition returned home, Stimpson had become the director of the Chicago Academy of Science,

> ... to which place nearly all the invertebrate materials of the expedition were transferred. . . . the memorable conflagration of 1871, which destroyed so large a part of Chicago, completely annihilated the entire collection there. . . . The only collections of marine invertebrates which escaped were the corals and a few of the Crustacea, which had been left for study at the Smithsonian Institution, the Museum of Comparative Zoology, and Yale College.[46]

After Stimpson's death in 1871, a manuscript that he prepared was discovered in Washington, D.C. It described and illustrated many of the specimens he had collected, which were lost in the 1871 fire, and for which only very brief Latin accounts had been published earlier. It is conjectured that this work had been paid for out of the $15,000 appropriated by Congress in 1857, but it was not until 1907 that the manuscript was published as *Report of the Crustacea* (Brachyura and Anomura) *Collected by the North Pacific Exploring Expedition, 1853–1856;* by William Stimpson (Smithsonian Miscellaneous Collections, 49, Washington, 1907).[47] Almost half of the species described in this work were previously unknown.[48]

New information about the floor of the Pacific basin was also given to science and the public by Jacob Whitman Bailey's work on the bottom samples gathered by the North Pacific expedition. Bailey was a professor of chemistry at West Point to whom Maury sent the samples. Maury had previously sent him specimens from the floor of the Atlantic, and his study of all this material enabled him to publish a series of important articles on ocean bed marine research. Maury also sent samples of the North Pacific and Bering Strait sea bed to the prominent scientist Christian von Ehrenberg.[49]

On their return to Washington, D.C., Ringgold, Rodgers, Brooke and William Gibson all worked on preparing the expedition's charts for publication but it appears that only a partial number of their finished productions were printed or engraved on copper plates before the Civil War brought a virtual end to their work. (Rodgers' contributions continued until 1866.) After the Civil War, the printed maps, those still in manuscript and those engraved on copper plates were modified as occasion demanded to include newer and more accurate information. During World War II, these up-dated charts were vital in planning U.S. military operations in the Pacific.[50]

Some of these charts and corresponding data, and the hydrometer and the thermometer readings obtained by the expedition, were used by Maury in the preparation of various editions after 1855 of his book *The Physical Geography of the Sea* and his *Explanations and Sailing Directions to Accompany the Wind and Current Charts*. In the eighth edition of his *Physical Geography of the Sea,* Maury quite freely used the hydrographic data obtained by Rodgers to strengthen his presentation; he even included a chart showing the curves of specific gravity and temperature "of the surface waters of the ocean, as observed by Captain John Rodgers in the U.S. Ship *Vincennes,* on a voyage from Behring's Strait via California and Cape Horn to New York." This material was also used in the preparation of the actual wind and current charts published under his direction.[51]

No official narrative report of the China Sea-North Pacific-Bering Strait Expedition was ever submitted to the Secretary of the Navy, to the President, or to the Congress.

On April 9, 1858, Lieutenant John M. Brooke, while working at the Naval Observatory preparing the scientific data of the North Pacific Expedition for publication, and still under the command of John Rodgers, received orders from the Secretary of the Navy to plan and command an expedition to chart a steamship route between San Francisco and China. The ship selected for this expedition was the *Fenimore Cooper,* still docked at San Francisco. Brooke was given a crew of 20 men, including one lieutenant, one clerk, one draftsman, two boatswain's mates, one carpenter's mate, one sailmaker's mate, one gunner's mate, one armorer's mate, one ship's steward, one hospital steward, two quartermasters, one cook, one boy, and five seamen.

By August 5, 1858, Brooke was in San Francisco preparing for the voyage. The *Fenimore Cooper* sailed on September 26 and on November 9 reached Honolulu.[52] During the passage Brooke and his men surveyed obstructions to navigation while charting their route so that other ships could follow them. Moreover, the *Polynesian,* a newspaper of Honolulu, reported that no natural obstacles were found to the laying of a Pacific cable.

On December 29, 1858, Brooke began a survey to the northwest of Honolulu, and during that survey took possession of French Frigate Shoals in the name of the United States. In his report to the Secretary of the Navy, Brooke enclosed a sketch of the islet by Edward M. Kern. A seal rookery, and guano, were found there. After visiting Gardner's Island and Saipan, the *Fenimore Cooper* returned to Honolulu on February 9 while Mauna Loa was in a violent state of eruption.

The ship spent a month in Honolulu preparing for the next stage of the expedition and sailed on March 9, 1859. By March 14 she was off Johnston Island, and after encountering a heavy gale, arrived at Gaspar Rico or Smyth's Island. On April 12 she anchored at Apra harbor in Guam.

Brooke visited the governor of Guam, and the ship rode out a typhoon while at anchor. She sailed on May 3 for Hong Kong, where she arrived on May 19. En route, the party made deep sea soundings, one of which reached a depth of 3,300 fathoms at a position several hundred miles due east of the northern end of Luzon Island.

Early in June, the *Fenimore Cooper* sailed for Kanagawa Bay, near Yokohama, surveying off Okinawa en route. On August 13 they reached Kanagawa Bay. Ten days later, while Brooke was in Tokyo, a typhoon hit the area. In an attempt to save the ship and her crew, Lieutenant Charles E. Thorburn ran her ashore. In spite of assistance rendered by a Russian squadron in the area, nothing could be done to make the *Fenimore Cooper* seaworthy again, since her timber frame was so decayed that repairs were not feasible.

Brooke and his officers and crew remained in Japan for about six months, during which time they were treated very considerately. On February 10, 1860, the Japanese war steamer *Kanrin Maru* sailed for San Francisco; Brooke and nine other Americans from the *Fenimore Cooper* sailed with her to aid in navigation. The rest of the crew sailed aboard the USS *Powhatan,* which had been sent to Japan to transport the first Japanese diplomatic mission to the United States.

The *Kanrin Maru* crossed the Pacific in 37 days, arriving in San Francisco on March 17, 1860. A week later she moved up to the Mare Island Navy Yard for overhaul. The *Powhatan* arrived in San Francisco on March 29, and for the next week Californians treated the Japanese to a round of festivities in which Brooke participated. When the *Powhatan* sailed a week later, Brooke and Kern went with her, as far as the Isthmus of Panama. They arrived in New York on April 27.

After a period of leave, Brooke was ordered to prepare his reports and charts for publication. He was still engaged in this work, nearly a year later, when the Civil War broke out. Brooke, born in Florida and admitted to the Navy from Virginia, decided to resign from the Navy to join the Confederacy. His resignation was not accepted and his name was stricken from the rolls of the United States Navy by order of the President. No comprehensive report of Brooke's expedition was ever published, but his hydrographic work received recognition by the Navy and scientific circles after the Civil War.

# Epilogue

During the Civil War, the Navy expanded rapidly, but despite such growth it was hard-pressed to satisfy the immediate military needs of the nation. There were no ships or personnel available to continue the pre-war program of exploration and discovery; such peaceful pursuits as charting and surveying had to be set aside. Once the nation returned to peace, however, there was again renewed public interest in the utilization of the Navy in overseas exploration and scientific discovery. Considering the widespread range of interest, and many different national and international demands for renewed endeavor in these fields, there was no common denominator under which all the new expeditions might be discussed collectively. One point of similarity, however, was that each involved men of varying degrees of vision, ambition, and curiosity, and that all government support for such expeditions was influenced by a variety of motives, considerations, and partisan political motives. In general, the government showed no great interest in overseas developments, except in relation to Central America and the Arctic, and only where Central America was concerned could its attitude be considered anything but hesitant and inconsistent.

From one point of view, this failure by Congress to establish a sound program of overseas exploration and discovery attests to the range and extent of what had been accomplished in the pre-war period. The government had opened the way, so to speak, and was prepared to defend it; private enterprise must take over the task of exploiting the opportunities so made available. It is indicative that after the Civil War the Navy, with congressional blessing, again resumed its distant station policy as the best method of promoting and protecting the commerce of the United States and American interests abroad.

Congressional unwillingness to underwrite special voyages for exploration and discovery can also be explained by the fact that the United States, in the period immediately after the Civil War, was preoccupied with the challenge and opportunity presented by the vast interior of the continent. It can be argued that until the Civil War, American character and development were affected by both the sea and the land. After the Civil War, the land became the dominant factor.

It should also be mentioned that after the Civil War, extended voyages for charting, surveying, exploration and discovery became increasingly more difficult and expensive due to the fuel and repair requirements of the steam-powered ships coming into use. There was no denying that sail, while slower, was also cheaper and simpler. Moreover, as scientific bodies such as the Smithsonian Institution acquired financial independence, they began to send out their own expeditions. Nevertheless, the scientific work of the Navy continued, especially with regard to charting the ocean floor.

In the transition from pre-Civil War to post-Civil War operations, in which the Navy was used to further the commercial, industrial, and scientific interests of the United States, there was at least one continuous element. Before the war, officers and men of the Navy had demonstrated that they could accomplish their tasks in the face of many obstacles and were quite willing to do so. After the war, it was again demonstrated that, when given the same opportunity, Naval personnel still had the same spirit and capability. The bond between commerce, science, and the Navy which had been forged in the trials and tribulations of the early exploring expeditions could not be broken and still remains strong.

In the past, both the Navy and the United States have benefitted from this bond. In the future, it is hoped, this beneficial relationship will continue.

# Notes on Sources

(Works cited without mention of publisher or publication date are properly identified in the Bibliography.)

CHAPTER 1

[1]James A. Field, Jr., *America and the Mediterranean World, 1776–1882,* (Princeton, New Jersey. c. 1967), p. 25–38.

[2]Harry James Carman, *Social and Economic History of the United States,* 2 Vols. (New York, 1968), II, p. 146–57; Lawrence Battistini, *The Rise of American Influence in Asia and the Pacific* (Lansing, Michigan, 1960), p. 17–18; Robert G. Albion, *Square Riggers on Schedule: The New York Sailing Packet to England, France, and the Cotton Ports* (Princeton, 1938), p. 1–272; Arthur H. Clark, *The Clipper Ship Era* (New York, 1911), p. 96–97.

[3]Harold and Margaret Sprout, *The Rise of American Naval Power, 1776–1918,* (Princeton, New Jersey, c. 1967), p. 25–38; Marshall Smelser, *The Congress Founds the Navy 1787–1798* (Notre Dame, Indiana, 1959), p. 48–63, 72–84.

[4]Charles Oscar Paullin, *Paullin's History of Naval Administration . . .* (Annapolis, Maryland, c. 1968), p. 186: Field, *America and the Mediterranean World,* p. 37–58.

[5]Philip I. Mitterling, *America in the Antartic to 1840* (Urbana, Illinois, 1959), p. 19–97; Ernest S. Dodge, *New England and the South Seas* (Cambridge, Massachusetts, 1965), p. 19–111; Charles Oscar Paullin, *American Voyages to the Orient, 1690–1865 . . .* (Annapolis, c. 1917), p. 9–41. Edward A. Stackpole, "The Voyage of the Huron and the Huntress; the American Sealers and the Discovery of the Continent of Antarctica," *Marine Historical Association* Publication No. 29 (Mystic, Conn. Copyright 1955), p. 1–86.

[6]After the expedition returned to the United States, many specimens were given to the Lyceum of Natural History in New York; some were sent to Philadelphia. Eights gave his specimens to the Albany Institute, while Reynolds' personal collection went to the Boston Society of Natural History. Subsequently, Eights published seven scholarly papers: Bertrand, "*Geographical Exploration . . . .*" p. 264, footnote 55.

[7]J. N. Reynolds, *Voyage of the United States Frigate* Potomac 3rd Edition, (New York, 1835).

[8]Mitterling, *America in the Antarctic.* p. 97–107.

[9]In 1819 the USS *Nonsuch* sailed up the Orinoco River into the interior and a journal kept at the time gives information about the voyage, which was not made primarily for exploration or scientific objectives. "*Journal of the Voyage of the U.S.S.* Nonsuch *up the Orinoco, 1819.*" Record Group 59, N.A., M83, Roll 1.

CHAPTER 2

[1]Rear Admiral Daniel Ammen, USN, *The Old Navy and the New: Personal Reminiscences,* pp. 1–52; Charles Oscar Paullin, *Paullin's History of Naval Administration,* pp. 159–203.

[2]This account of the relationship of the executive and legislative branches of the government to the Navy is based on Harold and Margaret Sprout, *The Rise of American Naval Power,* pp. 86–150.

[3]Paullin, *Paullin's History of Naval Administration,* pp. 181–85.

[4]Harold and Margaret Sprout, *The Rise of American Naval Power,* pp. 139–140. Frank M. Bennett, *The Steam Navy of the United States,* pp. 1–137.

[5]Gustavus A. Weber, *The Naval Observatory, Its History, Activities, and Organization,* Institute for Government Research Service Monographs of the United States Government No. 39, pp. 1–28. For an attempt to make Maury the "Grey Eminence" of the Navy's involvement in exploration work, see Edward L. Towle "Science, Commerce, and the Navy on the Seafaring Frontier (1842–1861), The Role of Lieutenant M. F. Maury and the U.S. Naval Hydrographic Office in Naval Exploration, Commercial Expansion, and Oceanography Before the Civil War," unpublished Ph.D. dissertation.

[6]This aspect of the Secretary of the Navy's work for the period before the Civil War has been neglected by historians. The only modern biography of John P. Kennedy, for example, is completely unsatisfactory with regard to his relationship to the exploring and surveying work of the Navy during the period of his secretaryship: Charles Bohner, *John Pendleton Kennedy, Gentleman from Baltimore.*

[7]Paullin, *Paullin's History of Naval Administration,* pp. 226–43.

[8]Harold D. Langley, *Social Reform in the United States Navy, 1798–1862.*

[9]James A. Field, *America and the Mediterranean World,* p. 151.

[10]Fitch W. Taylor, *A Voyage Around the World . . .* pp. 261–317.

[11]Diplomatic Missions Conducted by Naval officers to Siam and Muscat in the period 1832–1837 are discussed in Paullin's *American Voyages to the Orient 1690–1865,* pp. 53–61. *See also* Paullin's *Diplomatic Negotiations of American Naval Officers.* For a critical assessment of the Navy's activities in this regard see Peter Karsten, *The Naval Aristocracy,* pp. 140–267.

CHAPTER 3

[1]Niles' National Register 62 (August 20, 1842); 385, as cited in Philip I. Mitterling, *America in the Antarctic to 1840,* fn. 5, p. 124.

[2]For a different expression of the same position, *see* Lieut. Charles Wilkes, to James Kirk Paulding, Secretary of the Navy, Dec. 22, 1839 in "Records Relating to the U.S. Exploring Expedition Under the Command of Lieut. Charles Wilkes, 1836–42," Record Group 37, M-75, Roll 5. Hereafter ("Exploring Expedition").

[3]Mitterling, *America in the Antarctic,* p. 139.

[4]Journal of Lieut. Charles Wilkes, I, Jan. 30, 1840, ("Exploring Expedition"), Roll 7; Mitterling, p. 144.

[5]Journal of Lieut. Charles Wilkes, II, Feb. 12, 1840, ("Exploring Expedition"), Roll 8; Mitterling, p. 146.

[6]Journal of George T. Sinclair, Acting Master, Aboard the *Flying Fish,* Jan. 21, 1840, ("Exploring Expedition"), Roll 21; Mitterling, p. 152.

[7]The cost of the expedition under Wilkes' command was $928,183.62. A good

summary of the expedition's accomplishments is in Charles Wilkes, *Synopsis of the Cruise of the U.S. Exploring Expedition* (Washington, D.C.: 1842), 56 pp.

[8]David B. Tyler, *The Wilkes Expedition: The First United States Exploring Expedition (1838-1842)*, pp. 368-420.

### CHAPTER 4

[1]James Y. Mason, Secretary of the Navy, to Lieut. William F. Lynch, November 11, 1847 ("Confidential Letters,") Record Group 45, T-829, Roll 359, Nos. 372-73; James Y. Mason, Secretary of the Navy, to Lieut. William F. Lynch, November 9, 1847, "Letters Sent by the Secretary of the Navy to Officers" ("Officers, Ships of War"), 1798-1868, Record Group 45, M-149. Hereafter ("Officers, Ships of War").

[2]Lieut. William F. Lynch, USN, *Narrative of the United States Expedition to the River Jordan and the Dead Sea,* p. 18.

[3]Lieut. William F. Lynch to John Y. Mason, Secretary of the Navy, "Letters Received by the Secretary of the Navy from Officers Below the Rank of Commander ("Officers' Letters") 1802-1886," Record Group 45, M-148. Hereafter M-148 letters will be cited as ("Officers' Letters"); John Y. Mason, Secretary of the Navy, to Lieut. William F. Lynch, January 30, 1847 ("Officers, Ships of War"): William F. Lynch, U. S. Navy, Memo dated March 23, 1933, in the Office of Early Records Section, Naval History Division, Department of the Navy, National Archives.

[4]Lieut. William F. Lynch to John Y. Mason, Secretary of the Navy, May 8, 1847 ("Officers' Letters").

[5]Robert St. John, *Roll Jordan Roll: The Life Story of a River and Its People,* pp. 349-53.

[6]Marie Francois Arouet de Voltaire, *A Philosophical Dictionary,* ten volumes in two, 1: 149-51.

[7]Lieut. William F. Lynch to John Y. Mason, Secretary of the Navy, May 8, 1847 ("Officers' Letters").

[8]First published in 1837, Stephens' work had gone through 10 editions by 1839. J. S. Stephens, *Incidents of Travel in Egypt, Arabia, Petraea, and the Holy Land.* "By an American." 10th ed., with Additions, 2 vols. See also Victor von Hagen, *Maya Explorer John Lloyd Stephens and the Lost Cities of Central America and Yucatan,* pp. 67-69.

[9]John Y. Mason, Secretary of the Navy, to Lieut. William F. Lynch, May 27, 1847, July 31, 1847 ("Officers, Ships of War").

[10]Lynch, *Narrative,* p. 13.

[11]John Y. Mason, Secretary of the Navy, to Lieut. William F. Lynch August 14, 1847, October 26, 1847, November 4, 1847, November 12, 1847 ("Officers, Ships of War"); Lynch, *Narrative,* pp. vi-vii, 14-15; Lieut. William F. Lynch to John Y. Mason, Secretary of the Navy, October 4, 1847 ("Officers' Letters"). Lynch secured the help of Lieut. Matthew F. Maury in the matter of obtaining needed instruments as well as in the selection of personnel. Lieut. William F. Lynch to Lieut. Matthew F. Maury, August 2, 1847, Naval Historical Foundation Mss.; Lieut. William F. Lynch to Lieut. Matthew F. Maury, October 26, 1847, in Towle, *Science, Commerce and the Navy on the Seafaring Frontier (1842-1861),* p. 171; Lieut. Matthew F. Maury to Lieut. William F. Lynch, October 28, 1847, November 11, 1847, Record Group 78, microfilm, National Archives, No. NNO-546 (52),

"Letters Sent, Records of the Naval Observatory." Hereafter cited as ("Letters Sent, Naval Observatory").

[12]John Y. Mason, Secretary of the Navy, to Lieut. William F. Lynch, November 11, 1847 ("Confidential Letters") Roll 359, nos. 372–73.

[13]*New York Herald,* November 30, 1847, p. 2.

[14]*Littell's Living Age* 15 (October, November, December, 1847); No. 189 (December 25, 1847); 606.

[15]Unless otherwise noted, the following account of the expedition's departure from the United States to its return is based on Lynch's *Narrative,* as well as Lynch's letters collected in Record Group 45, T-829, Roll 438, *Expedition to the Dead Sea, Lt. Lynch, December 1847, to February 1849.* Hereafter cited as T-829, Roll 438.

[16]Yigael Yadin, *Masada: Herod's Fortress and the Zealot's Last Stand,* trans. from the Hebrew by Moshe Pearlman.

[17]Edward P. Montague, ed., *Narrative of the Late Expedition to the Dead Sea from a Diary by One of the Party,* pp. 335–36; John Y. Mason, Secretary of the Navy, to Lieut. William F. Lynch, January 10, 1849, February 7, 1849, February 27, 1849 ("Officers, Ships of War"); Lynch, *Narrative,* pp. v–vi; John Y. Mason, Secretary of the Navy, to Commander John D. Sloat, December 9, 1848, December 12, 1848, January 18, 1848 ("Officers, Ships of War"). For Read's story as to why the *Supply* was not at Beirut on July 1, *see* Comm. George Read to John Y. Mason, Secretary of the Navy, June 20, 1848, August 3, 1848, "Mediterranean Squadron Letters, 1842–1861," Record Group 5, M-89, Roll 78. See also log of USS *Supply,* June–September 1848.

[18]*New York Herald,* December 18, 1848, p. 2.

[19]As has been noted in Chapter 3, the Wilkes expedition was subjected to similar indifference upon its return to the United States.

[20]Lieut. M. [atthew] F. [ontaine] Maury, "The Dead Sea Expedition," *Southern Literary Messenger* 14 (September 1848): pp. 547–553; Benjamin Silliman, Sr., "Notice of the Narrative of Lynch's Expedition to the Dead Sea," *American Journal of Science and Arts* 58 (November 1849): pp. 137–138; Lieut. William F. Lynch to John Y. Mason, Secretary of the Navy, June 9, 1848, T-829, Roll 438. *Expedition to the Dead Sea, Lieut. Lynch; National Intelligencer* 37 (November 1, 1849). Lynch did not want to release his findings to Robinson. Lieut. William F. Lynch to John Y. Mason, Secretary of the Navy, November 4, 1847 ("Officers' Letters").

[21]"Report of the Secretary of the Navy, with a Report Made by Lieut. William F. Lynch of an Examination of the Dead Sea." February 26, 1849; (30th Cong., 2nd sess., *Senate Ex. Doc. No. 34*).

[22]*Littell's Living Age* 22 (July, August, September, 1849): pp. 157–62.

[23]Quoted in *Littell's Living Age* 22 (July, August, September, 1849): 160.

[24]"Critical Notices," *Southern Quarterly Review* 16 (October 1849): 233.

[25]Lieut. William F. Lynch, *Official Report of the United States Expedition to Explore the Dead Sea and the River Jordan by Lieut. W. F. Lynch, USN.* Published at the National Observatory by Lieut. M. F. Maury, USN, Superintendent, by the Authority of the Hon. William A. Graham, Secretary of the Navy (Baltimore: 1852).

[26]*Harper's New Monthly Magazine* 5 (June–November, 1852): 289–303, 433–450, 577–596, 721–738; Vol. 10 (December 1854–May 1855): 189.

[27]In a letter dated February 13, 1850, William B. Preston, Secretary of the Navy, told Lynch that the Commandant of the Gosport Navy Yard had been ordered to give Lynch an "Egyptian tent," "Bedouin Spear," and the "Tattered Flag" which Lynch had requested. *See* William B. Preston, Secretary of the Navy, to Lieut. William F. Lynch, February 13, 1850 ("Officers, Ships of War"). The *National Intelligencer* for January 1, 1849, described two "Arabian Calves" brought back by Lynch and given by the Secretary of the Navy for display at Richmond, Virginia; two days later, the same paper said that a specimen of rock salt from the salt cliff around the Dead Sea had been placed in the Library of Congress, "with a correct drawing of the cliffs . . . .": *National Intelligencer* no. 11, 37 (January 1, 1849; January 3, 1849): 185, 187.

[28]St. John, *Roll Jordan Roll*, p. 360.

[29]Lieut. William F. Lynch, USN, *Narrative* . . . pp. vi-vii; Fanny Corbaux, *Journal of Sacred Literature* (April 1852), quoted in Appendix B1, 324, of William Allen, *The Dead Sea, A New Route to India; With Other Fragments and Gleanings in the East;* Allen, *The Dead Sea,* pp. 238–269.

[30]Captain William F. Lynch to Edward Fitzgerald Beale, January 11, 1850, in Stephen Bonsal, *Edward Fitzgerald Beale: A Pioneer in the Path of Empire, 1822–1903* pp. 56–57.

[31]William F. Lynch, *Commerce and the Holy Land: A Lecture Delivered Before the N.Y. Kane Monument Association,* pp. 37–39.

[32]The Secretary of the Navy declined to allow Lynch to proceed to the mouth of the Euphrates because this would make his expedition commercial and political, for which the authorization of Congress would be necessary. *See* John Y. Mason, Secretary of the Navy, to Lieut. William F. Lynch March 31, 1848, ("Confidential Letters"), Roll 359, nos. 424–425.

CHAPTER 5

[1]John P. Harrison, "Science and Politics: Origin and Objectives of Mid-Nineteenth Century Government Expeditions to Latin America," *Hispanic American Historical Review,* 187–89; Donald Marquand Dozer, "Matthew Fontaine Maury's Letter of Instruction to William Lewis Herndon," *Hispanic American Historical Review,* 212–28. For a list of Maury's writings on the economic future of the South in relation to the Gulf of Mexico, the South Atlantic Ocean, and South America, *see* Francis L. Williams, *Matthew Fontaine Maury, Scientist of the Sea,* pp. 706–708.

[2]Herndon, *Exploration of the Valley of the Amazon* . . . (32nd Cong., 2d sess., *House Ex. Doc. No. 43,* Pt. I, 5. Lieut. William L. Herndon to Lieut. James M. Gilliss, September 1, 13, 20, 22, 1850, *"Letters Received, Correspondence of the Astronomical Expedition to the Southern Hemisphere, 1846-1861,"* Record Group 78, T-54. It appears that the timing of Maury's proposal for the expedition was determined in part by desire to see that Herndon received credit for its execution, and Herndon's presence aboard the *Vandalia*. Lieut. Matthew Fontaine Maury to William B. Preston, Secretary of the Navy, August 4, 1849, ("Letters Sent, Naval Observatory"), William B. Preston, Secretary of the Navy, to Lieut. William Lewis Herndon, July 27, 1849 ("Officers, Ships of War").

[3]Lieut. Matthew F. Maury to Lieut. William L. Herndon, November 13 (with addition dated November 16), 1850 ("Letters Sent, Naval Observatory"); Lieut. Matthew F. Maury to William Graham, Secretary of the Navy, August 14, 1850 ("Let-

ters Sent, Naval Observatory"). Unless otherwise noted, the following account of Herndon's exploration of the Amazon River Valley, including all quotations, is from *Exploration of the Valley of the Amazon, Part 1.* For an account of Herndon's problems while waiting for his orders, see Lieut. William L. Herndon to Lieut. James M. Gilliss, September 1, 13, 20, 22, 26, 1850; October 2, 1850; December 22, 1850 ("Letters Received, Astronomical Expedition").

[4]Herndon, *Exploration of the Valley of the Amazon, Part 1,* 10–11. Lieut. William L. Herndon to Lieut. James M. Gilliss, February 8, 1851 ("Letters Received, Astronomical Expedition"). *See also* Lieut. James M. Gilliss to Lieut. William L. Herndon, March 15, 1851, *"Letters Sent, Astronomical Expedition," 1846–1861,* Record Group 78, T-54.

[5]Dozer, "Matthew Fontaine Maury's Letter of Instruction to William Lewis Herndon," 216–28. This letter was sent to San Francisco, but Herndon received a duplicate in Valparaiso on December 20, 1850. Lieut. William L. Herndon to Lieut. James M. Gilliss, December 20, 1850 *"Letters Received, Astronomical Expedition."*

[6]Lieut. William L. Herndon to William Graham, Secretary of the Navy, July 10, 1841 ("Officers' Letters").

[7]Harrison, *"Science and Politics,"* pp. 191–92. In this article Harrison maintains that Maury's ultimate interest in the exploration of the Valley of the Amazon was concerned almost solely with the possibilities of colonization. For additional insight into this idea, see Matthew F. Maury to Ann Maury, March 7, 1851, *Matthew Fontaine Maury,* Mss., The Library of Congress, Manuscript Division. In this letter Maury wrote: "Lewis Herndon is off upon his Amazonian Expedition, as M. & E. how they would like to have a plantation there? I suppose Lewis will come back with extraordinary yarns and that he will give us all a country or two apiece at the very least."

[8]Herndon, *Exploration of the Valley of the Amazon,* part 1, 241. It appears that some sort of traveling circus preceded Herndon and that the commandant at Tabatinga compelled them to abandon their Peruvian-built raft and build another.

[9]Unless otherwise noted, the following account of Gibbon's trip, including all quotations, is from Lieut. Lardner Gibbon, *Exploration of the Valley of the Amazon,* Part II . . . (33rd Cong., 1st sess., House Ex. Doc. 53). As far as can be ascertained, this report has never been republished.

[10]*New York Times,* June 1, 1852; *New York Times,* July 5, 1842.

[11]Lieut. William L. Herndon to John P. Kennedy, Secretary of the Navy, January 26, 1853 ("Officers' Letters"); Herndon, *Exploration of the Valley of the Amazon,* 3–4. On December 8, 1853, the Secretary of the Navy wrote to Herndon to thank him for sending two copies of his report to the Department on December 7, 1853. James C. Dobbin, Secretary of the Navy, to Lieut. William L. Herndon, December 8, 1853 ("Officers, Ships of War").

[12]James C. Dobbin, Secretary of the Navy, to Lieut. William L. Herndon, May 28, 1853 ("Officers, Ships of War").

[13]*Littell's Living Age,* 41, 2d. ser., vol. 1 (April, May, June, 1854): 429–31. *New York Times,* January 10, 1854. It should be noted that Herndon mentions the trip of Smyth and Lowe in his account many times, and also refers to Henry Lester Maw, *Journal of a Passage from the Pacific to the Atlantic* . . . Herndon had read these accounts, knew the accomplishments of the men who had written them, and utilized

the information they provided about his route. Mark Twain's reading of Herndon's exploration of the Amazon was at least indirectly responsible for his adventures as a steamboat pilot on the Mississippi. There is also some indication that Herndon's book influenced Twain in the preparation of his Huckleberry Finn stories. Charles Neider, *The Autobiography of Mark Twain . . .* p. 98. *See also* Hamilton Basso, ed., *Exploration of the Valley of the Amazon . . .* pp. i-xxvii.

[14]Lieut. Lardner Gibbon to James C. Dobbin, Secretary of the Navy, June 18, 1853; February 22, 1854 ("Officers' Letters"); James C. Dobbin, Secretary of the Navy, to Lieut. Lardner Gibbon, April 19, 1853; May 11, 1853; June 1, 1853, ("Officers, Ships of War"); James C. Dobbin, Secretary of the Navy, to Lieut. William L. Herndon, May 4, 1853; May 11, 1853 ("Officers, Ships of War") Gibbon, *Exploration of the Valley of the Amazon,* p. iii.

[15]James C. Dobbin, Secretary of the Navy, to William L. Herndon, February 4, 1854 ("Officers, Ships of War"). *See also* John P. Kennedy, Secretary of the Navy, to Lieut. William L. Herndon, July 21, 1852 ("Officers, Ships of War"); James C. Dobbin, Secretary of the Navy, to Lieut. William L. Herndon, June 25, 1853; June 28, 1853 ("Officers, Ships of War"); William Graham, Secretary of the Navy, to Lieut. Matthew F. Maury, June 8, 1852 ("Officers, Ships of War").

[16]In the Annual Report for 1860 of the Smithsonian Institution, it was reported that John Cassin had the collection of bird specimens brought back to the United States by Herndon. Smithsonian Institution, *Annual Report of the Smithsonian Institution, Showing the Operations, Expenditures, and Condition of the Institution for the year 1860* (36th Cong., 2d sess., *House Misc. Doc.* (Washington, D.C.: 1861), 74-75. *See also* William Rhees, Jr., comp. and ed., *The Smithsonian Institution Documents Relative to its Origin and History, 1835-1899,* 2 vols. (Washington, D.C.: 1901), 1: 1011-14, for transfer of specimens from the National Institute to the Smithsonian.

[17]Lieut. William L. Herndon to James C. Dobbin, Secretary of the Navy, October 2, 1854 ("Officers' Letters").

[18]Lieut. Matthew Fontaine Maury to Isaac Toucey, Secretary of the Navy, October 19, 1857 ("Letters Sent, Naval Observatory").

[19]Record of Captain Lardner Gibbon, Gen. & Staff Officers (Capt. Art'y), Confederate National Archives, National Archives and Records Service (Washington, D.C.); *Official Records . . . of the War of the Rebellion,* ser. 1, vol. 12, 837.

CHAPTER 6
[1]John Y. Mason, Secretary of the Navy, to Lieut. James M. Gilliss, November 16, 1848, *Letters Received, Astronomical Expedition;* Passed Midshipman Archibald MacRae to Lieut. James M. Gilliss, July 11, 1849, July 17, 1849, *Letters Received, Astronomical Expedition;* William B. Preston, Secretary of the Navy, to Lieut. James M. Gilliss, August 6, 1849, ("Officers, Ships of War"); Lieut. James M. Gilliss to R. W. Patterson, with enclosed addressed to American Philosophical Society, July 11, 1848; Lieut. James M. Gilliss to John Y. Mason, Secretary of the Navy, September 25, 1848, in *Letters Sent, Astronomical Expedition.* Lieut. James M. Gilliss to William B. Preston, Secretary of the Navy, August 7, 1849, August 27 1849, October 13, 1849, October 25, 1849; *Letters Sent, Astronomical Expedition;* Lieut. James M. Gilliss to John P. Kennedy, Secretary of the Navy, November 15, 1852, *Letters Sent, Astronomical Expedition.*

[2]28th Cong., 2nd sess., "Report of the Secretary of the Navy Communicating a Report of the Plan and Construction of the Depot of Charts and Instruments with a Description of the Instruments, Feb. 18, 1845," *Senate Ex. Doc. No. 114,* (Washington, D.C., Gales and Seaton, 1845), 65. See also Benjamin A. Gould, "Memoir of James Melville Gilliss. 1811–1865" *National Academy of Sciences Biographical Memoirs,* Vol. I (Washington, D.C., 1877), 141, Gould's "Memoir of James Melville Gilliss," is an account and analysis of Gilliss' life; pages 137–145 deal with his career before his association with the Astronomical Expedition.

[3]*Astronomical Observations made at the Naval Observatory,* Washington, under orders of the Honorable Secretary of the Navy, dated August 13, 1838. By Lieutenant J. M. Gilliss, U.S.N. Printed by Order of the Senate of the United States. (Washington, D.C.: Gales and Seaton, Printers, 1846), p. iii. See also Allen Johnson and Dumas Malone, eds., "*Dictionary of American Biography,* 11 vols. (New York: 1927) 4, 292. A short account of Gilliss' life also is contained in this volume, pages 292–293.

[4]Gustavus A. Weber, *The Naval Observatory: Its History, Activities and Organization,* pp. 12–17.

[5]James Grant Wilson and John Fiske, eds., *Appleton's Encyclopedia of American Biography,* p. 653.

[6]James M. Gilliss, "Origin and Operations of the U.S. Naval Astronomical Expedition," in *The U.S. Naval Astronomical Expedition to the Southern Hemisphere, During the Years 1849—'50—'51–'52,* printed as 33rd Cong., 1st *Sess., House Ex. Doc. No. 121,* 4 vols. (Washington 1855–1856), 3, 1–2. Hereafter volume 3 noted here will be cited simply as "Origin and Operations of the U. S. Naval Astronomical Expedition." The content of all four of these volumes will be described later in the text of this chapter.

[7]*Proceedings of the American Philosophical Society,* 5 January–April, 18.

[8]Asa Gray, Corresponding Secretary, American Academy of Arts and Sciences, to Lieut. James M. Gilliss. January 15, 1858, in 30th Cong. 1 Sess. "Astronomical Observations" Report No. 470, April 13, 1848 [To Accompany bill H. R. No. 219], *House of Representatives, Reports of Committees* (Washington, 1848), pp. 43–44.

[9]30th Cong., 1 sess., *"Astronomical Observations,"* Report No. 470, April 13, 1848 [To Accompany bill H. R. No. 219], House of Representatives, Reports of Committees, pp. 1–4. The correspondence and events leading to this report by the Naval Committee of the House as noted in the text is contained on pages 5–55 of the aforementioned source.

[10]John Y. Mason, Secretary of the Navy, to Don Manuel Carrvallo Minister of Chile to the United States, November 16, 1848, *Letters Received, Astronomical Expedition.*

[11]Lieut. James M. Gilliss to John Y. Mason, Secretary of the Navy, August 4, 1848 ("Officers' Letters"); John Y. Mason, Secretary of the Navy, to Lieut. James M. Gilliss, August 29, 1848, *Letters Received, Astronomical Expedition.*

[12]James M. Gilliss to John Y. Mason, Secretary of the Navy, September 25, 1848, *Letters Sent, Astronomical Expedition.*

[13]John Y. Mason, Secretary of the Navy, to Lieut. James M. Gilliss, November 16, 1848 ("Offlcers, Ships of War"); Joseph Henry to Lieut. James M. Gilliss, September 27, 1848, October 2, 1848, October 26, 1848; William J. Young to Lieut. James M. Gilliss, November 6, 1848, *Letters Received, Astronomical Expedition;*

Lieut. James M. Gilliss to W. W. Windeman November 28, 1848, *Letters Sent, Astronomical Expedition.*

[14]Beaufort's interest in Gilliss' endeavor may be seen in W. H. Smyth to Lieut. James M. Gilliss, February 15, 1849, enclosing letter of Admiral Sir Francis Beaufort to W. H. Smyth, February 2, 1848, *Letters Received, Astronomical Expedition.* On March 19, 1849, Gilliss reported to the Secretary of the Navy that Beaufort had offered "to send for the use of the Expedition . . . 'any and every chart, plan, book or other document' which could be supplied by the Admiralty." Lieut. James M. Gilliss to William B. Preston, Secretary of the Navy, March 19, 1849, *Letters Sent, Astronomical Expedition. See also* Lieut. J. M. Gilliss to Admiral Sir Francis Beaufort, July, 1849, *Letters Sent, Astronomical Expedition;* William B. Preston, Secretary of the Navy, to Lieut. James M. Gilliss, April 16, 1849 ("Officers, Ships of War").

[15]Lieut. James M. Gilliss to Lt. Col. Edward Sabine, October 25, 1848 Letters Sent, Astronomical Expedition; Lt. Col. Edward Sabine to Lieut. James M. Gilliss, November 16, 1848, June, 1849, *Letters Received, Astronomical Expedition.*

[16]Mars and Venus Santiago Observations, Introduction, Description of the Observatory, *U.S. Naval Astronomical Expedition to the Southern Hemisphere,* 3: xlvi; John Y. Mason, Secretary of the Navy, to James M. Gilliss, March 15, 1849 ("Officers, Ships of War").

[17]Lieut. James M. Gilliss to F. P. Stanton, Chairman, Naval Committee House of Representatives, December 13, 1848; Lieut. James M. Gilliss to Professor Benjamin Pierce, November 29, 1849, *Letters Sent, Astronomical Expedition.*

[18]Lieut. James M. Gilliss to William B. Preston, Secretary of the Navy, August 7, 1849 ("Officers' Letters").

[19]Lieut. James M. Gilliss to W. Edmond Smith, November 28, 1848, *Letters Sent, Astronomical Expedition.*

[20]Matthew F. Maury, *Circular Prepared by Direction of the Hon. Wm. Ballard Preston, Secretary of the Navy, in Relation to the Astronomical Expedition to Chile.*

[21]Unless otherwise noted, the following account of the expedition's work in Chile is based on Lieut. James. M. Gilliss to John P. Kennedy, Secretary of the Navy, November 15, 1852, *Letters Sent, Astronomical Expedition.*

[22]In a letter dated January 17, 1853 Gilliss reminded the Secretary of the Navy that he had spent $650 for the collection and stated that "should the Department consider it proper to reimburse the cost ($650) and make the collection the property of the Government, I would respectfully suggest that an appropriation of $1,000 be asked from Congress for the purpose of arranging and mounting it." Lieut. James M. Gillisss to John P. Kennedy, Secretary of the Navy, January 17, 1853, *Letters Sent, Astronomical Expedition.*

[23]Spencer Fullerton Baird, Assistant Secretary, Smithsonian Institution, November 26, 1851, April 12, 1852, *Letters Received, Astronomical Expedition.* Letters to Gilliss from Baird about the study and exhibiting of Gilliss' specimens from Chile can be found in the series called Correspondence, Official Outgoing, Assistant Secretary, Smithsonian Institution Archives. Subsequent volumes of Gilliss' letters to Baird can also be found in Correspondence, Official Incoming, Assistant Secretary, 1854–1868, Smithsonian Institution Archives.

[24]William D. Brackenridge to Lieut. James M. Gilliss, June 27, 1850 (received on January 23, 1851), *Letters Received, Astronomical Expedition;* Lieut. James M. Gilliss to William D. Brackenridge, December 20, 1851, *Letters Sent, Astronomical Expedition;* Wayne D. Rasmussen, "The United States Astronomical Expedition to Chile, 1849–1852," *Hispanic American Historical Review* (1954): 107.

[25]Ignacio Domekyo, Rector, National Institute of Chile, to Lieut. James M. Gilliss, July 2, 1852, *Letters Received, Astronomical Expedition;* Lieut. James M. Gilliss to Ignacio Domekyo, Rector, National Institute of Chile, July 3, 1852; July 13, 1852; August 27, 1852, *Letters Sent, Astronomical Expedition.* On July 17, 1852, the Secretary of the Navy authorized Gilliss to give the buildings to Chile, but this authorization evidently did not reach Gilliss before he left Chile and the sale arrangements were not changed. See also Luis Galdames, *A History of Chile,* trans. and ed. by Isaac Joslin Cox (Chapel Hill, N.C., 1941), pp. 293–94.

[26]Lieut. James M. Gilliss to Lieut. Archibald MacRae, September 15, 1852, *Letters Sent, Astronomical Expedition;* Rasmussen, "The United States Astronomical Expedition to Chile," 109.

[27]The relationship of the work which was supposed to have been accomplished by the Naval Observatory in Washington to the lack of complete success in the primary mission of the Astronomical Expedition may be noted in "Mars and Venus Santiago Observations, No. 2, General Statement of the Problem," *U.S. Naval Astronomical Expedition to the Southern Hemisphere,* 3, lxvii–lxxii. *See also* F . . . "The U.S. Naval Expedition to the Southern Hemisphere, during the years 1849–1852," *Journal of the Franklin Institute,* 68, 3rd ser. (1859), 68–70; Gould, "Memoir of James Melville Gilliss," 161–71. For the start of his work at the Naval Observatory see Lieut. James M. Gilliss to John P. Kennedy, Secretary of the Navy, November 17, 1852, January 17, 1853, February 17, 1853, *Letters Sent, Astronomical Expedition;* John P. Kennedy, Secretary of the Navy, to Lieut. James M. Gilliss, November 18, 1852 ("Officers, Ships of War"); Rasmussen, "The United States Astronomical Expedition to Chile," 109–110.

[28]Lieut. James M. Gilliss to James C. Dobbin, Secretary of the Navy, March 18, 1853 ("Officers' Letters").

[29]John P. Kennedy, Secretary of the Navy, to Lieut. James M. Gilliss, February 26, 1853 ("Officers' Letters").

[30]Lieut. James M. Gilliss to James C. Dobbin, Secretary of the Navy, March 18, 1853, ("Officers' Letters").

[31]Lieut. James M. Gilliss to James C. Dobbin, Secretary of the Navy, May 9, 1853, ("Officers' Letters").

[32]James C. Dobbin, Secretary of the Navy, to Lieut. James M. Gilliss, May 30, 1853, *Letters Received, Astronomical Expedition;* Lieut. James M. Gilliss to Prof. Benjamin B. Stillman, Sr., June 7, 1853, *Letters Sent, Astronomical Expedition;* Lieut. James M. Gilliss to James C. Dobbin, Secretary of the Navy, June 7, 1853 ("Officers' Letters").

[33]Lieut. James M. Gilliss to James C. Dobbin, Secretary of the Navy, July 5, 1853 ("Officers' Letters").

[34]Lieut. James M. Gilliss to James C. Dobbin, Secretary of the Navy, July 8, 1854 ("Officers' Letters").

[35]In addition to the studies of Baird, Brackenridge, and Gray, the second volume included a report on bird specimens by J. Cassin, and one on reptiles and fishes by C.

Girard. For other published reports dealing with the specimens brought back by Gillis, see Max Meisel, *A Bibliography of American Natural History, the Pioneer Century,* 1769–1865, p. 111.

[36]See Bibliography for publisher, date and place of publication. Two other volumes were projected as 4 and 5 to contain the observations to determine the right ascensions and declinations of 1,963 fixed stars and the zone observations respectively. These volumes were not finished when Gilliss died. By 1866, the observations to be contained in volume 4 were ready for the printer, but the office of the Astronomical Expedition was closed; work came to a stop and all pertinent papers were deposited at the Naval Observatory. The material intended for volume 4 was printed in 1871 as "A Catalogue of 1963 Stars and of 290 Double Stars observed by U.S. Naval Astronomical Expedition to the Southern Hemisphere during the years 1850-'51-'52," *Astronomical and Meteorological Observations made at the United States Naval Observatory during the year 1868* Published by authority of the Hon. Secretary of the Navy. Commodore B. F. Sands, U.S.N., Superintendent. Appendix I (Washington: Government Printing Office, 1871), 1–73.

On March 3, 1873, Congress appropriated $1,500 for the reduction and publication of the material planned for volume 5, the zone observations. This sum did not prove adequate for the purpose, however, and work stopped in March, 1873, when the appropriation was exhausted. In 1881 work was resumed and in 1895 after some twenty years of intermitted labor, the zone observations were printed as "A Catalogue of 16,748 Southern Stars Deduced by the United States Naval Observatory from the Zone Observation Made at Santiago de Chile by the U.S. Naval Astronomical Expedition to the Southern Hemisphere During the Years 1849-'50-'51-'52." In 54th Cong., 1st sess., Astronomical Magnetic and Meteorological Observations Made during the year 1890 at the United States Naval Observatory Capt. Frederick V. McNair, U.S.N., Superintendent. Appendix I *House Ex. Doc.* No. 219 (Washington, D.C.: Government Printing Office, 1895), 1–420.

[37]"The U.S. Naval Astronomical Expedition to the Southern Hemisphere, during the years 1849-'52," *American Journal of Science and Arts,* 31, ser. 2 (January, 1856), 147–148; F . . . "The U.S. Naval Expedition to the Southern Hemisphere, during the years 1849–1852," *Journal of the Franklin Institute,* 68–70; Rasmussen, "U.S. Astronomical Expedition to Chile," 112.

[38]Lieut. James M. Gilliss to James C. Dobbin, Secretary of the Navy, October 17, 1855, *Letters Sent, Astronomical Expedition;* James C. Dobbin, Secretary of the Navy, to Lieut. James M. Gilliss, October, 1855 ("Officers' Letters").

[39]Gilliss acknowledged Moesta's report in Lieut. James M. Gilliss to D. C. W. Moesta, Santiago, Chile, January 15, 1854, *Letters Received, Astronomical Expedition.*

[40]Lieut. James M. Gilliss to Andres Bellow, June 3, 1854, *Letters Sent, Astronomical Expedition.*

[41]J.[ames] M. Gilliss, *An Account of the Total Eclipse of the Sun on September 7, 1858, as Observed over Olmos Peru.*

CHAPTER 7

[1]Lieut. Thomas J. Page to John P. Kennedy, Secretary of the Navy, February 5, 1853; February 8, 1853; Lieut. Thomas J. Page to James C. Dobbin, Secretary of

the Navy, May 28, 1853; August 31, 1853, "Letters &c From Lieutenant Thomas J. Page Exploration and Survey of the Rivers Plata Paraguay, January 6, 1853 and August 4, 1856," Record Group 45, T-829, Roll 445. Hereafter this collection will be cited as ("Letters, Exploration and Survey of the Rivers Plata"). *See also* Muster Roll of Crew of the U.S. Steamer *Water Witch,* Thomas J. Page, Lieut. Commander & Acting Purser, Old Military Records Division, National Archives and Records Service (Washington, D.C.).

²Pablo Max Ynsfran, "Sam Ward's Bargain with President Lopez of Paraguay," *Hispanic American Historical Review;* "Memorial of the American Geographical and Statistical Society, to the Hon. Wm. A. Graham, Secretary of the Navy, May 11, 1852," *Bulletin of the American Geographical and Statistical Society* I (1852): 66–72. *See also* H. Peterson, "Edward A. Hopkins, A Pioneer Promoter in Paraguay," *Hispanic American Historical Review;* John K. Wright, *Geography in the Making* (New York: American Geographical Society 1952), 27–9, and "Paper by Mr. E. A. Hopkins," *Bulletin of the American Geographical and Statistical Society* I (1852): 14–72. The interest of the American Geographical and Statistical Society in the LaPlata region ante-dated the talk of Hopkins, influenced possibly by Maury. S[imeon] DeWitt Bloodgood to Matthew Fontaine Maury, January 20, 1852, *Records of the Naval Observatory, Letters Received,* RG78, File 18, Part I.

³John P. Kennedy, Secretary of the Navy, to Commodore Isaac McKeever, Commdg. U.S. Squadron on the Coast of Brazil, January 29, 1853, Record Group 45, M-625, Area 4, *Area File of the Naval Records Collection.* William F. Lynch had solicited the command of an expedition to explore the La Plata and its tributaries during William Graham's tenure as Secretary of the Navy, but without success. William F. Lynch to Matthew Fontaine Maury, February 24, 1852, March 5, 1852, March 24, 1852, *Records of the Naval Observatory, Letters Received,* RG78, File 18, Part I; William F. Lynch to William Graham, Secretary of the Navy, February 24, 1852, *Letters Received by the* Secretary of the Navy from Captains' ("Captains' Letters") 1805–61, 1866–85, RG 45, M125.

⁴Thomas J. Page, USN, *La Plata, the Argentine Confederation, and Paraguay,* pp. xix–xxi. *See also* William Graham, Secretary of the Navy, to Lieut. Thomas J. Page, February 25, 1852; John P. Kennedy, Secretary of the Navy, to Lieut. Thomas J. Page, January 31, 1853 ("Officers, Ships of War").

⁵John P. Kennedy, Secretary of the Navy, to Lieut. Thomas J. Page, November 10, 1852; December 7, 1852; December 13, 1852; December 14, 1852; January 1, 1853; January 26, 1853 ("Officers, Ships of War").

⁶Lieut. Thomas J. Page to John P. Kennedy, Secretary of the Navy, January 21, 1853 ("Letters, Exploration and Survey of the Rivers Plata").

⁷John P. Kennedy, Secretary of the Navy, to Lieut. Thomas J. Page, January 31, 1853 ("Officers, Ships of War").

⁸For example, Lieut. Thomas J. Page to the Hon. J. C. Dobbin, Secretary of the Navy, August 1, 1854 ("Officers' Letters"); James C. Dobbin, Secretary of the Navy, to Lieut. Thomas J. Page, September 4, 1854 ("Officers, Ships of War").

⁹John P. Kennedy, Secretary of the Navy to Lieut. Thomas J. Page, January 29, 1853 (Confidential Letters), Roll 360, No. 422–25; Lieut. George Minor to Lieut. Thomas J. Page, Sept. 21, 1853 ("Letters Sent, Naval Observatory"). "The Records of the Hydrographic Office (Record Group 37) in the National Archives include the

notebooks kept aboard the *Water Witch* in 1853–54, and the following notebooks kept by junior officers while they were away from the ship: Lieut. Daniel Ammen, 2 vols., Aug. 31, 1853–May 14, 1854; Passed Midshipman W. H. Murdaugh, Feb. 10–24, 1854; and Lieut. William L. Powell, May 31–Aug. 21, 1854." Harrison, "Science and Politics" fn. 84, p. 197. Page's instruction to his officers dated April 21, 1853, can be found in U.S. Miscellany, Naval Historical Foundation Collection, Library of Congress.

· [10] Unless otherwise noted, the following account of Page's expedition to 1856 is based on the series of letters cited in footnote 6, supplemented by the official report Page submitted to the Secretary of the Navy ("Letters, Exploration and Survey of the Rivers Plata"), as well as by Page's book cited in footnote 4.

[11] Welsh reported his arrival in New York to the Secretary of the Navy in a letter dated November 25, 1854. Lieut. G. P. Welsh to James C. Dobbin, Secretary of the Navy, November 25, 1854 ("Officers' Letters").

[12] "Guayacan" and "Palosanto," in Francisco Santamaria, *Diccionario General de Americanismos,* pp. 71, 389.

[13] 2nd Assistant Engineer Wm. J. Lamdin to James C. Dobbin, Secretary of the Navy, October 2, 1854; 3rd Assistant Engineer T. B. C. Boggs to James C. Dobbin, Secretary of the Navy, October 3, 1854; Assistant Engineer R. C. Potts to James C. Dobbin, Secretary of the Navy October 3, 1854 ("Officers' Letters").

[14] *Congressional Globe,* 35th Cong., 1st sess. (April 15, 1858), 1604–05. For Page's orders to return home *see* James C. Dobbin, Secretary of the Navy, to Commander Thomas J. Page, December 20, 1855 ("Confidential Letters"), Roll 361, number 348. In a letter from Montevideo to the Secretary of the Navy dated January 28, 1856, Page wrote that he was returning to the United States on his own responsibility. In his book, he notes that he received orders to return home at Montevideo on June 24, 1856, when he returned from exploring the Uruguay River. Page, *La Plata,* p. 430.

[15] Notation on letter of Lieut. Thomas J. Page to James C. Dobbin, Secretary of the Navy, May 7, 1856, in ("Letters, Exploration and Survey of the Rivers Plata").

[16] *New York Herald,* February 1, 1855; Lieut. Thomas J. Page to James C. Dobbin, Secretary of the Navy, March 21, 1855 ("Letters, Exploration and Survey of the Rivers Plata"). For the Hunter affair, *see* Lieut. Charles G. Hunter to James C. Dobbin, Secretary of the Navy, January, 23, 1855; January 24, 1855, with notation on latter letter by President Franklin Pierce ("Officers' Letters"); *New York Times,* November 21, 1855, p. 1. Hunter, like Page, wanted to institute forceful action against Paraguay after the *Water Witch* incident and took the *Bainbridge* home without orders as a protest against Commodore Salter's inactivity. Harrison, *"Science and Politics,"* pp. 198–200, claims that this attitude was not too unusual for this period.

[17] "Annual Report of the Secretary of the Navy, December 3, 1857," 35th Cong., 1st sess., *House Ex. Doc. No. 2,* 580; Robert B. Forbes, *Personal Reminiscences,* p. 224.

[18] "Annual Report of the Secretary of the Navy, December 3, 1857," 580; Isaac Toucey, Secretary of the Navy, to Commander Thomas J. Page, January 28, 1858, April 10, 1858 ("Officers, Ships of War").

[19] Isaac Toucey, Secretary of the Navy, to Commander Thomas J. Page, May 13,

1858 ("Confidential Letters"), Roll 362. In addition to his other duties, Page was ordered to serve as Acting Purser of the expedition. Isaac Toucey, Secretary of the Navy, to Commander Thomas J. Page, May 12, 1858 ("Officers, Ships of War").

[20]*See,* for example, Commander Thomas J. Page to Spencer Fullerton Baird, January 7, 1858 (2 pages), U.S. Exploration and Government Reports, 2 vols. (Bound Letters) I, Smithsonian Institution.

[21]Forbes, *Personal Reminiscences,* 224–25; Isaac Toucey, Secretary of the Navy, to Commander Thomas J. Page, September 24, 1858 ("Officers, Ships of War"); "Annual Report of the Secretary of the Navy, December 6, 1858," 35th Cong., 2nd sess., *Senate Ex. Doc. No. 1,* 12.

[22]Lieut. C. R. McGary to Isaac Toucey, Secretary of the Navy, April 22, 1858 ("Officers' Letters"); "Annual Report of the Secretary of the Navy, December 6, 1858," 12.

[23]Muster Roll, USS *Argentina,* March 31, 1860. Signed Th. J. Page, Commander, enclosed with Commander Thomas J. Page to Isaac Toucey, Secretary of the Navy, March 31, 1860, *Letters Received by the Secretary of the Navy From Commanders* ("Master Commandant" through 1837, thereafter "Commanders' Letters"), 1804–86, Record Group 45, M-147. Hereafter M-147 letters will be cited as ("Commanders' Letters").

[24]Johnson and Malone, eds., *Dictionary of American Biography,* pp. 140–01; Harris Gaylord Warren, *Paraguay, an Informal History,* p. 195; Commander Thomas J. Page to Isaac Toucey, Secretary of the Navy, March 8, 1860 ("Commanders' Letters").

[25]Forbes, *Personal Reminiscences,* p. 241; for date of detachment of Page from USS *Salinas, see* Commander Thomas J. Page to Isaac Toucey, Secretary of the Navy, March 8, 1860 ("Commanders' Letters").

[26]Forbes, *Personal Reminiscences,* pp. 243–51.

[27]Commander Thomas J. Page to Isaac Toucey, Secretary of the Navy, July 28, 1859; November 6, 1859 (two letters, same date); March 9, 1860; May 25, 1860; August 26, 1860; October 6, 1860; October 12, 1860; December 9, 1860; December 12, 1860 ("Commanders' Letters"); Isaac Toucey, Secretary of the Navy, to Commander Thomas J. Page, January 20, 1860 ("Officers, Ships of War"). *See also* Isaac Toucey, Secretary of the Navy, to Commander Thomas J. Page, December 10, 1860; December 13, 1860 ("Officers, Ships of War").

[28]Commander Thomas J. Page to Isaac Toucey, Secretary of the Navy, December 10, 1860; December 31, 1860; January 21, 1861; January 31, 1861 ("Commanders' Letters"); Isaac Toucey, Secretary of the Navy, to Commander Thomas J. Page, December 14, 1860; January 3, 1861; April 17, 1961 ("Officers, Ships of War"); "Annual Report of the Secretary of the Navy, December 2, 1861," 37th Cong., 2nd sess., *Senate Ex. Doc. No. 1.* There are 56 manuscript maps from Page's 1859–1860 exploration under file 341.7, Cartographic and Audiovisual Records Division, National Archives.

[29]Lieut. Thomas J. Page to John P. Kennedy, Secretary of the Navy, "*Report of the Exploration and Survey of the River La Plata*" pp. 31, 36–38, in ("Letters, Exploration and Survey of the Rivers Plata"); Lieut. Thomas J. Page to Spencer Fullerton Baird, November 18, 1854, December 16, 1855; November 13, 1856; November 25, 1856; Lieut. Thomas J. Page to Joseph Henry, November 6, 1856, in *U.S. Explorations and Government Reports,* 1; Spencer Fullerton Baird to Lieut.

Thomas J. Page, April 30, 1855; February 20, 1856, Correspondence, Assistant Secretary, Official Outgoing, Smithsonian Institution Archives.

[30]*Littell's Living Age,* 63, 34d ser. vol. 7 (October, November, December, 1859), 308–312; *Harper's New Monthly Magazine,* vol. 18 (December, 1858; May, 1859)' 325–39. It is probable that Kern executed his drawings from sketches provided him in Washington, D.C. His originals are now in the Thomas Gilcrease Institute, Tulsa, Oklahoma. *See* Robert V. Hine, *Edward Kern and American Expansion* (New Haven, Conn.: 1962), p. 126.

### CHAPTER 8

[1]John P. Kennedy, Secretary of the Navy, to Commodore M. C. Perry, appointed to command the U.S. Squadron in the East India and China Seas, November 13, 1852, ("Confidential Letters"), Roll 361, nos. 390–394.

[2]Allan B. Cole, "Captain David Porter's Proposed Expedition to the Pacific and Japan, 1815," *Pacific Historical Review.*

[3]Arthur Walworth, *Black Ships Off Japan: The Story of Commodore Perry's Expedition with an Introduction by Sir George Sansom,* pp. 8–11.

[4]Richard A. von Doenhoff, "Biddle, Perry, and Japan," *United States Naval Institute Proceedings,* pp. 78–87.

[5]31st Cong., 1st sess., "Letter from the Secretary of the Navy Transmitting correspondence relative to the visit of Preble to the port of Nagasaki; for the purpose of demanding the release of imprisoned American seamen," *House Ex. Doc. No. 84,* August 28, 1850; Charles Oscar Paullin's *American Voyages to the Orient* . . . pp. 122–25; Walworth, *Black Ships,* pp. 13–29; Samuel Eliot Morison, "*Old Bruin,*" pp. 247–80; William Graham, Secretary of the Navy, to Commodore M. C. Perry, March 29, 1852 ("Confidential Letters"), Roll 360; Allan B. Cole, "The Ringgold-Rodgers-Brooke Expedition to Japan and the North Pacific, 1853–1859," *Pacific Historical Review:* 153–62. Congress refused to appropriate funds for a civilian scientific contingent similar to that which accompanied the Wilkes Expedition.

[6]C. M. Conrad, Acting Secretary of State, to John P. Kennedy, Secretary of the Navy, November 5, 1852, in Walworth, *Black Ships,* Appendix B, pp. 240–46; John P. Kennedy, Secretary of the Navy, to Commodore M. C. Perry, Appointed to command of the U.S. Squadron in the East India and China Seas, November 13, 1852 ("Confidential Letters"), Roll 361, nos. 390–394; Walworth, *Black Ships,* Appendix D, pp. 249–51; Morison, "*Old Bruin,*" p. 287.

[7]Unless otherwise noted, the following account of the expedition's movements is based on Francis L. Hawks, *Narrative of the Expedition of an American Squadron to the China Seas and Japan* . . .

[8]See Chapter 7, p. 109. P. S. Forbes was a cousin of R. B. Forbes.

[9]For the account of the squadron's activities in the Bay of Tokyo, Walworth's *Black Ships,* pp. 70–103, has been used to supplement the story in Hawks' *Narrative,* pp. 261–319; unless otherwise noted, however, all quotations are from the *Narrative.*

[10]S. Wells Williams, "A Journal of the Perry Expedition to Japan (1853–1854) with a prefatory note by F. W. Williams," *Transactions of the Asiatic Society of Japan:* 65.

[11]Hawks, *Narrative,* pp. 322. The account of the expedition's movements until its return to Tokyo Bay in 1854 is based on Hawks, *Narrative,* pp. 320–372.

[12]Ibid., pp. 338.

[13]The following account of the events surrounding the negotiations of Commodore Perry and the Japanese (as well as subsequent movements of the squadron) is taken from Hawks, *Narrative,* pp. 372–591, supplemented by Walworth, *Black Ships.*

[14]Walworth, *Black Ships,* p. 123.

[15]Ibid. pp. 259–60.

[16]Ibid. pp. 223–24; Hawks, *Narrative,* pp. 566–68.

[17]Ibid. pp. 229–30.

[18]Originally, most of the presents brought back by Perry were housed with the other collections of the National Institute in the Great Hall of the Patent House under the supervision of the Commissioner of Patents. In 1857–1858 these presents were transferred to the Smithsonian Institution and listed in the Smithsonian's Department of Anthropology catalog book Number 1, Numbers 1–445 under the date March 1859. In 1968–69, this collection was examined by the Smithsonian and 112 items of the original list were not found. The original list with notations indicating those items which were missing from the collection in 1968–69 can be found as Accession No. 199043 in files of the Registrar's Office of the Smithsonian. Some idea of what type and how many items found their way into private hands, as well as the number of private diaries extant, paintings held, and other items still extant, is indicated in the brochure called *The Japan Expedition 1852–1855 of Commodore Matthew Calbraith Perry* that the Smithsonian issued in connection with the Perry centennial and much more exhaustively in Morison, *"Old Bruin,"* pp. 461–464. Some recent publications of private accounts are Lieut. George Henry Preble, USN, *The Opening of Japan: A Diary of Discovery in the Far East, 1853–1856 From the Original Manuscript in the Massachusetts Historical Society;* and Roger Pineau, ed., *The Japan Expedition 1852–1854. The Personal Journal of Commodore Matthew Perry.* Other published contemporary accounts are listed in Morison, *"Old Bruin,"* p. 462.

[19]Walworth, *Black Ships,* pp. 233–234.

CHAPTER 9

[1]Unless otherwise noted, the following account is based on J. T. Headley, "Darien Exploring Expedition, Under Command of Lieut. Isaac C. Strain," *Harpers' New Monthly Magazine* 10 (March, April, May, 1855): 433–58, 600–15, 745–64; Lieut. Isaac G. Strain to James C. Dobbin, Secretary of the Navy; October 25, 1854, 33rd Cong., 2nd sess., *"Annual Report of the Secretary of the Navy, December 4, 1854,"* Appendix E, 407–27, *House Ex. Doc.* 1, part 2, 383–612; *New York Times,* May 10, 1854; File headed Isaac G. Strain, U.S. Navy, in Office of Early Records Section, Naval History Division, National Archives; J. T. Headley, *Darien Exploring Expedition Under Command of Lieutenant Isaac G. Strain, USN,* New York: Harpers' Franklin Square Library, 1885, no. 480 is a republication of the article in *Harpers' New Monthly Magazine* noted above.

[2]Isaac G. Strain, *Cordillera and Pampa, Mountain and Plain: Sketches of a Journey in Chile, and the Argentine Provinces in 1849.*

[3]Lieut. Isaac G. Strain to William B. Preston, Secretary of the Navy, January 8, 1850; January 20, 1850; February 6, 1851 ("Officers' Letters"). *See also* microfilm of the *Mexican Boundary Commission Papers of John Russell Bartlett 1850–1853,*

12 Reels, John Carter Brown Library, Providence, Rhode Island, Reel 1, nos. 3, 4, 13, 14, 15, 24, 35, and 46.

⁴James C. Dobbin, Secretary of the Navy, to Commander George Hollins, December 12, 1853, ("Confidential Letters"), Roll 361, No. 118. *See also New York Times,* March 23, 1853, p. 3; November 11, 1853, p. 1; November 14, 1853, p. 1.

⁵Gerstle Mack, *The Land Divided: A History of the Panama Canal and Other Isthmian Canal Projects* (New York: 1944), p. 251.

⁶Lieut. Isaac G. Strain to James C. Dobbin, Secretary of the Navy, January 10, 1854 ("Officers' Letters").

⁷*Harpers' New Monthly Magazine,* 8 (May 1854): 834; *Littell's Living Age,* 40 (February 1854): 303.

⁸*New York Times,* June 19, 1856; James C. Dobbin, Secretary of the Navy, to Lieut. Isaac G. Strain, May 18,1854 ("Officers, Ships of War").

⁹Lieut. Isaac G. Strain to James C. Dobbin, Secretary of the Navy, October 25, 1854, "Annual Report of the Secretary of the Navy, December 4, 1854" 426–7.

¹⁰*Harpers' New Monthly Magazine,* 10, (March, April, May, 1855): 433–58, 600–15, 745–64; Lieut. I. G. Strain, "A Paper on the History and Prospects of Interoceanic Communication read before the New York Historical Society," June 17, 1856. See also, Great Britain, Public Record Office, "Darien Surveying Expedition," *Admiralty, Secretary In-Letters* (Adm. 1, 5629).

¹¹Strain was detached from the Darien expedition in January, 1855, and placed in the status of awaiting orders. James C. Dobbin, Secretary of the Navy, to Lieut. Isaac G. Strain, January 10, 1855 ("Officers', Ships of War"). For his transfer to the *Cyane* see Lieut. Isaac G. Strain to James C. Dobbin, Secretary of the Navy, April 10, 1855, April 17, 1855, ("Officers' Letters"). For Paulding's letters of May 15, 1857, and May 19, 1857, see Comm. Hiram Paulding to James C. Dobbin, Secretary of the Navy, May 15, 1857, May 19, 1857, *Home Squadron Letters 1842–1861,* RG 45, M89.

¹²Dr. Edward Cullen to Editor, *New York Times,* July 23, 1855, in *New York Times,* July 26, 1855. Cullen also tried to get the British to sponsor another land expedition. Great Britain, Public Record Office, *Admiralty Digest 12424* (1856).

¹³Passed Assistant Surgeon W. C. Caldwell, USN, to Isaac Toucey, Secretary of the Navy, May 8, 1857, in "Papers" relating to the Exploration of Isthmus of Darien. 1854. RG 45, T-829; New York Times, May 20, 1857; May 22, 1857; May 29, 1857. For the story of the abortive 1859 Darien expedition see Flag Officer William J. McCluny to Isaac Toucey, Secretary of the Navy, with enclosures, October 13, 1859, *Home Squadron Letters.*

¹⁴Charles H. Davis, *Report on Interoceanic Canals and Railroads* (Washington, D.C., Government Printing Office), pp. 21–2, as cited in Mack, *Land Divided,* p. 168. There were at least two other investigations of possible canal routes across Central America between 1854 and 1861 financed by the government in which Naval officers were involved. Mack, *Land Divided,* pp. 241–42, 276. In 1858 Lieut. Nathaniel Michler, USA, and Lieut. T. A. Craven, USN, explored a proposed canal route based on utilization of the Atrato and Truando rivers, and Captain Frederick Engle, USN, led a private party to investigate the Chiriqui Lagoon area. Preliminary reports of the Chiriqui expedition accompanied the 36th Cong., 2nd sess., "Annual Report of the Secretary of the Navy, December 1, 1860," *Senate Ex. Doc.* No. 1, 36–44. Lieut. Michler's report to the Secretary of War is in 36th Cong.,

2nd sess., "Report of the Secretary of War Communicating in Compliance with a Resolution of the Senate, Lieutenant Michler's Report of His Survey for an Interoceanic Ship Canal Near the Isthmus of Darien," *Senate Ex. Doc.* No. 9, 1–457.

[15]Mack, *Land Divided*, pp. 168–9, 263.

[16]Ibid., pp. 263–65, 417–515.

CHAPTER 10

[1]Christopher Lloyd, *Mr. Barrow of the Admiralty: A Life of Sir John Barrow*, p. 188.

[2]Lloyd, *Mr. Barrow of the Admiralty*, p. 190; L. P. Kirwan, *A History of Polar Exploration*, pp. 161–74.

[3]John Edwards Caswell, *Arctic Frontiers: United States Explorations in the Far North*, pp. 13–14; Nellis M. Crouse, *The Search For the North Pole*, p. 16; *Congressional Globe*, 31st Cong., 1st sess., 1850, 21, pt. 1: 102.

[4]Crouse, *Search For the North Pole*, p. 16–17; *Congressional Globe*, p. 884–91; Enclosure with letter of Lieut. Edwin J. DeHaven to William B. Preston, Secretary of the Navy, New York, May 7, 1850 ("Officers' Letters"). *See also* Edward L. Towle, *Science, Commerce and the Navy on the Seafaring Frontier (1842–1861)*, p. 354–61, where Clay's role in the affair is minimized.

[5]William B. Preston, Secretary of the Navy, to Edwin J. DeHaven, Lieut. commanding the American Arctic Expedition, New York, May 15, 1850, Appendix A, of Elisha K. Kane, *The U.S. Grinnell Expedition in Search of Sir John Franklin: A Personal Narrative*, p. 491. Other officers were considered to command this expedition before DeHaven was finally chosen. Maury ultimately suggested DeHaven, but at one point he submitted the names of William F. Lynch and Raymond Rodgers for consideration. Lynch later withdrew from contention because in his opinion the size and poor equipment of the expedition made its success highly unlikely. Lieut. Matthew F. Maury to Lieut. William J. Lynch, February 12, 1850, February 14, 1850, ("Letters Sent, Naval Observatory"), Great Britain, *Parliamentary Papers*, 35, no. 107 (1850), p. 154; Towle, *Science, Commerce and the Navy on the Seafaring Frontier (1842–1851)*, p. 341.

[6]Jeannette Mirsky, *Elisha Kent Kane and the Seafaring Frontier*, p. 55. Kane volunteered for this assignment.

[7]The following account of the DeHaven expedition is based on Lieut. Edwin J. DeHaven to William A. Graham, Secretary of the Navy, U.S. Brig *Advance*, New York, October 4, 1851; Appendix B, of Kane, *U.S. Grinnell Expedition*, pp. 494–508, and excerpts from Kane's book.

[8]William B. Preston, Secretary of the Navy, to Edwin J. DeHaven, Lieut. Commanding the American Arctic Expedition, New York, May 15, 1850; Appendix A, of Kane, *U.S. Grinnell Expedition*, pp. 491–94. On May 13, 1850, the Secretary of the Navy sent DeHaven's instructions to Maury for Maury's examination and suggestions that were to be submitted the next day. Maury's letter of instruction to DeHaven of May 13, 1850, is in ("Letters Sent, Naval Observatory"). William A. Graham, Secretary of the Navy, to Lieut. Matthew F. Maury, May 13, 1850 ("Officers, Ships of War"). Maury's connection with and influence on the scientific objectives of the DeHaven expedition is recounted in Towle, *Science, Commerce and the Navy on the Seafaring Frontier (1842–1861)*, pp. 341–80.

[9]Lloyd, *Mr. Barrow of the Admiralty*, p. 191.

[10]Kane, *U.S. Grinnell Expedition*, p. 508.

[11]Lieut. Edwin J. DeHaven to William A. Graham, Secretary of the Navy, U.S. Brig *Advance*, New York, October 4, 1851; Appendix B, of Kane, *U.S. Grinnell Expedition*, pp. 494–508; Meteorological Abstract, Appendix C. Kane, *U.S. Grinnell Expedition*, pp. 509–42; George M. Justice, "The Protococcus nivalis brought to Dr. Kane from the Arctic Region . . . and a microscopical description of the plant," *Proceedings of the American Philosophical Society*, (1852): 262; Elisha K. Kane, "A Number of Specimens of Vegetable Matter found by him on the ice-plains of the Polar Seas," *Proceedings of the American Philosophical Society*, 5 (1852): 266–67; Chart of Cruise of American Expedition in search of Sir John Franklin in 1850 and 1851, fitted out by Henry Grinnell, commanded by E. J. DeHaven, brig *Advance*, Lieut. DeHaven, schooner *Rescue*, S.P. Griffin. Compiled by George P. Welsh under direction of Matthew F. Maury from materials in Bureau of Ordnance and Hydrography, 236 "K25" c 1853. *See also* Max Meisel, *A Bibliography of American Natural History: The Pioneer Century, 1796–1805*, pp. 142–43; "Meteorological Observations May 1, 1851, to July 31, 1851. Artic Temp. May 1850 to June 9, 1851," War Records Branch, National Archives; John Edwards Caswell, . . . *Utilization* . . . p. 64. 1 (1856).

[12]Elisha K. Kane to John P. Kennedy, November 15, 1852; November 22, 1852, John Pendleton Kennedy Mss., Letters to Kennedy, 8, no. 59, 60; Matthew Fontaine Maury to Elisha K. Kane, November 26, 1853 ("Letters Sent, Naval Observatory"); Elisha K. Kane to John Ethridge, March 18, 1853 (marked done March 21); Elisha K. Kane to James C. Dobbin, Secretary of the Navy, April 10, 1853; Elisha K. Kane to John P. Kennedy, Secretary of the Navy, January 8, 1853; January 11, 1853; January 26, 1853; February 7, 1854; February 26, 1853 ("Officers' Letters"); F. Beaufort, Rear Admiral and Hydrographer, Hydrographic Office, Admiralty, February 25, 1853 to Elisha K. Kane ("Officers' Letters"), with enclosures; Lecture on Access to Open Polar Sea, in Connection with the Search after Sir John Franklin and his Companions, read before the American Geographical regular monthly meeting, by Dr. Kane, December 14, 1852, Appendix F, Kane, *U.S. Grinnell Expedition*, pp. 543–52; *American Geographical and Statistical Society Bulletin*, 1 (1853), 84; Franklin Parker, "George Peabody and the Search for Sir John Franklin, 1852–1854," *The American Neptune*, 20 (April, 1960): 104–107; Wright, *Geography in the Making* p. 30.

[13]Elisha K. Kane to John P. Kennedy, Secretary of the Navy, Boston, February 16, 1853 ("Officers' Letters"). Kane acknowledged this latter order by saying that it was most agreeable to his own wishes and the interests of the expedition in search of Sir John Franklin. The first order was also in conformity with his wishes as seen in Elisha K. Kane to John P. Kennedy, Secretary of the Navy, November 22, 1852, John Pendleton Kennedy Mss., Letters to Kennedy, 8, no. 60.

[14]Elisha K. Kane to J. C. Dobbin, Secretary of the Navy, April 10, 1853 ("Officers' Letters"). In this letter, Kane also asked for six additional petty officer appointments in the naval service "which would render the party unfettered by jealousy, and Amenable to naval discipline."

[15]Unless otherwise noted, the following account of the Kane expedition until its return to New York is based on Elisha K. Kane, M.D., *Arctic Explorations in the*

*Years 1853, '54, '55;* Preliminary Report of Passed Assistant Surgeon Kane to the Secretary of the Navy, James C. Dobbin, n.d., Kane, *Arctic Explorations,* Appendix no. 2, pp. 300–319.

[16]The reports of these men are in Kane, *Arctic Explorations,* Appendix no. 5, pp. 365–80.

[17]Preliminary Report of Passed Assistant Surgeon Kane, p. 310.

[18]E. K. Kane to John P. Kennedy, Secretary of the Navy, November 20, 1854, John Pendleton Kennedy Mss., Letters to Kennedy, 8, no. 77; Memorandum by John Pendleton Kennedy, probably written in 1855 on Elisha K. Kane's letter to John P. Kennedy, Secretary of the Navy, November 14, 1852, John Pendleton Kennedy Mss., Letters to Kennedy, 8, no. 58; *Congressional Globe,* 33rd Cong., 2nd sess., 1853, pp. 27, 28, 229, 251–52, 444–46, 508, 567, 1125; Appendix, p. 396.

[19]Lieut. Henry J. Hartstene to James C. Dobbin, Secretary of the Navy, March 13, 1855; March 23, 1855 ("Officers' Letters").

[20]Lieut. Henry J. Hartstene to James C. Dobbin, Secretary of the Navy, March 24, 1855; March 28, 1855; April 5, 1855; April 6, 1855; April 13, 1855; April 28, 1855; May 7, 1855; May 10, 1855; May 14, 1855; n.d.; May 23, 1855; May 28, 1855; ("Officers' Letters").

[21]James C. Dobbin, Secretary of the Navy, to Lieut. Henry J. Hartstene, May 25, 1855, in Kane, *Arctic Explorations,* Appendix no. 4, pp. 322–4.

[22]Lieut. Henry J. Hartstene to James C. Dobbin, Secretary of the Navy, June 4, 1855; July 1855; July 15, 1855 ("Officers' Letters"); Lieut. Henry J. Hartstene to James C. Dobbin, Secretary of the Navy, September 8, 1855, in Kane, *Arctic Explorations,* Appendix no. 4, pp. 326–29; John K. Kane, "The Kane Relief Expedition," *Putnam's Magazine,* 7, no. 41 (May 1856), 449–63.

[23]John Edwards Caswell, *The Utilization of the Scientific Reports of United States Arctic Expeditions, 1850–1909,* p. 195. Mirsky states that sales were over 145,000 in the first three years. Mirsky, *Elisha Kent Kane,* p. 180.

[24]*See also* August Sonntag, *Thrilling Narrative of the Grinnell Exploring Expedition . . . in the Years 1853, 1854, and 1855.*

[25]For example, "Dr. Kane's Expedition," in the *Literary Gazette* of January 19, 1856, as reprinted in *Littell's Living Age,* 12 (from the beginning 48), (January, February, March, 1856), 675–6; "Dr. Kane: A Sketch by Dr. William Elder," in *Graham's Magazine,* as reprinted in *Littell's Living Age,* 12 (from the beginning 48), (January, February, March, 1856), 427–30.

[26]Caswell, *Utilization . . .* pp. 10–12, 20, 33, 38, 46, 47, 92, 100–03, 156–57, 168–69, 176, 185.

CHAPTER 11

[1]"Report of the Secretary of the Navy, December, 1852," *Congressional Globe,* 32nd Cong., 2nd sess., Appendix: p. 10.

[2]The following account of Lynch's trip is based on his report to the Secretary of the Navy, James C. Dobbin, dated U.S. Steamer *Alleghany,* Potomac River, October 17, 1853, in "Annual Report of the Secretary of the Navy, December 5, 1853," *House Ex. Doc. No. 1,* 33rd Cong., 1st sess., pt. 3: 329–89.

[3]Speech of Hon. J. W. Miller of New Jersey, in the Senate, March 3, 1853, *Congressional Globe,* 32nd Cong., 2nd sess., Appendix: 231–232; *Congressional*

*Globe,* 32nd Cong., 2nd sess., December 7, 1852 to March 3, 1853: 1064–65. For the interest of the United States in West Africa immediately after the Civil War, *see* James A. Field, *America and the Mediterranean World,* pp. 378–79.

CHAPTER 12

[1]John P. Kennedy, Secretary of the Navy, to Commander Cadwallader Ring-gold, February 28, 1853, ("Confidential Letters"), Roll 361; *Congressional Globe,* 33rd Cong., 2nd sess., 24, pt. 3: xx1; *Annual Report of the Board of Regents of the Smithsonian Institution,* 1854, 33rd Cong., 2nd sess., *Senate Mis. Doc. no. 24,* p. 89; Allan B. Cole, "The Ringgold-Rodgers-Brooke Expedition," pp. 153–62; 32nd Cong., 2nd sess., "Annual Report of the Secretary of the Navy, December 4, 1852," *Senate Ex. Doc.* no. 1; 297.

[2]Cole, "The Ringgold-Rodgers-Brooke Expedition," p. 155; John P. Kennedy, Secretary of the Navy, to Commodore Charles Morris, September 24, 1852, Record Group 78; Records of the Naval Observatory, Letters Received, File 20.

[3]John P. Kennedy, Secretary of the Navy, to Commander Cadwallader Ring-gold, March 2, 1853 ("Officers, Ships of War").

[4]John P. Kennedy, Secretary of the Navy, to Commander Cadwallader Ring-gold, March 2, 1853 ("Officers, Ships of War"). (Additional letter to above, written on same day.)

[5]John P. Kennedy to James C. Dobbin, Secretary of the Navy, December 26, 1853, *U.S. Exploration and Government Reports,* 2 vols. (Bound Letters), 1; Spencer Fullerton Baird to Kennedy, Dec. 22, 1853; March 7, 1854; ("Corre-spondence, Assistant Secretary, Official Outgoing").

[6]John P. Kennedy, Secretary of the Navy, to Commander Cadwallader Ring-gold, February 28, 1843 ("Confidential Letters"), Roll 361, no. 15; John P. Ken-nedy, Secretary of the Navy, to Commodore Charles Morris, September 24, 1852 Records of the Naval Observatory, Letters Received, File 20; Matthew Fon-taine Maury to Louis Agassiz, October 27, 1852; Matthew Fontaine Maury to Commander Charles Morris, Chief of the Bureau of Ordnance and Hydrography, October 27, 1852 ("Letters Sent, Naval Observatory"); "Mr. Maury's Letter to Henry Grinnell, Esp.," *Bulletin of the American Geographical and Statistical Society,* 1, no. 2 (January 1853):82–3, File 20.

[7]John P. Kennedy, Secretary of the Navy, to Commander Cadwallader Ring-gold, November 12, 1852; December 8, 1852; February 8, 1853; February 28, 1853; March 1, 1853 ("Officers, Ships of War"). For the departure of Ames and the em-ployment of Squires, see "Journals Kept Aboard the *John Hancock* June 11, 1853–May 29, 1855, *Records Relating to the United States Surveying Expedition to the North Pacific Ocean 1852–1863,* Record Group 45, M88, Roll 12. (Hereafter cited as *"Records . . . North Pacific . . ."*)

[8]John P. Kennedy, Secretary of the Navy, to Commander Cadwallader Ring-gold, November 12, 1852; December 13, 1852; December 14, 1852; December 17, 1852; January 7, 1853; January 12, 1853; February 4, 1853; March 3, 1853; ("Officers, Ships of War"); George Mercer Brooke, Jr., *John Mercer Brooke, Naval Scientist,* pp. 308–22.

[9]John P. Kennedy, Secretary of the Navy, to Commander Cadwallader Ring-gold, two letters dated February 28, 1853, ("Confidential Letters"), Roll 361.

[10]William Joseph Haffernan, *Edward M. Kern, The Travels of an Artist-Explorer*, p. 75-6.

[11]William Stimpson, *Journal of a Cruise in the U.S. Ship* Vincennes *to the North Pacific Ocean, China Seas, Behring Sts., etc., 1853-1855,* Mss. in Smithsonian Archives, no pagination. Hereafter this source will be cited as Stimpson, Mss. Journal.

[12]"Annual Report of the Secretary of the Navy, December 4, 1854," 33rd Cong., 2nd sess., *House Ex. Doc. no. 1,* pt. 2, 388-9.

[13]Allan B. Cole, ed., *Yankee Surveyors,* . . . p. 8 (*"Records . . . , North Pacific . . ."*) Roll 6 (Punctuation slightly altered.)

[14]Lieut. John Rodgers to James C. Dobbin, Secretary of the Navy, August, 1854, original in M. 88, Roll 4.

[15]James C. Dobbin, Secretary of the Navy, to Lieut. John Rodgers, November 18, 1854 ("Confidential Letters"), Roll 361, no. 223; William Stimpson to S. F. Baird, September 5, 1854, *U.S. Exploration and Government Reports* (Bound Letters), 2.

[16]Lieut. John Rodgers to Lieut. Matthew F. Maury, February 19, 1853, Records of the Naval Observatory, (*"Letters Received,"*) File 20; Lieut. John Rodgers to James C. Dobbin, Secretary of the Navy, September 8, 1854, in Cole, *Yankee Surveyors . . . ,* p. 28; Lieut. Matthew F. Maury to Lieut. John Rodgers, November 17, 1854 ("Letters Sent, Naval Observatory").

[17]Lieut. W. W. Habersham, *My Last Cruise . . . ,* pp. 125–26.

[18]Cole, *Yankee Surveyors,* pp. 27–34.

[19]Stimpson, Mss. Journal.

[20]Lieut. John Rodgers, USN, to James C. Dobbin, Secretary of the Navy, February 15, 1855, (*"Records . . . North Pacific . . ."*) Roll 6.

[21]Cole, *Yankee Surveyors,* p. 39–46.

[22]Lieut. John Rodgers, To James C. Dobbin, Secretary of the Navy, April 2, 1855, in Cole, *Yankee Surveyors,* pp. 53–4; James C. Dobbin, Secretary of the Navy, to Lieut. John Rodgers, December 9, 1854 ("Confidential Letters"), Roll 361, no. 227.

[23]Cole, *Yankee Surveyors,* p. 53.

[24]Heffernan, *Edward M. Kern,* p. 79.

[25]Act. Lieut. John M. Brooke to Lieut. John Rodgers, June 22, 1855, (*"Records . . . North Pacific . . ."*) Roll 4 (43).

[26]Ibid.

[27]Ibid.

[28]Cole, *Yankee Surveyors,* pp. 98–129.

[29]Heffernan, *Edward M. Kern,* p. 82.

[30]Lieut. Habersham, *My Last Cruise . . .* p. 356.

[31]Lieut. John Rodgers to James C. Dobbin, Secretary of the Navy, October 19, 1855, in (*"Records . . . North Pacific . . ."*) Roll 5.

[32]Matthew Fontaine Maury, *The Physical Geography of the Sea* and its *Meteorology,* pp. 201, 203, 234.

[33]John Rodgers to Nicolas Mauraviff, Governor General of Siberia, December 11, 1855, in Cole, *Yankee Surveyors;* pp. 134–5; Lieut. John Rodgers to James C. Dobbin, Secretary of the Navy, October 19, 1855, in (*"Records . . . North Pacific . . ."*), Roll 5. The quote from the Log of *Vincennes* is cited in Nourse, *American Explorations in the Ice Zones,* p. 127.

[34]*San Francisco Daily Herald,* October 19, 1855.

[35]Translated from the German as given in Wilhelm Heine, *Die Expedition . . . ,* vol. 3, p. 179–180.

[36]Ibid., vol. 3 pp. 182, 184, 186.

[37]Ibid., vol. 3, p. 191.

[38]Heffernan, *Edward M. Kern,* p. 85.

[39]Translated from the German as given in Wilhelm Heine, *Die Expedition . . . ,* vol. 3, pp. 172–73.

[40]Heffernan, *Edward M. Kern,* pp. 861–87.

[41]Cole, *Yankee Surveyors,* pp. 142–56.

[42]Commander John Rodgers to James C. Dobbin, Secretary of the Navy, June 23, 1855, in ("*Records . . . North Pacific . . .*") Roll 4.

[43]James C. Dobbin, Secretary of the Navy, to Commander John Rodgers, December 5, 1855, "Confidential Letters," Roll 361; Commander John Rodgers to James C. Dobbin, Secretary of the Navy, January 29, 1856, in Cole, *Yankee Surveyors,* pp. 159–61.

[44]*Annual Report of the Smithsonian Institution,* 1856, 34th Cong., 3rd Sess., *Senate Misc. Doc.* no. 54, pp. 53–54. In a letter to James Dwight Dana dated December, 1856, William Stimpson noted "The whole number of [zoological] species collected in all departments is about 5,300. The number of specimens may be stated approximately as 12,000." *American Journal of Science and Arts,* Series 2, No. 23 (1857), 136–138.

[45]United States *Statutes At Large,* 2, p. 247.

[46]Richard Rathbun, "Descriptive Catalogue of the Collection Illustrating the Scientific Investigation of the Sea and Fresh Waters," Great International Fisheries Exhibition, *Bulletin of the United States National Museum, No. 27,* 533–34.

[47]John Edwards Caswell, *The Utilization of the Scientific Reports,* pp. 129–30.

[48]No single work was ever published about the valuable and extensive herbarium collected at the Smithsonian. Nourse, *American Explorations in the Ice Zones,* pp. 455–56. For an indication of the number and types of reports which were published, see Max Meisel, *Bibliography of American Natural History, The Pioneer Century, 1769–1865,* 3, 223–8. In 1862, Ferdinand V. Hayden reported in the *American Journal of Science and Arts,* ser. 2, that the "following reports on the Natural History are in progress: On the Zoology, by Dr. William Stimpson, assisted by Dr. A. A. Gould, Mr. John Cassin, Dr. Hallowell, Dr. Uhler, Mr. Barnard and Professor Theo. Gill. The zoological portion will probably comprise about 3 volumes 4to, with an atlas of plates for each. A Report on the Botany by Professor Asa Gray and Charles Wright, is in progress." Ferdinand V. Hayden, "United States Government Surveys," *American Journal of Science and Arts,* 2, 34 (New Haven, Conn., 1862), 98–101.

[49]Jacob Whitman Bailey, "On Some Specimens of Deep Sea Bottom from the Sea of Kamtschatka," *American Journal of Science and Arts,* 21 (1856): 284–5; "On the Origin of Green Sand and its Formation in the Oceans of the Present Epoch," *American Journal of Science and Arts,* 22 (1856): 280–4; "Notice of Microscopic Forms found in the Soundings of the Sea of Kamtschatka," *American Journal of Science and Arts,* 22 (1856): 1–6. On the subject of Bailey's work and the relationship of Maury to Christian von Ehrenberg, see Edward L. Towle, *Science, Commerce and the Navy on the Seafaring Frontier* (1842–1861), pp. 459–63.

⁵⁰For an indication of the state of this work in 1860, see the reports of Ringgold and Rodgers in *Annual Report of the Secretary of the Navy, December, 1860*, 36th Cong., 2nd Sess., *Senate Ex. Doc.* no. 13: 44–9. For examples of the up-dating of these charts, *see* Caswell, *Utilization of the Scientific Reports*, pp. 24–9. The charts are now part of Record Group 37 of the Naval Archives and Records held in the Cartographic Archives Division of the National Archives. For a list of those charts printed and for sale, see *Catalog of Charts and Books*, United States Hydrographic Office, 1871, Washington, D.C., Government Printing Office, pp. 53, 63, 67. It has been impossible to locate photographs taken on any expedition discussed here.

⁵¹Maury, *Physical Geography of the Sea*, p. 203. *See also* Matthew Fontaine Maury, *Explanations and Sailing Directions*, pp. 155–6. An account of the launch trip commanded by Brooke is given in John Mercer Brooke, "Coasting in Japan," *The U.S. Nautical Magazine and Naval Journal*, 5 (December, 1856): 196–204; 5 (January, 1857): 278–87; 5 (February, 1857): 338–47; 5 (March, 1857): 411–22; 6 (April, 1857): 25–39.

⁵²The following account of Lieut. John M. Brooke's work in surveying a steamship route across the Pacific is based on George Mercer Brooke, Jr., *John Mercer Brooke, Naval Scientist*, pp. 583–734; Heffernan, *Edward M. Kern*, pp. 93–8; "*Annual Report of the Secretary of the Navy, December 1, 1860*," 36th Cong., 2nd sess., *Senate Ex. Doc. No. 1, 19; "Annual Report of the Secretary of the Navy, December 2, 1859*," *Congressional Globe*, 36th Cong., 1st sess., Appendix, pp. 16–17.

# Bibliography

Much of the manuscript material from the National Archives and other depositories used in the preparation of this study is on microfilm. The appropriate microfilm sets and rolls have been cited here rather than the file numbers of the photographed collections as they are held in their original state by the National Archives and other depositories. The microfilm copies of these records give the appropriate file and document numbers of the original material.

Archival sources, not on microfilm, have been listed with appropriate file or other reference indicators.

For the most part, only material cited in the footnotes appears in the bibliography. Thus, the list presented here is selective. Some exceptions have been allowed; a sample number of general histories of the Navy have been listed although they do not appear in the footnotes; the Prologue refers to such works and the reader may wish to consult some of them after or while reading this section of the present text.

Not cited in text or footnote, but of particular interest to those wishing to orient themselves geographically, is the *National Atlas of the United States of America*, United States Department of the Interior, Geological Survey, Washington, D.C., published in 1970. A map showing exploring expeditions conducted by the U.S. Navy, into the twentieth century, appears on page 150; Arctic and Antarctic expeditions are treated on pages 148–149.

## PRIMARY SOURCES

*Manuscripts*

The National Archives

Records of the Bureau of Naval Personnel, Record Group 24, File No. 148
Records of the Hydrographic Office, Record Group 37, Microcopy M-75
Records of the Offfice of Naval Records and Library, Record Group 45, Microcopy
    M-88 (rolls 4,5,6,12); M-89 (roll 78); M-125 (rolls 326–368); M-147 (rolls 34–
    67); M-148 (rolls 173–275); M-149 (rolls 41–64); M-517 (rolls 1–17); M-625
    (Area 4, rolls 15–16); T-829 (rolls 359–362, 438, 443, 445).*

---

*The General Records of the Department of the Navy, Record Group 80, contains material similar in type to Record Group 45, but for a later period mostly.

Records of the Department of State, Record Group 59, Microcopy, M 83, M-472 (roll 3)

Records of the Naval Observatory, Record Group 78, Microcopy T-54; Letters Sent, 1842–1862 (Volumes 1–19); Letters Received, 1840–1855 (Files 18–29)

Miscellaneous

Memo headed Isaac G. Strain, U.S. Navy, in Office of Early Records Section, Naval History Division, Department of the Navy

Ibid, William F. Lynch, U.S. Navy, March 23, 1833, Office of Early Records Section, Naval History Division, Department of the Navy

Muster Roll of Crew of the U.S. Steamer *Water Witch,* Thomas J. Page, Lieut. and Acting Purser, Old Military Records Division

Chart of cruise of American Expedition in Search of Sir John Franklin in 1850 and 1851, fitted out by Henry Grinnell, commanded by E. J. De Haven, schooner, *Rescue,* S. P. Griffin. Compiled by George P. Welsh under the direction of Matthew F. Maury from material in the Bureau of Ordnance and Hydrography, 236 "kas" c. 1853

"Meteorological Observations May 1, 1851, to July 31, 1851. Arctic temperature May 1850 to June 9, 1851," Small Volume, War Records Branch

Selected Pages from *Log of the U.S.S.* Supply (June–September 1848) on microfilm (NNMO-73-282-(685). Washington, D.C.: The National Archives: National Archives and Records Service, 1973

Foreign Archives

Great Britain, Public Record Office, *Admiralty, Secretary In-Letters* (Admin. 1, 5629–5645, 5672–5681); *Admiralty Digest* 12424.

Smithsonian Institution Archives

Accession Files, Office of the Registrar

Annual Reports of the Board of Regents of the Smithsonian Institution, 1848–1867

Catalogs and other material in the Divisions of the Museum of Natural History relating to the acquisition and distribution of specimens. Correspondence and private papers of Assistant Secretary Spencer Fullerton Baird, 1850–1879

Manuscript journal of a Cruise in the USS *Vincennes* to the North Pacific Ocean, China Seas, Behring's Sts., etc. by Wm. Stimpson (Zoologist to the Expedition) 1853–1854–1855 (Typescript copy obtained from David H. Johnson, former Curator, Division of Mammals, Museum of Natural History, Smithsonian Institution)

Material in the Library of the Museum of Natural History.

National Institute Mss.

North Pacific Exploring Expedition. Extracts of data on mammals from notebook in Division of Mammals, U.S. National Museum (apparently a record kept by Stimpson of the outfit provided for him and of the contents of various containers of specimens as they were packed for shipment home during the expedition). (Typescript copy obtained from David H. Johnson, former Curator, Division of Mammals, Museum of Natural History, Smithsonian Institution).

Collections of Private Papers

Kennedy, John Pendleton, Mss., Enoch Pratt Free Library, George Peabody Department, Baltimore, Maryland
Maury, Matthew Fontaine, Mss., The Library of Congress
Naval Historical Foundation Mss., The Library of Congress, Washington, D.C.
Bartlett, John Russell, Mexican Boundary Commission Papers, 1850–1853 (Available on Microfilm). John Carter Brown Library, Brown University.

Studies

Brooke, George Mercer. "John Mercer Brooke, Naval Scientist." Unpublished Ph.D. diss. Chapel Hill: University of North Carolina, 1955.
Coblentz, Catherine Cate. "Naval Lieutenant Matthew Fontaine Maury—First Citizen of the World." Unpublished biography. Washington, D.C.: Library of Congress (filed with M. F. Maury Collection)
Towle, Edward L. "Science, Commerce, and the Navy on the Seafaring Frontier (1842–1861), The Role of Lieutenant M. F. Maury and the U.S. Naval Hydrographic Office in Naval Exploration, Commercial Expansion, and Oceanography Before the Civil War." Ph.D. diss. Rochester, New York: University of Rochester, 1965.

*Published Material*

Public Documents: U.S. Congressional Documents, Listed Chronologically

28th Cong., 2nd sess., "Report of the Secretary of the Navy Communicating a Report of the Plan and Construction of the Depot of Charts and Instruments with a Description of the Instruments, Feb. 18, 1845," *Senate Ex. Doc. No. 114,* 1845
28th Cong., 2nd sess., "Magnetical and Meteorological Observations made at Washington, under orders of the Honorable Secretary of the Navy, dated August 13, 1838," *Senate Ex. Doc. No. 172,* Part I, 1846
30th Cong., 1st sess., "Astronomical Observation," *House Report No. 470 to accompany House of Representatives Bill No. 219,* April 13, 1848
30th Cong., 2nd sess., "Report of the Secretary of the Navy, with a Report made by Lieutenant William F. Lynch of an Examination of the Dead Sea. February 26, 1849; Read February 27, referred to the committee on Commerce and Ordered to be printed." *Senate Ex. Doc. No. 34,* 1849
31st Cong., 1st sess., "Message from the President of the United States. Transmitting copies of a correspondence with the Lady of Sir John Franklin relative to the expedition of Sir John Franklin," *House Ex. Doc. No. 16,* January 22, 1850. (Also printed in *Senate Ex. Doc. No. 8,* January 4, 1850)
31st Cong., 1st sess., "Letter from the Secretary of the Navy Transmitting Correspondence Relative to the Visit of the *Preble* to the Port of Nagasaki; for the Purpose of Demanding the Release of Imprisoned American Seamen," *House Ex. Doc. No. 84,* August 28, 1850
32nd Cong., 1st sess., "Exploration of the Valley of the Amazon, Made Under the Direction of the Navy Department by William Lewis Herndon and Lardner

Gibbon, Lieutenants, United States Navy, Part I by Lieutenant William L. Herndon," *House Ex. Doc. No. 43*, 1853

33rd Cong., 1st sess., "Exploration of the Valley of the Amazon, Made Under the Direction of the Navy Department, Part II by Lieutenant Lardner Gibbon," *House Ex. Doc. No. 53*, 1854.

33rd Cong., 1st sess., "U.S. Naval Astronomical Expedition to the Southern Hemisphere during the years 1849, '50, '51, & '52" 4 Vols. *House Ex. Doc. No. 121*, Parts 1–3, 6, 1855–1856

33rd Cong., 2nd sess., "Correspondence Relative to the Naval Expedition to Japan," *Senate Ex. Doc. No. 34*

33rd Cong., 2nd sess., "Narrative of the Expedition of an American Squadron to the China Seas and Japan performed in the years 1852, 1853, and 1854, under the Command of Commodore M. C. Perry, United States Navy," *Senate Ex. Doc., No. 79*, 3 parts, 1856. Also printed as *House Ex. Doc. No. 97*, 3 parts, 1856. (Part II actually published in 1857, part III in 1858.)

34th Cong., 3rd sess., "Report (Mr. Fish) of Committee on Naval Affairs to whom was referred petition of Commodore J. Page, in behalf of himself and other officers of U.S. Steamer *Water-Witch*, recently engaged in exploration and survey of river La Plata and its tributaries," asking increased compensation, *Senate Report No. 380*, February 12, 1857

35th Cong., 1st sess., "Report of the Secretary of the Navy, in answer to resolution of Senate for information in relation to publication of results of U.S. Naval Exploring and Surveying Expedition to North Pacific Ocean and China Seas, and also of results of U.S. Naval Expedition to La Plata River," *Senate Ex. Doc. No. 52*, May 3, 1858

36th Cong., 2nd sess., "Report of the Secretary of War Communicating, in Compliance with a Resolution of the Senate, Lieutenant Michler's Report of his Survey for an Interoceanic Ship Canal near the Isthmus of Darien," *Senate Ex. Doc. No. 9*, 1861.

54th Cong., 1st sess., "Washington Observations for 1890," Appendix I, *House Ex. Doc. No. 219*, 1895.

*Congressional Globe*, 1836–1861


U.S. Navy Department Documents

*Annual Reports of the Secretary of the Navy*, 1833–1861
*Antarctic Bibliography*, Washington D.C., 1951


Miscellaneous

United States, *Statutes at Large*
*Astronomical and Meteorological Observations Made at the United States Naval Observatory During the Year 1868*, Appendix I, Washington, D.C., Government Printing Office, 1871.
*Astronomical Observations made at Washington, D.C., under Orders of the Honorable Secretary of the Navy dated August 13, 1838*, by Lieut. J. M. Gilliss, USN., Washington, D.C., Giles and Seaton, 1846.
Great Britain, *Parliamentary Papers*, 35, no. 107 (1850).

Books, Memoirs, and Contemporary Pamphlets

Allen, William. *The Dead Sea, A New Route to India: With Other Fragments and Gleamings in the East.* London: Longmans, Brown, Green, and Longmans, 1855.

Ammen, Daniel. *The Old Navy and the New. Personal Reminiscences.* Philadelphia: J. B. Lippincott Co, 1891.

Forbes, Robert B. *Personal Reminiscences.* 2nd ed. rev., to which is added *Rambling Recollections Connected with China.* Boston: Little, Brown, and Company, 1882.

Gilliss, James M. *An Account of the Total Eclipse of the Sun on September 7, 1858, as Observed over Olmos, Peru.* Washington, D.C.: Smithsonian Institution,

Godfrey, William C. *Last Grinnell Arctic Exploring Expedition.* Philadelphia: J. T. Lloyd & Co., 1857.

Habersham, W. W., Lieutenant, USN. *My Last Cruise, or Where We Went and What We Saw Being an Account of Visits to the Malay and Loo-Choo Islands, the Coasts of China, Formosa, Japan, Kamtschatka, Siberia, and the Mouth of the Ammor River.* Philadelphia: J. B. Lippincott and Co., 1857.

Hawks, Francis L. *Narrative of the Expedition of an American Squadron to the China Seas and Japan, Performed in the Years 1852, 1853, and 1854, Under the Command of Commodore M. C. Perry, United States Navy, by Order of the Government of the United States, Compiled from the Original Notes and Journals of Commodore Perry and His Officers, at His Request and Under His Supervision, With Numerous Illustrations.* New York: D. Appleton and Company, 1856.

Headley, J. T. *Darien Exploring Expedition Under Command of Lieutenant Isaac C. Strain, USN.* New York: Harpers' Franklin Square Library, No. 480, 1855 (a republication of 1855 articles).

Heine, Wilhelm. *Die Expeditionen in die Seen von China, Japan und Ochotsk, unter Commando von Commodore Colin Ringgold and Commodore John Rodgers, im Auftrage der Regierung der Vereinegten Staaten unteinommen in der Jahren 1853–1856, unter Zuzrehung der Officiellen Autoritaten Quellen.* 3 vols. Leipzig: H. Costenoble, 1858–59.

Herndon, William Lewis, and Gibbon, Lardner. *Exploration of the Valley of the Amazon, made under direction of the Navy Department.* 2 vols. Vol. 1, Herndon, Washington, D.C.: Taylor & Maury, 1854. Vol. 2, Gibbon, Washington, D.C.: R. Armstrong, 1854.

Kane, Elisha Kent, M.D. *The U.S. Grinnell Expedition in Search of Sir John Franklin, a Personal Narrative.* New York: Harper & Bros., 1853.

————. *Arctic Explorations, the Second Grinnell Expedition in Search of Sir John Franklin in 1853, '54, and '55.* 2 vols. Philadelphia: Childs & Peterson, 1856.

Lowe, Frederick, and Smyth, William. *Narrative of a Journey from Lima to Para, across the Andes and down the Amazon: Undertaken with a View of Ascertaining the Practicability of a Navigable Communication with the Atlantic by the Rivers Pachitea, Ucayali, and Amazon.* London: W. Murray, 1836.

Lynch, William F., Lieut. *Official Report of the United States Expedition to Explore the Dead Sea and the River Jordan by Lieut. W. F. Lynch, USN.* Published at the National Observatory by Lieutenant M. F. Maury, USN, Superintendent, by the authority of the Hon. William A. Graham, Secretary of the Navy. Baltimore: J. Murphy, 1852.

Lynch, William F. *Narrative of the United States Expedition to the River Jordan and the Dead Sea.* Philadelphia: Lea and Blanchard, 1849.

———. *Narrative of the United States Expedition to the River Jordan and the Dead Sea, A New and Condensed Edition.* Philadelphia: Lea and Blanchard, 1850.

———. *Bericht Uber die Expedition der Verenighten Staaten nach dem Jordan.* Leipzig: 1859.

———. *Naval Life; or, Observations Afloat and on Shore.* New York: Scribner, 1851.

———. *Commerce and the Holy Land: A lecture Delivered Before the N.Y. Kane Monument Association.* Philadelphia: King & Baird, 1860.

Maury, Matthew F. *Circular Prepared by Direction of the Hon. Wm. Ballard Preston, Secretary of the Navy, in Relation to the Astronomical Expedition to Chile.* Washington, D.C.: Alexander, 1849.

———. *Explanations and Sailing Directions To Accompany the Wind and Current Charts.* 1st edition, n.p., 1850; 2nd edition, n.p., 1850; 3rd edition, Washington, D.C.: C. Alexander, 1851; 4th edition, Washington, D.C.: C. Alexander, 1852; 5th edition with supplement, Washington, D.C.: C. Alexander, 1853; 6th edition, Philadelphia: E. C. and J. Biddle, 1854; 8th edition, Washington, D.C.: William A. Harris, 1858.

———. *The Physical Geography of the Sea and its Meteorology.* New York: Harper & Bros., 1855.

———. *The Amazon and the Atlantic Slopes of South America.* Washington, D.C.: F. Taylor, 1853.

Maw, Henry Lester. *Journal of a Passage from the Pacific to the Atlantic Crossing the Andes in the Northern Provinces of Peru, and Descending the River Maranon or Amazon.* London: John Murray, 1829.

Montague, Edward P., ed. *Narrative of the Late Expedition to the Dead Sea From a Diary by One of the Party.* Philadelphia: Carey & Hart, 1849.

Morrell, Benjamin, *Narrative of Four Voyages, to the South Seas, North and South Pacific Ocean, Chinese Sea, Ethiopic and Southern Atlantic Ocean, Indian and Antarctic Ocean, from* the Year 1822 to 1831 . . . New York: J. & J. Harper, 1832.

Neider, Charles, ed. *The Autobiography of Mark Twain, Including Chapters Now Published for the First Time as arranged and Edited, with an Introduction and Notes.* New York: Harper & Brothers, 1959.

Page, Thomas J. *La Plata, The Argentine Confederation, and Paraguay.* New York: Harper & Brothers, 1859.

Perry, Matthew C., Commodore. *The Enlargement of Geographical Science, A Consequence to the Opening of New Avenues to Commercial Enterprise.* New York: D. Appleton and Company, 1856.

Pineau, Roger, ed. *The Japan Expedition 1852-1854. The Personal Journal of Commodore Matthew C. Perry.* Introduction by Samuel Eliot Morison. Washington, D.C.: Smithsonian Institution Press, 1968.

Preble, George Henry, Lieut. USN. *The Opening of Japan: A Diary of Discovery in the Far East, 1853-1856 From the Original Manuscript in the Massachusetts*

*Historical Society*. Edited by Boleslaw Szczesniak. Norman: University of Oklahoma Press, 1962.

Reynolds, J. N. *Voyages of the United States Frigate* Potomac, *under the command of Commodore John Downes, During the Circumnavigation of the Globe, in the Years 1831, 1832, 1833, and 1834.* 3rd ed. New York: Harper and Brothers, 1835.

Rhees, William J., comp. and ed. *The Smithsonian Institution Documents Relative to its Origin and History, 1835–1899.* 2 vols. Washington, D.C.: Smithsonian Institution, 1901.

Ross, Sir James Clark, Captain. *A Voyage of Discovery and Research in the Southern and Antarctic Regions, During the Years 1839–1843.* 2 vols. London: John Murray, 1847.

Sonntag, August. *Thrilling Narrative of the Grinnell Exploring Expedition . . . in the Years 1853, 1854, and 1855.* Philadelphia: J. T. Lloyd & Co., 1857.

Stephens, J. S. *Incidents of Travel in Egypt, Arabia, Petraea, and the Holy Land.* By an American. 10th ed., with additions. 2 vols. New York: Harper and Brothers, 1839.

Strain, I. G., Lieut. *A Paper on the History and Prospects of Interoceanic Communication Read Before the New York Historical Society, June 17, 1856.* New York: Charles Vinten, Printer, 1856.

Strain, Isaac G. *Cordillera and Pampa: Mountain and Plain, Sketches of a Journey in Chile, and the Argentine Provinces in 1849.* New York: H. H. Moore, 1853.

Taylor, Fitch W. *A Voyage Round the World and Visits to Various Foreign Countries in the United States Frigate* Columbia; *Attended by Her Consort the Sloop of War* John Adams, *and Commanded by Commodore George C. Read.* New York: D. Appleton & Co., 1843.

Wilkes, Charles. *Synopsis of the Cruise of the U.S. Exploring Expedition Delivered before the National Institute, June 20, 1842.* Washington, D.C.: P. Force, 1842.

Wilkes, Charles. *Narrative of the United States Exploring Expedition During the Years 1838, 1839, 1840, 1841, 1842.* 5 vols. Philadelphia: Lea & Blanchard, 1845.

*Contemporary Accounts In Periodicals*

Jacob Abbott "Memoirs of the Holy Land," *Harper's New Monthly Magazine* 5 (June-November, 1852) 289–303, 433–450, 577–596, 721–738.

*American Geographical and Statistical Society Bulletin*, 1 (1853), 84.

Jacob Whitman Bailey, "On Some Specimens of Deep Sea Bottom from the Sea of Kamtschatka," *American Journal of Science and Arts*, 21 (1856) 234–5; "On the Origin of Green Sand and its Formation in the Oceans of the Present Epoch," *American Journal of Science and Arts*, 22 (1856) 280–4; "Notice of Microscopic Forms found in the Soundings of the Sea of Kamtschatka," *American Journal of Science and Arts*, 22 (1856): 1–6.

John Mercer Brooke, "Coasting in Japan," *The U.S. Nautical Magazine and Naval Journal*, 5 (December, 1856): 196–204; 5 (January, 1857): 278–87; 5 (February, 1857): 338–47; 5 (March, 1857): 411–22; 6 (April, 1857): 25–39.

"Critical Notices," *Southern Quarterly Review*, 16 (October, 1849): 233.

"The Dead Sea, Sodom and Gommorah," *Harper's New Monthly Magazine* 10 (December, 1854–May, 1855), 187–193.

F . . . "The U.S. Naval Expedition to the Southern Hemisphere, during the years 1849–1852," *Journal of the Franklin Institute,* 68, 3rd ser. (1859), 68–70.

*Harper's New Monthly Magazine* 8 (May, 1854) 834; 18 (December, 1858–May, 1859) 325–339.

Ferdinand V. Hayden, "United States Government Surveys," *American Journal of Science and Arts,* 2, 34 (New Haven, Conn., 1862) 98–101.

J. T. Headley, "Darien Exploring Expedition, Under Command of Lieut. Isaac C. Strain," *Harper's New Monthly Magazine* 10 (March, April, May, 1855): 433–58, 600–15, 745–64.

George M. Justice, "The Protococcus nivalis brought to Dr. Kane from the Arctic Region . . . and a Microscopical Description of the Plant," *Proceedings of the American Philosophical Society,* 5 (1852): 262.

Elisha K. Kane, "A Number of Specimens of Vegetable Matter found by him on the Ice-Plains of the Polar Seas," *Proceedings of the American Philosophical Society,* 5 (1852): 266–67.

John K. Kane, "The Kane Relief Expedition," *Putnam's Magazine,* 6, no. 41 (May 1856): 449–63.

*Littell's Living Age,* 15 (October, November, December, 1847), 606; 22 (July, August, September, 1849), 160; 40 (February, 1854), 303; 48 (January, February, March, 1856), 227–301; 675–6; 63 (October, November, December, 1859) 308–312.

Lieutenant M [atthew] F [ontaine] Maury, "The Dead Sea Expedition," *Southern Literary Messenger,* 14 (September, 1848): 547–553.

"Memorial of the American Geographical and Statistical Society, to the Hon. Wm. A. Graham, Secretary of the Navy, May 11, 1852," *Bulletin of the American Geographical and Statistical Society,* 1 (1852): 66–72.

"Paper by Mr. E. A. Hopkins," *Bulletin of the American Geographical and* Statistical Society, 1 (1852): 14–72.

Benjamin Silliman, Sr., "Notice of the Narrative of Lynch's Expedition to the Dead Seas," *American Journal of Science and Arts,* 58, (November 1849): 137–138.

William Stimpson, Letter to James Dwight Dana, December, 1856, *American Journal of Science and Arts* 23, ser. 2 (1857) 136–138.

"The U.S. Naval Astronomical Expedition to the Southern Hemisphere, during the years 1849–'52," *American Journal of Science and Arts,* 21 ser. 2 (January, 1856), 147–148.

*Newspapers*

*National Intelligencer,* November 24, 1847; January 1, 3, November 1, 1849.

*New York Herald,* November 30, 1847; December 18, 1848; February 1, 1855.

*New York Times,* June 1, July 5, 1852; March 23, November 11, 14, 1853; January 10, May 10, 1854; July 26, November 21, 1855; June 19, 1856; May 20, 22, 29, 1857.

*San Francisco Daily Herald,* October 19, 1855.

## SECONDARY SOURCES

*Books*

General Histories of the Navy

Alden, Carroll S. and Westcott, Allan, *The United States Navy, A History.* 2d ed., rev. Philadelphia: J. B. Lippencott Co., 1945.

Chapelle, Howard I. *The History of the American Sailing Navy.* New York: W. W. Norton and Company, 1949.

Cooper, James Fenimore. *History of the Navy of the United States of America abridged in One Volume from the Octavo Edition by J. Fenimore Cooper Continued to 1756 from the Author's Manuscripts and Other Authentic Sources.* New York: Stringer and Townsend, 1856.

Emmons, George F. *The Navy of the United States from the Commencement, 1775–1853, with a Brief History of each Vessel's Service and Fate as Appears upon Record.* Washington, D.C.: Gideon and Co., 1853.

Knox, Dudley W. *A History of the United States Navy.* Rev. ed. New York: G. P. Putnam's Sons, 1948.

Maclay, Edgar S. *A History of the United States Navy from 1775 to 1901.* 3 vols. New York: D. Appleton and Co., 1901.

Neeser, Robert W. *Statistical and Chronological History of the United States Navy, 1776–1907.* 2 vols. New York: Macmillan Co., 1909.

Pratt, Fletcher. *The Navy: A History.* New York: Garden City Publishing Co., 1945.

Books related to Specific Topics in U.S. Naval History

Albion, Robert G. *Square Riggers on Schedule: The New York Sailing Packets to England, France, and the Cotton Ports.* Princeton, N.J.: Princeton University Press, 1938.

Basso, Hamilton, ed. *Exploration of the Valley of the Amazon by William Lewis Herndon, edited and with an introduction by Hamilton Basso, Illustrated with maps and reproductions of Contemporary Prints.* New York: McGraw-Hill Book Co., 1952.

Battistini, Lawrence. *The Rise of American Influence in Asia and the Pacific.* Lansing: Michigan State University Press, 1960.

Bemis, Samuel Flagg, ed. *The American Secretaries of State and Their Diplomacy.* 17 vols. New York: Pageant Book Co. and Cooper Square Publishers, 1958–67.

Bennett, Frank M. *The Steam Navy of the United States.* Pittsburgh: Warren and Co., 1896.

Bohner, Charles H. *John Pendleton Kennedy, Gentleman from Baltimore.* Baltimore, Md.: John Hopkins University Press, 1961.

Bonsal, Stephen. *Edward Fitzgerald Beale: A Pioneer in the Path of Empire, 1822–1903.* New York: G. P. Putnam's Sons, 1912.

Carman, Harry James. *Social and Economic History of the United States.* 2 vols. New York: D. C. Heath & Co., 1930; Johnson Reprint, 1868.

Carrell, Anna E. *The Star of the West.* New York: Miller, Orton & Mulligan, 1857.

Caswell, John Edwards. *Arctic Frontiers, United States Explorations in the Far North.* Norman: University of Oklahoma Press, 1956.

———. John Edwards. *The Utilization of the Scientific Reports of United States Arctic Expeditions, 1850–1909.* Palo Alto, Calif.: Stanford University Press, 1951.

Clark, Arthur H. *The Clipper Ship Era.* New York: G. P. Putnam's Sons, 1911.

Coker, Robert Ervin. *This Great and Wide Sea.* Rev. ed. Chapel Hill: University of North Carolina Press, 1949.

Cole, Allan B., ed. *Yankee Surveyors in the Shoguns' Seas, Records of the United States Surveying Expeditions to the North Pacific Ocean, 1853–1856.* Princeton, N.J.: Princeton University Press, 1947.

Crouse, Nellis M. *The Search for the North Pole.* New York: 1947.

———. *The Search for the Northwest Passage.* New York: Columbia University Press, 1934.

de Voltaire, Marie Francois Aroute. *A Philosophical Dictionary.* 10 vols. in 2. vol. 1. New York: Coventry House, 1932.

Dodge. Ernest S. *New England and the South Seas.* Cambridge, Mass.: Harvard University Press, 1965.

Elder, William. *Biography of Elisha Kent Kane.* Philadelphia; Childs and Peterson, 1857.

Field, James A., Jr. *America and the Mediterranean World, 1776–1882.* Princeton, N.J.: Princeton University Press, 1969.

Finne, David H. *Pioneers East, the Early American Experience in the Middle East. Harvard Middle Eastern Studies.* Cambridge, Mass.: Harvard University Press, 1967.

Galdames, Luis. *A History of Chile.* Translated and edited by Isaac Joslin Cox. Chapel Hill: University of North Carolina Press; 1941.

Goetzmann, William H. *Exploration and Empire: The Explorer and the Scientist in the Winning of the American West.* New York: Alfred A. Knopf, 1967.

Griffis, William E. *Matthew Calbraith Perry.* Boston: Cupples & Hurd, 1887.

Haffernan, William Joseph. *Edward M. Kern, The Travels of an Artist-Explorer.* Bakersfield, Calif.: Kern County Historical Society, 1953.

Haskell, Daniel C. *The United States Exploring Expedition, 1838–1842, and its Publications 1844–1875: A Bibliography.* New York: Greenwood, 1942.

Henderson, Daniel. *Hidden Coasts.* New York: William Sloane Associates, 1953.

Hine, Robert V. *Edward Kern and American Expansion.* New Haven: Yale University Press, 1962.

Jenkins, John S. *Recent Exploring Expeditions to the Pacific and the South Seas.* London and Edinburgh: T. Nelson & Sons, 1853.

———. *United States Exploring Expedition.* New York: J. C. Derby, 1850.

Johnson, Allen and Malone, Dumas, eds., *Dictionary of American Biography.* 21 vols. New York: Charles Scribner's Sons, 1928–37.

Johnson, Robert E. *Thence Round Cape Horn.* Annapolis, Md.: United States Naval Institute, 1963.

Karsten, Peter. *The Naval Aristocracy, The Golden Age of Annapolis and the Emergence of Modern American Navalism.* New York: The Free Press, 1972.

Kirwan, L. P. *A History of Polar Exploration.* New York: W. W. Norton, 1960.

Langley, Harold D. *Social Reform in the United States Navy, 1798–1862.* Urbana, Ill.: University of Illinois Press, 1967.

Leighly, John, ed. *Physical Geography of the Sea and Its Meteorology.* 1861 ed. Cambridge, Mass.: Harvard University Press, 1963.

Lewis, Charles Lee. *Admiral Franklin Buchanan.* Baltimore: Norman, Remington Co., 1929.

Lloyd, Christopher. *Mr. Barrow of the Admiralty: A Life of Sir John Barrow.* London: Collins, 1970.

Mack, Gerstle. *The Land Divided: A History of the Panama Canal and Other Isthmian Canal Projects.* New York: Alfred A. Knopf, 1944.

Meisel, Max. *A Bibliography of American Natural History: The Pioneer Century, 1769–1865.* 3 vols. Brooklyn, N.Y.: Premier Publishing Co., 1924–1929.

Mirsky, Jeannette. *To the Arctic: The Story of Northern Exploration from Earliest Times to the Present.* New York: Alfred A. Knopf, 1948; London: Allan Wingate, 1949.

————. *Elisha Kent Kane and the Seafaring Frontier.* Boston: Little, Brown, 1954.

Mitterling, Philip I. *America in the Antarctic to 1840.* Urbana, Ill.: University of Illinois Press, 1959.

Morison, Samuel Eliot. *"Old Bruin," Commodore Matthew C. Perry, 1794–1858. The American Naval Officer Who Helped Found Liberia, Hunted Pirates in the West Indies, Practised Diplomacy with the Sultan of Turkey and the King of the Two Sicilies; Commanded the Gulf Squadron in the Mexican War, Promoted the Steam Navy and the Schell Gun, and Conducted the Naval Expedition Which Opened Japan.* Boston: Little, Brown, 1967.

Nourse, J. E. *American Exploration in the Ice Zones.* Boston: D. Lothrop and Co., 1884.

Paullin, Charles Oscar. *American Voyages to the Orient, 1690–1865: A Collection of Articles from the United States Naval Institute Proceedings.* Annapolis, Md.: United States Naval Institute, 1971.

————. *Diplomatic Negotiations of American Naval Officers.* Baltimore, Md.: The Johns Hopkins Press, 1912.

————. *Paullin's History of Naval Administration, 1775–1911: A Collection of Articles from the U.S. Naval Institute Proceedings.* Annapolis, Md.: United States Naval Institute, 1968.

St. John, Robert. *Roll Jordan Roll: The Life Story of a River and Its People.* New York: Doubleday and Company, Inc., 1965.

Santamaria, Francisco. *Diccionario General de Americanismos.* 3 vols. Mexico, D.F.: Editorial Pedro Robredo, 1942.

Smelser, Marshall. *The Congress Founds the Navy, 1787–1798.* Notre Dame, Indiana: University of Notre Dame Press, 1959.

Sprout, Harold, and Margaret Sprout. *The Rise of American Naval Power, 1776–1918.* Fifth Printing. Princeton, N. J.: Princeton University Press, 1967.

Tyler, David B. *The Wilkes Expedition: The First United States Exploring Expedition 1838–1842.* Philadelphia: American Philosophical Society, 1968.

Tuckerman, Henry T. *The Life of John Pendleton Kennedy.* New York: G. P. Putnam & Sons, 1871.

Von Hagen, Victor W. *Maya Explorer John Lloyd Stephens and the Lost Cities of Central America and Yucatan.* Norman: University of Oklahoma Press, 1947.

Walworth, Arthur. *Black Ships off Japan: The Story of Commodore Perry's Expedition with an Introduction by Sir George Sausom.* Hamden, Conn.: Anchor Books, 1966.

Warren, Harris Gaylord, *Paraguay, an Informal History.* Norman: University of Oklahoma Press, 1949.

Weber, Gustavus Adolphus. *The Hydrographic Office, Its History, Activities and Organization.* Service Monograph for the U.S. Govt., No. 42. Baltimore, Md.: The Johns Hopkins Press; Institute for Government Research, 1926.

_____. *The Naval Observatory, Its History, Activities, and Organization.* Service Monograph for the U.S. Govt. No. 39. Baltimore, Md.: The Johns Hopkins Press; Institute for Government Research, 1962.

Williams, Francis L. *Matthew Fontaine Maury, Scientist of the Sea.* New Brunswick, N. J.: Rutgers University Press, 1963.

Wilson, James Grant, and John Fiske, eds. *Appleton's Cyclopaedia of American Biography.* 7 vols. New York: 1888.

Wright, John K. *Geography in the Making.* New York: American Geographical Society, 1952.

Yadin, Yigael. *Masada: Herod's Fortress and the Zealot's Last Stand.* Translated from the Hebrew by Moshe Pearlman. New York: Random House, 1966.


*Articles*

Bertrand, Kenneth. "Geographical Exploration by the United States." In *The Pacific Basin, A History of Its Geographical Exploration.* Edited by Herman R. Friis. New York: American Geographical Society, 1967.

Bolander, Louis H. "The Vincennes, World Traveler of the Old Navy." *United States Naval Institute Proceedings* 63 (July 1936): 823–31.

Bryan, G. S. "The Wilkes Exploring Expedition." *United States Naval Institute Proceedings* 65 (1939): 1452–64.

Caswell, John E. "Materials for the History of Arctic America." *Pacific Historical Review* 20 (1951): 219–26.

Cole, Allan B. "Captain David Porter's Proposed Expedition to the Pacific and Japan, 1815." *Pacific Historical Review* 9 (March 1940): 6–61.

_____. "The Ringgold-Rodgers-Brooke Expedition to Japan and the North Pacific, 1853–1859." *Pacific Historical Review* 16 (1947): 152–62.

Dozer, Donald Marquand. "Matthew Fontaine Maury's Letter of Instruction to William Lewis Herndon." *Hispanic American Historical Review* 28 (May 1948): 212–28.

Feipel, L. N. "The Wilkes Expedition." *United States Naval Institute Proceedings* 40 (1914): 1323–50.

Friis, Herman R. "A Brief History of Matthew Fontaine Maury's large role in the interest of the United States in the Arctic, especially in the Northwest Passage prior to 1861." *Etudes d'histoire maritime, presentées au XIIIe Congrès International des Sciences Historiques par la Commission Internationale d'Histoire Maritime a l'Occasion de son XIIe collogue, Moscow,* 16–23 Aout, 1970 (Paris, 1970): 147–80.

Gleaves, Albert, Rear Admiral, USN. "The De Haven Arctic Expedition." *United States Naval Institute Proceedings* 54 (July 1928): 579–91.

Gould, Benjamin Apthorp. "Memoir of James Melville Gilliss, 1811–1865." *National Academy of Sciences Biographical Memoirs* I (Washington, D. C., 1877): 137–39.

Harrison, John P. "Science and Politics: Origin and Objectives of Mid-Nineteenth Century Government Expeditions to Latin America." *Hispanic American Historical Review* 35 (1955): 175–202.

Hill, James D. "Charles Wilkes—Turbulent Scholar of the Old Navy." *United States Naval Institute Proceedings* 57 (1931): 867–88.

Krout, Mary Hannah. "Rear Admiral Charles Wilkes and His Exploits." *United States Naval Institute Proceedings* 50 (March 1924): 405–16.

Littlehales, G. W. "The Navy As a Motor in Geographical and Commercial Progress." *Bulletin of the American Geographical Society* 21 no. 2 (1899): 123–49.

Parker, Franklin. "George Peabody and the Search for Sir John Franklin, 1852–1854." *American Neptune* 20 (April 1960): 104–11.

Peterson, H. "Edward A. Hopkins, A Pioneer Promoter in Paraguay." *Hispanic American Historical Review* 22 (1942): 245–61.

Pickard, Madge E. "Government and Science in the United States: Historical Backgrounds." *Journal of the History of Medicine* 1 (April 1946): 254–89.

Pillsbury, John E., Rear Admiral USN. "Wilkes's and d'Urville's Discoveries in Wilkes Land." *United States Naval Institute Proceedings* 36 (June 1910): 465–68.

Rasmussen, Wayne D. "The United States Astronomical Expedition to Chile, 1849–1852." *Hispanic American Historical Review* 34 (1954): 102–13.

Rathbun, Richard. "Descriptive Catalogue of the Collection Illustrating the Scientific Investigation of the Sea and Fresh Waters." Great International Fisheries Exhibition, London, 1883. *Bulletin of the United States National Museum*, No. 27 (Washington, 1884): 513–621.

Strauss, W. Patrick. "Preparing the Wilkes Expedition: A Study in Disorganization." *Pacific Historical Review* 28 (1959): 221–32.

Thom, J. C. "The American Navy and The Dead Sea," *United States Naval Institute Proceedings* 52, No. 9; Whole No. 283 (September 1926): 1689–1700.

von Doenhoff, Richard A. "Biddle, Perry and Japan." *United States Naval Institute Proceedings* 92 (November 1966): 70–87.

Williams, S. Wells. "A Journal of the Perry Expedition to Japan (1853–1854), with a prefatory note by F. W. Williams." *Transactions of the Asiatic Society of Japan*, Series 1, 37, Part 2 (Tokyo, 1910): i–259.

Ynsfran, Pablo Max. "Sam Ward's Bargain with President Lopez of Paraguay." *Hispanic American Historical Review* 34 (1954): 315–17.

# Appendix - Ships' Data

*Characteristics of ships.* Data are approximate only; rigs, batteries, and engines varied from time to time. Some ships named in text were not commissioned, but obtained on charter. Where available, displacement is stated, followed by dimensions: length × beam × draft.

*Advance*  Brig, 144 tons, 88' × 21' × 8'. Abandoned in Arctic, 1855.

*Alpha*  Paddle wheel river steamer, 22 tons, 2' draft. Built in Boston, 1858, by R. B. Forbes; returned to Forbes in Buenos Aires, 1860.

*Arctic*  Screw steamer, 235 tons. Built in Keyport, N. J., in 1853 as *Thomas C. Haight.* Transferred to Lighthouse Service, 1859.

*Argentine*  Steamer, 98' × 16' × 4'. Built in Boston, 1857, by R. B. Forbes, returned to Forbes in Buenos Aires, 1860.

*Bainbridge*  Brig, 259 tons, 100' × 25' × 11'. Built at Boston Navy Yard, 1842; lost off Cape Hatteras 21 August 1863. Armament: 12 32-pdrs.

*Brandywine*  Frigate, 1,726 tons, 175' × 45' × 14'. Built at Washington Navy Yard, 1825; burned at Norfolk, 3 September 1861; razed and sold, 1867. Armament: 33 24-pdrs., 22 42-pdrs.

*Caprice*  (no data)

*Colonel Marney*  Steamer, 300 tons. Transferred from War Department to Navy after Seminole War; returned to War Department 1846.

*Colorado*  Screw-frigate, 3,425 tons, 263' × 52' × 22'. Single screw, 8 knots. Built at Norfolk Navy Yard, 1856; sold 1885. Armament: 24 9" guns, 14 8" guns

*Columbia*  Frigate, 1,726 tons, 175' × 45' × 14'. Built at Washington Navy Yard, 1836; burned at Norfolk, 1861; razed and sold, 1867. Armament: 4 8" shell guns, 25 32-pdrs., 22 42-pdrs.

*Columbus*  Ship-of-the-line, 2,480 tons, 193' × 52' × 21'. Built at Washington Navy Yard, 1819; burned at Norfolk, 1861. Armament: 63 32-pdrs., 24 32-pdrs.

*Consort*  Brig, 230 tons, 78' × 25' × —. Sold, Philadelphia. 1844.

*Constitution*   Frigate, 2,200 tons, 175' × 43' × 14'. Built in Boston, 1797; still on Navy List. Armament: 44 guns

*Cyane*   Sloop, 792 tons, 132' × 34' × —. Built at Boston Navy Yard, 1837; sold in California, 1887. Armament: 18 guns.

*Dolphin*   Brigantine, 224 tons, 88' × 25' × 11'. Built at New York Navy Yard, 1836; burned at Norfolk Navy Yard, 1861. Armament: 10 guns

*Fenimore Cooper*   Former New York pilot boat *Skiddy,* 95 tons. Purchased 1853; wrecked on Pacific Coast, 1859.

*Flying Fish*   Former New York pilot boat *Independence,* 96 tons, 85' × 22' × —. Sold at Singapore, 1842; became opium smuggler.

*Fulton*   (No. 1) Paddle wheel steamship, 2,475 tons, 156' × 56' × 20'. Built by Adam & Noah Brown, New York, 1814; exploded 1829.

*Fulton*   (No. 2) Paddle wheel steamship, 1,200 tons 180' × 34' × 12'. Sidewheels 22' in diameter. Built at New York Navy Yard, 1837; captured by Confederates at Pensacola, 1861, burned 1862.

*Greta*   Brig (no data)

*Independence*   Ship-of-the-line, 2,257 tons, 190' × 50' × 20'. Built at Charleston, Mass., 1814, as 74-gun ship; razed to 54-gun frigate in 1836. Sold, Mare Island, California, 1914.

*Jamestown*   Sloop, 982 tons, 157' × 35' × 16'. Built at Norfolk Navy Yard, 1843; transferred to Marine Hospital Service, 1892. Armament: 4 8″ shell guns, 18 32-pdrs.

*John Adams*   Sloop, 127' × 34' × 15'. Built at Norfolk Navy Yard, 1830; sold, Boston Navy Yard, 1867. Armament: 2 18-pdrs., 22 32-pdrs.

*John Hancock*   Steam tug, 328 tons, 164' × 22' × 12'. Built at Boston, Mass., 1850. Two engines, single screw; 7 knots, 112 tons coal. Armament: 3 howitzers.

*John P. Kennedy*   Storeship; merchant ship *Sea Nymph* purchased at New York, 1853. Armament: 3 guns.

*Lexington*   Sloop, 127' × 34' × 15'. Built at New York Navy Yard, 1825; sold, 1860. Converted to store ship, 1840–1853.

*Macedonian*   Frigate, 1,341 tons, 164' × 41' × 18'. Built at Norfolk Navy Yard, 1836; razed to first class sloop, 1852–1853; sold at Norfolk, 1875. Armament: 6 8″ shell guns, 16 32-pdrs.

*Merrimac*   Screw-frigate, 4,636 tons, 257' × 51½' × 23'. Built at Boston Navy Yard, 1855–1856; burned at Norfolk, 1861; razed and converted to ironclad ram CSS Virginia, 1862; blown up to prevent capture, May, 1862. Two engines, single screw, 8+ knots. Armament: original, 24 9″ smooth bore, 14 8″ shell guns, 2 10″ smooth bore.

*Minnesota*   Screw-frigate, 3,200 tons, 264' × 51' × —. Built at

Washington Navy Yard, 1855; sold 1885. Two engines, one screw, 8+ knots. Armament: 24 9″, 14 8″, 2 10″ smooth bore.

*Mississippi*  Paddle wheel frigate, 1,692 tons, 225′ × 40′ × 19′. Built at Philadelphia, 1841; destroyed by fire, Battle of Port Hudson, 14 March 1863. Armament: 8 8″ shell guns, 2 10″ shell guns.

*Niagara*  Screw sloop-of-war, 4,580 tons, 328′ × 55′ × —. One screw, speed 10+ knots.

*Ohio*  Ship-of-the-line, 197′ × 53′ × —. Built at New York Navy Yard, 1820; sold at Boston Navy Yard, 1883. Armament: 30 42-pdrs., 30 32-pdrs., 26 42-pdr. carronades.

*Oregon*  Brig, 250 tons. Purchased at Ft. Vancouver, 1841; sold 1845.

*Peacock*  Sloop-of-war, 119′ × 32′ × —. Built by Adam & Noah Brown, New York, 1813; broken up at New York, 1828. Armament: 2 12-pdrs., 20 32-pdr. carronades.

*Pilcomayo*  Steamer, 65′ × 14′ × 3′. Built in Paraguay by Navy officers for river survey work 1853–1856. Two engines, 12′ paddle wheels.

*Pilot*  Schooner, 120 tons, 65′ × 21′ × 9′. Sold at Baltimore, 1838.

*Pioneer*  Brig, built in 1836, sold in 1844.

*Plymouth*  Sloop, 189 tons, 147′ × 38′ × 17′. Built in 1843; burned at Norfolk, 1861. Armament: 4 8″ shell guns, 18 32-pdrs.

*Poinsett*  Steamship, 250 tons, transferred to Navy from War Department after Seminole War. Sold, 1845.

*Porpoise*  Brig; 224 tons, 88′ × 25′ × 11′. Built at Boston Navy Yard, 1836; lost at sea, 1854. Armament: 10 guns.

*Potomac*  Frigate 1,726 tons, 175′ × 45′ × 14′. Built at Washington Navy Yard, 1822; sold, Philadelphia, 1877. Armament: 44 guns.

*Preble*  Sloop, 566 tons, 118′ × 34′ × 15′. Built at Portsmouth Navy Yard, 1839; burned at Pensacola, 1863. Armament: 14 32-pdr. carronades, 2 9-pdrs.

*Princeton*  First screw steam war vessel in U.S. Navy, 954 tons, 164′ × 30′ × —. Built at Philadelphia Navy Yard, 1843; broken up at Boston Navy Yard, 1849.

*Powhatan*  Steam frigate, 3,765 tons, 254′ × 45′ × 18′. Two engines, 10+ knots, 630 tons coal. Built at Norfolk Navy Yard, 1847; sold, 1887. Armament: 16 9″ single bore guns.

*Raritan*  Frigate, 1,726 tons, 175′ × 45′ × 14′. Built at Philadelphia, 1843; burned at Norfolk, 1861. Armament: 8 8″ shell guns, 36 42-pdrs.

*Release*  (no data)

*Relief*  Storeship, 468 tons, 109' × 30' × 12'. Built at Philadelphia Navy Yard, 1836; sold 1865. Armament: 4 18-pdrs., 2 12-pdrs.

*Rescue*  Schooner, 90 tons, 65' long. Built in Maine for Henry Grinnell, re-rigged as brig.

*Roanoke*  Screw-frigate, 3,400 tons, 263' × 52' × —. Built at Norfolk Navy Yard, 1856; sold 1885. Two engines, one screw, 8+ knots.

*Salinas*  (no data)

*Saratoga*  Sloop, 882 tons, 146' × 35' × 16'. Built at Portsmouth, N. H., 1842; sold 1907. Armament: 4 8" shell guns, 18 32-pdrs.

*Sea Gull*  Former New York pilot boat *New Jersey,* 110 tons. Purchased 1838; lost in Antarctic same year.

*Shark*  Schooner, 178 tons, 86' × 25' × 10'. Built Washington Navy Yard, 1821; wrecked in Columbia River, 1846. Armament: 10 12-pdr. carronades, 2 18-pdrs.

*Southampton*  Storeship, 567 tons, 152' × 27' × 16'. Built, or purchased, Norfolk, 1845; sold, 1855. Armament: 2 42-pdr. carronades.

*Supply*  Storeship, 547 tons. Purchased in New York, 1846; sold, 1884. Armament: 4 24-pdr. carronades.

*Susquehanna*  Steam frigate, 2,213 tons, 257' × 69' × —. Armament: 6 8" shell guns, 3 64-pdrs.

*Vandalia*  Sloop, 700 tons, 127' × 33' × 15'. Built at Philadelphia Navy Yard, 1828; broken up at Portsmouth, N. H., 1870. Armament: 4 8" shell guns, 16 32-pdr. carronades.

*Vermont*  Ship-of-the-line, 2,633 tons, 196' × 53' × 21'. Built at Boston, 1818–1848; sold, 1902. Armament: 74 guns.

*Vincennes*  Sloop-of-war, 700 tons, 127' × 33' × 15'. Built at Philadelphia Navy Yard, 1826; sold, Boston Navy Yard, 1867. Armament: 18 32-pdr. carronades.

*Vixen*  Side-wheel steamer, 240 tons. Purchased for use in Mexican War; sold, 1855.

*Wabash*  Steamship, 3,200 tons, 262' × 51' × —. Built at Philadelphia Navy Yard, 1856.

*Water Witch*  (No. 1) Paddle wheel steamer, 190 tons. Two 16' diameter wheels, speed 6+ knots. Condemned, 1851.

*Water Witch*  (No. 2) Paddle wheel steamer, 378 tons, 180' × 23' × —. Two 19' diameter wheels. Sold, Washington Navy Yard, 1866.

# Index